HERMENEUTICS

An Introduction

Anthony C. Thiselton

WILLIAM B. EERDMANS PUBLISHING COMPANY

GRAND RAPIDS, MICHIGAN / CAMBRIDGE, U.K.

Published 2009 by

Wm. B. Eerdmans Publishing Co.

2140 Oak Industrial Drive N.E., Grand Rapids, Michigan 49505 /

P.O. Box 163, Cambridge CB3 9PU U.K.

Printed in the United States of America

14 13 12 11 10 09   7 6 5 4 3 2 1

Library of Congress Cataloging-in-Publication Data

Thiselton, Anthony C.

Hermeneutics: an introduction / Anthony C. Thiselton.

    p.   cm.

    Includes bibliographical references (p.   ) and indexes.

    ISBN 978-0-8028-6410-9 (pbk.: alk. paper)

    1. Bible — Hermeneutics.   I. Title.

BS476.T458   2009

220.601 — dc22

                            2009026551

www.eerdmans.com

Contents

Preface

This book was commissioned as a textbook on hermeneutics for the student and general reader. I have based it on nearly forty years of teaching the subject. I have regularly defined technical terms as they are introduced. My students over this time have helped me to decide what questions, writers, and subjects need coverage.

I have avoided repeating what I have said in other books, especially in *New Horizons in Hermeneutics* and *Thiselton on Hermeneutics.* There may be, however, a small overlap with the chapters on Bultmann in *The Two Horizons,* but that was written as a research book nearly thirty years ago. The chapter here is very much shorter. Neither can one write infinitely fresh things about Schleiermacher, because the scope of his writing on hermeneutics is small. But I have tried to present this subject differently and more simply than previously. For the remaining fourteen chapters, overlap scarcely occurs. No previous book of mine has been open while writing this.

Two years ago hardly any textbooks on hermeneutics existed, except that of David Jasper, which was very basic and short. It still offers a "taster" of the subject. Three others have appeared, but none is entirely adequate. In spite of their merits, they all remain too general and far too short, and a writer cannot cut corners in this subject without risking misunderstanding. None covers Gadamer and Ricoeur adequately, and none offers the range of writers and subjects offered here.

I am most grateful to my secretary, Mrs. Karen Woodward, for meticulously typing the whole manuscript, especially when my writing has been even worse than usual after a severe stroke last summer. I am grateful also to my wife Rosemary for proofreading and much of the indexing, and to Mrs.

Sheila Rees for proofreading. I thank Mr. Jon Pott, vice president of Eerdmans, for his personal encouragement.

Anthony C. Thiselton
Department of Theology and Religious Studies
University of Nottingham, U.K.
May 2008

CHAPTER I

The Aims and Scope of Hermeneutics

1. Toward a Definition of Hermeneutics

Hermeneutics explores how we read, understand, and handle texts, especially those written in another time or in a context of life different from our own. Biblical hermeneutics investigates more specifically how we read, understand, apply, and respond to biblical texts.

More broadly, from the early nineteenth century onward, notably following the work of Friedrich Schleiermacher (1768-1834), hermeneutics has involved more than one academic discipline. (1) Biblical hermeneutics raises *biblical* and theological questions. (2) It raises *philosophical* questions about how we come to understand, and the basis on which understanding is possible. (3) It involves *literary* questions about types of texts and processes of reading. (4) It includes *social,* critical, or sociological questions about how vested interests, sometimes of class, race, gender, or prior belief, may influence how we read. (5) It draws on theories of communication and sometimes general *linguistics* because it explores the whole process of communicating a content or effect *to readers* or to a community.

In the case of understanding biblical texts, responsible interpretation draws on the varied resources of biblical studies, including Old Testament and New Testament introduction and exegesis. In turn, this cannot ignore questions of Christian theology and the biblical canon, especially against the background of the history of interpretation or of "the reception" of texts.

It is impossible to divorce a number of sophisticated theoretical questions in hermeneutics from practical problems that concern almost everyone. For example: Are the meanings of texts "constructed" by readers, or are meanings "given" through texts by authors of texts? This is a complex question of hermeneutical theory, but on this depends how we seek to answer a basic practical question: Can the Bible mean anything we want it to mean? How can we agree about norms or criteria for the responsible or valid interpretation of Scripture?

In the era of the Church Fathers (up to around A.D. 500) and from the Reformation to the early nineteenth century, hermeneutics was regularly defined as "*rules* for the interpretation of Scripture." Among many writers, although not all, hermeneutics was almost equivalent to *exegesis,* or at least to *rules for going about exegesis* in a responsible way. Only in the nineteenth century with Schleiermacher and especially in the later twentieth century with Hans-Georg Gadamer (1900-2002) did the notion emerge that hermeneutics was an *art* rather than a *science.* Schleiermacher wrote in 1819: "Hermeneutics is part of the art of thinking, and is therefore philosophical."[1] Similarly Gadamer disengages the subject from formulating purely rationalist procedures of "method," observing: "Hermeneutics is above all a practice, the art of understanding. . . . In it what one has to exercise above all is the ear."[2] The very title of Gadamer's most important work, *Truth and Method,* indicates his suspicion of rationalist or mechanical "method" as a way of acquiring understanding and truth. He might have called his major book "Truth *or* Method."

Nevertheless, the notion that we can formulate "rules" for hermeneutics or for the interpretation of texts has a long history, and in some quarters it still persists today. It is not surprising that early rabbinic traditions of "rules for interpretation" should take this form. First, interpretations of the sacred biblical text became enshrined in fixed rabbinic traditions (even though these often developed to address new situations). Second, these early formulations had more to do with deductive logic than with hermeneutics in the broader sense of the term. Seven rules of interpretation were traditionally ascribed to Rabbi Hillel (about 30 B.C.). The first five of these were, in effect, rules of deductive and inductive logic. The first (called "light and heavy") related to drawing inferences. The second concerned the application of comparisons or analogy. The third, fourth, and fifth concerned deduction (draw-

---

1. Friedrich Schleiermacher, *Hermeneutics: The Handwritten Manuscripts,* ed. Heinz Kimmerle, trans. James Duke and J. Forstman (Missoula: Scholars Press, 1977), p. 97.

2. Hans-Georg Gadamer, "Reflections on My Philosophical Journey," in *The Philosophy of Hans-Georg Gadamer,* ed. Lewis Edwin Hahn (Chicago and La Salle, Ill.: Open Court, 1997); for the whole essay, see pp. 3-63.

ing inferences from a general principle to a particular case) and induction (formulating a general axiom on the basis of inferences from particular cases). The sixth and seventh rules, by contrast, were more genuinely hermeneutical. They asked: What is the bearing of one passage of Scripture on the meaning of another? How does the wider context of a passage elucidate its meaning?

We should not overstate the significance of these seven "rules" (or *middoth*), for they were often subsequently applied in arbitrary ways, and rabbinic inquiry (midrash) into the sacred text held together belief in the definitive authority of the text with the possibility of radically multiple interpretations and applications. The so-called rules also had much in common with principles formulated in Hellenistic rhetoric of the times.[3]

The notion of "rules" of interpretation has had a regular appeal to those conservative Christian writers for whom the concept of an infallible or inerrant biblical canon is essential, but for whom the notion of fallible human interpretation would seem to provide a weak link in the chain of communicating biblical authority in the actual use of biblical texts. It is no surprise that Milton S. Terry, for example, author of one of the most conservative textbooks on hermeneutics (1890), begins: "Hermeneutics is the science of interpretation."[4] Yet even Terry concedes that hermeneutics "is both a science and an art. As a science it enunciates principles . . . and classifies the facts and results. As an art, it teaches what application these principles should have . . . showing their practical value in the elucidation of more difficult scriptures."[5]

Terry's work, however, concentrates almost exclusively on the biblical text as a *"source"* in the process of communication. It reflects relatively little concern for the horizons of understanding that *readers* or communities of readers bring to the text. It is precisely attention to this "second" (or readers') horizon that leads Schleiermacher and Gadamer to redefine hermeneutics as "the art of *understanding.*" Communication, like teaching a class, describes not only what is *transmitted* by the text, or the source of the subject matter, but also what is *conveyed to,* and *understood* and *appropriated by,* the reader or the "target" audience. In communication theory and in general linguistics, writers often use the terms "sender" and "receiver" to denote the

3. A technical discussion can be found in David Daube, "Rabbinic Methods of Interpretation and Hellenistic Rhetoric," *Hebrew Union College Annual* 22 (1949): 234-64.

4. Milton S. Terry, *Biblical Hermeneutics: A Treatise on the Interpretation of the Old and New Testaments* (Grand Rapids: Zondervan, 1974), p. 17.

5. Terry, *Biblical Hermeneutics*, p. 20.

two sides of this process. This concern for *the whole process* as it involves author, text, and reader, as an act or event of communication, distinguishes hermeneutics from exegesis in one of several different ways.

Writers sometimes complain that the Jewish writer Philo, and later the Alexandrian Fathers of the Church from Clement and Origen onward, "allegorize" the text of the biblical writers, or go beyond the so-called literal meaning to an allegorical one. Those who complain insist that this approach often distorts the "literal" meaning intended by the author of the text. At a basic level there is some truth in this, but the issues involved are also more complex. Alexandrian hermeneutics consciously asked questions about the impact of texts upon the understanding and responses of hearers and readers, and the question, at least, is valid. I argue later in this book that the answer is more complex than a straight yes or no. This concern for readers contributes to the distinctive hermeneutic of the Alexandrians.[6] It is often stated that the opposite emphasis, associated by many with Diodore, Theodore of Mopsuestia, John Chrysostom, and the School of Antioch, champions the "literal" meaning. In broad terms this is true, but Chrysostom is also concerned with the role of the author of the text, especially in the case of Jesus, apostles, or prophets, to remain "in control" of the meaning of the text. This arguably provides a better and more accurate way of formulating the difference of emphasis here than comments about "literal" meaning. "Literal" is a slippery term that people use in many different ways.[7]

Finally, whereas *exegesis and interpretation* denote the *actual processes* of interpreting texts, *hermeneutics* also includes the second-order discipline of asking critically *what exactly we are doing when we read, understand, or apply* texts. Hermeneutics explores *the conditions and criteria* that operate to try to ensure responsible, valid, fruitful, or appropriate interpretation. This shows why, once again, hermeneutics has to call on various academic disciplines. It shows why we draw on philosophical questions about how we understand; psychological, social, and critical questions about selfhood, self-interest, and self-deception. It shows why we call on questions that arise in literary theory about the nature and effects of texts and textual forces. It also shows why we

---

6. Karen Jo Torjesen, *Hermeneutical Procedure and Theological Method in Origen's Exegesis* (Berlin: Walter de Gruyter, 1986), rightly underlines and explores the role of Origen's pastoral concern in his method.

7. An excellent discussion of the complex use of "literal" meaning can be found in R. W. L. Moberly, *The Bible, Theology, and Faith: A Study of Abraham and Jesus* (Cambridge: Cambridge University Press, 2000), pp. 225-32.

call on questions that arise in biblical studies, in interpretation in the history of the Church and other faith communities, and in doctrine and theology.

2. What Should We Hope to Gain from a Study of Hermeneutics?

What might we expect from a serious study of hermeneutics? I began teaching hermeneutics as a degree subject in the University of Sheffield in 1970. Since then I have taught hermeneutics in three other U.K. universities, as well as in America, Canada, Europe, and the Far East. Frequently I have asked my classes (from B.A. to Ph.D.) what they have gained, if anything at all, from this subject. Three answers have emerged with regularity.

First and most frequently, students say that by the time they have completed the course or module, *they have come to read the biblical writings in a different way* from before. If pressed, many will add that they have learned especially from Gadamer the importance of *listening* to a text on its own terms, rather than rushing in with premature assumptions or making the text fit in with prior concepts and expectations they may have. They have also gained from Paul Ricoeur (1913-2005) a realization of the need to examine the ways in which they read with a healthy measure of critical *suspicion,* knowing how easy it is to be seduced into self-deception by self-interest.[8] It is all too easy to opt for convenient or self-affirming interpretations.

Second, many find that hermeneutics, by virtue of its multidisciplinary nature, provides an *integrating dimension* to their theological and religious studies. If previously there had seemed to be little connection between biblical studies and fundamental philosophical problems, or between New Testament studies and the history of Christian thought, all these different areas and methods of approach *came together* in hermeneutics as *coherent, "joined up," interrelated* factors in the process of understanding texts.

Third, a number express the view that hermeneutics produces habits of respect for, and more sympathetic understanding of, views and arguments that at first seem alien or unacceptable. Hermeneutics seeks *to establish bridges* between opposing viewpoints. This does *not* necessitate *giving ground* to the other view, but sympathetically to understand the diverse *mo-*

---

8. Ricoeur explains this in many writings, but his classic study of this aspect is *Freud and Philosophy: An Essay on Interpretation,* trans. Denis Savage (New Haven: Yale University Press, 1970), e.g., p. 27.

tivations and journeys that have led in the first place to each respective view or argument.

This features as a persistent theme in multidisciplinary hermeneutics from Schleiermacher to the present. In his early aphorisms of 1805 and 1809, Schleiermacher writes: "In interpretation it is essential that one be able to step out of one's own frame of mind into that of the author."[9] Interpreters must use imagination and historical research to learn how the "first readers" of a text would understand it.[10] Wilhelm Dilthey (1833-1911), who effectively succeeded Schleiermacher in the development of hermeneutics, speaks of the need to try to step into the shoes of the author or dialogue-partner that one seeks *to understand*. This involves a measure of *empathy* (for which he uses the German word *Hineinversetzen*).[11]

In the mid–twentieth century the New Testament scholar Rudolf Bultmann (1884-1976) took up Dilthey's hermeneutics and insisted that understanding a person or a text must entail having "a living relationship" to what one seeks to understand.[12] He cites the examples of trying to understand a text of music or of mathematics. This would be almost impossible if music or mathematics played no part at all in the life of the reader or interpreter. In the second half of the twentieth century another New Testament specialist, Ernst Fuchs (1903-83), the main architect of "the new hermeneutic," insisted that *empathy* or *mutual understanding* stood at the very heart of hermeneutics. He used the broad German word *Einverständnis* to convey this.[13] One writer suggested that this word meant "penetrative understanding."

Emilio Betti (1890-1968) provides probably the most striking comments on what we might hope to gain from the study of hermeneutics. Betti wrote on philosophy, theology, and law, and many regard him as third in importance behind Gadamer and Ricoeur in twentieth-century hermeneutics. He argues that hermeneutics fosters "open-mindedness" and "receptiveness" to

9. Schleiermacher, *Hermeneutics*, p. 42.

10. Schleiermacher, *Hermeneutics*, p. 107.

11. Wilhelm Dilthey, *Gesammelte Schriften*, vol. 7 (Leipzig and Berlin: Teubner, 1927), pp. 213-14; translated in *Selected Writings*, ed. H. P. Rickman (Cambridge: Cambridge University Press, 1976), pp. 226-27.

12. Rudolf Bultmann, "The Problem of Hermeneutics," in *Essays Philosophical and Theological* (London: SCM, 1955), p. 242; the essay is on pp. 234-61.

13. Ernst Fuchs, "The Hermeneutical Problem," in *The Future of Our Religious Past: Essays in Honour of Rudolf Bultmann*, ed. J. M. Robinson, trans. C. E. Carlston and R. P. Scharlemann (London: SCM, 1971), pp. 267-68; the essay is on pp. 267-78.

such an extent that the subject should be obligatory in all universities. It nurtures tolerance, mutual respect, and *reciprocal listening* one to another with patience and integrity.[14]

A fourth benefit probably concerns Christians and biblical hermeneutics, although it also has relevance to wider religious interests. Hermeneutics helps to explain two types of phenomena. On one side hermeneutics shows that "understanding" can be a slow process in which disclosure of the truth can take many years. Understanding is not an on/off event in which we expect belief always to happen suddenly. Some take many years fully to come to faith. Yet it is equally otherwise with others. Some experience understanding dramatically and suddenly, as if scales fell from their eyes. Both means, however, are equally in accord with what it is to understand. To understand understanding helps people to see that both ways of belief are to be expected.

3. Differences between "Philosophical Hermeneutics" and More Traditional Philosophical Thought, and Their Relation to Explanation and Understanding

Most writers on philosophical hermeneutics, including especially Gadamer and Ricoeur, perceive the regular approach of philosophical hermeneutics to stand at a considerable distance from, and be almost opposite to, the rationalism of René Descartes (1596-1650) and the empiricism of David Hume (1711-76). It is far removed in spirit and outlook from the rationalism of the secular Enlightenment and its subsequent deification of the natural sciences as the controlling model for all human knowledge. We may identify several distinct points of difference between philosophical hermeneutics (or hermeneutical philosophy) and philosophy as more traditionally practiced.

1. While admittedly a rational dimension remains within the process of hermeneutical inquiry, the more creative dimension of hermeneutics depends more fundamentally on the receptivity of the hearer or reader to *listen with openness*. To appreciate and to appropriate what we seek to understand with sensitivity have priority over the traditional method of scrutinizing

---

14. Emilio Betti, *Allgemeine Auslegungslehre als Methodik der Geisteswissenschaften*, German translation and edition of the Italian (Tübingen: Mohr, 1967), p. 21. As yet, it appears that no full English translation has been made, although this appears to be in progress, and extracts can be found in Josef Bleicher, *Contemporary Hermeneutics: Hermeneutics as Method, Philosophy, and Critique* (London and Boston: Routledge and Kegan Paul, 1980), pp. 51-94.

"objects" of perception, thought, and knowledge. This "listening" dimension is often described as part of the process of *"understanding"* in contrast to the more rational, cognitive, or critical dimension of *"explanation."* Some writers, including James Robinson, expound this principle as a "reversal of the traditional flow" in epistemology, or in the theory of knowledge.[15] In the rationalism of Descartes and other rationalist philosophers, the human self, *as active subject,* scrutinizes and reflects upon what it seeks to know as a *passive object* (diagram below). But in hermeneutics *the text itself* (or what a person seeks *to understand*) operates almost, in effect, as the *active subject,* exposing and interrogating the human inquirer as *its object* of scrutiny.

Figure 1

Human Subject → Object of Knowledge   Human Inquirer ← **Active Text**
The Traditional Philosophical Approach   *The More Hermeneutical Model*

Ernst Fuchs (whose emphasis upon mutual understanding we have already noted) insists: "*The texts must translate us* before we can translate them."[16] The interpreter of texts is not a neutral observer, on the analogy of the supposed stance of the natural scientist or empiricist. *Understanding* in the fullest sense demands *engagement and self-involvement.* Virtually every exponent of contemporary hermeneutics supports this view, originating with Schleiermacher and Dilthey, developed through the biblical scholars Bultmann and Fuchs, and explicated most fully by the great hermeneutical figures of the late twentieth century, Gadamer and Ricoeur.

Robert Funk, who acknowledges his indebtedness to Fuchs for his approach, illustrates the dynamics of this epistemological flow of understanding with reference to the parable of the prodigal son (Luke 15:11-32). The parable traces the journey of the younger son from his desire for independence into estrangement, destitution, dereliction, and finally utter remorse. At his wit's end, he determines to return to his father, seeking only the status of a hired laborer. Yet his father runs to welcome him, and restores his personal dignity through the gifts of a ring, a robe, and shoes. However, the parable turns also on the attitude of the elder son. He resents the generous and lavish

---

15. James M. Robinson, "Hermeneutics since Barth," in *New Frontiers in Theology,* vol. 2, *The New Hermeneutic,* ed. James M. Robinson and John B. Cobb, Jr. (New York and London: Harper and Row, 1964), pp. 23-24.

16. Fuchs, "The Hermeneutical Problem," p. 277.

welcome for the prodigal, and refuses to join in the welcome in angry indignation, because he views the comparison between the younger son's conduct and his welcome as flagrantly unjust to him.

Of the elder son Funk writes: "He refuses to be identified as a sinner because he is righteous and has no need of the grace of God. The word of grace and the deed of grace divide the audience into younger sons and elder sons — into sinners and Pharisees. This is what Ernst Fuchs means when he says that one does not interpret the parables: *the parables interpret him*."[17] (We refer to this again briefly when discussing the parables and the new hermeneutic.)

All the same, in hermeneutical theory it is widely recognized that the more traditional approach to texts as "objects" of scrutiny still has its place, even if not the most important place. Most exponents of hermeneutics agree on the need for a *critical check* on the process of interpretation. Credibility is different from mere credulity. Hence many writers on hermeneutics distinguish between the two valid dimensions of *explanation* and *understanding*. The axis of *explanation* is more akin to the traditional flow of *knowing; understanding* entails a more personal, intuitive, or suprarational dimension. Schleiermacher draws a contrast between what he called the "masculine" activity of criticism and comparison, and the "feminine" quality of interpersonal understanding or *rapport*, as when we seek to understand a friend. He called these, respectively, "the comparative" and "the divinatory" (his German word is similar to the English translation, namely, *divinatorische*).[18] We need both as complementary processes, he insists, although the feminine quality of divinatory understanding or rapport is more creative than the merely critical and comparative.

The parallel contrast between *explanation* and *understanding* has become so firmly rooted and so widespread in Continental European hermeneutics that the respective German terms *Erklärung* (explanation) and *Verstehen* (understanding) are widely used even by English-speaking writers. In Germany Karl-Otto Apel has not only published *Die Erklären-Verstehen-Kontroverse* (translated by Georgia Warnke under the inverted title *Understanding and Explanation*), but also refers regularly in shorthand to the "E-V" debate in philosophical method.[19] This relates closely, in turn, to Paul

---

17. Robert W. Funk, *Language, Hermeneutic, and Word of God* (New York: Harper and Row, 1966), p. 16, italics in original.

18. Schleiermacher *Hermeneutics*, pp. 150-51.

19. Karl-Otto Apel, *Understanding and Explanation: A Transcendental-Pragmatic Per-*

Ricoeur's parallel distinction between the critical task of "doing away with idols" by countering self-deception through a hermeneutic of suspicion, and the more distinctively hermeneutical task of "retrieving" symbols, metaphors, narratives, and other texts through openness and listening.[20]

2. A second contrast between hermeneutical philosophy and more traditional philosophical thought emerges from what Gadamer perceives as a fundamental contrast between confronting philosophical *"problems"* in *abstraction* from what gave rise to them in human life, and exploring *"questions that arise"* within a chain of question-and-answer that reflects concrete situations in human life.[21]

I encountered the significance of this contrast at first hand in my first year as professor of Christian theology in the University of Nottingham, when I inherited from my predecessor a joint honors class on God, freedom, and evil, attended by final-year honors students from the Department of Philosophy and the Department of Theology. The philosophy students made it clear that, on their side, they perceived only arguments or ideas deliberately abstracted from life and in effect *"self-contained" as problems* as worthy of evaluation and assessment. By contrast, students in theology inquired about the settings and motivations of arguments in human life, as their biblical and historical studies had accustomed them.

By way of example, students in the Department of Theology appreciated and examined the varied motivations and changes of audience that led to different emphases on the question of God, freedom, and evil in the varied writings of Augustine (354-430). Since the aim varies, audience and agenda are different in different works, and Augustine's emphasis will vary between the following: his early writings against the Manicheans (397-99); his theological autobiographical testimony to divine grace, the *Confessions* (398-400); his works against Pelagius (411-21); his philosophy of history and providence, *The City of God* (416-22); the *Enchiridion* (421-23); and his later writings against the semi-Pelagians, including *Of Grace and Free Will* (426-27). Terrence Tilley argues that only the *Enchiridion* comes near to providing a "theodicy." Most of his other works, he suggests, take the form of

---

spective (Cambridge: MIT Press, 1984); the full German title is *Die Erklären-Verstehen-Kontroverse in transzendental-pragmatischer Sicht.*

20. Ricoeur, *Freud and Philosophy,* pp. 27-28.

21. Hans-Georg Gadamer, *Truth and Method,* 2nd English ed. (London: Sheed and Ward, 1989), pp. 369-79, especially pp. 376-77.

"performative speech acts" written *to perform* specific tasks. The *Enchiridion*, Tilley rightly concludes, "is not an argument but an instruction."[22]

Gadamer expounds this fundamental contrast between abstract "problems" and processes of questioning embedded in life as a key philosophical divide. "The logic of question and answer that Collingwood elaborated puts an end to talk about permanent *problems*. . . . The identity of the problem is an empty abstraction. . . . There is no such thing, in fact, as a point outside history from which the identity of a problem can be conceived."[23] Gadamer continues: "The concept of the problem is clearly an abstraction, namely the detachment of the *content* of the question from the *question* that in fact *first reveals it*. . . . Such a 'problem' has fallen out of the motivated context of questioning."[24] Problems are not fixed, self-contained entities, like "stars in the sky."[25] Gadamer concludes: "Reflection on hermeneutical experience transforms problems back to questions that arise and that derive their source from this motivation."[26]

This is no minor or hairsplitting distinction. It underlines almost the whole of Gadamer's approach and his formulation of philosophical hermeneutics. It is also the launchpad that gave my recent work *The Hermeneutics of Doctrine* much of its distinctive approach to Christian doctrine.[27] It also reflects the distinctive approach of the later philosophy of Ludwig Wittgenstein (1889-1951), who argues that conceptual questions cannot be asked and answered "outside" a particular language game, by which he means "the whole, consisting of language and the actions into which it is woven."[28] Uses of language are said to become intelligible in their "home" language-game. Confusions and ambiguities occur when language is considered in the abstract "like an engine idling."[29] They arise when "the language-game in which they are to be applied is missing."[30]

---

22. Terrence W. Tilley, *The Evils of Theodicy* (Washington, D.C.: Georgetown University Press, 1991), p. 121.

23. Gadamer, *Truth and Method*, p. 375.

24. Gadamer, *Truth and Method*, p. 376, italics mine.

25. Gadamer, *Truth and Method*, p. 377.

26. Gadamer, *Truth and Method*, p. 377.

27. Anthony C. Thiselton, *The Hermeneutics of Doctrine* (Grand Rapids: Eerdmans, 2007).

28. Ludwig Wittgenstein, *Philosophical Investigations,* 2nd ed., German and English (Oxford: Blackwell, 1958), sections 7, 19, and 47.

29. Wittgenstein, *Philosophical Investigations,* section 132.

30. Wittgenstein, *Philosophical Investigations,* section 96.

3. Descartes also formulated a philosophical method in which we begin with *doubt* in contrast to *inherited understanding*, with the *individual* rather than with the *community*, and with the fallible *human subject* rather than with *what* we seek to understand. On all three counts the major exponents of hermeneutics, including Gadamer and Ricoeur, adopt a thoroughly different, indeed opposite, approach.

The famous (or infamous) *cogito ergo sum* ("I am thinking, therefore I exist") of Descartes rests on the notion that to doubt all other knowledge except my own processes of conscious reflection provides an authentic starting point for philosophical thinking. In the context of hermeneutics, however, Bernard Lonergan calls this "the principle of the empty head," and exposes its uselessness and inadequacy for embarking upon any process of interpretation.

> The principle of the empty head . . . bids the interpreter forget his own views, look at what is out there, let the author interpret himself. In fact, what is out there? There is just a series of signs. Anything over and above a re-issue of the same signs in the same order will be mediated by the experience, intelligence, and judgement of the interpreter. The less that experience, the less cultivated that intelligence, the less formed that judgement, the greater will be the likelihood that the interpreter will impute to the author an opinion that the author never intentioned.[31]

In contrast to the commendation of *doubt* as a starting point (as commended by Descartes), exponents of hermeneutics commend as a more fruitful starting point for "understanding" what has come to be denoted by the technical term *pre-understanding*. The English might more idiomatically be rendered *preliminary understanding*. It denotes an initial and provisional stage in the journey toward understanding something more fully. Of course, not all philosophy is "Cartesian" or rationalist. But Descartes has left an indelible mark on the discipline, and even Hume and the empiricists share the same mind-set in this respect. It is the mind-set largely of the Enlightenment. Some philosophers are very different. The later Wittgenstein is one. Existentialists and postmodernists, whatever their failings, represent others.

---

31. Bernard J. F. Lonergan, *Method in Theology* (London: Darton, Longman and Todd, 1972), p. 157.

4. Preliminary and Provisional Understanding (Pre-understanding) and the Hermeneutical Circle

"Pre-understanding" is not a term that seems natural for English-speakers to use. Not surprisingly it is an English translation of a term widely used in German thought from Schleiermacher onward, namely, *Vorverständnis.* As will be apparent, the term adds the prefix *Vor-* to the German noun for "understanding," *Verständnis,* which in turn relates to the verb *verstehen,* "to understand," or to the noun *Verstehen,* "understanding."

This notion is not opposed to the role of doubt as a dialogue partner. For the very purpose of speaking of *preliminary* understanding is to underline that it offers no more than a *provisional* way of finding a bridge or starting point toward further, more secure understanding. From the very first it is *capable of correction* and *readjustment.* It signifies the initial application of a tentative working assumption to set understanding going and on its journey toward a fuller appreciation of all that this might entail. In discussions of theology on the Church of England doctrine commission, I recall a particular bishop often opening the exploration of a new idea with the words: "Let's try this for size." As understanding begins to move and to grow, we may discover that certain aspects of our preliminary understanding need to be corrected while other aspects seem to be proving their value. Some aspects seem to fit the larger picture as "the right size"; others begin on the wrong track. This is why understanding is more often a *process* and seldom a sudden event (although a disclosure or new idea may sometimes have the force of "Now I see!" — until subsequent testing reveals whether it is valid or illusory).

I often suggest to my students the analogy of beginning to put together a jigsaw puzzle. We hold a puzzle piece in our hands and surmise that the color blue may represent sky or perhaps sea. We try it here and there. Another piece has a dark line that is shaped in such a way that it might represent the leg of an animal; but it might be something else. Piece by piece we begin to build a picture as some initial guesses or judgments are proved wrong and others retained as promising and probably right. To progress at all, we must entertain *some* working assumption about what the piece might represent and how it fits into the larger picture. But in the end, it is only as the larger picture emerges that we can be sure about where the piece belongs and what it signifies.

This analogy applies not only to pre-understanding. It also constitutes a parable that introduces us to *the hermeneutical circle*. The term "circle" is misleading here, although it is used because it has become part of the standard technical terminology of hermeneutics from the nineteenth century, following Friedrich Ast (1778-1841) and Schleiermacher. The philosophers Martin Heidegger (1889-1976) and Gadamer use the term. Grant Osborne has more accurately used the term "the hermeneutical spiral" as the title of his book on hermeneutics for two reasons. First, it denotes an *upward and constructive* process of moving from earlier pre-understanding to fuller understanding, and then returning back to check and to review the need for correction or change in this preliminary understanding. Second, this dialogue between pre-understanding and understanding merges into a further process of examining the parts or pieces of the puzzle that we handled initially and relating them to an understanding of the whole picture.[32] We cannot arrive at a picture of the whole without scrutinizing the parts or pieces, but we cannot tell what the individual pieces mean until we have some sense of the wider picture as a whole.

We shall explore this principle more fully when we examine Schleiermacher's hermeneutics. Meanwhile, however, students of biblical studies will readily perceive how the hermeneutical circle (or spiral) operates constantly in their reading of biblical texts. The exegesis and interpretation of verses or passages in the Pauline epistles, for example, shed light on Paul's theology as a whole. At the same time, in the opposite direction, a careful and judicious understanding of Pauline theology is of immeasurable value in advancing our wrestling with issues of exegesis and interpretation at the level of individual passages. As I have observed elsewhere, one Pauline scholar who demonstrates this principle admirably is J. Christiaan Beker.[33]

This provides one explanation of why certain theologians and historians tend to interpret certain texts in ways that are almost predictable by those who know their work. This should not give rise to skepticism. It is to be expected that how we understand a wider picture should influence how we understand the elements that build it up. The cynic or skeptic may be tempted to bow out under the illusion that "Everything depends on your presuppositions." This is often a cheap way of foreclosing further discussion,

---

32. Grant R. Osborne, *The Hermeneutical Spiral: A Comprehensive Introduction to Biblical Interpretation* (Downers Grove, Ill.: InterVarsity, 1991).

33. J. Christiaan Beker, *Paul the Apostle: The Triumph of God in Life and Thought* (Edinburgh: T. & T. Clarke; Philadelphia: Fortress, 1980).

especially when a student disagrees with a professor! But a greater familiarity with hermeneutics reveals that negotiating between a given view and provisional pre-understandings is not in any sense a matter of warfare between nonnegotiable fixed presuppositions. Preliminary understandings and responsible journeys into fuller understanding leave room for renegotiation, reshaping, and correction in the light of subsequent wrestling with the parts and the whole.

This is the point of our comments above about the way hermeneutics at a serious philosophical level nurtures respect for "the other," patience, and mutual understanding, without undermining the integrity of a belief that is sincerely and responsibly held. We noted Betti's comments on the need for hermeneutics in all universities and academia. The hermeneutical circle, as Heidegger insists, is not a vicious circle.[34] It invites not skepticism, but hard work and renewed "listening," albeit without surrender of one's critical capacities. This is why Grant Osborne's term "the hermeneutical spiral" more accurately suggests what all this implies.

Hermeneutics does not encourage the production of tight, brittle, fully formed systems of thought that are "closed" against modification or further development. The horizons of interpreters in hermeneutical inquiry are always moving and expanding, and always subject to fresh appraisal. Nevertheless, this does not exclude the importance of reasonable and coherent thought, or the emerging of "system" in a loose and flexible sense. This kind of coherence is compatible with the metaphor of the "nest" described by the later Wittgenstein. What a believer *"believes,"* he observes, is "not a single proposition, but a system of propositions (light dawns gradually over *the whole*)."[35] The child forms a flexible system of belief "bit by bit . . . some things stand unshakeably fast, and others are more or less liable to shift. . . . It is held fast by what lies around it."[36] Even a system of beliefs is not rigid; it is "a nest of propositions."[37] When might a belief system lose its identity or its integrity? The simile of the nest is appropriate. A *nest* might remain intact as an entity if a few of its twigs are lost or displaced; but if twig after twig is torn from it, this nest would cease to exist as a nest. Here perhaps is another

---

34. Martin Heidegger, *Being and Time* (Oxford: Blackwell, 1962), p. 194 (German edition, p. 153).

35. Ludwig Wittgenstein, *On Certainty,* German and English (Oxford: Blackwell, 1969), section 141, italics mine.

36. Wittgenstein, *On Certainty,* section 144.

37. Wittgenstein, *On Certainty,* section 225.

analogy of the relations between the parts and the whole in hermeneutics. Wittgenstein writes, "All testing . . . takes place already *within a system*"; but in opposition to Descartes, "Doubt comes *after* belief."[38] This is a different process from that adopted in more traditional philosophy, and we shall very shortly explore these differences further.

Meanwhile, we may note that although Gadamer shares Wittgenstein's concern for the importance of particular cases over against sweeping generalizations, even Gadamer appeals to the ancient Roman concept of *sensus communis* as a way of understanding that avoids the fragmentation of "technical" reason. He seeks some shared coming together of understanding in human life that relates the "parts" to a kind of working "whole," even in provisional ways that are still en route. In the terminology of the Greco-Roman classical world, he seeks *wisdom (phronēsis)* rather than "instrumental" or technical knowledge *(technē).*[39] Hermeneutics operates within this tension (or dialectic) between particular cases and a broader frame of reference. The latter provides a provisional coherence within the context of human history, human language, and human life.

5. Recommended Initial Reading

Jasper, David, *A Short Introduction to Hermeneutics* (Louisville and London: Westminster John Knox, 2004), pp. 7-28.

Jensen, Alexander S., *Theological Hermeneutics* (London: SCM, 2007), pp. 1-8.

Oeming, Manfred, *Contemporary Biblical Hermeneutics: An Introduction,* translated by Joachim Vette (Aldershot and Burlington, Vt.: Ashgate, 2006), pp. 7-10 and 15-27.

Thiselton, Anthony C., *New Horizons in Hermeneutics: The Theory and Practice of Transforming Biblical Reading* (London: HarperCollins; Grand Rapids: Zondervan, 1992), pp. 31-46.

————, *The Two Horizons: New Testament Hermeneutics and Philosophical Description* (Grand Rapids: Eerdmans; Exeter: Paternoster, 1980), pp. 3-23.

---

38. Wittgenstein, *On Certainty,* sections 105 and 160.
39. Gadamer, *Truth and Method,* pp. 19-30.

CHAPTER II

Hermeneutics in the Contexts of Philosophy, Biblical Studies, Literary Theory, and the Social Self

1. Further Differences from More Traditional Philosophical Thought: Community and Tradition; Wisdom or Knowledge?

There are further differences between hermeneutical thinking and more traditional philosophical thought. These arise in the first place from the contrast between a strong emphasis upon community and communal traditions in hermeneutics, and the emphasis placed upon individual consciousness mainly in rationalism but also in empiricism.

Descartes begins his philosophical reflection with the lone individual as "thinking subject," abstracted from the world. It is fundamental for Descartes that everything else is shut away and suppressed, to leave the individual alone with his or her thoughts. Archbishop William Temple, outraged at the unreality of such a posture and its implications about society, declares (even if with some overstatement) that this formulation marks "perhaps the most disastrous moment in the history of Europe."[1] Equally in the classic British empiricism of Locke, Berkeley, and Hume, it is likewise the individual's perceptions of sense impressions that begin the process of "knowledge," whether or not Locke also had wider social concerns in other contexts.

Gadamer, Ricoeur, Betti, and the major exponents of hermeneutical theory firmly oppose such an individualistic starting point. They also reject what they consider to be a naive and false "objectivity." Preliminary understanding begins with what we inherit from the wisdom or common sense of the community and traditions into which we were born and educated.

---

1. William Temple, *Nature, Man, and God* (London: Macmillan, 1940), p. 57.

Gadamer insists that the transmitted wisdom of communities ranks above the subjective data of the fallible individual "consciousness." To Gadamer this contrast probably ranks second in importance only to his contrast between "abstract problems" and "questions that arise."[2]

Ricoeur argues that psychoanalysis, psychology, and the social sciences provide a deeper understanding of the fallibility of individual consciousness than was available to Descartes in his time. This is emphatically *not* to reduce human "rationality" to the level of what is caused and conditioned by social or historical forces. Social factors and the historical era that shapes us do influence how we think and how we reason, but reasoning and reasonableness are not mere *products* or *constructions* of social or historical conditions, as in postmodern "social constructionism." On the other hand, Ricoeur rightly suggests that psychological and sociological advances do call into question the supposed sovereignty and "autonomy" of the individual's power of rational reflection and judgment. Pannenberg rightly also questions its theological validity.

Exponents of hermeneutics distance themselves, then, on one side from the naive overconfidence in human reason adopted by those who fail to recognize the influence of historical and social factors in shaping how we reason. On the other side they distance themselves from the pessimistic retreat from reason and rationality adopted by those who ascribe everything to social, historical, and economic forces. The latter represent the roots of postmodernism, not hermeneutics. In theological terms hermeneutics is distanced from a naive overconfidence in human reason that underestimates the distorting effects of human sin; and on the other side from those who hold a quasi-determinist view of socioeconomic forces as if these were all that counted in life.

Nevertheless, with Jürgen Habermas and with other sociocritical theorists, exponents of hermeneutics recognize the part played by "interests" of power, desire, self-affirmation, self-aggrandizement, and forces of oppression.[3] These may distort how people read and interpret texts, and in handling the sacred scriptures of faith communities these factors may lead to abuse. Yet on the other side they ascribe a positive role, even if within historical limits, to rational judgment and coherence among criteria of explana-

---

2. Hans-Georg Gadamer, *Truth and Method,* 2nd English ed. (London: Sheed and Ward, 1989), pp. 362-79.

3. Jürgen Habermas, *Knowledge and Human Interest,* 2nd ed. (London: Heinemann, 1978).

tion and understanding. Responsible interpretation entails both critical explanation and creative understanding. It is arguable that Gadamer pays insufficient attention to criteria of "true" interpretation, but in the terminology of Ricoeur, this entails both a hermeneutic of suspicion and a hermeneutic of retrieval.

Gadamer sees the role of the community as being of key importance for processes of understanding, just as Ricoeur sees interaction with "the other" as important for the ethical discussion of avoiding "narcissism."[4] Both thinkers demand and seek to cultivate openness to what speaks *from beyond* the individual self. Gadamer respects and accepts the humanism and concern for communal traditions that Giambattista Vico (1668-1744) championed, in contrast to the Enlightenment. Vico and Gadamer oppose excessive individualism and "the idle speculations of the Sophists."[5] Self-reflection by the individual, as entailed by the "method" of Descartes, can take the form of "a distorting mirror."[6]

Contrary to the rationalism of the secular Enlightenment, which elevates the autonomous individual above inherited traditions and values, Gadamer calls for "the rehabilitation of authority and tradition."[7] Recognition of these, he declares, "rests on . . . an act of reason itself which, aware of its own limitations, trusts to the better insight of others."[8] He rejects any supposed antithesis between inherited historical traditions and human knowledge. This coheres well with Christian theology. Pannenberg accepts that in one sense "autonomy" makes responsible agency possible, but in another sense the notion of moral autonomy has been "replaced by the caprice of individual self-determination," which reflects the self-centeredness of human sin and overlooks human destiny as fellowship with God and other persons.[9]

Ricoeur examines the impact of Nietzsche, Marx, and Freud upon the philosophy of Descartes. "The philosopher trained in the school of Descartes knows that things are doubtful . . . but he never doubts that consciousness is as it appears to itself. . . . Meaning and the consciousness of

---

4. Paul Ricoeur, *Oneself as Another,* trans. K. Blamey (Chicago and London: University of Chicago Press, 1992), especially pp. 113-297.

5. Gadamer, *Truth and Method,* p. 19.

6. Gadamer, *Truth and Method,* p. 276.

7. Gadamer, *Truth and Method,* pp. 277-85.

8. Gadamer, *Truth and Method,* p. 279.

9. Wolfhart Pannenberg, *Systematic Theology,* trans. G. W. Bromiley, 3 vols. (Edinburgh: T. & T. Clark; Grand Rapids: Eerdmans, 1991, 1994, 1998), 2:224-25.

meaning coincide. . . . For the first time comprehension (understanding) is hermeneutics."[10] Psychoanalysis and the biblical writings share a common witness, even if from different angles, concerning self-deception and "resistance to truth" on the part of individual consciousness or the "heart" (cf. Jer. 17:9 and 1 Cor. 4:4-5).

This resistance, Ricoeur explains, stems from "a primitive and persistent narcissism . . . a narcissistic humiliation" that involves "suspicion [and] guile" and is trapped within attempts to shelter the self from disclosures that come from beyond the self.[11] Ricoeur accuses Descartes of finding certitude devoid of truth.[12] For individual "consciousness" falls victim to thoughts and desires that are ultimately central in the self. Hermeneutics engages with wider, multiple horizons of meaning and understanding.

2. Approaches in Traditional Biblical Studies: The Rootedness of Texts Located in Time and Place

The metaphor of the "rootedness" of texts comes from Schleiermacher's comment on biblical interpretation, and we shall refer to it shortly. From around the sixteenth or seventeenth century to mid or late twentieth century, traditional approaches to interpretation in *biblical studies* took as their starting point the intention of the biblical writer or author, together with the historical context out of which the text emerged.

In historical terms, many in the early Church also placed a strong emphasis upon the mind and purpose of the authors or writers, especially in their commissioned role as apostles or prophets, as the starting point for meaning and interpretation. This is explicit in Diodore of Tarsus (died ca. 390) and John Chrysostom (ca. 347-407), and is prominent in Theodore of Mopsuestia (ca. 350-428), as well as in other interpreters within the "Antiochene" tradition. Theodore of Mopsuestia suffered some misunderstanding until relatively recently.[13] In the medieval period Peter Lombard

---

10. Paul Ricoeur, *The Conflict of Interpretations: Essays in Hermeneutics*, trans. D. Ihde (Evanston, Ill.: Northwestern University Press, 1974), pp. 148-49.

11. Ricoeur, *The Conflict of Interpretations*, p. 152; cf. also pp. 151-53.

12. Paul Ricoeur, *Freud and Philosophy: An Essay on Interpretation*, trans. Denis Savage (New Haven: Yale University Press, 1970), p. 44.

13. Dimitri Z. Zaharopoulos, *Theodore of Mopsuestia on the Bible: A Study of His Old Testament Exegesis* (New York: Paulist, 1989), especially pp. 103-41.

(ca. 1100-1160) and Andrew of St. Victor (1110-75) maintained an author-focused emphasis alongside a cautious use of allegorical interpretation.

Many think of John Calvin (1509-64) as the first "modern" biblical commentator. He brought to biblical exegesis the training of a Renaissance humanist in the universities of Orléans and Paris, and training in legal studies in which the "new" method was to begin with original historical contexts rather than with later legal commentaries. This harmonized well with Calvin's theological concern to go back to the original writings of the prophets and of the apostles and to the sayings of Jesus in contrast to later commentaries and strata of church tradition. At the same time, his approach remained contextual rather than atomistic, and like Luther, he retained a clear respect for the traditions of the earliest Church Fathers. He regarded these as regularly worthy of consideration, but not of uncritical replication. In his dedicatory preface to his commentary on Romans, Calvin states explicitly that the first duty of the commentator is to lay bare the mind of the author.[14]

Together with Martin Luther (1483-1546), Calvin stressed the importance of careful historical and linguistic research and inquiry, although with one theological proviso: biblical interpretation should remain mindful of the central place of Jesus Christ in divine revelation. Christ himself interpreted the Hebrew Bible in such a way that his work as Messiah shed light on it (Luke 24:27) and it also shed light on his work as Messiah (Luke 24:45-46). We shall look more closely at biblical interpretation of the Antiochene writers and the Reformers in later chapters.

In the nineteenth century Schleiermacher similarly argued that meaning and interpretation began with the intention of the author of a biblical text, with due regard also to the historical context and situation out of which the author wrote. "Only historical interpretation can do justice to the rootedness of the New Testament authors in their time and place."[15] In our later chapter on Schleiermacher, I argue that he did not merely have in mind some shadowy "mental state" or inner psychological process of "intending," but rather the goal and purpose behind and within a text that signal an author's desire, will, and action as evidenced in and by the text and its sur-

---

14. John Calvin, *Iohannis Calvini Commentarius in Epistolam Pauli ad Romanos*, ed. T. H. L. Parker (Leiden: Brill, 1981), p. 1. See also T. H. L. Parker, *Calvin's Old Testament Commentaries* (Edinburgh: T. & T. Clark, 1986), pp. 81-82.

15. Friedrich Schleiermacher, *Hermeneutics: The Handwritten Manuscripts*, ed. Heinz Kimmerle, trans. James Duke and Jack Forstman (Missoula: Scholars Press, 1977), p. 104.

roundings. Meaning and interpretation include more than these; but these remain his starting point.

It is sometimes forgotten that Schleiermacher's formulations of hermeneutics were motivated equally by both his concern for academic integrity and his vision for effective Christian preaching. While he was professor of theology in the University of Berlin, Schleiermacher also preached Sunday by Sunday in Berlin's Church of the Trinity. Effective biblical preaching, he wrote, involves "striking up the music" and awaking "the slumbering spark."[16] But this can be done only if the preacher catches the vision that inspired the biblical writer first to put pen to paper. Thus his pioneering the new discipline (then) of New Testament introduction was not to produce bare facts about the dates of documents, their integrity, or the editorial sequences of Gospels. Many students today often find "introduction" dull, tedious, and uninspiring. Yet its purpose was precisely the opposite: to provide an understanding of how New Testament documents are rooted in specific times, places, and historical situations. Nor was it to determine what linguistic repertoire was at their authors' disposal. New Testament introduction was meant truly to bring the documents alive as their authors wanted them to live and to speak.

This approach held sway in biblical studies until the second half of the twentieth century, and three grounds make it plausible at first sight. First, an author selects a specific language, vocabulary, grammar, syntax, and genre to serve *the purpose* for which he or she writes. Second, even in everyday speech, if we need to clarify the meaning of an utterance, we regularly ask the speaker or writer to explain further "what he or she meant." Third, in theology, the status of sacred texts as revelation often derives from the divine commission of the author or writer as prophet or apostle, or stems from the words of Jesus Christ.

The history of biblical interpretation and of the "reception" of biblical texts (discussed in chapter XV) well illustrates the necessity of considering the situation behind the text, and the purpose for which it was written. In a public lecture I delivered in the University of Chester, I cited several examples, including an episode drawn from the story of Jacob and Laban (Gen. 29–31).[17] In Genesis 31:49 Laban exclaims, "The Lord watch between you and

---

16. F. D. E. Schleiermacher, *On Religion: Speeches to Its Cultured Despisers*, trans. J. Oman (New York: Harper, 1958; original in German, 1799), pp. 119-20.

17. Anthony C. Thiselton, *Can the Bible Mean Whatever We Want It to Mean?* (Chester, U.K.: Chester Academic Press, 2005), pp. 10-11.

me when we are absent from each other." Numerous devout Christians have used this text as a fond commitment of a loved one or a dear friend to God as they part for a period of time. It is used as a kind of blessing and commitment each of the other to God's protection.

Is this what the verse means? One writer calls this "an un-meant" meaning. The Hebrew word for "to watch" *(tsaphah)* used here *can* bear this meaning in some contexts, but more often it denotes *watching out* for someone or something, typically for an enemy. The context from Genesis 29 onward portrays Jacob and Laban playing one dastardly trick after another against each other, each worse than the one before. These range from cheating the other out of flocks of sheep to ensuring that the other is lumbered with the wrong wife. The Hebrew of Genesis 29:25 is dramatic. Jacob had married, he thought, his beloved Rachel, presumably heavily veiled, and took her to bed. The Hebrew reads *bhabhoqer hinneh-hu' Leah:* "And in the morning: behold [choose any interjection that strongly expresses incredulous dismay] — Leah!" So *would* Laban have said to Jacob, "I do hope that the Lord will lovingly take care of you while we are parted, and commit your safety to him"? The verse means: "May the Lord glue his eyes on you, and avenge me if you try another trick!"

Without understanding the situation behind the text, the meaning may escape us. *Can* this text mean what it is sometimes taken to mean within a tradition of religious pietism? In a purely descriptive sense it *can.* But is this a *textual* meaning when everything in the context excludes such a meaning on the part of the text, the narrator, and the speaker? We shall return to these questions again, especially when we discuss the claim that readers, not authors, "make" meaning.

In the same lecture I used another example from 1 Corinthians 6:1-8. Here Paul declares, "If one of you has a dispute with another, how dare he go to law before a pagan court" (6:1). "Must Christian go to law with Christian? . . . You suffer defeat if you go to law" (vv. 6-7). A widespread assumption is that these verses condemn any resort to the law on the part of Christians. But is this the point at issue, not least for twenty-first-century readers? Historical and archaeological research demonstrates that although Corinth was a Greek city in the geographical sense, the constitution, politics, law, and government of Corinth were modeled on the institutions of Rome, not Greece, in Paul's day. Julius Caesar had refounded it as a Roman *colonia* in 44 B.C., and from Paul's time to that of Hadrian virtually all inscriptions were in Latin, not Greek. This bears on our passage, for while Roman *criminal* law was relatively impartial, *civil* lawsuits operated differently. It was expected that both parties to a dispute would offer incentives to the judge (and when applicable, to the jury) to grant a favorable verdict. This might be an unashamed financial bribe, or offering the benefit of business contacts, invitations to prestigious social events, gifts of property or slaves, or whatever.

In such a situation, only rich and influential Christians would consider taking a fellow Christian to the civil courts. Paul attacks not a responsible use of law; indeed, he himself appeals to Roman law. Here he attacks the inappropriate *manipulation* of a fellow Christian through the use of superior wealth, power, patronage, social influence, or business networks. This amounts to using indirect force to gain what the wealthier party covets. Prohibition of resort to law as such is not what these verses *mean*. They can mean whatever we want them to mean only if we fly in the face of the historical situation that illuminates Paul's purpose in writing these words. Careful inquiry into Paul's purpose, the responsible use of reason, and respect for contextual constraints discern the meaning of the passage in relation to its rootedness in time and place. Traditional approaches in biblical studies have honored and observed this principle since at least the time of the Reformation, and in many cases, long before then.

3. The Impact of Literary Theory on Hermeneutics and Biblical Interpretation: The New Criticism

Why, then, did anyone challenge such an apparently reasonable, time-honored approach? Challenges arose at first not from within biblical studies or classical philology, but *from within literary theory*. A text was often deemed to be "literary" if it seemed to carry with it layers and levels of meaning that very often transcended the immediate conscious thoughts of the writer. Many literary theorists came to believe that texts conveyed meanings in effect as autonomous systems of signs and meanings in their own right, apart from the writer or author who had produced them.

Such a view came to prominence in the late 1930s and in the 1940s with the literary theory of John C. Ransom (1938), René Wellek (1949), Monroe C. Beardsley (1946 and 1954), and others. The movement of thought they represented came to be known under two names: the New Criticism and literary formalism. Their immediate target for attack was nineteenth-century Romanticism, in which J. G. Herder, Schleiermacher, and Wilhelm Dilthey, among others, had looked to causes "behind" texts, especially the vision that moved the authors, to account for their meaning and to promote their understanding. Wellek and Warren began their *Theory of Literature* (1949) with an attack of Dilthey's notion of the "causal antecedents" of texts.[18] Romanticism tended to stress (indeed to overstress) the role of the individual genius of a creative author in producing great literature.

In 1946 Wimsatt and Beardsley produced a famous, or infamous, essay that carried enormous influence at the time, called "The Intentional Fallacy." They attacked what they perceived as a conceptual confusion between a poem itself and the *origin* of the poem. They aimed at a supposed "objectivity" that rejected the notion of a poem as the "personal expression" of a poet, and perceived it as having independent, autonomous existence as an entity in its own right. They defined "intention" as a "design or plan in the author's mind," and on this basis questioned whether such an inner, mental entity could readily be discovered. Even if it could be discovered, they insisted, it would not be relevant to a poem's meaning. They formulated what became a famous (or, later, infamous) axiom: "The design or intention of the author is neither available nor desirable as a standard for judging the success of a work of literary art."[19] Any material "outside" the text, namely, what they called "external evidence," belongs to literary *biography,* not to literary criticism or to questions about the *text.* This material "leads away from" the poem; the text is detached from the author.

We need not pursue the development of the New Criticism or literary formalism further, except to note that in 1968 Roland Barthes revived the notion of a text as a self-contained system in his well-known essay "The Death of the Author."[20] We touch on this further in chapters X and XVI when we consider the impact of structuralism and postmodernism, respectively, on hermeneutics.

For roughly twenty years (very broadly, 1950-70) approaches in biblical studies and in literary theory tended to go in separate ways. But from the 1970s a number of biblical specialists became increasingly captivated by vari-

18. René Wellek and Austin Warren, *Theory of Literature* (London: Jonathan Cape, 1949; 3rd ed., Pegasus, 1973), p. 17.

19. W. K. Wimsatt and Monroe C. Beardsley, "The Intentional Fallacy," *Sewanee Review* 4 (1946): 468-88; revised and republished in Wimsatt and Beardsley, *The Verbal Icon: Studies in the Meaning of Poetry* (Lexington: University Press of Kentucky, 1954), pp. 3-18.

20. Roland Barthes, "The Death of the Author" (1968), in *Image-Music-Text,* trans. Stephen Heath (London: Fontana, 1977), especially pp. 145-47.

ous approaches and assumptions in literary theory. In a positive direction this opened up new understandings of the nature of biblical narrative, narrative devices, including "points of view." In a more negative direction some biblical specialists became uncritically seduced by notions of the autonomy of the text, even if the text was not clearly "literary." Some biblical scholars appealed to "the intentional fallacy," even calling it more explicitly "the genetic fallacy." They followed Wimsatt and Beardsley in asserting that the traditional approach confused meaning with the historical origins. This was unfortunately made more plausible by a different confusion between meaning and origins in lexicography and linguistics about the meanings of *words*. This different point reflects the valid principle in general linguistics, identified and expounded most notably by James Barr, that *etymology* very often said more about the history of a word than about its meaning.[21] This is discussed in chapter X. The notion of the autonomy of a *text*, however, belongs to a quite different set of ideas.

Several points that arise in the context of the New Criticism, however, clearly fail to apply to biblical interpretation. These suggest that we think further about this matter before being seduced by what was once "modern."

First, it is transparently false to claim that *in all cases* "external" factors fail to shed light on the meaning of a biblical text. We have just seen in the previous section that in Genesis 31:49 and in 1 Corinthians 6:1-8 the *meaning* of the words of Laban and of Paul's language about going to law is constrained and restricted by its context in the historical situation out of which the texts grew. The same principle applies to the meaning of Paul's language about the wearing of hoods or veils in 1 Corinthians 11:2-16, or about divisions in the Lord's Supper in 11:17-34. These passages can be fully *understood* only in the light of dress codes expected of respectable Roman married women in the mid–first century, and in the light of Roman dining customs and dining space as evidenced by such writers as Tacitus.[22] We cannot "understand" the point of the parable of the Pharisee and the tax collector (Luke 18:9-14) *today* unless we know from "external" evidence that Pharisees were admired and respected for their devotion to the law in the time of Jesus.

21. James Barr, *The Semantics of Biblical Language* (Oxford: Oxford University Press, 1961), pp. 107-60.

22. Anthony C. Thiselton, *The Epistle to the Corinthians: A Commentary on the Greek Text*, New International Greek Testament Commentary (Grand Rapids: Eerdmans; Carlisle: Paternoster, 2000), pp. 418-40 and 799-899; and Thiselton, *1 Corinthians: A Shorter Exegetical and Pastoral Commentary* (Grand Rapids: Eerdmans, 2006), pp. 88-92 and 169-91.

They were not considered a metaphor for self-righteousness or hypocrisy, as the term "Pharisee" too readily and unhistorically suggests today.

Second, Wimsatt and Beardsley explicitly apply their "literary" approach to *poems* and *poetry* in their essay, not to texts that address a specific message to a specific audience at a specific time for a specific purpose related to that situation. In Schleiermacher's phrase, they were not concerned with texts that were "rooted in time and place." Admittedly the Bible contains much poetry. Some texts were deliberately written in poetic form. In such cases, and indeed in some self-contained parabolic narratives, the point made by literary theorists merits careful consideration and due weight. It may well apply in general terms, although careful exegesis will judge each case on its own merits. The Bible contains many examples in which a prophetic promise that a writer clearly applied to Israel may seem to have further extended applications, perhaps to Christ as Messiah of Israel. James Smart insists that the "first step" of all interpretation must be to hear the text as it was first spoken or written; but, he asks: "May there not be a meaning in words of scripture that was not fully known or understood by the person who spoke or wrote them?"[23] He applies this to Isaiah 40–55, which includes the Suffering Servant passage of 53:1-12.

Third, intention does not always denote an inner mental state of the kind that remains known only to the person who does the intending. It is misleading to think of it as a "mental state" at all in many cases. In my book *New Horizons in Hermeneutics* I have suggested that we can avoid such an assumption and probable misunderstanding if we call this *directedness,* or *intentional directedness.*[24] "Intention" is best understood when we use the term as an adverb, as in "Did you do it *intentionally?*" In such terms a supposedly mysterious quest to discover an inner state is exposed as irrelevant. Wimsatt and Beardsley attack an overeasy target. In law a court often needs to judge whether a deed was done by accident or intentionally, even "with malice aforethought." The complexity of the logical "grammar" of intention has been discussed in philosophy in meticulous detail by such writers as Elizabeth Anscombe and Ludwig Wittgenstein. Some concepts of intention, they argue, too easily direct our attention to the wrong thing.[25]

23. James Smart, *The Interpretation of Scripture* (London: SCM, 1961), pp. 34-35.

24. Anthony C. Thiselton, *New Horizons in Hermeneutics: The Theory and Practice of Transforming Biblical Reading* (London: HarperCollins; Grand Rapids: Zondervan, 1992), pp. 558-61.

25. Ludwig Wittgenstein, *Philosophical Investigations,* German and English (Oxford: Blackwell, 1967), sections 334-37.

We might perhaps summarize the differences between traditional approaches in biblical interpretation (as those of Calvin and of Schleiermacher) and approaches characteristic of the New Criticism or literary formalism (such as those of Wimsatt and Beardsley) in the following way:

Figure 2

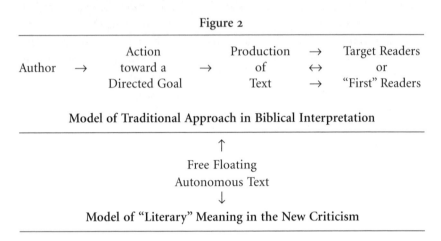

Model of Traditional Approach in Biblical Interpretation

Model of "Literary" Meaning in the New Criticism

There are also further gains to the impact of literary theory on biblical studies. Robert Morgan and John Barton have traced some of these at the level of method in their book *Biblical Interpretation* (1988). Morgan claims that this approach can bridge "the gulf between critical scholarship and religious faith."[26] One such example is Robert Alter's *Art of Biblical Narrative* (1981), which includes a reflection on the two different accounts of the call of David in 1 Samuel 16:1-23 and 1 Samuel 17–2 Samuel 5, respectively. Alter interprets these as representing, stereoscopically, as it were, divine control (1 Sam. 16:12, 13) and the hurly-burly of human life (1 Sam. 17:1–2 Sam. 5:5).[27] David Gunn, Stephen Prickett, and in his own way Hans Frei have also explored this approach to advantage. But, as we are seeing, there are also disadvantages.[28] To avoid placing a

26. Robert Morgan (with John Barton), *Biblical Interpretation* (Oxford: Oxford University Press, 1988), pp. 10, 25, and 198.

27. Robert Alter, *The Art of Biblical Narrative* (New York: Basic Books, 1981), pp. 147-53.

28. Anthony C. Thiselton, "On Models and Methods: A Conversation with Robert Morgan," in *The Bible in Three Dimensions: Essays in Celebration of Forty Years of Biblical Studies in the University of Sheffield,* ed. David J. Clines, Stephen Fowl, and Stanley E. Porter, Journal for the Study of the Old Testament: Supplement Series 87 (Sheffield: Sheffield Academic, 1990), pp. 337-56.

high emphasis on biblical criticism also means placing a low emphasis on historical reference and enfleshment or "bodiliness." It becomes docetic.

4. The Impact of Literary Theory: Reader-Response Theories

Before we leave the subject of the impact of literary criticism, at least for the present, we may note one further development that followed the realization, even among literary theorists, that the New Criticism failed to address certain problems. The next generation of literary theorists after the New Criticism were not slow to acknowledge that notions of an "autonomous" text seemed to leave the text detached not only from its author, but also from the subject matter to which it referred, and even from its readers. It appeared to lose any anchorage in the public world, or reality. It is reasonably well established in literary theory that whether texts are deemed "literary" or nonliterary depends on judgments made by *readers.*

Hence, by the late 1960s and certainly during the 1970s and 1980s, there emerged a movement that in effect tended to supersede the New Criticism. This movement promoted the view that the key determinant for the production of meaning was the *reader* or *readers.* Meaning was less a product of the author or the text as such, or even of the relation between the text and its author, than a product of the relation between *the text and its readers. How readers responded to the text* came to be regarded as the main source and determinant of meaning. This approach came to be known as *reader-response theory.* Again, as in the New Criticism, this theory emerged in literary criticism before it entered the discipline of biblical studies. We devote half of chapter XV to reader-response theory.

One of the more sophisticated literary critics, Frank Lentricchia, considers the 1950s and 1960s retrospectively from the vantage point of 1980, and comments: "The great hope for literary critics in 1957, when the hegemony of the New Criticism was breaking, was . . . that younger critics would somehow link up poetry with the world again."[29] But "the world" was not now primarily that of the author, nor that to which the text referred, but the readers or community of readers and what *they made of* the text. A number of textbooks and volumes of essays were produced that carried such titles as

---

29. Frank Lentricchia, *After the New Criticism* (Chicago: University of Chicago Press, 1980), p. 7.

The Reader in the Text, which also included an essay under the title "Do Readers Make Meaning?"[30] In this essay Robert Crosman concludes: "Meaning is made precisely as we *want* it to be made."[31]

We can now begin to see some of the theoretical questions that lie behind what is a very practical question about the Bible for Christian believers: "Can the Bible mean whatever we want it to mean?" How we answer this question relates very closely indeed to the theory of texts and the theory of meaning that we hold. An answer cannot be given without stating our theory of text and meaning; or, in different language, our theory of hermeneutics.

Later we shall trace how these issues are related to structuralism, post-structuralism, and postmodern thought. Reader-response theories vary widely in their outlooks from moderate and largely constructive versions to more radical and more questionable formulations, as we see in chapter XV. Many place Roman Ingarden among the earlier New Critics, but because he called attention to the open-endedness or "indeterminacy" of many texts, Ingarden more notably paved the way for the idea that readers "fill in" gaps left in texts in their own particular ways. He thus laid the foundation for reader-response theory. He compared the ways in which we tend to "fill in" gaps in our daily perceptions of the world to make sense of it, or interpret it. We might perceive in fact only three sides of a cube, or only three legs of a table, but we then project an interpretation that ascribes six faces to the cube, or four legs to the table.

Wolfgang Iser developed this approach in greater detail. Readers, Iser argued, always *bring* something of their own *to* the text. In effect, they "fill in gaps" the text may have left open, or where it is nonexplicit. Iser's books *The Implied Reader* and *The Act of Reading* are classic sources for "moderate" reader-response theory.[32]

Nevertheless, differences among reader-response theorists became so radical that one of the most extreme advocates of the theory (he would say, one of the most consistent), namely, Stanley Fish, attacks Iser's moderate version with more ferocity than he displays in various other discussions. He

30. Susan R. Suleiman and Inge Crosman, eds., *The Reader in the Text: Essays on Audience and Interpretation* (Princeton: Princeton University Press, 1980); cf. Robert Crosman, "Do Readers Make Meaning?" in *The Reader in the Text,* pp. 149-64.

31. Crosman, "Do Readers Make Meaning?" p. 164.

32. Wolfgang Iser, *The Implied Reader: Patterns of Communication in Prose Fiction from Bunyan to Beckett* (Baltimore: Johns Hopkins University Press, 1974), and *The Act of Reading: A Theory of Aesthetic Response* (Baltimore: Johns Hopkins University Press, 1978, 1980).

attacks Iser not only for being too cautious, but also for being "objectivist." Fish maintains that there is nothing "in" the text to interpret, because, like Nietzsche, he believes that everything that exists is only interpretations. We can ask of a text not what it means, but only: "What does this text *do?*" He declares, "The reader's response is not *to* the meaning; it *is* the meaning."[33]

We reserve for chapter XV a fuller discussion of reader-response theories. I shall argue that, depending on the text in view and the type of theory under consideration, this approach *either* encourages more active participation and engagement by the reader *or* leads to the kind of self-projection into the text that Ricoeur rightly associates with self-centered narcissism and idolatry. This may refer to the corporate self-interest of a like-minded community of readers. In its most radical form (Fish would call this its most consistent form) it is difficult to see how any text, including the Bible, could confront its readers as "other," in grace or judgment, if it is first preshaped into what accords with the desires and selfhood of the readers. Dietrich Bonhoeffer declares that we meet with no more than an idol if through the text we encounter "what accords with me."[34] Once again, a diagram may indicate the different models of reading that are under discussion.

Figure 3

Author	→	Text	↔	Readers

A Moderate Version of Reader-Response Theory

Readers	↔	Constructed
	→	Text

A More Radical Reader-Response Mode

5. Wider Dimensions of Hermeneutics: Interest, Social Sciences, Critical Theory, Historical Reason, and Theology

One positive gain reader-response theory has produced is: it has underlined the part played inevitably by the beliefs and assumptions that readers

33. Stanley Fish, *Is There a Text in This Class? The Authority of Interpretive Communities* (Cambridge: Harvard University Press, 1980), p. 3; cf. pp. 12, 13, and 1-17.

34. Dietrich Bonhoeffer, *Meditating on the Word* (Cambridge, Mass.: Cowley, 1986), pp. 44-45.

and interpreters bring with them to texts. Not only is it the case that *authors and texts* are shaped by their place in history, but *readers* are no less shaped by their own place in history and in society as readers and interpreters. This brings together what Gadamer calls historically conditioned reason (which relates to "effective history") and what Jürgen Habermas calls *interest.*

Interest, in this technical sense, relates very closely to what Schleiermacher, Bultmann, and Gadamer mean by a *preliminary understanding,* or to use their technical term, "pre-understanding" (discussed in chapter I, section 4). To be sure, *pre-understanding* is a *negotiable and provisional* starting point, for which the word "presupposition" may sometimes be misleading, since it often seems to suggest fixed beliefs that cannot be changed. Nevertheless, the idea of *interest* goes further than pre-understanding, because it denotes a specific kind of pre-understanding, namely, that which serves *self-interest* especially in terms of *power,* self-affirmation, or the gratification of desire by the self. Interest arises in part from distorted perspectives that arise from self-centered values.

Georg W. Hegel (1770-1831), Schleiermacher's contemporary and rival in the University of Berlin, first fully expounded the notion of *historical reason* as embedded in processes of history and tradition. Hegel saw how the ongoing process of history shapes human ways of thinking, and more especially how our place within history governs our values. Kierkegaard insisted that his speculative idealism, or philosophy of the Absolute as Spirit, represented a denial of this very insight. Nevertheless, Hegel initiated a new, "historical" way of understanding, which became central for philosophical hermeneutics, especially in Dilthey, Heidegger, and Gadamer. Furthermore, it opened the way for a more socially orientated way of thinking, in contrast to the individualism of Descartes, the British empiricists, and Kant.

Thus Karl Marx (1818-83), Wilhelm Dilthey (1833-1911), Max Weber (1864-1920), Karl Mannheim (1893-1947), and more recently Jürgen Habermas (b. 1929) all attempted to bring such a social dimension to *"historical"* theories of interpretation in the wake of Hegel. In effect they applied theories of understanding, or hermeneutics, not only to texts, but also to *social institutions* and social theory. Marx attempted a theory of history and society based on the formative power of economic forces and social action alone. Mannheim and Habermas allowed for the role of distortion, partiality, and *interest* on the part of the interpreters, as rooted and situated in a given time. For Dilthey, *"life" (Leben)* took the place of spirit or mind *(Geist)* in Hegel, and arguably Dilthey was the first to introduce hermeneutics systematically into the social sciences.

Habermas attacks *positivist* theories of knowledge mainly because of their mistaken claims to be value-neutral or genuinely "objective." "Consciousness," he claims, is largely shaped by social life as well as by historical existence. Like Ricoeur, Habermas draws on Freudian psychoanalysis as a resource for formulating a critique of human self-interest and misdirected desire. Both thinkers believe that unconscious drives can "block" factors that the human agent or interpreter wants to suppress. Habermas addresses the debate that constantly arises about the relation between rationality and social theory. In his *Theory of Communicative Action* he seeks to provide a place for the particularities of hermeneutics in relation to communication and to social worlds. Some of his critics, however, claim that he tends to reduce genuine hermeneutics to social theory. On his side, Habermas criticizes Gadamer for neglecting the social realities of hermeneutics.

In Christian theology the concept of *misdirected desire* brings us to the heart of the nature of human sin. I have discussed this at length in my *Hermeneutics of Doctrine*.[35] Habermas shares with biblical traditions and with Christian theology the recognition that *positivism* (or in more theological terms, a secular-scientific worldview) is far from "neutral" with respect to values, and is just as likely to distort understanding and communication as any other ideology or system of belief. To exclude theism or theology from the interpretation of texts is just as biased or value-laden as to impose any other belief onto the enterprise. It is an example of secular or antitheist *interest*. Indeed, arguably theological interpretation in biblical studies pays more respect to the nature of the text in question than to its exclusion. A hermeneutic of suspicion must be exercised against false, often secular pretensions to a false objectivity,

Several writers in biblical studies and theology have recently underlined this point with convincing force. Francis Watson argues that, like every other discipline, biblical interpretation has its "social base" outside the academy, and this is legitimately the worshiping community of the Church. He attacks as other than neutral "a commitment to academic secularity." He writes: "The assumption that faith is incompatible with proper academic standards or with openness to alternative viewpoints is ultimately a mere prejudice, what-

---

35. Anthony C. Thiselton, *The Hermeneutics of Doctrine* (Grand Rapids: Eerdmans, 2007), chapters 12 and 13. See also Pannenberg, *Systematic Theology*, 2:231-76.

ever the practical grounds for caution over the issue."[36] R. W. L. Moberly rightly exposes and laments the ironic self-contradiction that characterizes the work of the Bible and Culture Collective, which produced *The Postmodern Bible*.[37] These "postmodern" writers ought to have been more aware than others of the role of "interest"; but, Moberly writes, "In practice their ignoring the concerns of Christian and Jewish faith performs precisely the function of marginalizing such concerns in favour of a wholly secularized agenda. Theirs is an exercise in persuasive definition."[38] Peter Balla, Christopher Seitz, and Jens Zimmermann, among others, make similar points.[39]

The problem of interest, self-affirmation, desire, and self-deception may emerge in greater detail, not least in Ricoeur's "hermeneutic of suspicion" (in chapter XII). In these first two chapters our aim has been to indicate something of the nature and scope of hermeneutics as an academic and practical discipline. Hermeneutics, including biblical hermeneutics, cannot be true to its task unless it is genuinely multidisciplinary and interdisciplinary.

6. Recommended Initial Reading

Jensen, Alexander, *Theological Hermeneutics*, SCM Core Text (London: SCM, 2007), pp. 207-17.

Oeming, Manfred, *Contemporary Hermeneutics* (Aldershot and Burlington, Vt.: Ashgate, 2006), pp. 31-54 and 60-74.

Palmer, Richard E., *Hermeneutics: Interpretation Theory in Schleiermacher, Dilthey, Heidegger, and Gadamer* (Evanston, Ill.: Northwestern University Press, 1969), pp. 43-71 (in most libraries, but may be out of print).

Thiselton, Anthony C., *New Horizons in Hermeneutics* (London: Harper-Collins; Grand Rapids: Zondervan, 1992), pp. 55-71.

---

36. Francis Watson, *Text, Church, and World: Biblical Interpretation in Theological Perspective* (Edinburgh: T. & T. Clark, 1994), p. 9; see also pp. 1-17.

37. Bible and Culture Collective, *The Postmodern Bible* (New Haven: Yale University Press, 1997), and R. W. L. Moberly, *The Bible, Theology, and Faith: A Study of Abraham and Jesus* (Cambridge: Cambridge University Press, 2000), pp. 26-39.

38. Moberly, *Bible, Theology, and Faith*, p. 35.

39. For example: Jens Zimmermann, *Recovering Theological Hermeneutics: An Incarnational-Trinitarian Theory of Interpretation* (Grand Rapids: Baker Academic, 2004); Christopher R. Seitz, *Figured Out: Typology and Providence in Christian Scripture* (Louisville: Westminster John Knox, 2001).

CHAPTER III

An Example of Hermeneutical Methods:
The Parables of Jesus

We turn next to the interpretation of the parables of Jesus because the parables offer an excellent workshop of examples in which few hermeneutical approaches can be called "wrong," and many are fruitful. The historical or literal approach places the parables in a historical situation, which illuminates them, but some of the parables also invite a very different approach.

Some parables verge on allegory in their original form; many open up a narrative "world," anticipating Gadamer and Ricoeur; some invite a reader-response approach; many are "existential," and require attention even to the characters of the parable. At the same time, many of the parables show the utterly different dynamic of interpretation used in parable and allegory respectively. Perhaps some parables also show both the value and the limits of reader-response theory, and the limited freedom of an interpreter to use what psychological or semiotic (sign) theories he or she wishes.

1. The Definition of a Parable and Its Relation to Allegory

Charles H. Dodd provided a definition of the parable proper more than half a century ago that is still as relevant as ever. In *The Parables of the Kingdom* he wrote, "At its simplest the parable is a metaphor or simile drawn from nature or common life, arresting the hearer by its vividness or strangeness, and leaving the mind in sufficient doubt about its precise application to provoke it into active thought."[1] According to Joachim Jeremias, "The parables are a fragment

---

1. Charles H. Dodd, *The Parables of the Kingdom* (London: Nisbet, 1935), p. 16.

of the original bedrock of tradition. . . . Pictures leave a deeper impress on the mind than abstractions."[2] Robert Funk comments on each of Dodd's four elements. First, metaphor is deeper than symbol or analogy, and involves the whole person. Second, parables may be vivid because of their supposedly contrasting values. For example, an unjust manager is commended (Luke 16:8) and an unjust judge is bullied and pestered by a widow (Luke 18:5-6). Sometimes the vividness arises not from contrast but because the hearers actually see or hear of the event, as when the tower-builder left his work half-done because he ran out of money (Luke 14:28-30). The parable is vivid but simple. Third, the parable is certainly drawn from everyday life. For example, it may be about measures of flour, or weeds and wheat (Matt. 13:24-29). Fourth, and this is Funk's main point, the parable arrests hearers by an imprecise application that makes them think for themselves, such as the commendation of the unscrupulous manager (Luke 16:8).[3] Funk comments, "The parable is not closed, so to speak, until the listener is drawn into it as a participant."[4] Already we are beginning to look at some examples of reader-response theory.

Does Dodd's definition of a parable, however, include all parables? Do not some offer self-evident truths from life, and have an obvious application bordering on aphorism? Adolf Jülicher, over a hundred years ago, saw self-evident example stories as evidence that a parable originated authentically with Jesus. Such "authentic" examples included the parable of the rich fool (Luke 12:16-21).[5] But Dodd makes it clear that, contrary to Jülicher, he is considering what he regards as "proper" parables, which are distinctive parables with a dynamic of their own.

Neither Dodd nor Jülicher appears to be entirely right. Amos Wilder rightly argues, "Jesus uses figures of speech in an immense number of ways. . . . Indeed we must say that the term 'parable' is misleading since it suggests a simple pattern, and often distorts our understanding of this or that special case."[6] Jeremias similarly points out, "The Hebrew *mashal* and

---

2. Joachim Jeremias, *The Parables of Jesus,* trans. S. A. Hooke, rev. ed. (London: SCM, 1963), p. 11.

3. Robert W. Funk, *Language, Hermeneutic, and Word of God* (New York: Harper and Row, 1966), p. 133.

4. Funk, *Language,* p. 133.

5. Adolf Jülicher, *Die Gleichnisreden Jesu,* 2nd ed., 2 vols. (Freiburg: Mohr, 1899-1900), pp. 92-111.

6. Amos M. Wilder, *Early Christian Rhetoric* (Cambridge: Harvard University Press; London: SCM, 1964), p. 81.

the Aramaic *mathla* embraced all these categories . . . parables, similitude, allegory, fable, proverb, apocalyptic revelation, riddle, symbol . . . jest. Similarly parable in the New Testament has not only the meaning 'parable,' but also 'comparison' (Luke 5:36; Mark 3:23) and 'symbol.' . . . In Mark 7:17 it means 'riddle,' and in Luke 14:7 simply 'rule.'"[7] Jeremias makes a similar point about the Greek word *paroimia* in John 10:6 and John 16:25, 29. This offers a challenge to hermeneutics. Craig Blomberg states, "The dominant approaches in the twentieth century to the interpretation of the parables are misguided and require rethinking."[8]

Blomberg argues that for many centuries the Christian Church interpreted parables as allegories, but modern critical scholarship follows Jülicher and Jeremias in rejecting allegorical interpretation. But, Blomberg comments, many parables contain allegorical elements, and even the New Testament interprets some as allegorical. The scholarly consensus, he argues, is unduly selective. The latest scholarship recognizes that parables include more than the simple comparisons that Jülicher and others supposed.

All the same, the dynamics of interpreting parables and allegories are very different. A parable proper catches a listener off guard. It wounds from behind. How did the prophet Nathan approach King David when God told him to expose his adultery with Bathsheba? He could simply have confronted him, but confrontation is seldom wise with Oriental kings, even an Israelite king. He told him a story. A passerby visited a rich man, and the wealthy man determined to show him the best of hospitality. But he ignored what his own flocks could amply have provided and stole the one ewe lamb of his neighbor, which had been his pride and joy. "Who is the fellow?" David asked. "He should be flogged to death!" "You are the man," Nathan explained. "In spite of your many concubines and riches, you have plundered the one delight of your neighbor Uriah." At this point David broke down to acknowledge his fault. The parable draws the listener into a narrative world, and gently the application places him under attack (2 Sam. 12:1-15).

The dynamics or function of the allegory is quite different. An allegory is like a code. In Ezekiel 17:1-10 "the mighty eagle" represents Nebuchadnezzar, who comes to "Lebanon," which stands for Jerusalem. He seizes the topmost branch of the "cedar," which represents Jehoiachin, and carries it off to the "land of trade," which clearly in this context means Babylon. This is an alle-

---

7. Jeremias, *The Parables of Jesus,* p. 20.
8. Craig L. Blomberg, *Interpreting the Parables* (Leicester: Apollos, 1990), p. 14.

gory addressed to "insiders," who can work out the code. Most scholars regard Matthew 22:1-14 as also ending in an allegory. It might seem extreme and certainly not part of everyday life for a person to send troops to deal with someone who declines an invitation. So this is more than a parable. Israel invites judgment on herself here. Eta Linnemann comments, "An allegory cannot therefore be understood unless one knows . . . the state of affairs to which it refers. Anyone who does not have this Key can read the words, but the deeper meaning is hidden from him. Allegories therefore may serve to transmit encoded information, which is only intelligible to the initiated."[9]

An allegory therefore *presupposes* shared understanding; a parable *creates* shared understanding. There are two further differences. An allegory addresses *insiders* who are in the know; a parable attacks, or seeks to win over, *outsiders.* Further, it is crucial that on the whole a parable presents an entirely *coherent narrative world;* an allegory can contain a string of *independent applications.* Often this is expressed by insisting that a parable has only one point. But although this often follows, it does not always follow, and this view has been attacked.

The principle is broadly true if it is not used in a doctrinaire and universal way to determine what parables come from Jesus rather than the early Church. In English literature the best-known example of an allegory is John Bunyan's *Pilgrim's Progress.* Here the purpose is didactic, and it *assumes* an intimate knowledge of the Bible. The lost coin in the New Testament (Luke 15:8-10), however, is a real coin in a real, ordinary, everyday room. In *A Pilgrim's Progress* the Holy Spirit sweeps a room, which is code for his cleansing the heart. Mr. Worldly Wiseman is not a genuine character, but a biblical mind-set. The Slough of Despond is not a real location, but code for passing through despondency. The same can be said of being a prisoner of Giant Despair. All this is allegory.

So does it matter whether we find parable or allegory in the New Testament? It matters greatly, for each is to be interpreted differently. In many parables (though not in all) the listener is drawn into a narrative world. Funk is right in his assessment of the parable of the prodigal son and envious brother (Luke 15:11-32). The word of grace divides the audience into elder and younger sons. Funk writes, "The Pharisees are those who insist on interpreting the word of grace rather than letting themselves be interpreted

9. Eta Linnemann, *Parables of Jesus: Introduction and Exposition,* translated by John Sturdy from 3rd edition (London: SPCK, 1966), p. 7.

by it. The elder son is he who insists that his loyalty counts for something: his loyalty must be the basis of interpretation."[10] The repentant people in the audience identify with the younger son and share his delight at welcome.

Yet as soon as the father becomes "God," is this not an allegory? It goes beyond most parables, but its dynamics of interpretation are not those of an allegory. It works, or has its effects, only when the listener is "lost" in a coherent, real narrative world. The well-worn question: "Is this parable or allegory?" must be answered according to its hermeneutical function and the textual genre. The answer is seldom a simple one. Meanwhile Funk insists, "The parables as pieces of everyday lives have an unexpected 'turn' in them which looks through the commonplace to a new view of reality."[11] Anticipating or following Gadamer's view that understanding is inseparable from application, Funk comments, "Response does not follow but accompanies the parable."[12] "Younger sons" in the audience find themselves welcomed; "elder sons" find themselves rebuffed. In Wolfgang Iser's reader-response theory, they "understand" as their response to the parable completes its meaning.[13]

2. The Plots of Parables and Their Existential Interpretation

Not all the parables of Jesus share the same hermeneutical dynamic. Bultmann and Jeremias distinguish the similitude, which draws from typical or recurrent situations in life, from parables that draw from particular, probably unrepeatable situations. The parable of the leaven depicts what always happens when leaven is added to the meal (Matt. 13:33). It is therefore classed as a similitude. The parable of the mustard seed also depicts its flourishing to relative greatness regularly (Matt. 13:31-32). The respective attitudes of masters and servants also depict a typical situation (Luke 17:7-10).

Other parables depict what someone once did. Jülicher observes, "We are not shown what everyone does, but what someone did once, whether or

---

10. Funk, *Language*, p. 17.

11. Funk, *Language*, p. 161.

12. Funk, *Language*, p. 180.

13. Wolfgang Iser, *The Act of Reading: A Theory of Aesthetic Response* (Baltimore and London: Johns Hopkins University Press, 1978), pp. ix-x and 163-232. Cf. Anthony C. Thiselton, *New Horizons in Hermeneutics: The Theory and Practice of Transforming Biblical Reading* (London: HarperCollins; Grand Rapids: Zondervan, 1992), pp. 515-23.

not other people would do it the same way."[14] The parable of the dishonest manager (Luke 16:1-8) is a good example. Jülicher comments, "The similitude appeals to what is universally valid: the parable proper to what happens only once. . . . The similitude guards against opposition because it speaks of only established facts."[15] The parable guards against opposition by its warm, fresh, or gripping narrative. Nowadays we might say "narrative world." It is also often fictional, and catches the listener off guard. The parable of the Good Samaritan offers another good example (Luke 10:29-37). It is not usual for a Samaritan to help a Jew, but on this one occasion a "world" is opened up where love conquers convention or justice. This kind of parable, as Ernst Fuchs observes, gives up the use of force.

Jülicher and Linnemann insist that the parable has only one point, in contrast to allegory, which produces a string of independent applications. Linnemann writes, "In the parable the evaluation that the narrative compels one to make has to be carried over to another level" (i.e., from picture to reality, or in German scholarship since Jülicher, from the picture-half [Bildhälfte] to the content-half [Sachhälfte]).[16] Linnemann describes the parables as having "narrative laws."[17] This comes largely from Bultmann, who argues that the parables reflect the "laws" of popular storytelling, often with a buildup that he calls "end stress," the sending of the servants to the vineyard (Mark 12:2-8). They often involve groups of three (the priest, the Levite, and the Samaritan [Luke 10:24-37]); and those who make excuses, in the parable of the great supper or marriage feast (Matt. 22:1-10; Luke 14:16-24); and especially the "rule" of contrast, in the wise and foolish virgins (Matt. 25:1-11) and in the rich man and Lazarus (Luke 16:19-31).[18] Bultmann, too, argues that a parable has only one point, uses contrast and antithesis, and often uses gradation. All this shows the artistry of Jesus, although also supposed embellishments of the early Church or of the Synoptic tradition. The parables also often involve high emotional intensity. Finally, parables are often told with an economy of detail.

Sometimes exceptions can be found to these so-called rules. Via is right in distinguishing between "comic" and "tragic" plots. In the so-called comic

14. Jülicher, *Die Gleichnisreden Jesu*, 1:93.

15. Jülicher, *Die Gleichnisreden Jesu*, 1:97.

16. Linnemann, *Parables of Jesus*, pp. 4-7.

17. Linnemann, *Parables of Jesus*, pp. 8-16.

18. Rudolf Bultmann, *History of the Synoptic Tradition*, trans. John Marsh (Oxford: Blackwell, 1963), pp. 188-92.

parables, everything comes right in the end. These include, he observes, the workers in the vineyard (Matt. 20:1-16), the dishonest manager (Luke 16:1-9), and the prodigal son (Luke 15:11-32).[19] In the tragic parables, like all tragedies, the hero or heroine faces disaster, which the audience, but not the hero or heroine, can see coming. These include the parable of the talents and one-talent man (Matt. 25:14-30), the ten maidens (Matt. 25:1-13), and the man without a wedding garment (Matt. 22:11-14). All these parables have a clear and discernible plot, with an upward dynamic into well-being or a downward dynamic into tragedy.

Moreover, Via brings out the existential dimension of the parables. In the parable of the laborers in the vineyard (Matt. 20:1-16), each worker receives at least an agreed-upon, fair day's wage. Some, it is true, receive even more, to the consternation of those who dislike the notion that grace supersedes justice. Generosity is even greater than, and eclipses, justice. "When he [the employer] pays the last workers a full day's wage for one hour's work . . . our very existence depends on whether we will accept God's gracious dealings; his dealings shelter our calculations about how things ought to be ordered."[20] The dishonest manager "lived beyond the world of communal norms."[21] He showed shrewd action in a crisis (Luke 16:1-9). The story of the prodigal son is about reconciliation, remorse, status as a person (the shoes, ring, and robe), and welcome or envy and bitterness (Luke 15:11-32).

The tragic parables are even more clearly existential. The one-talent man saw himself as a victim: "I knew that you were a harsh man," he tells the employer. Hence his desire to be rid of responsibility and accountability leads to, indeed constitutes, his loss of opportunity.[22] He does not wish to take a risk; therefore risks will be removed: he will not be given the rule over any city. The punishment is one of "internal grammar." On the parable of the foolish maidens Via writes, "The foolish maidens too presumptuously believed that their well-being was guaranteed, no matter what they did. . . . They supposed that someone else would take care of them, that someone else will pay the bill."[23] They are not in control of the time of coming, chosen by the bridegroom, but live and act as though they are, self-deceived because

---

19. Don Otto Via, *The Parables: Their Literary and Existential Dimension* (Philadelphia: Fortress, 1967), pp. 147-76.

20. Via, *The Parables,* p. 154.

21. Via, *The Parables,* p. 160.

22. Via, *The Parables,* p. 120.

23. Via, *The Parables,* p. 126.

for a long time nothing seems to happen (Matt. 25:1-13). The third parable is about a man who attempts to attend a wedding in dirty clothes. His attempt "manifests his split existence. . . . Man is limited in that he cannot choose certain courses and stances and also avoid disastrous consequences."[24] He tried to get the best of both worlds.

It cannot but cross our mind to ask, however, whether Via draws too many details from a main-point parable. This reaches huge proportions in Geraint Vaughan Jones's exposition of the existential significance of the parable of the prodigal son.[25] Jones addresses the concerns of Bultmann and Jeremias in detail but rejects their "one-point" rule as owing more to theory than practice. Parables, he argues, involve the whole existential human condition. The historical approach, he insists, is too restrictive. Many less well-known interpreters of the parables have explored their details. He names C. G. van Koestveld and J. A. Findlay among these, citing also the Old Testament background and especially the Wisdom literature, where there are various kinds of comparisons. He also looks at the rabbinic background.[26] He cites Paul Fiebig's use of a number of parables from the Talmud. The parables, he argues, are a work of art. Whatever tradition has done, like all good art, the parables transcend time and place.

Jones wrote at a time when reader-response theory was only just beginning to make an impact on biblical studies. Whether the details of parables have the place that he demands may depend on how the reader responds, although this already takes them from the realm of history. He particularly makes his case with a superb interpretation of the parable of the prodigal son (Luke 15:11-32). This is a parable, Jones argues, about the personalness of life, freedom, and estrangement, and decision and reconciliation. These are all existential themes. The defiant younger son thinks he chooses freedom and independence, but "the new self living in destitution and abandonment is in a sense different from the confident, defiant, self, at the moment of departure. . . . He is a stranger, unwanted and anonymous, experiencing the utter nausea of dereliction." Jones continues, "The Parable is the flight into estrangement and the return through longing."[27] Jones explores the existential themes of nausea, anxiety, anonymity, and despair. "When the Prodigal

---

24. Via, *The Parables*, p. 132.

25. Geraint Vaughan Jones, *Art and Truth of the Parables* (London: SPCK, 1964), pp. 135-66.

26. Jones, *Art and Truth*, pp. ix-xii and 59-64.

27. Jones, *Art and Truth*, p. 175.

walks out of his father's house, and when Adam leaves the Garden of Eden, they enter a disenchanted world in which they are not at home."[28] It is a microcosm of the human situation. The younger son is in anguish. "When the crash comes, he is deserted: his friends and associates abandon him for they were bound to him only by money, the flimsiest of all bonds. He finds life empty and meaningless without personal relationships, and he becomes desperate. . . . Nobody wants him."[29] Even after his return, the elder son treats him less as a person than as a type, to be dealt with by a standardized approach.

The father, however, restores the younger son's personhood. He bestows upon him a ring, a robe, and shoes, signs of personhood. "He is regaining his character through once more being treated as a person."[30] It is part of the archetypal restoration of all things, which is the heart of the gospel. But exclusion from the feast is not peculiar to this parable. The foolish virgins and the man without the wedding garment make voluntary choices that lead to their exclusion and hence isolation.

Does Jones make too much of the details? He certainly explicates what is implicit in the parables. Whether this is legitimate depends in part on whether we give priority to historical interpretation or to reader-response theory. As we shall see below, there are various versions of the latter.

3. The Strictly Historical Approach: Jülicher, Dodd, and Jeremias

Jülicher was professor of New Testament at Marburg from 1888 to 1923, and one of Rudolf Bultmann's teachers. He is typical of the liberal ascendancy represented by Adolf von Harnack and others. Much of his two volumes on the parables relates to their authenticity as words of Jesus. He reversed the trend of nineteenth-century writers to interpret the parables as having a series of independent points, as if they were allegories. The best known of these writers is Archbishop R. C. Trench.

Jülicher distinguished sharply between parable as simile, which he believed went back to Jesus, and parable as puzzling metaphor, which he believed was due to the destructive editing of the Synoptic tradition or the

---

28. Jones, *Art and Truth,* p. 177.
29. Jones, *Art and Truth,* p. 185.
30. Jones, *Art and Truth,* p. 191.

early Church. Similes *(Vergleichung)* are obvious or straightforward in meaning. Metaphors are puzzling, unless the reader or audience knows the code. There is all the difference between saying "A lion rushed on" as a metaphor for Achilles, and saying "Achilles rushed on like a lion," which is a simile. Metaphor is nonliteral speech, and for this Jülicher used the German *uneigentliche Rede*. By contrast, the simile is described as "literal speech," for which the German is *eigentliche Rede*. Unfortunately these terms also may mean inauthentic speech and authentic speech, respectively.

It was a short step, therefore, for Jülicher to regard metaphor as inauthentic, and similes as authentic, words of Jesus.[31] He was convinced that Jesus would have taught only simple, generalizing truths that were easy to understand. He believed that "example stories" *(Beispielerzählung)* were typical of Jesus. The parable of the Good Samaritan (Luke 10:29-37) is supposedly simple, obvious, and authentic to Jesus. The parable of the talents simply meant "Wise use of the present is the condition of a happy future," or "A reward is earned only by forbearance."[32] The parable of the sons of the bridechamber, who do not fast, means only "Religious sentiment is valuable only if it expresses a proper sentiment."[33] The parable of the rich man and Lazarus (Luke 16:19-31) means only that a life of suffering can be followed by great joy.[34]

J. D. Kingsbury rightly claims that Jülicher inaugurated the modern era of parable interpretation, and Warren Kissinger calls him "a colossus in the history of the interpretation of parables."[35] Nevertheless, he has been severely criticized. His liberal premises meant that he saw Jesus as a teacher of general truths rather than as a preacher who demanded an active response and often used indirect communication. Archibald M. Hunter is scathing. Hunter asks why a man who goes about Galilee drawing innocuous morals from life should be nailed to a cross and crucified. Would people have crucified someone who told picturesque tales to reinforce prudential platitudes?[36]

Nearer to Jülicher's time, Christian A. Bugge in 1903 and Paul Fiebig in

---

31. Jülicher, *Die Gleichnisreden Jesu*, 1:92-111.

32. Jülicher, *Die Gleichnisreden Jesu*, 2:495 and 511.

33. Jülicher, *Die Gleichnisreden Jesu*, 2:188.

34. Jülicher, *Die Gleichnisreden Jesu*, 2:638.

35. Warren S. Kissinger, *The Parables of Jesus: A History of Interpretation and Bibliography* (Metuchen, N.J., and London: Scarecrow, 1979), pp. 71-72.

36. A. M. Hunter, *Interpreting the Parables* (London: SCM, 1964); cf. Hunter, *The Parables Then and Now* (London: SCM, 1971).

1904 and 1912 put forward serious criticisms of Jülicher based on the Old Testament and Judaism. Bugge admitted that some parables were clear, and their meaning self-evident. But the Hebrew *mashal* could include dark sayings, riddles, and puzzles (Ezek. 17:22; Dan. 4:10). Both Bugge and Fiebig argued that Jülicher's view owed more to Aristotle's Greek definition of parable as a comparison than to the Hebrew background that would have been familiar to Jesus. His definition of parables offers no good reason for deciding which parables are authentic to Jesus.[37] Fiebig insists on the originality and lifelikeness of the parables of Jesus. They concern grace, prayer, mercy, love, and the rule or kingdom of God. In 1912 Fiebig published a second volume on the parables of Jesus.[38] Here he considers thirty-six parables from the Babylonian and Jerusalem Talmuds, the rabbinic midrash, and the Mishnah.[39] Again, he attacks Jülicher for his reliance on Greek thought.

It is surprising that Jülicher's work is regarded as foundational by so many in the light of criticisms by Bugge and Fiebig. It may have something to do with the liberal spirit of the times, and with the fact that the allegorical method of Trench and of the nineteenth century was dominant and needed correction. Jülicher did point out the difference between parable and allegory, and the need for a historical approach. Yet today Robert Stein and Craig Blomberg are among many who point out its severe limitations.[40] Stein calls attention to his doctrinaire approach to "one point" parables and his emphasis on general moral truths. Funk argues that an exclusively didactic approach violates the hermeneutical dynamics of many parables.

In spite of its historical skepticism, Albert Schweitzer's *Quest of the Historical Jesus* did at least draw attention to the preaching of Jesus as eschatological proclamation, as Johannes Weiss had done before him.[41] The kingdom of God was a matter of God's dynamic reign. Schweitzer also believed that the message of the parables was not obvious to all, but to a chosen few.

Next came the era of form criticism, with Martin Dibelius and Rudolf

---

37. C. A. Bugge, *Die Haupt-Parabeln Jesu* (Geissen: Ricker, 1903), and Paul Fiebig, *Altjüdische Gleichnisse und die Gleichnisse Jesu* (Tübingen: Mohr, 1904), pp. 14-73.

38. Paul Fiebig, *Die Gleichnisreden Jesu im Licht der rabbinirohen Gleichnisse der neutestamentlichen Zeitalters* (Tübingen: Mohr, 1912).

39. Fiebig, *Die Gleichnisreden Jesu*, pp. 6-118.

40. Robert H. Stein, *An Introduction to the Parables of Jesus* (Philadelphia: Westminster, 1981), pp. 54-58.

41. Albert Schweitzer, *The Quest of the Historical Jesus*, trans. W. Montgomery (London: Black, 1931).

Bultmann.[42] Both emphasized eschatological crisis, such as we have in the parable of the dishonest manager. But both made questionable claims about the *Sitz im Leben* (setting in life) of parables, locating too many in the life of the early Church. Bultmann argued that the parables were "word pictures" *(Bildworte)*, while similitudes *(Gleichnisse)* were different. There are also example stories *(Beispielerzählungen)*. Bultmann assigned many to early Christian tradition. But on the whole, British scholarship was more cautious. Vincent Taylor, T. W. Manson, and Charles H. Dodd valued form criticism, but not as a way of evaluating the origins or authenticity of all parables. In 1935 Dodd delivered his more moderate lectures at Yale on *The Parables of the Kingdom,* which proved to be a further milestone in the historical interpretation of parables.

Dodd argued that the parables were perhaps the most characteristic element in the teaching and preaching of Jesus. For centuries they had been interpreted allegorically, but Dodd agreed with Jülicher and Bultmann that this was misguided. Dodd also stressed the eschatological nature of many parables, and looked cautiously to form criticism to establish a *Sitz im Leben,* where possible. Often the "crisis" moved, in his view, from the end time to the ministry of Jesus. Dodd rejected Jülicher's emphasis on "general truths," seeing many parables as applying to specific situations. The parable of the pearl of great price, for example, concerns the specific quest of a pearl merchant. But the parable, in contrast to the allegory, had one point.

In accordance with form criticism, Dodd also distinguishes between a typical setting in the life of Jesus and a setting in the life of the early Church. We should not exclude beforehand the possibility of more than a single setting *(Sitz im Leben),* not least because the parable of the lost sheep has an evangelistic setting in Luke 15:3-7 and a pastoral setting in Matthew 18:12-14. Clearly the context in Matthew 18 concerns the Church and its leaders, while Luke 15 concerns Pharisaic criticisms of Jesus' reaching out to the lost. In Luke the parable is about celebration when the lost are found; in Matthew 18 it is pastoral concern for the vulnerable flock (18:10, 11). The same parable is used in two settings with more than one application.

Dodd extends this principle to "the Day of the Son of Man" and the parables' "setting in life" *(Sitz im Leben).* He cites the parables in Q, Matthew,

---

42. Martin Dibelius, *From Tradition to Gospel,* trans. B. L. Woolf (London: Clarke, 1971), throughout, and Bultmann, *History,* especially pp. 39-68.

and Luke that refer to the coming of the Son of Man, and suggests that often "It is not clear therefore that the saying originally conveyed an explicit prediction of the 'coming' of the Son of Man."[43] What is the relation between the resurrection of the Son of Man and his "coming"? In the parable of the wicked husbandmen (Mark 12:1-8), for example, the reference may be to "an allegory constructed by the early Church" about the death of Jesus, as Jülicher argued. Dodd thinks the original parable has a genuine historical setting in the life of Jesus, but that the *testimonium* from the Old Testament used by all three Synoptic Evangelists has been added by the early Church (Mark 12:10 and parallels). Luke, he believes, has added a further saying about a stone that brings disaster upon those on whom it falls (Luke 20:18). Moreover, the Evangelists may well have increased the number of servants in this parable, to represent "the long toll of the prophets."[44] "The beloved Son" also suggests the hand of the early Church.

This is a relatively cautious but serious application of form criticism. To the parable of the dishonest manager Dodd believes the Evangelist has added three moralizing endings about acting in a crisis (Luke 16:1-7). "Realizing the seriousness of his position, he [the manager] does some strenuous thinking, and finds out a drastic means of coping with the situation."[45] This is the basic message of Jesus, with a comment about "the sons of this age" being more prudent than the sons of light. But the further applications come from Luke or the Synoptic tradition. In particular, most of "the parables of crisis," including the faithful and unfaithful servants, the thief at night, and the ten virgins (Matt. 24:45-51; 24:43-44, cf. Luke 12:39-40; Matt. 25:1-13), "were originally intended to refer to a situation already existing. . . . When the immediate crisis passed, the parables were naturally re-applied to the situation . . . after the death of Jesus . . . the expectation of the second advent."[46] But a parable can have more than one setting.

Joachim Jeremias builds on Dodd in his standard work on the parables, the sixth German edition of which was published in 1962.[47] Funk is right to say that Jeremias largely ignores the hermeneutical dynamic of many of the parables. His aim is wholly that of retrospective historical reconstruction. He wants to establish the original teaching of Jesus. But "as none has better

43. Dodd, *Parables of the Kingdom*, pp. 94-95.
44. Dodd, *Parables of the Kingdom*, p. 129.
45. Dodd, *Parables of the Kingdom*, p. 30.
46. Dodd, *Parables of the Kingdom*, pp. 170-71; cf. pp. 154-74.
47. Jeremias, *The Parables of Jesus*.

shown than C. H. Dodd, Jülicher left the work half done."[48] Like Dodd, he rejects Jülicher's aim of rediscovering "a single idea of the widest possible generality," believing that Jülicher missed the scope of the Hebrew *mashal*.[49] He argues, "It was C. H. Dodd's book which achieved the break-through."[50]

Jeremias traces a series of events that he believes take us from Jesus to the early Christian Church. These include the translation from Aramaic to Greek; changes in vocabulary; embellishment; the influence of the Old Testament in the Church; change of audience; the hortatory use of parables; the Church's situation; allegorization; and examples in which some parables are conflated with others. Change of setting *(Sitz im Leben)* also contributes significantly to this change. Jeremias claims for example that in the parable of the wheat and the tares (Matt. 13:36-43), certain peculiarities are out of place in the teaching of Jesus. He argues that 13:37 goes back to Matthew himself. In 13:40-43 and 49-50 there is mainly the requirement for patience. But in verse 37 it is impressed upon the *Church* that the time of separation has not yet come.

4. The Limits of the Historical Approach: A Retrospective View?

In the first half of his book, however, even Jeremias is not always right. We have already seen that the original parables as Jesus told them contain allegorization. Further, Jeremias's use of the *Gospel of Thomas* remains controversial as a means of establishing what comes from Jesus. The "crisis" that accompanies the word of Jesus may equally apply to the second advent. The use of vocabulary in the Epistles need not imply its prior use in the early Church; it may be the other way round. The Epistles may reflect at times the language of Jesus. I tried to show as long ago as 1970 that the endings of such parables as Luke 16:1-8 were not necessarily at odds with the intention of Jesus, through dialogue with linguistic philosophy.[51] Above all, it is not contradictory to say that parables can both conceal and reveal. The parable of the sower (Mark 4:1-9) does not necessarily contradict the interpretation of the parable of the sower (Mark 4:11-20). Both tell the preacher to go on sowing, despite disappointments. The section on the purpose of parables (Mark

---

48. Jeremias, *The Parables of Jesus*, p. 19.

49. Jeremias, *The Parables of Jesus*, pp. 19-20.

50. Jeremias, *The Parables of Jesus*, p. 21.

51. *Thiselton on Hermeneutics: Collected Works with New Essays* (Grand Rapids: Eerdmans; Aldershot: Ashgate, 2006), pp. 417-40.

4:11-12) holds together divine decree (Mark's "in order that," Greek *hina*) with the "so that" of Matthew and Luke. We have seen that the parable of the prodigal son confirms some of the audience as repentant younger sons but others as complacent elder sons. This passage is true to the intention of Jesus, and the citation of Isaiah 6:9-10 is not necessarily due to the artifice of the early Church, as Lane, Jones, and Cranfield rightly insist.[52]

Nevertheless, Jeremias recounts the themes of the parables well in the second half of his book. The kingdom of God comes and grows with the proclamation of the new age, and of Christ as deliverer. He is the shepherd of the oppressed flock (Matt. 15:24; Luke 19:10). Jesus is the physician come to heal the sick (Mark 2:17). He plunders the house of the strong man bound (Mark 3:27; Matt. 12:29). There are no half measures. The new wine is for new wineskins (Mark 2:21-22; Matt. 9:16; Luke 5:36-38); the new garment does not have a patch. Moreover, great endings will come from this beginning. The mustard seed becomes great (Mark 4:30-32; Matt. 13:31-32; Luke 13:18-19). Leaven permeates the dough (Matt. 13:33; Luke 13:21; *Gos. Thom.* 96). Here is a growth that cannot be stopped. The small band of the disciples of Jesus will become the great people of the new covenant. The parable of the sower (Mark 4:3-8; Matt. 13:3-9; Luke 8:5-8; *Gos. Thom.* 9) guarantees this, as does the parable of the seed growing secretly (Mark 4:26-29).

The parables also speak of God's mercy for sinners. These parables "are the most familiar and most important."[53] They include, again, the parable of the mustard seed, and of the leaven; the parables of the lost sheep and lost coin (Luke 15:1-10), the prodigal son and elder brother (Luke 15:11-32), and the parable of the tax collector and the Pharisee (Luke 18:9-14). The meaning of the latter is lost unless we reconstruct historically the religious status and piety of the genuine Pharisee. The parable is a shocking tale, which reverses expected values. These parables both attack opponents and are a veiled assertion of the authority of Jesus.

Third, many parables, Jeremias continues, are designed to give "the great assurance."[54] These include, again, the parables of the mustard seed

---

52. Cf. William L. Lane, *The Gospel of Mark* (London: Marshall, Morgan and Scott, 1974), pp. 156-63, and Charles E. B. Cranfield, *The Gospel according to St. Mark: A Commentary*, Cambridge Greek Testament (Cambridge: Cambridge University Press, 1959), pp. 150-63. Geraint Vaughan Jones also attacks the "one-point" view as doctrinaire in *Art and Truth*, pp. 41-166.

53. Jeremias, *The Parables of Jesus*, p. 124.

54. Jeremias, *The Parables of Jesus*, pp. 146-60.

and of the leaven. Jeremias also includes the seed growing secretly, the unjust judge (Luke 18:2-8), and the friend who arrived at night (Luke 11:5-8). The point of all these is that "the petition will be granted."[55]

Under these headings Jeremias includes parables of judgment or warnings of urgency. His headings are "The Imminence of Catastrophe" (the parable of the children in the marketplace, Matt. 11:16-17; Luke 7:31-32; and the parable of the rich fool, Luke 12:16-20; *Gos. Thom.* 63); the theme "It May Be Too Late" (the parable of the ten virgins, Matt. 25:1-13; and the parable of the great supper, Matt. 22:1-10; Luke 14:15-24); and "The Challenge of the Hour" (the rich man and Lazarus, Luke 16:19-31; the parable of the man without a wedding garment, Matt. 22:11-13).

Finally there are "Realized Discipleship," "The Via Dolorosa and the Exaltation of the Son of Man," "The Consummation," and "Parabolic Actions." The twin parables of the pearl of great price (Matt. 13:45-46; *Gos. Thom.* 76) and treasure in the field (Matt. 13:44; *Gos. Thom.* 109) stress not the cost of discipleship but its wonder and joy. "The same thought finds expression in the Parable of the Great Fish presented in the Gospel of Thomas 8."[56] Jeremias includes the Good Samaritan and the parable of the unmerciful servant. The theme of the consummation includes the parables of the tares and wheat (Matt. 13:24-30) and dragnet (Matt. 13:47-48), but some of the traditional crises are assigned only to the setting of the ministry of Jesus.

A purely historical approach sheds considerable light on the parables and saves us from wild, irresponsible application. Jeremias is largely followed by Eta Linnemann, whose approach is broadly historical but perhaps less restrictive. But *this was not the approach of most writers in the patristic and medieval eras.* We select here five examples from the patristic period. We return to the subject in chapters V and VI.

1. *Irenaeus* (ca. A.D. 180) approached most parables allegorically. For example, the treasure in the field was Christ (Matt. 13:44).[57] Since the joy of discipleship *is* Christ, arguably this is not allegory. But the parable of the wedding garment is used allegorically to expound doctrine, with an emphasis on "outer darkness."[58] Certainly he treats the parables of the laborer in

55. Jeremias, *The Parables of Jesus*, p. 159.
56. Jeremias, *The Parables of Jesus*, p. 201.
57. Irenaeus, *Against Heresies* 4.26.1.
58. Irenaeus, *Against Heresies* 4.26.6.

the vineyard, the fig tree, the wheat and the tares, and the Good Samaritan as detailed allegorical sources of doctrine.

2. *Tertullian* (ca. 210) treated many parables allegorically, including for example that of the prodigal son. The elder son stands for the Jew; the younger for the Gentile or the Christian. The ring represents baptism; the feast is the Lord's Supper or Eucharist; the fatted calf stands for Jesus.[59] Sometimes he is more cautious and gives only a "historical" application, as with the parable of the lost coin.[60]

3. *Clement of Alexandria,* Tertullian's near contemporary, regarded all Scripture as parabolic and looked regularly for its hidden meanings. The parable of the mustard seed, he argues, witnesses both to the unstoppable nature of the Church and to the medicinal properties of mustard. The fowls of the air who perch in its branches are the angels.[61] In the parable of the vineyard and laborers (Matt. 20:1-16), the day's wage is salvation, in accordance with appropriate "mansions" (from John 14:2).[62] Clement gives an elaboration of the details of the parable of the prodigal son (Luke 15).

4. *Origen* (ca. 240) allegorizes much of Scripture, as if the text represented "body, soul and spirit" with a literal, moral, and spiritual meaning.[63] We explore this in more detail below. In the parable of the Good Samaritan (Luke 10:30-33), for example, the man who goes down from Jerusalem is Adam; Jerusalem represents Paradise; Jericho is the world; the robbers are demons or false prophets; the priest represents the powerlessness of the law; the Levite represents the prophets; the Samaritan is Christ; the wine is the word of God; the oil is the doctrine of mercy; the inn is the Church; the innkeeper represents the apostles and their successors; and the two denarii or pence (AV/KJV) are the two Testaments.[64]

5. *Augustine* also interprets the man half-dead as Adam or the human race, fallen into partial knowledge of God. The Samaritan is Christ. Baptism is the oil and wine, and the inn is the Church. The Samaritan's promise to return becomes the return of Christ at the parousia.[65] Augustine admits that

---

59. Tertullian, *On Modesty* 9.2.
60. Tertullian, *Against Marcion* 30.11.2.
61. Clement, *Fragments from the Hypotyposes* 4.
62. Clement, *The Stromata* 4.6.
63. Origen, *De principiis* 4.1.11.
64. Origen, *Homilies on Luke* 34, and *Fragment* 71.
65. Augustine, *Questionam evangeliorum* 2.19, and *Sermon* 69.7. Cf. also Kissinger, *The Parables of Jesus,* pp. 26-27.

allegorical interpretation helps preaching because it allows the preacher to use ingenuity, but on the whole he is cautious about allegorical interpretation, except in parables. (See chapter VI.)

In this light one may sympathize with Jülicher, Dodd, Jeremias, and Linnemann about "one point." The historical approach provides necessary restraint and discipline in the interpretation of parables. Nevertheless, there is often "more" than the historical approach allows, including the veiled Christology that many parables convey. Each parable must be assessed and interpreted on its own merits.

5. The Rhetorical Approach and Literary Criticism

1. *Amos Wilder* set in motion a new movement, especially in America, that owed much to literary criticism. His method was to reveal the rhetorical dynamic of the New Testament. Norman Perrin, Robert Funk, Dan Otto Via, and John Dominic Crossan owed much to his pioneering work. Wilder called this a "transhistorical approach." The approach is not without cost, however, for it concentrates on the literary at the expense of the historical and theological, except in certain cases.

Wilder emphasizes the poetic nature of much of the language of Jesus.[66] He uses "speech-event" loosely to mean a renewal of language. Genre is also important to Wilder. Gospel, Acts, Letter, and Apocalypse are all different, and must be interpreted differently. In contrast to dialogue and poetry, he stresses the continuity of the parable form with prophets and apocalyptists. They are revelatory. Citing Ernst Fuchs, Wilder sees parables as calling forth faith. They offer "a potent and dynamic word."[67] The parables also come from the wisdom tradition, where communication is often indirect or "from behind." Finally they permit the hearer to make his or her own response. In his later book *Jesus' Parables and the War of Myths,* Wilder is a little more cautious.

2. Clearly *Robert Funk* appropriates much of this. We have seen how he criticizes Jülicher and Jeremias for missing the hermeneutical function of

---

66. Amos N. Wilder, *Early Christian Rhetoric* (Cambridge: Harvard University Press; London: SCM, 1964; the second edition of *Jesus and the Language of the Gospel* [Philadelphia: Fortress, reprinted 1976, 1982]), p. 23.

67. Wilder, *Early Christian Rhetoric,* p. 86.

parables. They are more than a storehouse of cognitive statements.[68] He recognizes the part played by Ernst Fuchs and Gerhard Ebeling. He sees that parables interpret the hearer, not the hearer the parables. He prefers the power of metaphor to mere didactic writing. "Metaphor shatters the conventions of predication in the interests of a new vision. . . . The metaphor is a means of modifying the tradition."[69] "Parables as pieces of everydayness have an unexpected 'turn' in them."[70] Yet Funk does not entirely abandon a "historical" approach. Matthew "corrects" Luke's parable of the great supper in view of the situation of the Church of his time.

3. I have discussed the work of *Dan Otto Via* in *New Horizons in Hermeneutics,* and we commented above on his book *The Parables: Their Literary and Existential Dimensions* with reference to the plots of "comic" and "tragic" parables.[71] Via later wrote *Kerygma and Comedy in the New Testament* (1975) and *The Revelation of God and Human Reception in the New Testament* (1997), as well as some smaller books including some on ethics.[72] In *Kerygma and Comedy* he takes a semiotic or formalist approach that represses or bypasses historical questions, but he is sensitive to the limitations of such approaches.

4. Successive numbers of the journal *Semeia* also explored semiotic and structuralist approaches, but many consider this a blind alley. The volumes *Semiology and Parables* and *Signs and Parables* are also formalist collections of essays.[73] Semiotics and literary formalism have a strictly limited usefulness in showing how elements of a text relate to each other. In Via's language, this approach may explain *from what* a text derives its functions and power.[74] But it remains debatable whether or how far this bracketing out of history genuinely sheds light on the meaning of parables.

---

68. Funk, *Language,* pp. 126-35.

69. Funk, *Language,* p. 139; cf. pp. 133-62.

70. Funk, *Language,* p. 161.

71. Thiselton, *New Horizons in Hermeneutics,* pp. 492-94.

72. Dan Otto Via, *The Revelation of God and/as Human Reception in the New Testament* (Harrisburg, Pa.: Trinity; London: Continuum, 1997) and *Kerygma and Comedy in the New Testament Parables* (Philadelphia: Fortress, 1975).

73. Daniel Patte, ed., *Semiology and Parables: Exploration of the Possibilities Offered by Structuralism for Exegesis* (Pittsburgh: Pickwick, 1976), and the Entrevernes Group, *Signs and Parables: Semiotics and Gospel Texts,* with a study by Jacques Geninasca, postface by A. J. Greimas, trans. Gary Phillips, Pittsburgh Theological Monograph 23 (Pittsburgh: Pickwick, 1978).

74. Patte, *Semiology and Parables,* pp. 1-70; cf. pp. 71-179; and John Dominic Crossan, *In Parables: The Challenge of the Historical Jesus* (New York: Harper and Row, 1973), pp. 247-372.

5. The work of the Irish American *John Dominic Crossan* (b. 1934) does shed light on the meaning of parables, at least in his earlier work. In his book *In Parables* (1973) he discusses parable in relation to allegory and metaphor, but perhaps his greatest contribution is on "parables of reversal."[75] He concedes that some parables are simply example stories. But many are not. The parable of the Good Samaritan, for example, would not have had a Samaritan as hero if it were an example story. "The Jews have no dealings with the Samaritans" (John 4:9) is the historical and sociological background. Hence "neighbor" and "Samaritan" seem a contradiction in terms to the Jewish audience. If we were hearing a mere example story, "it would have been far better to have made the wounded man a Samaritan and the helper a Jewish man."[76] The hearers were confronted with "the impossible, and having their world turned upside down and radically questioned."[77] The word "good" does not go with "Samaritan."[78] Nowadays we do not share these presuppositions. One former student of mine learned this lesson too well. He told the parable to a Northern Irish Protestant congregation, with a Catholic priest as the hero and an Orangeman as the villain who passed by "on the other side" (Luke 10:31).

This explains why the parable of the rich man and Lazarus (Luke 16:19-31) falls within the context of the love of worldly goods. It is still a parable of reversal. It runs counter to the expectations of the audience. Crossan writes, "Its metaphorical point was the reversal of expectation and situation, of value and judgement, which is the concomitant of the Kingdom's advent."[79] Similarly the parable of the Pharisee and the tax collector (Luke 18:10-14) reverses the expectation of the audience about a devout religious observer of the Law and a cruel, greedy collaboration with Romans. Nowadays most people miss the point by unhistorically and anachronistically construing "Pharisee" as synonymous with hypocrisy. Thus the parable becomes a cozy Victorian moral tale about rewarding humility, which is the opposite of its purpose. Walter Wink makes this point the same year as Crossan. In addition to the reversal of expectation, these parables underline the phenomenon of historical distance.

Other parables of reversal cited by Crossan include the rich fool, the

75. Crossan, *In Parables*, especially pp. 53-78.
76. Crossan, *In Parables*, p. 64.
77. Crossan, *In Parables*, p. 65.
78. Crossan, *In Parables*, pp. 57-66.
79. Crossan, *In Parables*, p. 68; cf. pp. 56-68.

vineyard workers (Matt. 20:1-16), the wedding guest (Luke 14:1-14), the great supper (Matt. 22:1-10), and the prodigal son and elder brother (Luke 15:11-32). Crossan writes, "Can you imagine, like Jesus, a vagabond and a wastrel son being feted by his father, and a dutiful and obedient son left outside in the cold?"[80]

In his next book, *The Dark Interval* (1975), Crossan makes more use of the term "world" in the parable.[81] Myth, he argues, creates "world" while parable subverts it. Parables are iconoclastic. We may ask whether this applies to all parables, but it certainly applies to some. Surprisingly, Crossan turns partly to structuralism and semiotics, partly to postmodernism, in his next book, *Raid on the Articulate* (1976).[82] The title comes from Eliot, and here he follows Roland Barthes in divorcing language from history. Jesus becomes essentially a destroyer of fixed and stable idols. V. Shklovsky's device of "defamiliarization" (making strange what is familiar or habitual) forms part of his program. He writes, "An allegorical parable will generate interpretations that are both multiple and paradoxical." Postmodernity becomes a major theme in *Finding Is the First Act* (1979), and *Cliffs of Fall* (1980) completes this process.[83] Obtaining the field in the parable provides space for discovery, and *Raid on the Articulate* combines allegedly "waking the Bible" with arguments for paradox and polyvalency. The parables can mean what a person makes of them, and Lynn Poland rightly criticizes what could equally well go under the name "ambiguity." In the end God's action is present "only as void."[84]

After the early 1980s Crossan turned his attention to reconstructing a "historical" Jesus, founding the Jesus Seminar at the Society of Biblical Literature. His later books *The Historical Jesus* (1991), *Jesus: A Revolutionary Biography* (1994), and *God and Empire: Jesus against Rome* (2007) increasingly depict Jesus controversially as a Jewish cynic from a peasant background

---

80. Crossan, *In Parables*, p. 74; cf. pp. 69-75.

81. John Dominic Crossan, *The Dark Interval: Towards a Theology of Story* (Niles, Ill.: Angus Communications, 1975).

82. John Dominic Crossan, *Raid on the Articulate: Comic Eschatology in Jesus and Borges* (New York: Harper and Row, 1976), p. 129.

83. John Dominic Crossan, *Finding Is the First Act: Trove Folktales and Jesus' Treasure Parable* (Missoula: Scholars Press, 1979) and *Cliffs of Fall: Paradox and Polyvalence in the Parables of Jesus* (New York: Seabury Press, 1980).

84. Lynn M. Poland, *Literary Criticism and Biblical Hermeneutics: A Critique of Formative Approaches* (Chico, Calif.: Scholars Press, 1985), p. 119.

who taught liberation and tolerance. In spite of his Irish Catholic background, Crossan distances Jesus from mainline orthodox Christian theology, which he sees as the construction of the Church. Lynn Poland has shown the limitations of his work on the parables, and William Lane Craig and Tom Wright have publicly debated his portrayal of Jesus.

6. *Bernard B. Scott* was similarly a participant of the Jesus Seminar, which was founded in 1985. He shares Crossan's interest in literary criticism and defines a parable as "a *mashal* that employs a short narrative fiction to reference a transcendent symbol."[85] He looks to rabbinic parables and to the Gnostic *Gospel of Thomas* more than most. In spite of his interest in the sociology of the New Testament, he sees many parables as pointing to the transcendent in symbolic language. At the same time, more traditional, historical studies continue, for example, in David Wenham's *Parables of Jesus*.[86]

6. Other Approaches: The New Hermeneutic, Narrative Worlds, Postmodernity, Reader Response, and Allegory

1. We have not said much about the new hermeneutic of Ernst Fuchs and Gerhard Ebeling. This is partly because I have included a separate section on them in a later chapter, partly because I have written so much on this elsewhere, and partly because the movement seems largely to have burnt itself out.[87] As I have remarked elsewhere, central to Fuchs's work on Jesus and the parables is the question: "What do we have to do at our desks if we want later to set the text in front of us in the pulpit?"[88] Fuchs and Ebeling argue that the text of the New Testament does not presuppose faith, but on the contrary creates faith.

The parables of Jesus seek a decision, but it is the decision of the hearer.

---

85. Bernard B. Scott, *Hear Then the Parable: A Commentary on the Parables of Jesus* (Minneapolis: Fortress, 1989), p. 8.

86. David Wenham, *The Parables of Jesus: Pictures of a Revolution* (London: Hodder and Stoughton, 1989).

87. Anthony C. Thiselton, *The Two Horizons: New Testament Hermeneutics and Philosophical Description* (Grand Rapids: Eerdmans; Exeter: Paternoster, 1980), pp. 330-47; *Thiselton on Hermeneutics*, pp. 417-40; and Thiselton, "The New Hermeneutic," in *New Testament Interpretation*, ed. I. H. Marshall (Exeter: Paternoster, 1972), pp. 308-31.

88. Ernst Fuchs, *Studies of the Historical Jesus*, trans. A. Scobie (London: SCM, 1964), p. 8.

In this there is risk. In the parable of the workers in the vineyard, for example (Matt. 20:1-16), Fuchs writes, this word "singles out the individual and grasps him deep down."[89] The parable affects and demands a decision. In this parable the hearers may begin, with the crowd, to expect "justice" on behalf of those who had worked the longest. But when, finally, they hear the words of the master about undeserved generosity, they "are drawn over to God's side and learn to see everything with God's eyes."[90] Leaving the short-term day workers to the end is deliberate. Fuchs writes, "Is not this the way of true love? Love does not just burst out. Instead it provides in advance the sphere in which meeting takes place."[91] We shall reserve further comments on the new hermeneutic for chapter X.

2. The emphasis on the *"world"* created by the text as a place of meeting, understanding, and seeing anew has been expressed in other contexts and in other forms. Paul Ricoeur is eminent among those who have explored the idea of the narrative world, not least because he, too, has studied Martin Heidegger with his notions of "possibility" and "world," and is familiar with narrative theory.

The concept of the "narrative world" of the parable comes ultimately from Heidegger, is mediated through Hans-Georg Gadamer, and finds direct expression in Ricoeur. In chapter XI we shall see that Gadamer makes much of the "world" of the game, of art, and of the festival. All these are "performed" by participants, whose practical involvement is greater than that of mere spectators.

In chapter XII we shall see that Ricoeur sees the "world" of the acting agent or self as a narrative world. Ricoeur traces its coherence or "concordance" to Aristotle's notion of "plot," and its extension in time and its "discordance" to Augustine. *Time and Narrative* shows the importance of "plot," which parables embody, while his book *Oneself as Another* shows the importance of temporal agency, decision, and accountability, which parables also enshrine.

3. We mentioned that Crossan moved from "parables of reversal" to seeing parables as radically *pluralist and ambivalent in meaning.* A number of other writers find legitimacy in the parables for indeterminate *"postmodern"* meanings. Crossan wrote controversially that "Myth establishes world . . .

89. Fuchs, *Studies,* p. 35.
90. Fuchs, *Studies,* p. 155.
91. Fuchs, *Studies,* p. 129.

satire attacks world. Parable subverts world."[92] P. S. Hawkins claims that a parable is "the utterance but not the unveiling of what has been hidden."[93] Stanley Fish combines a radical reader-response theory with postmodernism akin to the postmodern neopragmatic philosopher Richard Rorty. He asks of parables and other texts not "What does this text mean?" but only "What does this text do?" The community of readers who receive the text are those who, in effect, create it. There is no "given content" lying innocently in the text. The text is what readers make of it. Reader-response theorists are not all postmodern. Wolfgang Iser and Umberto Eco work out a more moderate and sober version of reader-response theory. We look at this further in chapter XV.

4. *Semiotic* approaches (theories of signs) sometimes lead to pluralist or postmodern interpretations. Mary Ann Tolbert attempts an interpretation of the parable of the prodigal son in which "there is no one correct interpretation . . . though there may be limits of congruency that invalidate some readings."[94] This seems reasonable until we learn that according to her "Freudian" interpretation, the father, the elder son, and the younger son respectively represent the ego, the superego, and the id of Freudian psychology. "The younger son embodies some of the aspects of Freud's conception of the id; the elder son exhibits striking analogies with the ego ideal or 'conscience.' The superego is the seat of morality."[95] All this work is a version of reader response, since she often speaks of "the reader's point of view." This does not yet represent a fully postmodern perspective, where a parable has no clear content, but we are journeying in that direction.

5. We have not the space to explore the impact of *redaction criticism,* which seeks to underline the distinctive editorial activity of each Evangelist. This began perhaps with J. D. Kingsbury's *Parables of Matthew 13* (1969) and includes the more recent book by G. W. Forbes, *The God of Old: The Role of Lukan Parables in the Purpose of Luke's Gospel* (2001).[96] It is scarcely surprising that in view of so many diverse approaches some should argue that the

92. Crossan, *The Dark Interval,* p. 59.

93. P. S. Hawkins, "Parables as Metaphor," *Christian Scholar's Review* 12 (1983): 226; cf. pp. 226-36.

94. Mary Ann Tolbert, *Perspectives on the Parables* (Philadelphia: Fortress, 1978), p. 99.

95. Tolbert, *Perspectives on the Parables,* p. 104.

96. G. W. Forbes, *The God of Old: The Role of Lukan Parables in the Purpose of Luke's Gospel,* Journal for the Study of the New Testament, Supplement Series, no. 198 (Sheffield: Sheffield Academic Press, 2001).

distinction between parable and allegory has become seriously overdrawn to the detriment of allegory. Madeline Boucher's *Mysterious Parable* stresses the allegorical nature of many parables, and Craig Blomberg, Ian Lambrecht, Mary Ford, and Mikeal Parsons have defended certain allegorical elements strongly.[97]

6. The conclusion of all this is that the interpreter should *not generalize* about "*the* parables." With many, there is a case for strict historical interpretation as proposed by Dodd, Jeremias, and Linnemann. There is a case for a cautious or "controlled" use of allegorical interpretation, reader-response criticism, and existential interpretation in some parables. Literary criticism is valuable, but within limits and not at the expense of theology. We run into difficulty when one single approach is thought to be the key to all the parables of Jesus.

7. Recommended Initial Reading

Blomberg, Craig L., *Interpreting the Parables* (Leicester: Apollos, 1990), pp. 13-170.

Crossan, John Dominic, *In Parables: The Challenge of the Historical Jesus* (New York: Harper and Row, 1973), pp. 8-15 and 57-78.

Jeremias, Joachim, *The Parables of Jesus,* translated by S. H. Hooke, rev. ed. (London: SCM, 1963), pp. 11-66 and 115-60.

Stein, Robert H., *An Introduction to the Parables of Jesus* (Philadelphia: Westminster, 1981), pp. 15-81.

Thiselton, Anthony C., "Reader-Response Hermeneutics, Action Models, and the Parables of Jesus," in Roger Lundin, Anthony C. Thiselton, and Clarence Walhout, *The Responsibility of Hermeneutics* (Grand Rapids: Eerdmans; Exeter: Paternoster, 1985), pp. 79-115.

---

97. Madeline Boucher, *The Mysterious Parable: A Literary Study* (Washington, D.C.: American Catholic Biblical Association, 1977), especially pp. 17-20; Craig L. Blomberg, *Interpreting Parables* (Leicester: Apollos, 1990), pp. 36-49 and 309-28; Ian Lambrecht, *Once More Astonished: The Parables of Jesus* (New York: Crossroad, 1981); J. M. Ford, "Towards the Reinstatement of Allegory," *St. Vladimir's Theological Quarterly* 34 (1990): 161-95; and Mikeal Parsons, "Allegorizing Allegory: Narrative Analysis and Parable Interpretation," *Perspectives in Religious Studies* 15 (1988): 147-64.

CHAPTER IV

A Legacy of Perennial Questions from the Ancient World: Judaism and the Ancient Greeks

1. The Christian Inheritance: The Hermeneutics of Rabbinic Judaism

Some may find this chapter one of the most tedious. Inevitably it may read simply as a string of names and facts. But its purpose is to show that (1) in Judaism no single method of interpretation absolutely prevailed over all others, and (2) as early as the first century (and earlier still) issues arose about the interpretation of the Hebrew Bible that have found no universally accepted solution and command no universal assent now. Judaism has never been one uniform thing, especially with respect to the differences between rabbinic Judaism, Greek-speaking Judaism, Qumran (the community that produced the Dead Sea Scrolls) and what we might call apocalyptic Judaism, let alone modern Judaism. Within rabbinic Judaism (if we may perhaps date its beginnings from A.D. 70 or a little earlier) the devout and lay Pharisees differed from the priestly Sadducees, even though the Sanhedrin, or ruling council, contained both groups. Their methods of interpreting Scripture were relatively similar.

Judaism at the beginning of the Christian era used multiple methods of interpretation. There is controversy about dating the beginning of the rabbinic period, but so-called rabbinic Judaism contemporary with Christ could use a historical or fairly literalistic approach. On the other hand, it was also a fairly atomistic method of interpretation. However, the rabbis were far from consistent in this respect, and other streams of Judaism used midrash (homiletical material) and, as occasion seemed to suggest, allegorical interpretation. They also used "pesher" (mainly eschatological) exegesis, and symbolic interpretation. Christianity inherited all these approaches. One lesson for Christianity is that the Church inherited various perennial problems, and ways of interpreting Scripture, and most of these are still with us.

A study of modes of interpretation in Judaism also has value in its own right, not least because Greek-speaking Judaism is so different from rabbinic Judaism. In spite of cross-fertilization between the two, we cannot simply speak of ancient Jewish interpretation as a single thing. In Diaspora Judaism Philo and others used symbolic or allegorical interpretation extensively, although not exclusively. The sources are abundant and varied in their interpretation of the Old Testament or of the Jewish and earliest Christian Scriptures.

We should first note Jewish attitudes toward Scripture. Virtually all Jews believed that every part of Scripture was inspired by the Holy Spirit. Scripture constituted a coherent unity and mediated the truth of God. For the most part Jews equated Scripture with the wisdom of God, and believed that every word of Scripture carried some meaning or purpose.[1] One of the earliest examples of interpretation is probably the Palestinian Targum, which presents a mixture of translation into Aramaic and interpretation of texts for the synagogue audience. Many in the synagogue depended on a Targum, not the Hebrew text, for their understanding of Scripture. This began as a translation for synagogue use of every part of the Old Testament, except those few already written largely in Aramaic, namely, Daniel, Ezra, and Nehemiah. Any member of the synagogue could make the translation, and in later years this became interpretation also.[2]

The Haggadic (or mainly narrative) Targum appeared in different sources. In spite of their similarities, each of the following has its individual characteristics: the Neofiti Targum, the Fragment Targum, the Cairo Geniza Targum Fragments, the Onkelos (or Onqelos) Targum, and Pseudo-Jonathan.[3] The Onkelos Fragments Targum, Later Pseudo-Jonathan, and newly discovered Neofiti I (sometimes rendered Neophyty) are Targums to the Pentateuch. Pseudo-Jonathan is a Targum on the Prophets; Targums to the Writings are more individualistic.[4] The discovery of Targums at Qumran

1. Daniel Patte, *Early Jewish Hermeneutic in Palestine*, Society of Biblical Literature Dissertation Series 22 (Missoula: Scholars Press, 1975), pp. 19-29.

2. The process is described in Mishnah *Megillah* 4:4.

3. Richard Longenecker, *Biblical Exegesis in the Apostolic Period* (Grand Rapids: Eerdmans, 1975), pp. 21-23; cf. P. Grelot, *What Are the Targums? Selected Texts* (Collegeville, Minn.: Liturgical Press, 1992).

4. Craig A. Evans, "Targum," in *Dictionary of Biblical Criticism and Interpretation*, ed. Stanley E. Porter (London and New York: Routledge, 2007), pp. 347-49.

(among the Dead Sea Scrolls) places the date of some in the first century B.C. or earlier (namely, 11QTgJob and 4QTgJob).

The Targums began as translations. In Exodus 33:3 the Hebrew text reads: "I will not go up among you." Targum Neofiti reads: "I will not remove my presence from you." The best translations are seldom woodenly literalist word-for-word renderings. Genesis 4:14 reads: "Behold, you have driven me this day from the land, and from your face I shall be hidden." In the Neofiti and Onkelos Targums we read: "Behold, You have driven me this day from upon the land, but it is not possible to be hidden from You." All translation almost unavoidably becomes interpretation. The creators of the Targums believed that they could not ignore what they already knew of God, to make a fresh point.

Sometimes a Targum expands a Scripture passage. The Palestinian Targum on Genesis 6:3, for example, reads: "Behold, I have given them a hundred and twenty years in case they might repent; but they failed to do so." The NSRV text simply reads, "Their days shall be one hundred twenty years." Another example comes from Exodus 3:1. Targum Neofiti reads, "And he [Moses] reached the mount over which the glory of the Shekinah of the Lord was revealed." The Hebrew of Exodus 3:1 reads, "He came to Horeb, the mountain of God." Chilton argues that in spite of difficulties,

> Certain readings from the extant Targumim are strikingly similar to passages in the N.T. Examples from Jesus' sayings include Luke 6: 36, "Be merciful, just as your Father is merciful." This is comparable to Targum Pseudo-Jonathan Lev. 22: 28. Mark 4: 11-12 begins, "And he said to them, 'To you is given the secret of the Kingdom of God, but for those outside everything in parables, in order that they may indeed look, but not perceive.'" This appears to reflect an understanding of Isa. 6: 9-10 such as *Jonathan* preserves.[5]

Finally, the Targums were formulated in writings and gave rise to the Talmud, which included greater detail than a Targum. Although the Palestinian Targum appeared only in the second century A.D., much of it is attributed to a considerably earlier oral tradition. The Mishnah also comes from before the middle of the second century, and its codification is attributed to

5. Bruce D. Chilton, "Targum," in *Dictionary of Biblical Interpretation*, ed. John H. Hayes, 2 vols. (Nashville: Abingdon, 1999), 2:533; cf. pp. 531-34; and Chilton, *A Galilean Rabbi and His Bible: Jesus' Use of the Interpreted Scripture of His Time* (London: SPCK, 1984).

Rabbi Judah "the Prince" in A.D. 135. Rabbi Judah organized it into six parts and sixty-three tractates of material. Scripture is interpreted in the light of other scriptural passages, and it is believed that Scripture *applies to every aspect of life.* Rabbi Judah is attributed with the saying "If one translates a verse [of Scripture] literally, he is a liar; if he adds thereto, he is a blasphemer and a libeller."[6] Yet the Targums contain different vocalizations from the Masoretic Text (the established rabbinic Hebrew text), which may represent an earlier text, or are probably alterations and rewritings. The Targumim often expanded the text, for example, when the son of Esther is identified as Darius. Traditions are often "telescoped" in time and place.

The Tosefta is a supplement to the Mishnah, written by a rabbinic pupil of Rabbi Judah. The Gemara consists of legal discussions that seek to apply the Mishnah to every area of life, but is of a later date. This brings us to homily, or midrash (from *darash,* to inquire or to search), and back again to the exegesis and interpretation of Scripture.

In the synagogue Scripture was read (seder and haftarah) and preached (midrash). Midrash, or homily, could be loosely based on Scripture. On the other hand, Rabbi Hillel (born ca. 25 B.C. in Babylon) formulated seven "rules" *(middoth)* of interpretation.[7] The seven "rules" arose initially, for example, from the controversy about whether the Passover had precedence over the Sabbath or vice versa. As we earlier stated, the first five are largely a matter of deductive logic and do not strictly come under the heading of "hermeneutics." The first "rule" is that the greater includes the less. The sixth and seventh, however, are genuinely hermeneutical. The sixth concerns finding support in another Scripture, and the seventh declares that a meaning depends on its context. Rabbi Ishmael Ben Elisha, Hillel's pupil, expanded these into thirteen rules, which served to restrain the looser innovations of Rabbi Akiba. Thirty-two rules were later ascribed to Rabbi Eliezer Ben Jose the Galilean. But midrash continued for the most part to be atomistic and fairly free.[8] Rabbi Akiba (A.D. 50-135) interpreted the Song of Songs allegorically to denote God's love for Israel. Midrash included especially Sifre on Leviticus and Sifre on Numbers and Deuteronomy (they belonged to the cate-

---

6. Babylonian Talmud *Kiddushim* (Betrothals) 49a; Patte, *Early Jewish Hermeneutic,* p. 63 n.

7. Babylonian Talmud *Shabbat* (The Sabbath) 31a; on the rules, cf. Patte, *Early Jewish Hermeneutic,* pp. 109-10; and Longenecker, *Biblical Exegesis,* pp. 32-35.

8. J. V. Doeve, *Jewish Hermeneutic in the Synoptic Gospels and Acts* (Assen: Van Gorcum, 1954), pp. 65-75.

gory of conduct, law, or Halakha, in contrast to the narrative Haggadah). These were formulated probably in the middle or late second century. The Haggadic Midrash on Genesis is probably third century.

Many are accustomed in the Christian Church today to following lectionary readings for particular days and seasons. Readings of Scripture first in the temple and soon after in synagogues also began in the pre-Christian period to be set for the main festivals and later for the Sabbath. Their origins and dating are uncertain. Eventually a three-year cycle was followed. Considerably later the Mishnah, going back to an earlier tradition, was expanded into the Talmud. The Palestinian Talmud was earlier than the Babylonian Talmud, but the latter represents rabbinic Judaism between the second century and the sixth or even tenth centuries, although the Palestinian Talmud may go back to earlier oral traditions. Their origin is obscure.

Even more clearly than the Mishnah, the Talmud represents the belief that Scripture applies to every aspect of life. It therefore remains a supplement to Scripture, not a substitute, and seeks to apply Scripture to situations not fully envisaged by the biblical writer. Ernst von Dobschütz believed that all hermeneutics necessarily "supplements" the text.[9] The Talmud goes further than the Mishnah, although it is organized with the same headings and sections. It provides an invaluable guide to the development of rabbinic Judaism. Sometimes, for example, the name "God" is softened or eliminated in the interests of divine transcendence, although this also occurs in the Targums. Sometimes "Glory," "Presence," or "Word" *(Memra)* is used.

Meanwhile an early example of interpreting Scripture also originated at Qumran in the Dead Sea Scrolls. The community of Qumran flourished from pre-Christian times (ca. 200 or 150 B.C.–A.D. 70), but it was a distinctive Jewish heterodoxy. The community must be firmly distinguished from rabbinic Judaism. Members tended to regard other Jews as compromisers of their inheritance and even as impure sinners. They had withdrawn from the world and thought they were living at the end of times. They regarded themselves as the favored recipients of the revelation found in Scripture. To them was given a special revelation or gift of interpretation. Sometimes this was "pesher" interpretation, namely, that they lived in the end times, and they saw much Scripture, especially prophecy, as addressed specifically to them, and to be fulfilled in their time.

---

9. Ernst von Dobschütz, "Interpretation," in *Encyclopedia of Religion and Ethics,* vol. 7, ed. James Hastings (Edinburgh: T. & T. Clark, 1926), p. 391; cf. pp. 391-95.

The interpretation of Qumran did not therefore represent that of mainstream Judaism, nor was Qumran's tradition of interpretation "public" as it would be for Irenaeus among the Church Fathers, and many rabbinic Jews. The writings of the Qumran community are saturated with biblical interpretation. Some are commentaries, such as the well-known *Commentary on Habakkuk.* On Habakkuk 1:5 the writer at Qumran writes concerning the Teacher of Righteousness of their particular generation (1QpHab 2:1-3). Their distinctive and different understandings of the text are explained at greater length by Peter Enns.[10] Hanson discusses their different interpretation of Nahum 2:11.[11] Here the lion becomes Demetrius king of Greece, just as in Habakkuk 3:2 the "Kittim" become the Romans. Some compare this pesher interpretation with Luke 24:27, where Jesus sees certain events in Scripture as applying to himself. This is widely accepted, but it also remains controversial.

2. The Literature of Greek-Speaking Judaism

What are we to make of the literature of Greek-speaking or Hellenistic Judaism?

1. First, we encounter the Greek translation of the Hebrew Bible known as the *Septuagint,* or LXX. Richard Longenecker and others argue that we cannot compare the Septuagint with the Targums as a witness to Jewish interpretation of Scripture.[12] Although the texts of the LXX are older than the Hebrew Masoretic (standard rabbinic) Text, the Septuagint and its cognate versions constitute in some places a rewritten or expanded translation of the Hebrew. Martin Hengel and others have rightly shown that no watertight division exists between Palestinian and Hellenistic Judaism, in spite of the differences between Targumim and the LXX.[13] Yet the LXX is a consciously propagandistic collection of books in a way that the Targumim were not. The well-known story in the *Letter of Aristeas* (200-50 B.C.) tells us that King

10. Peter Enns, *Inspiration and Incarnation: Evangelicals and the Problem of the Old Testament* (Grand Rapids: Baker Academic, 2005), pp. 124-26.

11. Anthony Tyrrell Hanson, *The Living Utterances of God: The New Testament Exegesis of the Old* (London: Darton, Longman and Todd, 1983), pp. 15-16.

12. Longenecker, *Biblical Exegesis,* pp. 20-21.

13. Martin Hengel, *Judaism and Hellenism: A Study of Their Encounter in Palestine during the Early Hellenistic Period* (London: SCM, 1974), and Hengel, in collaboration with Christoph Markschies, *The "Hellenization" of Judaea in the First Century after Christ* (London: SCM, 1991).

Ptolemy of Egypt wrote to Eleazar the high priest and commissioned a definitive translation. It further says that Eleazar secured the services of seventy-two translators. Unfortunately the story has no historical basis, although it is repeated by Philo and Josephus. It is not universally accepted as historical fact today. Many regard it, too, as a propagandistic account of the Septuagint's origin.

Paul Kahle argued in 1915 that there never was a single "Septuagint" text, although Paul de Lagarde believed that the various texts were derived from a single text, which is now lost. Today many follow Emanuel Tov, who argued in 1981 and again in 1986 that there was an original, but also varied textual traditions, each followed by separate "schools." A degree of stabilization toward a single text occurred in the first or second century A.D. Longenecker responds that such *Tendenzen* as belief in the final resurrection and a doctrine of angels disqualify the candidacy of the LXX as a witness to Jewish interpretation. One writer calls the status of the Septuagint as a serious or accurate translation "dangerous," and even "dishonest."[14] Its translation of Job 42:17 adds to the Hebrew text, "[Job] will rise again with those whom the Lord raises up." The translation of Isaiah 26:19 adds to the Hebrew text: "They shall live," and Daniel 12:2 reads, "They shall awake." Exodus 35–40 differs significantly from the Hebrew Masoretic Text. The same applies to Jeremiah.

The LXX also tended to avoid the anthropomorphisms that the Hebrew text retained. In Exodus 15:3 the Hebrew text reads, "The Lord is a man of war," but the LXX reads, "The Lord crushes wars." Numbers 12:8 says of Moses in Hebrew, "He beholds the form of the Lord." The LXX has: "He beheld the glory of the Lord."[15] There are geographical alterations such as the change of Ekron to Askelon in 1 Samuel 5:10. Finally, some verses tidy up the Hebrew in the interests of intelligibility. For example, in Psalm 40:6 (LXX 39:7) the Hebrew reads: "Sacrifice and offering hast Thou not desired; ears hast Thou cut for me." To make it more intelligible, LXX renders it: "Ears hast Thou prepared for me."

Some dissent from the usual view, partly on the ground that the LXX was the Bible of the early Church, and this poses a problem for many. Paul cites the Septuagint more often than the Masoretic Text.[16] Many claim that the

---

14. Melvin K. H. Peters, "Septuagint," in *The Anchor Bible Dictionary*, ed. David Noel Freedman (New York: Doubleday, 1992), 5:1100; cf. pp. 1093-1104.

15. More examples can be found in Hanson, *Living Utterances of God*, pp. 12-13.

16. Christopher D. Stanley, *Paul and the Language of Scripture: Citation Technique in the Pauline Epistles and Contemporary Literature* (Cambridge: Cambridge University Press, 1992).

Fourth Gospel and the book of Revelation use the LXX, although Paul and the author of the Johannine writings probably knew both versions of Scripture. The author of Hebrews may have known only the LXX. Origen and most other Church Fathers used the LXX, although one or two knew Hebrew. But most scholars today believe that the LXX is mainly important for the light it sheds on the mind of Judaism in the third or possibly second centuries B.C.

The opening of the Holy Land to Hellenistic influences was partly due to Herod the Great (43-4 B.C.), who wanted to impress the Romans with his openness to Greco-Roman culture. The Sadducees and Pharisees opposed what they regarded as a Hellenizing compromise of their Jewish inheritance. After 4 B.C., upon Herod's death, Philip the Tetrarch ruled Ituraea and Trachonitis; Antipater ruled (under Rome) Galilee and Perea; and Archelaus at first ruled Judea, under Rome, until he was deposed. A line of successive procurators or governors took over, appointed directly by Augustus, emperor of Rome, and later, under the emperor Tiberius, Pilate took over as governor. Galilee ("Galilee of the Gentiles") was far more "Hellenistic" than Judea. Many spoke Greek, not least for trade and commerce.

At all events, a literature of Greek-speaking Judaism grew up that deserves brief mention here. Commerce and war meant that Diaspora Judaism was significant in numbers and power by the first century. Jews lived in large numbers in Rome, Alexandria, Antioch in Syria, and other Greek-speaking centers. Apart from works by Philo and Josephus, probably the most important are 4 Maccabees and the pseudonymous Wisdom of Solomon, although we shall also consider briefly the *Letter of Aristeas.*

2. *4 Maccabees* (probably ca. A.D. 18-37) is a quasi-philosophical treatise in the style of Greek diatribe. It is a good piece of Greek oratory, though with elements of homily. It recollects and embroiders the martyrdom of the Maccabean martyrs and loyalists, at the same time urging the supremacy of reason. It portrays Eleazar the high priest preeminently as a philosopher. Like the Christian book of Revelation, it portrays martyrdom as conquest *(nikaō)*. The Jewish Law is seen as the "truest" philosophy. Reason is the intellect choosing the "life of wisdom" (4 Macc. 1:15). For Eleazar, reason was "the shield of sanctity" (7:4): "O priest . . . O confessor of the Law and philosopher" (7:7). It is easy to see how Platonism flourished in Greek-speaking Judaism as an arbiter of interpretation. Moreover, although there is a doctrine of "souls" and immortality, this is not resurrection, whose agent is God alone. 4 Maccabees extols the expiatory power of martyrs, among whom it ranks Eleazar and Socrates.

3. The *Wisdom of Solomon* (ca. 40 B.C., or between 80 and 10 B.C.) is not to be confused with the earlier book of the Wisdom of Ben Sirach (also known as Ecclesiasticus). It defends belief in God and attacks idolatry, but uses the methods of Hellenistic rhetoric and learning to do so. Again, it teaches immortality rather than resurrection. The condemnation of idolatry is similar to Paul's in Romans 1:18-32. Wisdom of Solomon 1–5, and especially 14:24-26 and chapters 13–15 in general, reflects this, and probably represents standard synagogue homily material. Like 4 Maccabees and Philo, this book explains the fascination of Platonism for Greek-speaking Jews but cannot serve as a primary model for Jewish biblical interpretation.

4. The *Letter of Aristeas* (ca. 100 B.C.), as we have seen, purports to offer an eyewitness account of the origin of the Septuagint, but in fact represents a pseudonymous defense of the Jewish Scriptures for Hellenistic readers by a Jew of Alexandria. The writer aims to show that the Law of Moses accords with the philosophical maxims that would be shared by most educated Greeks of the day. Hence anything that might appear arbitrary or glaringly culture-relative to this wider readership would be reinterpreted to avoid such an understanding. For example, the verse that permits the eating of "whatever (animal) parts the hoof and is cloven-footed and chews the cud" (Lev. 11:3) is understood as an allegory that promotes wise discernment. The traces of allegorical interpretation found in 4 Maccabees and the Wisdom of Solomon do not reach this scale.

5. The classic Jewish exponent of allegorical interpretation is *Philo of Alexandria* (ca. 20 B.C.–A.D. 50). Specialists still disagree over whether (with E. R. Goodenough) we should take his thought as representative of a wider stream of Hellenistic Jewish thought in the Diaspora or whether (with C. K. Barrett) we should view him as a maverick and unrepresentative figure. He is first and foremost an apologist, committed to the authority of the Scriptures as "the holy word" of God, or "the divine word," but he seeks to commend the Scriptures to the educated Greek.[17] While he reveres Moses, Philo speaks also of "the great Plato," and quotes often from Homer, Pindar, Euripides, and other Greek writers. He is saturated in the philosophy of Zeno, Cleanthes, the Pythagoreans, and especially Plato. He is a man of two worlds and outdoes all others in allegorical interpretation of a sacred text.

Philo excludes the "surface" meaning (or literal meaning) of the text

---

17. Philo, *On Change of Names* 8; *The Heir of Divine Things* 53; and *On the Life of Moses* 3.23.

when it appears to say anything unworthy of God, or to limit God's wisdom, or to reduce his transcendence. Thus Adam cannot be said "to hide" from God (Gen. 3:8) since this would presuppose the possibility of divine ignorance; Adam cannot try to "hide" from an omniscient God. Some "other" *(allos)* meaning must be sought. The surface meaning of "God planted fruit trees" (Gen. 2:8-9) is unacceptable to educated Alexandrians, Greeks, and Romans. It is sheer "silliness"; the passage speaks allegorically of God's implanting virtues in the soul.[18] The story of Babel (Gen. 11:1-9) has little to do with the apparent surface meaning of accounting for the origin of languages, but speaks of divine sovereignty and human folly.[19] Philo calls allegorical interpretation into play to handle such supposedly "modern" difficulties as where Cain found a wife and how he built "a city" (Gen. 4:17).[20] The two accounts of creation in Genesis 1:1–2:3 and in 2:4-25 allude respectively to the heavenly or "spiritual" Adam (Gen. 1:27) and to the earthly, fleshly Adam (Gen. 2:7).[21] Numbers seldom denote actual numerals or numerical quantities; they usually denote symbolic qualities, as for example when *one* denotes the uniquely one God.[22]

Although his hermeneutics grew from apologetic concerns, and although he presupposes Plato's contrast between the earthly and spiritual realm, Philo does seek also to defend his method from the nature or genre of texts. Since it is inconceivable, he argues, for a serpent to speak (Gen. 3:1), this verse of necessity says something more than, and different from, a statement about a snake. Further, Philo cannot believe that the Mosaic Scripture speaks primarily about contingent or particular situations, rather than expounding broader principles that transcend time and place. The journey of Abraham from Ur of the Chaldees, for example (Gen. 12:1–25:8), represents the journey of the human soul or spirit in its growth of wisdom. Jacob crossing the Jordan with his staff (Gen. 32:10) signifies that baseness (represented by the Jordan) is overcome by discipline (represented by the staff).

Philo has a concept of the transcendence of God that dominates his biblical interpretation. Henry Chadwick writes, "Of all the non-Christian writers of the first century Philo is the one from whom the historian of emergent

18. Philo, *On Husbandry* 8-9.
19. Philo, *On the Confusion of Tongues* 38.
20. Philo, *On the Posterity and Exile of Cain* 11 and 14.
21. Philo, *On Allegorical Interpretation* 3.12 and 3.16.
22. Philo, *On Allegorical Interpretation* 2.1.

Christianity has most to learn."[23] He sought to be loyal to the Bible and Judaism while commending Judaism to educated Romans who had knowledge of Greek philosophy, including Platonism and Stoicism as well as neo-Pythagorean philosophy. Sometimes Philo regarded Scripture as containing a historical core, which was not to be allegorized away. His influence reaches indirectly to the Church Fathers. He shares Paul's condemnation of pagan idolatry and its consequences (cf. Rom. 1:18-32). Like Paul, he says our citizenship is in heaven, and our present knowledge of God is as in a mirror. His literature is vast and considerable.

6. *Flavius Josephus* (ca. A.D. 37-100) was born in Jerusalem of a priestly family and studied the ways of the Pharisees, the Sadducees, and the Essenes. At nineteen he became a Pharisee.[24] He was twenty-six when he traveled to Rome, in 64, to try to secure the release of certain priests who had been taken prisoner. He returned with success, and in 66 he advised against war with Rome.[25] During the siege of Jerusalem that followed, he called on Jews to surrender to Titus. After the war he went with Titus to Rome and was given Roman citizenship, an income, and an estate. All his writings, especially *The Jewish War* and his *Life,* are strongly pro-Roman. *The Antiquity of the Jews* recounts in twenty books Jewish history from creation. But as an interpreter of Scripture Josephus modifies Scripture to remove anything offensive to Romans.

3. Jewish Apocalyptic Literature around the Time of Christ

We conclude with a brief survey of the more important apocalyptic writings (ca. 200 B.C.–A.D. 100). The general view is that the world is too evil to be reformed. Humankind must await the decisive inbreaking of God into history, when God will bring about new creation and possibly also resurrection. This may be soon.

1. One apocalyptic document of relatively early times is *1 Enoch 37–71* (ca. 100-80 B.C.). This portrays the two ages and judgment, and has messianic overtones.

---

23. Henry Chadwick, "St. Paul and Philo of Alexandria," *Bulletin of the John Rylands Library* 40 (1965-66): 288; cf. pp. 286ff.

24. Josephus, *Life* 2.12.

25. Josephus, *Life* 4.17-19.

2. Of more direct interest to our concerns is the pseudonymous *Psalms of Solomon* (ca. 50-40). Pompey's capture of Jerusalem was still fresh in the mind, and *Psalms of Solomon* attacks the foreign oppressors of the day, by extending the immediate reference of Scripture passages to the present. The covenant with David is celebrated in the hope for a king who will purge Jerusalem of all the heathen, including "Latin men." This application of the Scripture to the present time reminds us in part of the pesher interpretation of Qumran.

3-4. *2 Esdras* (4 Ezra) and *2 Baruch* (the Apocalypse of Baruch) (ca. A.D. 50-90) are also eschatological in outlook. 2 Esdras reminds us of the apocalyptic parts of Daniel, where "One like a man from the depths of the sea" also "flies on the clouds of heaven," and the Lion of David delivers the remnant at the time appointed (13:3; cf. Gal. 4:4). The judgment is the harvest of the world. Of the Apocalypse of Baruch, Klausner comments, "There is no pseudepigraphic book in which are found so many Messianic expectations."[26] 2 Esdras is also "historical" in its portrayal of God's dealings with Israel, in contrast to *2 Enoch,* which is more visionary. The visionary books undoubtedly lend themselves to symbolic interpretation. Albert Schweitzer and others see 2 Esdras and *2 Baruch* as being of great importance for understanding Paul.[27] The visionary apocalypses are more like the book of Revelation. Unlike *2 Baruch,* 2 Esdras portrays the fall of Adam as a universal catastrophe.

5-6. *The Testaments of the Twelve Patriarchs* includes a free expansion of the Genesis narratives, providing also examples of virtue and vice, with moral admonitions. "The historical narrative of the Bible is filled out in the manner of a haggadic midrash in order to give ethical guidance."[28] The book of *Jubilees* in effect rewrites the scriptural account. It develops the material in Genesis 1 to Exodus 12 for its own purposes. It is so far from "interpretation" that some consider that it presupposes no firsthand knowledge of Scripture. But others, including Goppelt, see it as "a classic model of this Haggadic treatment of Scripture."[29]

---

26. J. Klausner, *The Messianic Idea in Israel,* trans. W. F. Stinespring (London: Allen and Unwin, 1956), p. 331.

27. Albert Schweitzer, *The Mysticism of Paul the Apostle,* trans. W. Montgomery (London: Black, 1931), chapter 3.

28. Leonhard Goppelt, *Typos: The Typological Interpretation of the Old Testament in the New,* trans. D. H. Hadvig (Grand Rapids: Eerdmans, 2006), p. 25.

29. Goppelt, *Typos,* p. 25.

4. The Greek Roots of Interpretation: The Stoics

The earliest issue for discussion in Greece between the sixth and fourth century B.C. concerned an allegorical method of interpretation. Was an allegorical reading of the texts of Homer and Hesiod legitimate? The allegorical interpretation of biblical texts became and remained an issue of controversy in the early Church, and was revived as a controversial question at the Reformation.

The origins of allegorical interpretation among the Greeks go back to Theagenes of Rhegium and Hecataeus the geographer and historian in the sixth century B.C. Theagenes flourished circa 525, and his writings are no longer extant. However, according to reliable traditions, he interpreted parts of Homer allegorically with the primary aim of defending this "sacred" or revered text from rationalist attacks on its polytheism and questionable morality. Stories of Homer about wars and jealousies among the gods and goddesses of the Greek pantheon were interpreted as allegories of natural forces, or as myths to encourage prudent conduct. Apollo and Hephaestus stand for fire; Poseidon stands for water; Hera for air; and so on.

In the fifth century Metrodorus of Lampsacus (or Lampsakos) understood Homeric tales of the gods as allegories that denoted parts of the human body. Apollo signified bile; Demeter represented the liver. This allegorical code went beyond physiology; it also reflected the orderliness of the universe and of humankind as a serious philosophical system, supported by respected literature. Zeno (ca. 334-262), founder of the Stoic School, read Hesiod in this way. Cleanthes (ca. 331-232) interpreted the Pantheon (with the exception of Zeus) as forces of nature, with Zeus as a symbol of divine order or control.

The early Stoic philosophers and rhetoricians used allegorical interpretation. Plato (ca. 428-348) expressed serious reservations about doing this. We need to distinguish between *allegorical interpretation* of texts that may or may not be allegorical, and *allegorical texts*. Allegorical interpretation denotes a hermeneutical procedure that presupposes a meaning different or "other" *(allos)* from the text's grammatical or normal everyday "dictionary" meaning. It is different from that which the reader or interpreter deems to underlie the text. Plato and most earlier writers prefer to use the term *hyponoia* (undermeaning, or a meaning beneath the surface) to the later word *allegoria*. *Allegorical texts* use ordinary, everyday language to convey symbolic, additional, or out-of-the-ordinary meanings.

Plato had recognized that some passages of Homer may convey a mythological meaning that is deeper than that of literal, descriptive, referential language. Nevertheless, he disapproves of *unrestrained* allegorical interpretation as representing a "rustic sort of wisdom."[30] In *Phaedrus* Socrates argues for a rational interpretation, over against flights of fancy.

In the first century A.D. Heracleitus (or Heraclitus or Heraclides) and Cornutus discuss the principles of interpretation used by the earlier Stoics and by the Platonists respectively. Heracleitus is sympathetic with the Stoic view of reading Homer as if the text merely and really described the goddess Athene pulling the hair of Achilles or as if the gods plotted against Zeus. This is to misunderstand and to devalue it. The former example describes only the subjective indecision or psychological state of mind of Achilles, while the latter example describes the interaction of air (Hera), sun (Apollo), and water (Poseidon) with ether (Zeus). Indeed, Heracleitus insists, Homer "says one thing but means something other. . . . It is called allegory (Greek, *allēgoria kaleitai*)."[31] Readers who look "below the surface" will perceive that Homer conveys a profound philosophy of life.

Platonist philosophers tended to be divided in their assessment of allegorical interpretation. For some a difference between a theoretical rejection and a practical acceptance emerged. For his part Plutarch adopted a cautious attitude. He rejected any overreadiness to read cosmological theories about the nature of the world in the text. However, he accepted the principle that mythology conveyed symbolic or practical meanings above and beyond flat, objective description. In our chapter on demythologizing we shall note that Rudolf Bultmann appeals to a long-standing recognition that "myth" has more to do with inviting or promoting human *attitudes* than with describing events or states of affairs "objectively."

While Greek thinkers were applying allegorical interpretation to Homer and Hesiod, some Jewish thinkers, as we have seen, were drawing on allegorical interpretation of the Hebrew Bible. Some passages in the Old Testament were arguably already allegorical *texts*. For example, the great eagle, the cedar, and the vine in Ezekiel 17:1-10 seem to be an allegory respectively for the king of Babylon, the king of Judah, and political relations between them. The text of Ezekiel is so full of symbolism and metaphor that extended meaning or even allegorical meaning would not seem out of place.

Nevertheless, more systematic allegorical interpretation arose less from

---

30. Plato, *Phaedrus* 229e.
31. Heracleitus, *Quaestiones Homericae* 22.

concern about the genre of the text than from anxieties about divine transcendence and anthropomorphism. Aristobulus in the first half of the second century showed such concerns about those biblical passages that appeared to portray God in anthropomorphic terms. These included not only such an obvious metaphor as understanding "the hands of God" to denote the power of God in action, but also "the descent" of God onto Sinai, or God's "resting" on the seventh day of creation (Gen. 2:2). Aristobulus read this to denote not cessation of action but the establishment of permanent order. R. P. C. Hanson accurately describes this less as allegorical interpretation than as "trembling on the verge of allegory." Nevertheless, Hanson adds, Aristobulus is "borrowing his allegory from Hellenistic models."[32]

Umberto Eco offers an illuminating comment on this. Philo, he points out, employs allegorical interpretation largely *to broaden* the focus of the text from particular, time-bound situations to general philosophical or theological principles. By contrast, allegory's use among the Alexandrian Church Fathers has the converse effect, namely, of *narrowing* the focus of the text specifically to *christological* applications.[33] He also suggests that pre-Christian allegorical interpretation tended to replace more "religious" meanings by more philosophical or secular ones, while early Christian allegorical interpretation tended to replace secular or ordinary meanings by more religious ones.

When we reach the New Testament and second century in the next chapter, we must examine the relationship between allegorical interpretation and the use of *typology*. We have already seen something of its complexity in the parables. We shall see more of this when we consider the third century to the thirteenth (chapter VI); the material on reform, the Enlightenment, and the rise of biblical criticism (chapter VII); and elsewhere in our chapters.

5. Recommended Initial Reading

Hanson, R. P. C., *Allegory and Event: A Study of the Sources and Significance of Origen's Interpretation of Scripture* (London: SCM, 1959), pp. 11-64.

32. R. P. C. Hanson, *Allegory and Event: A Study of the Sources and Significance of Origen's Interpretation of Scripture* (London: SCM, 1959), p. 43.
33. Umberto Eco, *Semiotics and the Philosophy of Language* (London: Macmillan, 1984), pp. 147-48.

Jensen, Alexander, *Theological Hermeneutics*, SCM Core Text (London: SCM, 2007), pp. 9-23.

Patte, Daniel, *Early Jewish Hermeneutic in Palestine*, Society of Biblical Literature Dissertation Series 22 (Missoula: Scholars Press, 1975), pp. 49-129.

CHAPTER V

The New Testament and the Second Century

The New Testament raises at least three kinds of issues about interpretation. Some passages take Jesus and the Old Testament as a *frame of reference* for God's dealings with the world. A second group of texts appear to use *typological* or allegorical interpretation to make a particular point. Yet a third group of passages identify *Jesus of Nazareth* as the one long foretold by the prophets and Old Testament writers, such as the cluster of texts in Matthew 1–3. We shall first consider examples that look to the Old Testament as a frame of reference or as providing a valid *pre-understanding* for interpreting the Gospel of Jesus Christ. For the Old Testament was in effect the Bible of the New Testament Church.

1. The Old Testament as a Frame of Reference or Pre-understanding: Paul and the Gospels

If we begin with the earliest pre-Pauline formulae, we find that according to the tradition that is earlier even than Paul's letters (i.e., before about A.D. 51), "Christ died for our sins in accordance with the Scriptures, that he was buried, and that he was raised on the third day in accordance with the Scriptures" (1 Cor. 15:3-4). This does not implicitly identify one particular verse. It tells us that the key to understanding the death and resurrection of Christ lies in its being "according to the Scriptures" *(kata tas graphas;* plural, *scriptures).* Ulrich Luz writes, "For Paul the Old Testament is not in the first place something to understand; but it itself creates understanding."[1] What is at

---

1. Ulrich Luz, *Das Geschichtsverständnis des Paulus* (Munich: Kaiser, 1968), p. 134.

stake here is not one single proof text about "the third day" (Hos. 6:2), but the whole Old Testament principle of God allowing his Servant to undergo suffering and to be ultimately vindicated.[2]

Anders Eriksson has shown the importance of shared pre-Pauline apostolic traditions for Pauline argumentation and the Church.[3] The historical horizon of the Jewish Scriptures provides the basis for understanding what God has done through Christ, "When the time had fully come" (Gal. 4:4). According to Luke, Jesus told his disciples that "everything written about me in the Law of Moses, the prophets, and the psalms must be fulfilled. Then he opened their eyes to understand the scriptures" (Luke 24:44-45). In Luke 24:26-27, the matter is expressed conversely: "Was it not necessary that the Messiah should suffer these things, and enter into his glory? Then beginning with Moses and all the prophets he interpreted to them (Greek *diermēneusen autois*) the things about himself in all the scriptures (Greek *en pasais tais graphais*)."[4]

This speaks to the modern debate about hermeneutics. Ever since Marcion in the second century (see below), many have in effect virtually set aside the Old Testament, ignoring or neglecting the fact that it constituted the Scripture of Jesus and the New Testament Church. The Old Testament or Hebrew Bible forms the preliminary understanding that paves the way for an authentic understanding of the New Testament. Even Schleiermacher might have written a different theology if he had been saturated in the Old Testament as much as in the New Testament, Kant, philosophy, the Enlightenment, and the German culture of his day. He taught almost every other theological subdiscipline. Bultmann is perhaps a worse culprit.

If we follow A. T. Hanson, Otto Michel, Ulrich Luz, Richard Longenecker, Moody Smith, J. W. Aageson, and other experts in the field, we shall find that at various points the New Testament writers see the Hebrew Scriptures as offering a pre-understanding or a frame of reference for interpreting the coming of Christ, his work, and the gospel.[5] Paul in his major epistles

---

2. Anthony C. Thiselton, *The First Epistle to the Corinthians: A Commentary on the Greek Text,* New International Greek Testament Commentary (Grand Rapids: Eerdmans; Carlisle: Paternoster, 2000), pp. 1186-1203.

3. Anders Eriksson, *Tradition as Rhetorical Proof: Pauline Argumentation in 1 Corinthians* (Stockholm: Almqvist & Wiksell, 1998), especially pp. 86-97 and 332-78.

4. Richard Palmer, *Hermeneutics: Interpretation Theory in Schleiermacher, Dilthey, Heidegger, and Gadamer* (Evanston, Ill.: Northwestern University Press, 1969), pp. 23-26.

5. Cf., for example, J. W. Aageson, *Written Also for Our Sake: Paul and the Art of Biblical*

sees the gospel as "proclaimed through the prophets in the holy scriptures" (Rom. 1:2). He repeats the same idea in Romans 3:21-22. In Romans 15:4 Paul tells his readers that these writings were written "for our instruction," also providing "the encouragement of the Scriptures." In Romans 4:1-15 Paul cites the example of Abraham, whom he calls "our ancestor" (4:1) since he is justified on the basis of God's promise. Romans 9–11 concern Israel, "my kindred according to the flesh" (9:3). Many, admittedly, especially Albert Schweitzer, have argued that we should expect ad hominem references to the Old Testament in Romans and Galatians, where Paul may be partly addressing "Judaizers" or Jewish Christians who would expect appeals to Scripture. But 1 and 2 Corinthians hardly fall into this category. In 1 Corinthians 10:1-13 Paul calls Israel not only a model of the Christian Church, but more. He writes, "These things occurred as examples for us" (10:6). They were "written down to instruct *us*" (10:11). In 2 Corinthians 1:20 Paul confirms divine promises in Christ recorded in the Old Testament, and in 2 Corinthians 3:14-18 he says the veil that hides the Old Covenant (or *Testament;* Greek *diathēkē* can mean either) has been removed for Christian believers.

This frame of reference is more than a matter of individual texts. It extends to major themes. In Paul Christ is the new or the "last" (eschatological) Adam (Rom. 5:12-21; 1 Cor. 15:45-50). The gospel brings new creation (Gal. 3:27-28; 2 Cor. 5:17). The Church is the "spiritual" Israel (Rom. 9:4-5). Paul takes up the example of Abraham in Genesis 15 (cf. Gal. 4:21-31).[6] Tom Holland has also shown recently how much Paul's thought owes to the Old Testament.[7] Many metaphors, such as that of the olive tree, would be unintelligible without their scriptural background (Rom. 11:17-24).

In the Synoptic Gospels the baptism of Jesus places Jesus in solidarity with Israel as one of the people of God. He is called as God's Servant and Son, in accordance with Isaiah 40–55 and some of the psalms (Ps. 2:7; Mark 1:11). At the transfiguration Moses and Elijah represent the Law and the Prophets. The Sermon on the Mount presupposes various comparisons with the Old Testament. Jesus regularly contrasts himself with Moses. He is the

---

Interpretation (Louisville: Westminster John Knox, 1993), and Richard N. Longenecker, *Biblical Exegesis in the Apostolic Period* (Grand Rapids: Eerdmans, 1975).

6. These themes are listed in Leonhard Goppelt, *Typos: The Typological Interpretation of the Old Testament in the New,* trans. D. H. Hadvig (Grand Rapids: Eerdmans, 2006), pp. 127-52.

7. Tom Holland, *Contours of Pauline Theology: A Radical New Survey of the Influences on Paul's Biblical Writings* (Fearn, Scotland: Christian Focus, 2004).

new Moses. Some of the miracles assume parallels with Old Testament events, which cannot all be dismissed as a "reading back," as with the raising of the young man from Nain (Luke 7:11-17) and the story of Elijah in 1 Kings 17:17-24 (or 2 Kings 4:18-37). The deceased is the "only son of a widow" in these episodes. The death of Jesus as "a ransom for many" (Mark 10:45) is understood in the light of the Scriptures (Luke 24:26-27, 44-45). Jesus is Son of David (Matt. 12:23), especially in Matthew. He is also "Son of Man" (Mark 2:10), which may look back to Daniel 7.[8] Even in the Gospels Jesus is the last Adam and the Righteous Sufferer.[9] The Lord's Supper occurs in the context of the Passover meal.

In Acts, Pentecost and the communal gift of the Holy Spirit (Acts 2:14-21) are understandable only in the light of Jeremiah 31:33-34, together with Ezekiel 36:27-32, and especially Joel 2:28-32, where the eschatological promise receives its significance. The appointment of the seven in Acts 6:1-6 may perhaps reflect Exodus 18:17-23. The "Twelve" in the first half of Acts presumably reflects the twelve tribes of Israel.

John's prologue, "in the beginning was the Word," looks to the creation account of Genesis 1:1-5.[10] The Word is the Christ "through whom all things were made" (John 1:3). The word "tent" or "tabernacle" *(skēnē)* may reflect the tent of the glory of God in Exodus 33:9 or Numbers 12:5. In the Book of Signs (John 1:19–12:50) Jesus is the source of *manna,* or the Bread of Life, who is "bread from heaven" (John 6:32; cf. 6:35, 41, 48, 50, 51). The Moses narrative in the Old Testament provides a necessary *pre-understanding* for the bread discourse in John 6.[11] The Son of Man will be "lifted up" on the cross,

---

8. Cf. Maurice Casey, *The Son of Man: The Interpretation and Influence of Daniel 7* (London: SPCK, 1979); A. J. B. Higgins, *The Son of Man in the Teaching of Jesus* (Cambridge: Cambridge University Press, 1980); and Seyoon K. Kim, *The "Son of Man" as the Son of God* (Tübingen: Mohr, 1983); cf. Anthony Tyrrell Hanson, *The Living Utterances of God: The New Testament Exegesis of the Old* (London: Darton, Longman and Todd, 1983), pp. 27-63, 177-89.

9. Cf. Goppelt, *Typos,* pp. 61-106.

10. See Rudolf Schnackenburg, *The Gospel according to St. John,* 3 vols. (London: Burns and Oates; New York: Herder and Herder, 1968-82), 1:236-41.

11. Joachim Jeremias, "Mōusēs," in *Theological Dictionary of the New Testament,* ed. G. Kittel, vol. 4 (Grand Rapids: Eerdmans, 1967), pp. 873-74, cf. pp. 864-74; T. F. Glasson, *Moses in the Fourth Gospel* (London: SCM, 1963). Cf. Hanson, *Living Utterances of God,* pp. 111-32; Goppelt, *Typos,* pp. 165-98; P. Borgen, *Bread from Heaven: An Exegetical Study of the Concept of Manna in the Gospel of John* (Leiden: Brill, 1965); and Raymond Brown, *The Gospel according to John,* 2 vols. (New York: Doubleday; London: Geoffrey Chapman, 1966 and 1971), 1:273-304.

just as Moses "lifted up" the serpent in the wilderness (John 3:14).[12] The Feast of Tabernacles (John 7:2) and especially the Passover (John 2:13; 6:4; 11:55; 12:1; 13:1; 18:28, 39; 19:14; Greek *to pascha*) play an important role. They were Jewish (Old Testament) festivals. Jesus is the true temple, the true vine, the true water-giving rock. In the Book of the Passion (from John 13:1) Jesus is the paschal sacrifice.[13]

2. Hebrews, 1 Peter, and Revelation:
The Old Testament as Pre-understanding

We look briefly at the Epistle to the Hebrews, which is saturated with Old Testament allusions. We also look briefly at 1 Peter, which reminds new converts of their new life and of the significance of the Hebrew Bible, or Old Testament. Finally we shall glance at the book of Revelation. Hebrews was not written by Paul, but by a major theologian of the very early Church, whose name has been lost, although some have argued for Apollos or Priscilla as the writer. So we are considering three (or two) distinct traditions in the New Testament, in addition to the three we have outlined in the previous section.

Clearly the whole of Hebrews centers on the notion of Jesus as mediator or high priest. Rather than justification by faith or reconciliation, as in Paul, or new life, as in John, the theme is access, or approach, to God based on the model of a liturgical approach.[14] This includes approach to the mercy seat, based on the Day of Atonement in Leviticus 16. Hebrews begins by introducing Jesus as the high priest who opens the way to God, and quotes Psalm 2:7 (Heb. 1:5) as pointing to "today." The homily then quotes 2 Samuel 7:14, Deuteronomy 32:43, and Psalms 104:4, 45:6-7, 102:25-27, all in the space of some ten verses in a single chapter (Heb. 1:5-13). The letter or homily then returns to the key frame of reference, namely, Psalm 110 (LXX Ps. 109), quoted in Hebrews 1:3, 10:12, and 12:2. William Lane, A. Vanhoye, and many other writers stress the book's homiletic character and the importance of Psalm 110. Jesus is contrasted with angels, with Moses (Heb. 3:1-19), and with Joshua (4:1-13),

12. Longenecker, *Biblical Exegesis*, pp. 153-54; cf. pp. 152-57.

13. Longenecker, *Biblical Exegesis*, p. 154; cf. Goppelt, *Typos*, pp. 188-94.

14. William L. Lane, *The Epistle to the Hebrews*, 2 vols., Word Biblical Commentaries, vol. 47 (Dallas: Word, 1991), and H. W. Attridge, *Commentary on the Epistle to the Hebrews* (Philadelphia: Fortress, 1989).

who failed to fulfill Israel's hopes of a full entry into the Promised Land. *Joshua* is Greek for *Jesus*.

The writer then considers four qualifications for genuine high priesthood. Jesus, like Aaronic high priests, lived in full solidarity with humanity, and he was appointed by God. But in contrast to high priests of the Aaronic line, only Jesus was "for ever," and only Jesus could offer a sacrifice "once for all" wholly for the sins of others, rather than for himself. He is therefore the perfect priest-king "after the order of Melchizedek" (cf. Gen. 14:17-20), who offered himself for sins "once for all" *(ephapax)*. People may therefore approach the throne of grace "boldly" (Heb. 4:14-16). Like Israelites of old, they also wait in faith for the final eschatological glory (Heb. 11:1-3, 13-40). Melchizedek is the priest-king who blessed Abraham (Gen. 14:19), received tithes from him (14:20), and thereby proves to be his "superior" (Heb. 7:4-7). He, like Jesus, is always a priest; or (in the text) "for ever" (Heb. 5:6; Ps. 110:4). The writer also stresses the inadequacy of the Old Testament or old covenant worship (Heb. 9:1-10). Something "better" is promised. Chapter 11 on faith is full of case studies from the Old Testament. The readers or hearers must not fall away. They must abandon false securities within the world (Heb. 11:9-13). Jesus provides a perfect model of faith (12:1-3).[15]

We cannot argue that *1 Peter* was addressed only to *Jewish* Christians or even to Judaizing Christians. The readers or hearers were new converts, whom the author of this epistle teaches to use the Old Testament as a frame of reference for understanding the gospel.[16] 1 Peter 2:4-10 tells them that this community is a holy priesthood, a spiritual temple, and the true people of God. They would not understand this fully without references to Scripture. In 1 Peter 1:18 they are delivered or redeemed, and while the purchase of slaves in the Greco-Roman world sheds some light on this, an understanding of redemption from Egypt in the Old Testament provides their fullest pre-understanding of redemption by Christ (cf. 2:10, 25). The reference to the blood of Christ (1:2, 19) presupposes some understanding of the Old Testament sacrificial system. The

15. Robert Jewett, *Letter to Pilgrims: A Commentary on the Epistle to the Hebrews* (New York: Pilgrim Press, 1981), and Ernst Käsemann, *The Wandering People of God: An Investigation into the Epistle to the Hebrews,* trans. R. Harrisville and A. Sandberg (Minneapolis: Augsburg, 1984).

16. Cf. Edward G. Selwyn, *The First Epistle of St. Peter: The Greek Text with Introduction, Notes, and Essays,* 2nd ed. (London: Macmillan, 1947); Francis W. Beire, *The First Epistle of Peter: The Greek Text,* 3rd ed. (Oxford: Blackwell, 1970); and Ernest Best, *1 Peter* (London: Oliphants, 1971).

theme of suffering and vindication also looks back to the Old Testament (1:11). The same applies to the theme of promise and hope (1:3-5, 10, 11). There are nine Old Testament quotations (1:16, 24, 25; 2:6; and others). There are perhaps up to thirty more allusions to the Old Testament.

The complex symbols of the *book of Revelation* invite endless puzzlement until the background of many symbols in the Old Testament comes to be explained. Anthony T. Hanson writes, "We meet bizarre symbols at every turn; a figure with a sword proceeding from his mouth (Rev. 1:16); four living creatures with six wings each (Rev. 4:8), horses with heads like lions and tails like serpents (9:17-19), a harlot seated on a scarlet, seven-headed beast (17:3-4), gates each made up of a single pearl (21:21). But these symbols are nearly all taken from scripture."[17]

The author of Revelation uses the Old Testament not to make explicit quotations of fulfillment in Christ or to prove the doctrine he promotes, but as a repertoire of symbols, emphasizing the continuity of divine revelation in the Old Testament and Christ. Jesus is "the first and the last, who died and came to life" (Rev. 2:8). In Isaiah 44:6 we read, "I am the first and the last; besides me there is no God." In Revelation 13:1-8 a beast rises from the sea with ten horns and seven heads, but also having the qualities of a leopard, a bear, and a lion. As Hanson comments, "Nearly all these features are taken from Daniel 7:1-7, where they belong to a succession of beasts, each one more terrible than the last."[18] In Daniel they are symbols of successive empires that enslaved Israel. In Revelation they are symbolic of the Church's adversary.

In Revelation 19:11-16 a man sits on a white horse, with his robe dipped in blood, while he pronounces judgment and wages war. In Isaiah 63:1-6, Hanson comments, we have a grim picture of God returning from war against Israel's enemy Edom in garments stained in blood. "The figure in Revelation 19:11-16 is undoubtedly that of the risen and victorious Christ. The blood on his garments is therefore his own blood shed on the cross."[19] The visions of Revelation 4 and 5 mostly are based on Isaiah 6 and Ezekiel 1, with their theme, the winged creatures and angels, with a hymn. Hanson writes, "The lamps of fire, the lightning, the crystal sea, the rainbow colours, the diverse characteristics of the living creatures come from Ezekiel's vi-

17. Hanson, *Living Utterances of God*, p. 159; cf. pp. 159-77.

18. Hanson, *Living Utterances of God*, p. 160; cf. George B. Caird, *The Revelation of St. John the Divine* (London: Black, 1966), pp. 161-69; Caird also sees allusions to Gen. 1:2; 7:11; and Job 28:14; 38:26.

19. Hanson, *Living Utterances of God*, p. 160. Cf. Caird, *Revelation*, pp. 239-48.

sion."[20] John has combined two well-known symbolic visions as a pre-understanding for his own.

This use of Scripture, Hanson urges, has close links with *typology,* rather than with so-called pesher exegesis. The author weaves Old Testament language into his own visions, as a frame of interpretation for the events of the Christian era, the Old Testament, and his visions. Many of the metaphors borrowed by Revelation have their origins in the Old Testament. Opening a scroll is a common metaphor for unfolding a plan. A terrible beast is a natural symbol or metaphor for a tyrannical force or empire. The apocalyptic background shares this in common with Revelation. Although writers speak of "the creative freedom" with which John the Seer uses Old Testament Scripture, this is not to prove doctrine but to open the understanding. G. B. Caird writes, "The symbolism is drawn from the Old Testament, but modified to carry a radically new meaning. Zechariah had two visions, one of four horsemen, one of four chariots . . . (Zech. 1:8-11; 6:1-8). But in John's vision four colours indicate a difference of commission."[21] There are both continuity and contrast with the Old Testament.

3. Does the New Testament Employ Allegorical Interpretation or Typology?

Many argue that the New Testament writers use allegorical interpretation of the Old Testament. But the matter is more complicated. One counterargument is that they used not allegory but typology. But even this is complex. Alexander Jensen believes that typology has too modern a ring to be taken seriously by New Testament writers.[22] On the other hand, the use of typology is vital to Leonhard Goppelt, and Richard P. C. Hanson sees allegory as reflecting a parallel between objects, persons, or *ideas,* while typology is based on a parallel between *events.*[23]

20. Hanson, *Living Utterances of God,* p. 161. Cf. Caird, *Revelation,* pp. 13 and 60-77. Caird adds 1 Kings 22:19-21; Jer. 23:18; Ps. 18:10; Isa. 65:17; 66:22; and numerous other references.

21. Caird, *Revelation,* pp. 79-80.

22. Alexander Jensen, *Theological Hermeneutics,* SCM Core Text (London: SCM, 2007), pp. 15-25.

23. Richard P. C. Hanson, *Allegory and Event: A Study of the Sources and Significance of Origen's Interpretation of Scripture* (London: SCM, 1959), p. 7; Goppelt, *Typos,* throughout.

Philo's date broadly coincides with that of the writing of Paul's earlier epistles. Did Paul and other New Testament writers ever interpret the Old Testament allegorically? In Galatians 4:21-31 Paul discusses the contrast between Hagar and Sarah found in Genesis 16:1-16; 17; 18; and 21:1-21. Concerning the respective status and significance of Hagar and Ishmael, and of Sarah and Isaac, Paul comments: *hatina estin allēgoroumena,* which the NRSV translates as "Now this is an allegory" (Gal. 4:24); although, strictly speaking, the Greek is in a verbal form. Nevertheless, F. F. Bruce rightly states in his commentary: "He is not thinking of allegory in the Philonic sense. . . . He has in mind that form of allegory which is commonly called typology."[24] Otto Michel and Leonhard Goppelt make this point even more emphatically.[25] By contrast Andrew Louth and others reject any sharp distinction between allegory and typology and insist that here Paul uses allegory.[26] But Louth has a theological agenda, to which we shall refer more fully in chapter XV.

There is in fact a significant difference between allegory, in Philo's sense of the term, and typology. Allegory postulates a parallel, correspondence, or resonance between *two sets of ideas;* typology (broadly speaking) postulates a parallel or correspondence between *two sets of events or persons.* It is not adequate to call both, as Jensen does, "pre-figuration." James Smart expresses this contrast in theological terms. "Typology is distinguished from allegory by the fact that it fastens onto the historical reality of the event, where allegory disregards the historical reality and draws out a contemporary meaning that has nothing to do with the original event."[27] Richard Hanson makes a similar point. Paul, he writes, is "not here trying to emancipate the meaning of the passage from its historical context" in order to transpose it into some "timeless" moral or philosophical truth.[28]

Some writers insist that Paul uses "allegory" in this passage, but it is unwise to use a term that has already developed such a different meaning in Philo (if misunderstanding is to be avoided). In his volume on typological interpretations, Leonhard Goppelt expresses the issue well. "For Philo,

24. F. F. Bruce, *The Epistle to the Galatians: A Commentary on the Greek Text* (Grand Rapids: Eerdmans; Carlisle: Paternoster, 1982), p. 217.

25. Otto Michel, *Paulus und seine Bibel* (Gütersloh: Bertelsmann, 1929), p. 110; Goppelt, *Typos,* pp. 151-52.

26. Andrew Louth, *Discerning the Mystery: An Essay on the Nature of Theology* (Oxford: Clarendon, 1983), pp. 138-39.

27. James Smart, *The Interpretation of Scripture* (London: SCM, 1961), p. 123.

28. Hanson, *Allegory and Event,* p. 82.

allegorizing is the same as advancing from the visible world to the higher world of ideas," often in terms of analogy with the body and the soul.[29] In the classic work *Essays on Typology,* Lampe and Woollcombe define typology as "the establishment of historical connections between certain events, persons, or things in the Old Testament and similar events, persons, or things in the New Testament."[30] More recent research by J. W. Aageson and others confirms, rather than questions, this axiom.[31] Philo, in fact, had already offered a more fully allegorical interpretation of these Genesis passages, which is very different from Paul's. In Philo Abraham, Sarah, and Isaac represent virtue and wisdom in their quest for the true God; Hagar represents the lower learning of the schools; her son Ishmael represents the more arbitrary arguments of the sophist.[32] Paul's approach is entirely different.

Within the historical situation that Paul addresses, no doubt his readers in Galatia would have argued that to show themselves true heirs of Isaac they should retain their observance of the Jewish ordinances and signs of the covenant. To be outside this Jewish covenant is to be abandoned, like Hagar, to the wilderness. Paul inverts this exegesis. The deeper significance of Isaac is that he is "free," whereas Hagar and Ishmael are in bondage as hand servants. Hence the deeper parallel is that between law and gospel, or between slavery and grace. "Hagar corresponds to Mount Sinai, bearing children for slavery" (Gal. 4:24b). Sarah corresponds "to the Jerusalem above: she is free, and she is our mother. . . . You are the children of the promise, like Isaac" (Gal. 4:26, 28). The argument concludes: "We are children of the free woman" (4:31).

Paul takes up a passage probably used by the Galatians, and by moving to what F. F. Bruce terms a different "level of meaning," he is able to allow the text to point in a different direction from that envisaged in Galatia. But the notion of bondage and freedom, and of promise and inheritance, remains grounded in the historical or event dimensions of the text, without dissipating the historical into what is abstract or timeless.

Paul is also accused of allegorical interpretation in his use of Deuteronomy 25:4, "You shall not muzzle any ox while it is treading out the grain," in 1 Corinthians 9:8-10. Hans Conzelmann, for example, insists that Deuteron-

---

29. Goppelt, *Typos,* p. 52.

30. Geoffrey W. H. Lampe and K. J. Woollcombe, *Essays on Typology* (London: SCM, 1957), p. 39.

31. Aageson, *Written Also for Our Sake.*

32. Philo, *On Abraham* 11.53, 54; 33.177; *On Flight and Finding* 30.166-68; 38.208-11; *On the Change of Names* 39.216-19; cf. further, Bruce, *Galatians,* p. 215.

omy 25:4 serves solely as a protection for animals, which is "contrary to Paul's exegesis."[33] The RSV translation of the Greek *pantōs* (v. 10) to mean "written for our sake" would exclude the straightforward meaning of Deuteronomy 25:4. It is better to translate it "of course," "undoubtedly," or "certainly." Richard Hays rightly understands Paul to mean that *ultimately* Scripture, in Paul's view, serves the eschatological people of God in a sense that includes, that moves beyond, more immediate, contingent examples.[34] J. W. Aageson also understands Paul to be referring to an extended context concerning the sheer routine of endlessly repetitive labor without hope of encouragement or recognition.[35] The parallel is at least typological rather than allegorical. I have discussed this verse in detail elsewhere.[36]

Adolf Jülicher attempts to distinguish very sharply between parable and allegory in the teaching and proclamation of Jesus. But Joachim Jeremias and others rightly insist that while there are clear differences of dynamic and function, some instances are borderline cases, or ones in which parable and allegory may overlap. Mark 12:1-9 (parallel, Matt. 21:33-41) seems to begin as a parable, but in the light of Isaiah 5:1-2 (which portrays Israel as a vineyard), the details of throwing the son and heir out of the vineyard and killing him (Mark 12:6-8) become an allegorical representation of the death of Jesus. The same has been said of the wedding banquet in Matthew 22:2-10. This, too, appears at first to run parallel with the parable in Luke, but then concludes with an allegorical turn, in which the king "sent troops, destroyed those murderers, and burned their city" (Matt. 22:7). Neither example, however, is one of allegorical interpretation of a sacred text in the sense discussed above. They are examples in which Jesus untypically uses the mode of allegory (as in Ezek. 17:1-10) in place of his usual mode of parable discourse. These have a different hermeneutical dynamic, as in chapter III.

In spite of the insistence of some writers, including R. M. Grant, that the New Testament writers use allegorical interpretations in the style of the Alexandrians, such judgments invite extreme caution. C. H. Dodd, in his earlier but classic study *According to the Scriptures,* declares that the New Testament writers interpreted the Old Testament "along lines which start from their first, historical, intention," viewing them "as *wholes.* . . . It is the

---

33. Hans Conzelmann, *1 Corinthians: A Commentary,* Hermeneia (Philadelphia: Fortress, 1975), pp. 154-55.

34. Richard B. Hays, *First Corinthians* (Louisville: John Knox, 1997), p. 151.

35. Aagerson, *Written Also,* pp. 49-53.

36. Thiselton, *First Epistle,* pp. 685-88.

total context that is in view," and this "upon the basis of a certain understanding of history."[37] Their interpretations, Dodd concludes, "in general remain true to the main intention of their writer."[38]

Most of these problems form perennial issues in biblical hermeneutics: the status of the Old Testament; the place and role of allegorical interpretation; the distinction between allegory and typology; and the extension of the original text in pesher fashion to refer to the present. All these issues concerned the patristic, medieval, and modern Church, even after the Enlightenment and the rise of biblical criticism. But we must first consider other issues in the New Testament.

4. Passages in Paul That Might Be "Difficult": Septuagint or Hebrew?

The New Testament writers often used the Septuagint (LXX), or Greek version of the Old Testament. From the first, Jewish rabbis from Hillel to Aquila criticized its translation as an inaccurate rendering of the Hebrew Bible. But it is understandable that if most of the New Testament was addressed to Greek-speaking people, New Testament writers would often use the Septuagint. The early Church after the second century would also regularly use the Septuagint. It would be like a writer today choosing the NRSV rather than Greek or Hebrew. These criticisms led to a second version of the Septuagint, known as the Symmachus. Jerome used the Symmachus in his Latin translation, the Vulgate. Meanwhile a third version named the Theodotion represents a Palestinian revision of the Septuagint, parts of which are older than the second century.

In the Pauline writings, Christopher D. Stanley carefully compares and discusses quotations from the Hebrew or Septuagint respectively.[39] We broadly follow Stanley's order.

1. First, he considers Romans 1:17, quoting Habakkuk 2:4b. Paul's wording almost represents the Septuagint but omits *mou*, "my," from the Septuagint. Stanley points out, however, that the problem hinges on the relation between three different manuscript readings of the Septuagint. But regard-

---

37. Charles H. Dodd, *According to the Scriptures* (London: Collins/Fontana, 1965), pp. 109 and 126, italics in original.

38. Dodd, *According to the Scriptures,* p. 130.

39. Christopher D. Stanley, *Paul and the Language of Scripture: Citation Technique in the Pauline Epistles and Contemporary Literature,* Society for New Testament Studies Monograph Series, no. 69 (Cambridge: Cambridge University Press, 1992).

less of this, the retention of *mou* "would have been incongruous with Paul's argument."[40]

2. In Romans 2:24 Paul quotes Isaiah 52:5 but has a different order of words from the LXX. Several words are changed to the second-person plural. But this strengthens Paul's argument. The hypocritical deeds of the Jews have caused the Gentiles to cast aspersions on the name of God. The mission of *dia pantos* may be due to variations in the LXX tradition, and the substantive of *tou Theou* ("of God") for *mou* ("of me") avoids God's speaking of himself in the third person. "Among the Gentiles" agrees with most LXX manuscripts.

3. Romans 3:10-12 is drawn from Psalm 13:1-3 (LXX). Psalm 52 has a similar passage. Paul declares, "There is no one who is righteous, not even one; there is no one who has understanding; there is no one who seeks after God. All have turned aside, together they have become worthless." The words "righteous, not even one" are regarded as added by Paul, but they are part of his exposition, not quotation. The Septuagint has "foolish" *(aphrōn)*, which is not suited to Paul's argument. The insertion of "righteous" makes Paul's point. Stanley considers more passages from Romans, but we have sampled enough to see his method. We may move to 1 Corinthians.

4. 1 Corinthians 3:19 alludes to Job 5:13. Paul uses "in their craftiness." The Greek once meant *being able to turn one's hand to anything* (to all things), but denotes *being cunning* or *crafty*. Paul, however, seems to be closer to the Hebrew text *'ārmāh*. Similarly, with "craftiness" he uses the word "catch" *(drassomai)*, which translates the Hebrew word *lākad*, "to grasp." He also uses "to take by surprise" (*katalambanein*, with the *kata*, intensive). Hence he conveys the picture portrayed by the Hebrew text of Job 5:13. Brendt Schaller argues that Paul's quotation has close affinities with the Hebrew Masoretic Text.[41] Stanley goes further, arguing that Paul and the LXX are independent translations of the Hebrew text.[42] 1 Corinthians 3:19 is one of some half a dozen texts that imply Paul's probable use of the Hebrew.

5. 1 Corinthians 9:8-10 is said by Conzelmann and Senft to be "contrary to Paul's exegesis . . . of God's concern with higher things," whereas Deuteronomy 25:4, which Paul quotes, is concerned to protect animals.[43] Yet the larger context surrounding Deuteronomy 25:4, Deuteronomy 24 and 25 (es-

---

40. Stanley, *Paul*, p. 84.

41. Thiselton, *First Epistle*, p. 322.

42. Stanley, *Paul*, pp. 190-94.

43. Conzelmann, *1 Corinthians*, pp. 54-55; C. Senft, *La Première Épitre de S. Paul aux Corinthiens*, 2nd ed. (Geneva: Labor et Fides, 1990), p. 119 n. 17.

pecially 24:6-7, 10, 22; 25:1-3), promotes the dignity of, and justice for, human beings. Deuteronomy 25:1-10 concerns levirate marriage. Hence Paul writes concerning Deuteronomy 25:4: "Is he not speaking in our interest?" (1 Cor. 9:10). Staab therefore writes that Deuteronomy 25:4 "functions as an elegant metaphor for just the point that Paul wants to make: the ox being drawn around and around on the threshing floor should not be cruelly restrained from eating food that his own labour is making available. . . . So, too, with apostles."[44] Hays, Fee, and I have supported and strengthened such a regard for the broader context.[45] C. H. Dodd claims that Paul and other New Testament writers used Old Testament passages in their proper context.

6. 1 Corinthians 14:21 quotes Isaiah 28:11-12, but it reflects neither the Septuagint nor the Hebrew text precisely. Stanley sees this as virtually unresolvable, and as "one of the greatest challenges in the entire corpus of Pauline citations."[46] But Origen claims to have encountered Paul's wording in Aquila's text.[47] Further, Paul may be combining exegesis and application. Paul writes, "By strange tongues *(en heteroglōssois)* and by the lips of foreigners I will speak to this people," but there are six differences from the LXX tradition. Yet the passage, as quoted, truly conveys the feeling of "being a stranger or foreigner," which was the lot of Israelites in Assyria, or Christians in a church community where many "spoke in tongues." In neither case did people feel that they "belonged." This is precisely Paul's point.[48]

Stanley has considered forty-five quotations in Romans and twelve in 1 Corinthians. We have considered only six, three from each epistle. But they are probably a representative sample.

5. Old Testament Quotations in the Gospels, 1 Peter, and the Epistle to the Hebrews

Many writers have addressed the peculiarities of the use of the Old Testament in the Gospels, and particularly in Matthew's Gospel. R. T. France has

---

44. W. Staab, *Der Bildersprache des Apostels Paulus* (Tübingen: Mohr, 1937), pp. 81-82.

45. Hays, *First Corinthians*, p. 151; Richard B. Hays, *Echoes of Scripture in the Letters of Paul* (New Haven: Yale University Press, 1989), pp. 165-66; Gordon D. Fee, *First Epistle to the Corinthians* (Grand Rapids: Eerdmans, 1987), p. 408. Thiselton, *First Epistle*, pp. 684-88.

46. Stanley, *Paul*, p. 198.

47. Origen, *Philocalia* 9.

48. Thiselton, *First Epistle*, pp. 1120-22.

published *Jesus and the Old Testament;* Robert H. Gundry, *The Use of the Old Testament in St. Matthew's Gospel with Special Reference to the Messianic Hope;* D. J. Moo, *The Old Testament in the Gospel Passion Narratives;* Krister Stendahl, *The School of St. Matthew and Its Use of the Old Testament;* and Don Hagner has produced several essays on the subject.[49] We must leave most of the discussion to the specialists.

1. *Matthew* contains over sixty explicit quotations from the Old Testament, and many further allusions to it. Matthew is especially concerned with the fulfillment of the Old Testament in the person and work of Jesus. Often this is done by way of additional comment by the Evangelist, or, according to Stendahl, by Matthew's "school" of disciples. A standard formula appears for example in Matthew 1:22-23: "in order that the word of the Lord [spoken] through the prophets might be fulfilled, [which says], 'Look, a virgin shall conceive and bear a son, and they shall call him "Emmanuel," which means "God is with us."'"

The quotation comes from Isaiah 7:14, where the Septuagint speaks of a virgin *(parthenos)* and gives a sign to King Ahaz and to the House of David that there will take place the birth of a royal son, who will bring victory and security to Israel. This links with calling Jesus the Son of David. The Hebrew word used in Isaiah 7:14 is not "virgin" but "young woman" *('almâ)*. Stendahl proposes that the fulfillment aspect is not only the product of a "school," but also represents the pesher exegesis ("this is that") discussed in chapter IV, on Judaism. But not all scholars accept his arguments. B. Gärtner and R. Gundry dispute the claim. Matthew includes eleven "fulfillment" quotations. Radical writers suggest that Matthew and others recast events to make the events fit the prophecy, but this rests on assumptions about the "supernatural" rather than on clear evidence.

Matthew does use "in order that," or the preposition in Greek *(hina)* usually translated "in order that" (Matt. 1:22). But P. Lampe, F. Danker, and C. F. D. Moule point out that sixteen of the thirty-nine occurrences in this context in Matthew are borrowed from Mark, who uses colloquial Greek loosely. In Mark the preposition *hina* often loses its purposive force in the

---

49. R. T. France, *Jesus and the Old Testament* (London: Tyndale Press, 1971); Robert H. Gundry, *The Use of the Old Testament in St. Matthew's Gospel with Special Reference to the Messianic Hope* (Leiden: Brill, 1967); Douglas J. Moo, *The Old Testament in the Gospel Passion Narratives* (Sheffield: Almond, 1983); Krister Stendahl, *The School of St. Matthew and Its Use of the Old Testament,* 2nd ed. (Lund: Gleerup, 1968); and Donald H. Hagner, *The Gospel of Matthew,* 2 vols. (Dallas: Word, 1993), 1:liii-lvii.

New Testament and Hellenistic or *koinē* Greek. It embraces a variety of uses, including those that denote consequence or result.[50]

2. Another quotation formula (we omit Matt. 2:5-6) occurs in Matthew 2:15, "Out of Egypt have I called my Son," where the quotation is probably from Hosea 11:1, reflecting the Hebrew Masoretic Text rather than the Septuagint. Hosea is alluding to the exodus, where Israel comes "out of" Egypt. But Jesus is taken "into" Egypt. Nevertheless, events are often telescoped in prophecy. Jesus had to enter Egypt in solidarity with God's people before he could come "out" of Egypt. Hence Hagner refers to this as "a matter of typological correspondence."[51] Luz concurs in speaking of "typology."[52]

3. Hanson considers the especially problematic formula-quotation that comes in Matthew 8:17, which quotes Isaiah 53:4, "Surely he has borne our griefs and carried our sorrows." The Septuagint, Hanson argues, has "spiritualized" the text, making it refer to our "sins." But Hanson, Hagner, Stendahl, and Luz believe Matthew has translated directly from the Hebrew, and well captured its meaning.

4. In Matthew 21:4-5 Matthew quotes Zechariah 9:9, "humble (or meek) and riding upon an ass, and on a colt the foal of an ass." The uninformed suggest that in Matthew Jesus rides upon two animals. But anyone who has Matthew's knowledge of Hebrew text knows that this is poetic parallelism, which repeats in the second line the context of the first. One example would be "In the presence is fullness of joy; at thy right hand are pleasures for evermore." We do not have space to explore Matthew further.

5. *Mark* has much less interest and expertise in the Old Testament than Matthew, but he still uses it as a frame of reference for Jesus and the gospel. Yet there remains at least one notorious use of an Old Testament quotation, namely, Mark 4:12, where Mark says the parables of the kingdom were misunderstood "in order that *(hina)* 'they may indeed look, but not perceive, and may indeed listen but not understand, so that they may not turn again and be forgiven.'" This comes from Isaiah 6:9-10 (LXX) and is an exact quo-

50. P. Lampe, "Hina," in *Exegetical Dictionary of the New Testament*, ed. Horst Balz and G. Schneider, 3 vols. (Grand Rapids: Eerdmans, 1981), 2:188-90; W. Bauer and Frederick W. Danker, eds., *Greek-English Lexicon*, 3rd ed. (Chicago: University of Chicago Press, 2000), pp. 475-77, abbreviated BDAG; C. F. D. Moule, *An Idiom Book of New Testament Greek*, 2nd ed. (Cambridge: Cambridge University Press, 1959), s.v. "hina."

51. Hagner, *The Gospel of Matthew*, 1:36.

52. Ulrich Luz, *Matthew 1–7: A Commentary*, trans. W. C. Linns (Minneapolis: Augsburg Fortress; Edinburgh: T. & T. Clark, 1989), pp. 146-47.

tation from the Targum of Isaiah 6.[53] The problem lies not in the quotation as such, but in Mark's introducing it with *hina,* while the parallels omit *hina,* as in Matthew 13:14-15, which has "because" (*hoti,* v. 13). Some consider *hina* original, which would mean that parables prevent premature belief, which Matthew modifies to avoid possible misunderstanding.

6. *Luke* alone among the Evangelists attributes to Jesus a direct quotation of Isaiah 53:12, "He was reckoned with the transgressors," in his passion narrative at Luke 22:37. The quotation matches the Septuagint (except for a trivial variant), which we should expect from one who writes for Greek-speaking readers. Granting that Luke's readers were Gentiles or Gentile Christians, it is noteworthy that he shares with Matthew and Mark the view that the Old Testament forms their frame of reference for his proclamation of the gospel, and that his quotations or allusions are frequent. Luke's interest is often in the providential purposes of God for the world, and he sees Christ as antitype to Abraham, Moses, and David. Luke's use of Scripture is fully discussed and documented by François Bovon in an impressive study.[54]

7. *John,* Hanson observes, "believes as firmly as any Pharisee that 'the scripture cannot be broken'" (John 10:35). The reference to "searching the scriptures" in vain "does not mean that searching the scriptures was in vain" (John 5:39-40, 46-47).[55] As Hanson reminds us, John includes traditional citations from Scripture (e.g., John 1:23, "the voice of one crying in the wilderness," from Isa. 40:3); Scripture cited with an introductory formula (e.g., John 17:12, probably from either Ps. 41:9 or Ps. 109:8, and John 19:28-29 from Ps. 69:21); explicit citings of Scripture (e.g., John 2:17 quotes Ps. 69:9a); and subtle allusions to Scripture as providing the basis for John's thought. Perhaps this is most characteristic of John. For example, the language of John 1:14, "The Word became flesh, and tabernacled among us, full of grace and truth; and we have beheld his glory . . . ," reproduces some words of Exodus 34:6. There God abounds in love (or grace) and faithfulness (or truth). The significance of John's language emerges in the light of

53. Longenecker, *Biblical Exegesis,* p. 59; Charles E. B. Cranfield, *The Gospel according to St. Mark: A Commentary,* Cambridge Greek Testament (Cambridge: Cambridge University Press, 1959), pp. 155-58; cf. Morna D. Hooker, *The Gospel according to St. Mark* (Peabody, Mass.: Hendrickson; London: Black, 1991), pp. 130-31.

54. François Bovon, *Luke the Theologian,* 2nd ed. (Waco, Tex.: Baylor University Press, 2006), pp. 87-122; cf. also Joel Green, *The Gospel of Luke* (Grand Rapids: Eerdmans, 1997), pp. 51-59.

55. Hanson, *Living Utterances of God,* p. 123.

Exodus 34:6, or as we should say today, with its intertextual resonances. Similarly John 1:51 ("You shall see heaven opened, and the angels of God ascending and descending on the Son of Man") has as its background Genesis 28:1-16 (the narrative of Jacob).[56]

8. *1 Peter* clearly regards the prophets as inspired by the Holy Spirit (1 Pet. 1:10-12). 1 Peter 1:19 and 2:22-25 quote the fourth Servant Song from Isaiah 52:13–53:12. Jesus is the lamb whose precious blood is shed. 1 Peter 2:6-8 quotes Isaiah 28:16: "The stone which the builders rejected has become the cornerstone." In 1 Peter 2:9 the author quotes Isaiah 43:20, about "a chosen race." But the most "difficult" passage is 1 Peter 3:19-22 about Noah and Christ's "preaching to the spirits in prison." In a small commentary of less than 200 pages, Ernest Best devotes 16 pages to the passage.[57] Not very often this is taken to mean that Christ preached to inhabitants of hades between his death and resurrection. Some view "spirits" as the fallen angels of Genesis 6:1-4 or *1 Enoch*. Augustine thought the "preaching" took place before the incarnation. Many think it happened after the ascension. 1 Peter 4:6 says the gospel was preached to the dead. But this may mean "to those who are dead at the time of writing." Clearly 3:19-22 has some reference to the Noah narrative in Genesis 6:12–9:29, possibly to readers or hearers who are being baptized (or have recently been baptized). In this sense they have put to death the old life and are made alive in the Spirit (1 Pet. 3:18). The Noah story is then introduced as an analogy or antitype of cleansing and new life. The proclamation may refer to Jesus' preaching to those "who did not obey" and are now, at the time of writing, in "prison." It need not refer to a descent to hades. The earliest references to such a doctrine otherwise occur in Justin, *Dialogue with Trypho* 72. Irenaeus knows of the doctrine but does not relate it to 1 Peter. Noah regularly features, for example, in Ezekiel 14:14, 20 and Wisdom 10:4.

9. The author of the *Epistle to the Hebrews* uses the Old Testament with considerable skill in a variety of ways.[58] The quotations from the Old Testament are all pivotal to the argument of Hebrews. The most important is Psalm 110:1-4. G. W. Buchanan has proposed that the whole of Hebrews 1–12 is a homily on Psalm 110; but Psalms 8:4-6 and 95:7-11 and Jeremiah 31:31-34

56. Cf. Brown, *Gospel according to John,* pp. 88-92.

57. Best, *1 Peter,* pp. 135-50. Cf. Selwyn, *First Epistle,* pp. 313-62.

58. Lane, *Epistle to the Hebrews,* 1:cxii-cxvii, and L. D. Hurst, *The Epistle to the Hebrews: Its Background of Thought,* Society for New Testament Studies Monograph Series, no. 65 (Cambridge: Cambridge University Press, 1990).

also deserve note.[59] Hebrews 2:5-18 begins this exposition. The Melchizedek theme is expounded in Hebrews 7:1-19, which reflects Psalm 110 as well as Genesis 14. We have already argued that Jesus is seen as the unique kingly high priest. He is no Aaronic priest, but our great High Priest "after the order of Melchizedek." Psalm 95:7-11 stresses the "today," which is so important for the readers or hearers. Hebrews 8:1–10:31 stresses the new covenant of Jeremiah 31:31-34. For reasons of space, we must move on to the second century.

6. Second-Century Interpretation and Hermeneutics

In the light of the New Testament, it may come as a surprise to learn that with Marcion the first hermeneutical battle of the second century was over the status of the Old Testament. The debate affected many in the second century, including Irenaeus, who defended the Christian view, as well as Marcion himself and some of the Gnostics. Justin and other apologists were less immediately involved.

Marcion (ca. 85-160) was born in Pontus in Asia Minor, but circa 140 came to Rome. There he came under the influence of some Gnostic teachers, who believed that the God of the Jews, in contrast to the God of the Christians, inspired the Old Testament, or Jewish Scriptures. Marcion rejected reinterpreting parts of the Bible by allegorical interpretation, insisting on its literal meaning. He rejected the Old Testament as not for Christians, but for Jews only. He defined his own canon, which also excluded the Gospels except for a mangled Luke. He excluded the Pastorals but accepted ten letters of Paul, which he edited to remove remnants of Judaism. In 144 the church in Rome excommunicated him. Marcion established his own "church."

Irenaeus tells us that Marcion taught "that the God proclaimed by the law and the prophets was *not* the Father of our Lord Jesus Christ."[60] The Father of Jesus, said Marcion, according to Irenaeus, "is above the God who made the world. . . . He mutilates the Gospel according to Luke, removing all that is written respecting the birth of our Lord."[61] Tertullian writes, "The

59. George B. Caird, "The Exegetical Method of the Epistle to the Hebrews," *Canadian Journal of Theology* 5 (1959): 44-51.

60. Irenaeus, *Against Heresies* 1.18.1. Cf. also E. C. Blackman, *Marcion and His Influence* (London: SPCK, 1948), and R. Joseph Hoffmann, *Marcion: On the Restitution of Christianity* (Chico, Calif.: Scholars Press, 1984).

61. Irenaeus, *Against Heresies* 1.18.2.

heretic of Pontus introduces two gods."[62] Tertullian argues for the unity of God.[63] Why, he asks, should revelation begin only with Paul? Indeed, Jesus reveals the Creator, and he is foretold by the prophets.[64] Many of the laws revealed in the Old Testament are good, including the command to keep the Sabbath.[65] God made promises in the Old Testament, and Moses was his true servant who "prefigured" Christ as a type of Christ.[66]

Gnostic writers use a considerable amount of New Testament language. Both their dating and definition are complex and controversial. But most regard Gnosticism as a mainly second-century movement with far later effects and influence, and many Gnostic writings have been discovered among the Nag Hammadi texts, found in 1945. Otherwise our chief source of knowledge comes through the Church Fathers. Probably the Valentinian sect within Gnosticism is most widely known, and the Manichees survived until at least the time of Augustine. Hans Jonas has shown that much Gnostic cosmological and mythological speculation had behind it an existential purpose.[67] The Gnostics were generally anti-Jewish, and the "Sethian" (or "Scithian") sect described many Old Testament characters as "a laughingstock."[68] Yet because of their interest in cosmology and creation, many also used Old Testament texts, even if creation was due to the Demiurge, not to the Father of Jesus.

Samuel Laeuchli is perhaps one of the best exponents of the Gnostic use of the language of the New Testament.[69] Laeuchli shows that Gnostic texts, including those of the Valentinian sect, abounded in New Testament terms. These included: *kosmos* (world or universe); *plērōma* (fullness); *gnōsis* (knowledge); *aiōn* (age); *sophia* (wisdom); *agapē* (love); *alētheia* (truth); *patēr* (father); *huios* (son); *heis* or *hen* (one); *dikaiosunē* (righteousness); *sarx* (flesh); *pneuma* (spirit); *sōma* (body); *mustērion* (mystery or revelation); *phōs*

---

62. Tertullian, *Against Marcion* 1.2.

63. Tertullian, *Against Marcion* 1.3 and 8.

64. Tertullian, *Against Marcion* 1.19 and 20.

65. Tertullian, *Against Marcion* 2.18 and 21.

66. Tertullian, *Against Marcion* 2.26.

67. Hans Jonas, *The Gnostic Religion: The Message of the Alien God and the Beginnings of Christianity*, 2nd ed. (Boston: Beacon Press, 1963).

68. "Tractate Seth," in *Nag Hammadi Codex*, ed. James M. Robinson and others (Leiden: Brill, 1972-84), 7.2.

69. Samuel Laeuchli, *The Language of Faith: An Introduction to the Semantic Dilemma of the Early Church*, introduction by C. K. Barrett (London: Epworth, 1965; Nashville: Abingdon, 1962).

(light); *pistis* (faith); *chronos* (time); *zōē* (life); and many more.[70] Many phrases at first seem similar to those of the New Testament. But Laeuchli carefully quotes from Basilides, *Gospel of Truth, Epistle to Flora, Excerpta ex Theodoto, Apocryphon of John,* Valentinus, and elsewhere. He shows that many terms come from Paul or the Synoptics. But he insists, "*There is a tension between the meaning in the original frame* [i.e. of the Bible] *and the new frame into which it is inserted.*"[71] He adds, "The same words have other implications; phrases stand in another light."[72] As Wittgenstein urged, the use of a word does not always correspond with its appearance on the surface.

Irenaeus precisely stressed the atomistic and incoherent use of Scripture by the Gnostics. "They abuse the scriptures by endeavouring to support their own system out of them."[73] In a famous passage he asserts, "They disregard the order and the connection of scriptures . . . just as if one, when a beautiful image of a king has been constructed . . . out of precious jewels, should this take the likeness of the man all to pieces, should re-arrange the gems, and so fit them together as to make them into the form of a dog or of a fox . . . and should then maintain and declare that *this* was the beautiful image of the king."[74] Irenaeus calls, in effect, for a proper attention to context and genre, and attention to other parts of the Bible.

No doubt the Gnostics claim a rationality of their own, and argue that the Fathers of the Church interpreted everything christologically. But Justin Martyr (ca. 100–ca. 165), an early Christian apologist, writes of appealing to the universal logos of reason, as it was revealed in Christ. His *Dialogues* are probably to be dated around 130 or 135. He taught at Ephesus and then in Rome. He addressed his apologia to Antoninus Pius, the Roman emperor, and to Marcus Aurelius, his adopted son and successor. He is among the most outstanding of the apologists of the second century.

Justin's *First Apology* and *Second Apology* have many references to the Old Testament. He sees Genesis 49:10-11 as an allegory of Christ, and in his

70. Laeuchli, *The Language of Faith,* pp. 15-55. Cf. Elaine Pagels, *The Johannine Gospel in Gnostic Exegesis* (Nashville and New York: Abingdon, 1973), and Pagels, *The Gnostic Paul: Gnostic Exegesis of the Pauline Letters* (Philadelphia: Fortress, 1975).

71. Laeuchli, *The Language of Faith,* p. 19, italics mine.

72. Laeuchli, *The Language of Faith,* p. 19.

73. Irenaeus, *Against Heresies* 1.9.1; cf. 1.3.1.

74. Irenaeus, *Against Heresies* 1.8.1. See further, Kendrick Grobel, *The Gospel of Truth: A Valentinian Meditation on the Gospel* (London: Black, 1960), and Werner Foerster, *Gnosis: A Selection of Gnostic Texts,* trans. R. McL. Wilson, 2 vols. (Oxford: Clarendon, 1972).

Dialogue with Trypho sees Micah 4:1-7 as pointing to the two advents of Christ.[75] Leah in Genesis prefigures Israel; but Rachel, the Church.[76] He interprets the law in the Old Testament as a moral guide, although he concedes that the law alone does not bring salvation. But the important point in relation to the Gnostics and heresies is his appeal to the logos (reason) in every human being, which reaches its truest expression in Christ. Shotwell stresses this in his study of Justin's use of the Bible.[77]

Justin argues that divine revelation took two forms: God's revelation in Christ as the Logos, and Scripture as a written text. He regards Scripture as inspired by the Holy Spirit.[78] He often quotes from the Old Testament, including Isaiah 7:14, "A virgin shall conceive . . . ," and Psalm 22, the cry from the cross.[79] Justin uses the Septuagint, and calls it "Scripture." Many events or persons in the Old Testament "prefigure" Christ, and he explicitly uses the term "types" (e.g., of Deut. 21:23). Some describe this as allegory, and he does use this, but also analogy.[80] The Old Testament "foretells," "announces," and even "predicts." He frequently uses the word *sēmainō,* "to signify" (Shotwell claims thirty-five times); or *sēmeion,* "sign," some twenty-eight times.[81] In *Dialogue* 96.4 "type" and "sign" together denote a provision made by Moses. Shotwell claims that the word "type" occurs in Justin eighteen times, including Moses' raising of the bronze serpent.[82]

Finally, Justin uses the New Testament, including Acts, Romans, 1 Corinthians, Galatians, Philippians, Colossians, 2 Thessalonians, and even Hebrews and 1 John, and refers to the Gospels as "Memories" of the apostles, alongside the prophets. He does not often use literal interpretation, but whether he uses mostly allegory or typology is debated. At all events, Scripture offers a frame of reference for his arguments, and individual passages often prefigure God's deed in Christ.[83]

---

75. Justin, *Apology* 1.52.43; 53.1-6; *Dialogue* 109.1; 110.1-6.

76. Justin, *Dialogue* 134.3-6.

77. Willis A. Shotwell, *The Biblical Exegesis of Justin Martyr* (London: SPCK, 1965), pp. 2-3.

78. Justin, *Dialogue* 7, 32, and 34.

79. Justin, *Dialogue* 98-106 (on Ps. 22); *Dialogue* 4.1; 68.7 (on Isa. 7); and *Apology* 1.25.

80. Justin, *Dialogue* 129.2.

81. Justin, *Dialogue* 14.7; 21.2; 42.5; 66.1; and Shotwell, *Exegesis,* p. 15.

82. Justin, *Apology* 1.60.3, 5; cf. Shotwell, *Exegesis,* pp. 18-19.

83. Shotwell, *Exegesis,* pp. 29-47, and L. W. Bernard, *Justin Martyr: His Life and Thought* (Cambridge: Cambridge University Press, 1967).

Aristides is a second-century apologist, but we mainly know his writing on others. Theophilus writes as an apologist of the late second century, but his writing against Marcion is lost. Tatian was a pupil of Justin. Tertullian (ca. 160–ca. 225) is mainly a third-century writer. But we have still to consider some of the subapostolic writings and Clement of Alexandria (ca. 150–ca. 215). Among the subapostolic writings, the *Epistle of Barnabas* (often dated between 75 and 150) uses the Old Testament, but often does so allegorically. Its author is probably Alexandrian, and regards animal sacrifices and the material temple as mistaken products of Judaism. By his use of allegory, however, the author believes that the Old Testament points to Christ. For example, the red heifer on the Day of Atonement is regarded as a type or prefiguring of Christ.[84] Water from the rock in the wilderness is a metaphor or allegory of Christian baptism.[85] Similarly, *Clement of Rome*, the author of *1 Clement*, writes on the brink of the second century (ca. 96) that "the scarlet thread" of Rahab in Joshua 2 points forward to the blood of Christ.[86]

Ignatius of Antioch (ca. 35–ca. 110), by contrast, uses neither allegory nor typology. But he often paraphrases the content of the Gospels, and argues that there can be no ambiguity about "it is written" in relation to Christ.[87] The *Didache* (dating uncertain, but probably early second century) has no allegorical interpretation, and little typology. But the *Didache* speaks of David as made known through Christ, and in another place applies Malachi 1:11, 14.[88]

Irenaeus quotes Isaiah 45:1 to show that "my anointed Cyrus" points to Christ. Hanson argues that Irenaeus (and Justin) shows no trace of Alexandrian allegorization. But he does see a *typological* correspondence between the tree of Eden and the cross. He probably does allegorize, however, Isaiah 11:6-9 to describe the harmony of animals in the messianic age.[89] In his later work he moves more into allegorical interpretation, providing a christological focus. In the parable of the Good Samaritan, he sees the injured man as Adam, the inn as the Church, and so on.[90] But we must not forget Irenaeus's emphasis on context and genre, and his work of the unity of the

---

84. *Barnabas* 8.
85. *Barnabas* 11.
86. *1 Clement* 12.
87. Ignatius, *Epistle to the Philadelphians* 8.2; cf. Hanson, *Allegory and Event*, p. 101.
88. *Didache* 9.2 and 14.2. ·
89. See also Irenaeus, *Against Heresies* 5.23.4.
90. Irenaeus, *Against Heresies* 4.30.3 and 4; *Fragments* 52; *Against Heresies* 3.17.3, respectively.

two Testaments, and the "rule of faith."[91] He insisted that there was no "secret" tradition as claimed by Gnostics, but that tradition was public and verifiable. He declared that the Gospels were four in number, as the "canonical" Gospels of the Church.[92]

By contrast, Clement of Alexandria believed in a secret quasi-gnostic tradition. This cannot be plain and open, because truth is conveyed only, he said, "in enigmas and symbols, in allegories and metaphor, and in similar figures."[93] Veiled teaching is said to stimulate inquiry. The style of the Scriptures is parabolic. Hanson observes, "With Clement of Alexandria we reach an author whose allegory is not only Alexandrian but openly and unashamedly Philonic."[94] Hidden meanings abound everywhere. He alludes to Sarah in Genesis as wisdom, and to Hagar as the wisdom of the world.[95] In the Garden of Eden the tree of life meant "divine thought."[96] Clement's interpretation of Scripture conveys a great contrast to Justin and especially Irenaeus. He prepares the way for Origen, his successor. But it is also different from most writers of the New Testament. Already we see a wide range of Christian interpretation, and its response to some key issues.

7. Recommended Initial Reading

Goppelt, Leonhard, *Typos: The Typological Interpretation of the Old Testament in the New* (Grand Rapids: Eerdmans, 1982), pp. 61-106, 127-40, 161-70, and 179-85.

Hanson, Anthony Tyrrell, *The Living Utterances of God: The New Testament Exegesis of the Old* (London: Darton, Longman and Todd, 1983), pp. 44-132.

Longenecker, Richard, *Biblical Exegesis in the Apostolic Period* (Grand Rapids: Eerdmans, 1975), pp. 51-75 and 104-57.

McKim, Donald K., ed., *Dictionary of Major Biblical Interpreters* (Downers Grove, Ill., and Nottingham: IVP, 2007), s.v. "Marcion," "Gnosticism," "Justin," "Irenaeus."

91. Irenaeus, *Against Heresies* 1.10.1, 2.
92. Irenaeus, *Against Heresies* 3.11.8.
93. Clement, *Stromata* 5.4.1-3; cf. 5.5-8.
94. Hanson, *Allegory and Event*, p. 117.
95. Clement, *Stromata* 5.12.80.
96. Clement, *Stromata* 5.11.72.

CHAPTER VI

From the Third to the Thirteenth Centuries

1. The Latin West: Hippolytus, Tertullian, Ambrose, Jerome

1. Apart from Tertullian, *Hippolytus* (ca. 170–ca. 236) is the earliest major biblical writer of the third century in the Latin West. Some regard him as the most important theologian of the church at Rome in the earliest Church. He rejected Callistus bishop of Rome as a heretic, and was elected as a rival bishop of Rome. In his hermeneutics he used christological interpretation, stressed the value of the Old Testament for Christians, respected accordance with apostolic tradition, and produced many exegetical writings.

Hippolytus was among the earliest Christian commentators. Among his extensive commentaries are those on Genesis 27 and 29 (the Jacob narratives); Deuteronomy 33 (the blessing of Moses); 1 Samuel 17 (on David and Goliath); Song of Songs 1–3; Daniel; and Revelation 19–22. He was especially interested in prophecy and apocalyptic, although many of his writings have been lost. He followed Justin and Irenaeus in focusing on christological interpretation, and the latter in stressing apostolic creedal tradition, or "the rule of faith." There is no doubt about the status of the Old Testament in Hippolytus. Many of his comments on apocalyptic literature also appear in his *Treatise on Christ and the Antichrist,* including Mark 13:14-37, 2 Thessalonians 2:1-11, and Revelation 12:1-6.[1] Some additional material survives in *Fragments from Commentaries.* His commentaries are on the Greek text.

2. *Tertullian* (ca. 160–ca. 225) was a North African convert to Christianity, educated in Carthage in law and rhetoric. He was converted to the Chris-

---

1. Hippolytus, *Treatise on Christ and the Antichrist* 63 and 61, respectively.

tian faith in about 197, when he was nearly forty. Toward the end of his life he adhered to the Montanists. In his earliest Christian works, he wrote largely as an apologist for the faith, but he wrote against fellow Christians whom he considered not rigorous enough in their faith. In his middle and later writings he used the Bible to condemn what he regarded as heresy or "corruptions" of the faith. His writings on the Trinity and *Against Praxeas* belong to his late Montanist phase. He stressed the importance of apostolic teaching and resisted any compromise with secular philosophy. Many of his writings are polemical.

In his earlier and middle works Tertullian attacks the Gnostics and Marcion in *Prescription against Heretics* and *Against Marcion*, respectively, seeking to rescue the Bible from their abuse of it. He rejected the notion that one could read Scripture *to satisfy "curiosity"; the Bible belonged to the Church.* He passionately defended the use of the Old Testament against Marcion's attacks on it. Christ is present, he argued, in the utterances of Moses. The Bible proves that God revealed himself from earliest times as Creator; Marcion implies an unduly recent revelation.[2] The Creator is the Father of Jesus Christ, not a different god (2.2.1). Was God willing, he asks ironically, "to remain hidden for ever" (2.3.1, 2)? The Law serves several purposes, including keeping people dependent on God. Tertullian also uses the Bible literally; for example, God's "repentance," or change of mind, is not smoothed over by allegory (2.19.1). God's taking an oath or showing wrath is no reason to discard the Old Testament. Moreover, the coming of Christ was promised and announced (2.24.1). Scripture also disproves Marcion's Docetism (3.2, 7, 17-19 and 5.4). Luke's Gospel is to be defended as it stands. Tertullian expounds the nature of grace from the New Testament writings (4.2, 5). He interprets 1 Corinthians as a running commentary, applicable to charges against Marcion (5.5-10).

Tertullian interweaves doctrine and biblical exposition. He defends the doctrine of resurrection, grace, and the unity of God, from the Bible.[3] He considers pagan appeals to the problem of evil. He also seeks a basis in the Bible for a rigorous ethic. He is entirely confident that he has understood Scripture aright, and that it supports and coheres with Christian doctrine as he understands it. His rhetoric is uncompromising and robust.

---

2. Tertullian, *Against Marcion* 1.25.1-4. Parenthetical references in this paragraph are to *Against Marcion.*

3. Tertullian, *Apology* 17.

3. *Ambrose of Milan* (ca. 338-97) brings us to the fourth century (if we bypass Tertullian's successor in North Africa, Cyprian, as contributing little that is distinctive to biblical interpretation). Ambrose was educated in Rome and was elected bishop of Milan by popular acclamation. He knew Greek as well as Latin, and became well read in Philo, Origen, Athanasius, and Basil on biblical interpretation. Ambrose was essentially a pastoral and teaching bishop. Indeed, in his three books *On the Duties of the Clergy* he insists on the role of the bishop or teacher, quoting: "I will teach you the fear of the Lord" (Ps. 34:11) and "God gave some, apostles; and some, prophets; and some, evangelists; and some, pastors and teachers" (Eph. 4:11).[4]

Most of Ambrose's interpretations of the Bible emerged in the service of oral preaching, and were often written down by someone else. Ambrose produced commentaries on Genesis 1:1-26, on parts of 1 and 2 Samuel and 1 Kings (Elijah and David), and on Psalms, Isaiah, Song of Songs, and Luke. Much of the purpose of this was to preach Christ or to assist practical Christian living. From Genesis 1 he argues that the resurrection is no more incredible than that God should create all things from nothing.[5] He argues that all three persons of the Trinity were involved in creation: "In the beginning *God* created the heaven and the earth" (Gen. 1:1); "*the Spirit* was upon the face of the water" (Gen. 1:2); "Let us make man in our image" (Gen. 1:26).[6] "Say *the Word,* and he shall be healed" (Matt. 8:8). David showed patience and absence of anger when Shimei cursed him (2 Sam. 16:12).[7] Ambrose expounds Psalm 118, stressing, "The Lord is my helper, I will not fear what humankind can do to me" (Ps. 118:6).[8] He provides a christological interpretation of the Song of Songs (Song 1:2, 3).[9] He often uses the New Testament, including the sayings in John. He quotes Isaiah, "Though your sins be as scarlet, I will make them as white as snow" (Isa. 1:18).[10] Ambrose uses many parts of the biblical writings seriously and responsibly, both to promote Christ and for moral teaching and spiritual or "devotional" aims.

4. *Ambrosiaster,* or pseudo-Ambrose, also features in the fourth century. We do not know the identity of Ambrosiaster, but he wrote during the

---

4. Ambrose, *Three Books on the Duties of the Clergy* 1.11.

5. Ambrose, *On Belief in the Resurrection* 2.2.84.

6. Ambrose, *Of the Holy Spirit* 2.1.1-3.

7. Ambrose, *Duties of the Clergy* 1.48.245.

8. Ambrose, *Of the Christian Faith* 5.3.42.

9. Ambrose, *On the Mysteries* 6.29.

10. Ambrose, *On the Mysteries* 7.34.

time of Damasus, bishop of Rome (366-84), and wrote a commentary on all thirteen of Paul's epistles, as well as other fragments of biblical expositions. For part or all of his adult life he lived in Rome. He showed a familiarity with Judaism. He argued that bishops and presbyters share "one ordination." He was a careful commentator, who respected the "literal" sense of Scripture. He also observed the historical and linguistic context of individual passages.[11]

5. *Jerome* (ca. 340-420) bridged the fourth and fifth centuries and was an impressive translator and textual critic. He was heavily influenced by Philo, Clement of Alexandria, and especially Origen; but he was also familiar with the Antiochenes: Diodore, Theodore, and John Chrysostom. Jerome is one of the few at the time to know *Hebrew* and Jewish methods of interpretation. Indeed, he worked hard to establish *the text* in Hebrew, Greek, and Latin, and provided a Latin *translation* (the Vulgate) from Hebrew and Greek. In addition to his work on textual criticism and translation, he wrote extensive commentaries on the biblical writings, of which his stated aim was to explain and to clarify what was obscure. Unlike Tertullian, he wished also to present different traditions and options to his readers. He recognized that to try to interpret Scripture is "a labour of love," but at the same time both "perilous and presumptuous."[12]

Jerome was fully aware of the Alexandrian method of finding a "spiritual" meaning in the biblical text, sometimes by allegorical interpretation. But he begins with the *literal meaning* of the biblical writings in their historical context. Then he often does move on to a "spiritual" interpretation, some drawn from Origen. His extant commentaries on the New Testament include those on Matthew, Galatians, Ephesians, Titus, and Philemon, and on the Old Testament, Isaiah, Jeremiah, Ezekiel, Daniel, Jonah, and the Minor Prophets. He engaged in a small amount of what from the early nineteenth century onward was called "New Testament introduction."[13] He notes the poetry of Isaiah, and calls him more of an evangelist than a prophet.[14] In Rome, in later years, he became the mentor of some notable women, and in 384 he left Rome for the monastic life in Antioch and the Holy Land. This was partly due to an alleged scandal. Ignorance of the Scriptures, he de-

---

11. Cf. A. Souter, *A Study of Ambrosiaster,* Texts and Studies 7 (Cambridge: Cambridge University Press, 1905).

12. Jerome, preface to *The Four Gospels* 1.

13. Jerome, *Matthew* 1.

14. Jerome, *Isaiah,* preface.

clared, is ignorance of Christ.[15] He qualifies his concern for "literal" meaning by saying that he translates not the "word" but the "sense."[16] Like Clement, he sees the Bible as full of obscurities and mysteries.[17]

2. Alexandrian Traditions: Origen; with Athanasius, Didymus, and Cyril

1. Origen (ca. 185–ca. 254) followed Clement of Alexandria as head of the catechetical school at the early age of seventeen. He was known as a versatile and creative scholar of prodigious output. He was an apologist and preacher, a philosophical theologian, a textual critic, and a biblical commentator. Three-quarters of his numerous writings expound Scripture. Eusebius the ecclesiastical historian tells us that his wealthy friend Ambrosius paid for a staff of seven shorthand writers and a number of women or girls to act as copyists for him.[18] He was educated in Greek philosophical traditions, exegetical methods, and Christian doctrine. Alexandria was at the time probably the greatest intellectual center of the Roman Empire. Origen would have been thoroughly familiar with the classical literature and philosophies of Greece. Origen also debated with proponents of various forms of Gnosticism. Yet his speculation led to a real or supposed deviation from orthodoxy, and his teaching was eventually condemned at the Fifth Ecumenical Council of 553. Subsequently many of his writings were lost or suppressed.

The question of what constitutes the Bible and how it was to be understood stood at the heart of Origen's concerns. One of his achievements was the production of the Hexapla, an exhaustive six-column comparison of biblical texts in original languages and their translated versions. The first column contained the Hebrew text of the Old Testament, which was not widely known at the time. The second column constituted a transliteration of the Hebrew in Greek letters. The other four columns contained different versions of the Septuagint: those of Aquila and Symmachus, a revised LXX, and that of Theodotion. The project took intense labor and lasted for some thirty years. It shows Origen's persistence in establishing

---

15. Cf. Jerome, *Letter 47: To John the Oeconomus.*
16. Jerome, *Letter* 126.29 and *Letter* 112.19.
17. Origen, *Commentary on John* 10.11-13.
18. Eusebius, *Ecclesiastical History* 6.25.2.

the best text of the Bible. Trigg examines the Hexapla, however, and believes that Origen's knowledge of Hebrew was rudimentary and largely secondhand.[19]

Origen believed in the importance of apostolic tradition, or "the rule of faith." He believed that Scripture was inspired by the Holy Spirit.[20] He is said to have written commentaries on all the books of the Bible. Jerome divided Origen's works into commentaries; *Scholia,* or marginal notes; and sermons. From 228 to 231 Origen produced his *Commentary on John, Commentary on Genesis,* and other biblical expositions, *The Miscellanies,* and *De principiis.* The work on John is one of his best biblical commentaries. *De principiis* is a major work of theology and doctrine.

In 231, owing largely to the resentment of the bishop of Alexandria, Origen left Alexandria and its superb libraries for Caesarea. But he continued to write commentaries, as well as his *Exhortation to Martyrdom.* Between 238 and 240 he wrote his *Commentary on Ezekiel.* Between 241 and 245 he wrote various homilies on the Old Testament, and New Testament commentaries, and concluded the monumental Hexapla. From 245 until his death he wrote the eight books of apologetics *Against Celsus,* a harsh pagan critic of Christianity. After his death Gregory of Nazianzus and Basil produced extracts of his work called the *Philocalia.*

Origen argued that every word of Scripture has a profound meaning. Indeed, every historical passage has a literal meaning comparable to a body, a moral meaning comparable to a soul, and a spiritual sense comparable to the spirit.[21] His exegetical method is largely borrowed from Philo of Alexandria (discussed in chapter IV). The meaning, he suggested, is like a ladder. The starting point and also the lowest rung constitute the "body," or "literal" meaning. At the literal level, he argues, Scripture contains contradictions, but he says, "The spiritual truth was often preserved in the material falsehood. Statements which are verbally contrary to each other are made," but spiritually the statement "is true."[22] Hence, often he uses the allegorical meaning as an apologetic tool. At times Origen sounds like Philo, and at times like Clement. Like Philo, he dismisses the literal meaning of God's

---

19. Joseph W. Trigg, *Origen: The Bible and Philosophy in the Third-Century Church* (London: SCM; Louisville: John Knox, 1983, 1985), pp. 82-86.

20. Origen, preface to *De principiis* 4; cf. *De principiis* 1.3; 4.1. The Hexapla is no longer extant in full but is partially reconstructed.

21. Origen, *De principiis* 4.2.4. Cf. Trigg, *Origen,* pp. 125-26 and 204-5.

22. Origen, *Commentary on John* 10.4.

planting trees in Eden.[23] On a literal level he compares Hesiod favorably with Genesis. Like Clement, Origen sees the Bible as full of obscurities and mysteries.

In his great work *De principiis* Origen writes,

> The way in which we ought to deal with the Scriptures and extract from them their meaning, is the following. . . . In a threefold manner (Greek, *trissōs*) . . . the simple man may be edified by the "flesh," as it were, of the Scriptures . . . the obvious sense; he who has ascended a certain way by the "soul" as it were (Greek, *apo tēs hōsperei pseuchēs autēs*). The perfect man (Greek, *ho teleios*) . . . not with the wisdom of the world . . . but the wisdom of God in a mystery, the hidden wisdom . . . from the spiritual law . . . learned from the Spirit (Greek, *tou Pneumatos*).[24]

He declares further, "The interpretation is 'spiritual' when one is able to show of what heavenly things the Jews 'according to the flesh' served as an example and a shadow *(hupodeigma kai skia)*."[25]

Origen believed that all Scripture is coherent and harmonious: "one perfect instrument of God."[26] All of it has meaning. Origen believes that the Song of Songs is a marriage poem written as a drama. His commentary and homilies on the book well illustrate its "spiritual" meaning. Names there apply to "the inner man."[27] The words *(logoi)* of a "bodiless" text lead the reader to "spiritual thought" *(pneumatika noēta)*.[28] In the New Testament his exposition is heavily influenced by Plato, especially in John, where he makes much of the Logos. The Logos is, in effect, the world of spirit *(ho kosmos noētos)*.[29] The Son is eternal and "unchanging," in accordance with the Platonic contrast between the contingent and material copy, and the realm of ideas or forms. Christ as the Logos is truth and wisdom. Some came to regard this as also too close to Gnostic exegesis. Even the soul is eternal,

23. Origen, *Against Celsus* 4.38, 39.

24. Origen, *De principiis* 4.2.4 (Greek, Jacques-Paul Migne, *Patrologiae Graecae Cursus Completus*, 81 vols. [Paris: Garnier, 1856-61; reprint, 1912], vol. 11, col. 364).

25. Origen, *De principiis* 4.2.4 (Migne, vol. 11, col. 264).

26. Origen, *Commentary on Matthew* 2; cf. R. B. Tollinton, ed., *Selections from the Commentaries and Homilies of Origen* (London: SPCK, 1928), pp. 47-49.

27. Origen, *Commentary on the Song of Songs* 2.21.

28. J. Christopher King, *Origen on the Song of Songs as the Spirit of Scripture: The Bridegroom's Perfect Marriage Song* (Oxford: Oxford University Press, 2006), p. 74.

29. Origen, *Commentary on John* 19.5; cf. *De principiis* 2.3.

according to Origen (as well as to Plato), and therefore Christ as Logos is also preexistent. Origen also taught subordinationism, namely, that the Son is inferior to the Father, and the Spirit to the Son, although there was "not a time when the Son did not exist."[30]

It is often thought that through looking for the "spiritual" meaning Origen sat loose to the "literal meaning" of Scripture, and we can sympathize with the reaction of the "Antiochene" school (set out below). But this partly, as Karen Jo Torjesen has pointed out, arose from Origen's pastoral concern for the readers.[31] If Chrysostom and the Antiochenes were primarily concerned with the aim or intention of the biblical *author* or *writer,* Origen and the Alexandrians were primarily concerned about the *readers,* and the *effect* of the text upon them. Indeed, Origen's apologetic concerns are as important as his pastoral ones. In defending the Christian faith against Gnosticism, it is easy for him to follow Philo and Clement in their method of "rescuing" the rationality of the Old Testament. In many Gospel passages, Origen is less inclined to dismiss the "bodily" meaning than in the Song of Songs or Leviticus. In Matthew he discusses Peter's standing "afar off" in the trial of Jesus.[32] The false witnesses at the passion show that "Jesus did no sin."[33] The high priest "rent his clothes," which displayed his shame and nakedness of soul.[34]

Yet Henri de Lubac quotes Origen as saying, "In all of Scripture there is a difference between the soul and the spirit."[35] Lubac argues that Origen's bold threefold division enriched medieval exegesis, and is based on 1 Thessalonians 5:23 and Romans 8:16, according to some. (These, however, are far from conclusive: "Your spirit and soul and body" in 1 Thessalonians 5:23 means only "your whole self"; and "The Spirit bears witness with our spirit" in Romans 8:16 means only "with us" or "with our inner self.") At all events, Lubac sees Origen's influence as great and positive.

---

30. Origen, *De principiis* 4.28; cf. 1.3.

31. Karen Jo Torjesen, *Hermeneutical Procedure and Theological Method in Origen's Exegesis* (Berlin: Walter de Gruyter, 1986), especially pp. 36ff. Cf. Gerald Bostock, "Allegory and the Interpretation of the Bible in Origen," *Journal of Literature and Theology* 1 (1987): 39-53.

32. Origen, *Commentary on Matthew* 105.

33. Origen, *Commentary on Matthew* 107.

34. Origen, *Commentary on Matthew* 112.

35. Origen, *Commentary on John* 32.18 (455); *De principiis* 2.8.4 (162). Cf. Henri de Lubac, *Medieval Exegesis,* 2 vols. (Grand Rapids: Eerdmans; Edinburgh: T. & T. Clark, 2000), 1:142.

2. *Athanasius* (ca. 296-373) is one of the most important theologians of the fourth century. He was educated and trained in Alexandria, was made deacon in 319, and played a key role in the Council of Nicea in 325. He served as bishop of Alexandria, succeeding Alexander, until 366, and was decisive in opposing the Arians and defending orthodox Chalcedonian Christology. He defended the clause "of the same substance as the Father" *(homoousion)* and laid the foundations for the Council of Constantinople (385) and the Nicene Creed. But he was known as a systematic theologian and apologist rather than a biblical commentator.

Indeed, Athanasius's use of Scripture was primarily to serve apologetic and theological concerns, although he also stressed that individual verses should be used with an eye to the whole of Scripture. Passages are to be interpreted in accord with the rule of faith *(regula fidei)*. "The Lord in Wisdom founded the earth" (Prov. 3:19) shows that "Wisdom" existed before the world, and since Christ is our Wisdom, this suggests that he existed before creation, and opposes and confounds the Arians.[36] Christians are to search the Scriptures to be ready for the coming of Christ as judge.[37] Athanasius writes, "If they (Arians) deny Scripture, they are at once aliens to their name . . . Christ's enemies. But if they agree that the sayings of Scripture are divinely inspired, let them dare to say openly . . . that God is without Wisdom, and 'There was a time once when He (Christ) did not exist.'"[38] "No holy Scripture has used such language of the Saviour" as the Arians, who use such verses as John 1:14 out of this context.[39] Occasionally he seems to quote Scripture inaccurately.[40] But he seems to respect the "bodily" meaning more than Origen, although he sees the Old Testament as primarily about Christ.

(3) *Didymus the Blind* (ca. 313–ca. 397) is known for biblical interpretation in the exegetical tradition of Origen. He defended Nicea and was a leader in the ascetic movement, like Jerome. He was too closely associated with Origen for many of his works to survive. But some of his work was discovered in 1941, including commentaries on Genesis, Job, and Zechariah, and lectures on Psalms 20 to 44. He continues the Alexandrian tradition of an apologetic and pastoral concern for the reader of the text. He was concerned that the reader should advance to "spiritual" maturity and under-

---

36. Athanasius, *Against the Arians,* discourse 2.22.73.

37. Athanasius, *Incarnation of the Word* 56.

38. Athanasius, *De decretis* (or *Defense of the Nicene Definition*) 4.

39. Athanasius, *Against the Arians,* discourse 1.4.11.

40. Athanasius, *Defense of His Flight* 13 and 17.

standing. Interpretation took place on the literal and "spiritual" (often figurative) levels. Didymus labeled his opponents "literalists" and debated vigorously with exponents of the "Antiochene" school.

(4) *Cyril of Alexandria* (ca. 378-444) was archbishop (or patriarch) of Alexandria, and is known primarily for his pro-Nicene Christology. He also was trained in the Alexandrian tradition of exegesis, seeking the higher level of meaning beyond the literal. His work on the Old Testament is primarily christological, but his work on the New Testament is more restrained and cautious than Origen's. His conflict with the Antiochene or Syrian church is not confined to exegetical method; he opposed Nestorius, archbishop of Constantinople and a Syrian, on Christology. Nestorius had studied under the Antiochene exegete Theodore of Mopsuestia, and Cyril denounced both. They were condemned at the Council of Ephesus (431). Meanwhile Cyril based his exegesis on Origen, producing commentaries on Isaiah, the Minor Prophets, Matthew, Luke, John, Romans, 1 and 2 Corinthians, and Hebrews.[41]

3. The Antiochene School: Diodore, Theodore, John Chrysostom, and Theodoret

1. *Diodore of Tarsus* (ca. 330-90, but dates not entirely certain) is generally regarded as the founder of the Antiochene School of biblical interpretation. It is not surprising that the Antiochenes reacted against Origen's exegesis, arguing that Origen's concern for readers, rather than authors, and the "spiritual" meaning of the biblical text led to the text's too easily becoming *a mirror of the interpreter's or reader's concerns.* We prefer, wrote Diodore, "the *historical* understanding of the text rather than the allegorical."[42]

By "historical" or "literal," however, we should not suppose that the Antiochenes were wooden literalists who rejected metaphorical, figurative, or typological reading.[43] By "historical" meaning, Diodore meant that texts and authors are conditioned by their situations or settings-in-life. Diodore described this as a guiding principle in exegesis. He had been head of the

---

41. Cf., for example, Cyril, *Commentary on the Gospel according to St. John,* ed. T. Randell (Oxford: J. Parker, 1885), and N. Russell, ed., *Cyril of Alexandria* (London: Routledge, 2000), which gives selections from Isaiah.

42. Cited in Dimitri Z. Zaharopoulos, *Theodore of Mopsuestia on the Bible: A Study of His Old Testament Exegesis* (New York: Paulist, 1989), p. 12.

43. James D. Wood, *The Interpretation of the Bible* (London: Duckworth, 1958), p. 59.

exegetical school in Antioch, Syria, prior to his election as bishop of Tarsus in 378. Diodore explicitly writes, "We do not forbid the higher interpretation of *theoria* [allegory], for the historical narrative does not exclude it. . . . We must, however, be on our guard against letting the *theoria* [allegory] do away with the historical basis, for the result would then be not *theoria,* but allegory."[44]

Clearly the distinction between *theoria* and allegory is a fine one, but crucial. Because of Diodore's involvement in christological controversy, most of his writings were lost or destroyed. Only the fairly recently discovered *Commentary on the Psalms* survives, in versions edited by J. M. Oliver and others.[45] The Arians destroyed many, and Diodore was judged guilty by association with Theodore when the latter was condemned. He was also opposed by Apollonarius. Both sides accused him of incipient Nestorianism (the doctrine that Jesus Christ was two distinct persons rather than two natures "of the same substance"). Yet in fact Diodore suggested a Nicene Christology, and contributed decisively to the first ecumenical Council of Constantinople (381).

2. *Theodore of Mopsuestia* (ca. 350-428) studied under Diodore at his exegetical school in Antioch, and was the friend of John Chrysostom. He studied in the Antioch school for nearly ten years, before becoming bishop of Mopsuestia in Cilicia in 392. At the Council of Ephesus, Cyril of Alexandria exposed the Nestorian heresy, and Theodore was condemned, with Diodore, for Nestorianism after his death. Whether he genuinely held the views of Nestorius, however, remains open to doubt. He insisted that Christ is both perfect God and "perfect" man, although his view of *how* these two natures are united as a single person is not clear. He used only biblical language and rejected the use of metaphysical speculation.[46]

Theodore wrote commentaries on nearly all the books of the Bible, examining their date and authorship, their structure and unity, their historical background, canonicity, and inspiration. But because of his association with Nestorianism, few of his commentaries have survived. Rabboula of Edessa was the first to anathematize him. He wrote three volumes on the book of Genesis. Photius (ca. 819-915) quotes from the first book.[47] Ex-

---

44. Diodore, preface to *Commentary on the Psalms;* cf. J. N. D. Kelly, *Early Christian Doctrines,* 5th ed. (London: Black, 1977), pp. 75-79.

45. Cf. J. M. Oliver, ed., *Diodore: Commentary on the Psalms,* in *Corpus Christianorum, Series Graeca,* 6 vols. (Turnhout: Brepols, 2006).

46. Zaharopoulos, *Theodore,* pp. 18-26.

47. Migne, *Patrologia Graeca,* 103:72; cf. 66:123-632.

cerpts from his commentary on Exodus have survived, including Exodus 25:8-20 on the ark of the covenant. We also possess short extracts from Judges 13:25 and 16:17. We know that he wrote on the Psalms, on 1 and 2 Samuel, on Job, on Ecclesiastes, and on the Song of Songs. On the New Testament there are allusions to his work on Matthew, Luke, and John, and on the Pauline Epistles.[48]

Many of Theodore's conclusions about biblical books accord with modern historical criticism. He rejected the titles of the psalms, and dated some psalms in the Maccabean period, and argued that different psalms represent different viewpoints. On the other hand, he shared with his contemporaries in the early Church a strong view of the inspiration of Scripture as God-breathed (2 Tim. 3:16). Zaharopoulos links his view of inspiration with his exegetical method. He writes, "His first exegetical principle held that, since Scripture is inspired by God, it can never mean anything that would be unworthy of God or useless to man."[49] Hence he does not altogether reject Philo and Origen, and their use of allegory. But allegory must not dominate, he urged, or reduce historical reality. *Theoria* amounts not to allegory but to *typology*. Yet Theodore recognized the christological exegesis of some psalms, especially Psalm 2 and Psalm 110, which are used christologically in Acts and in Hebrews. But for the most part, typological interpretation is restrained and seldom appears in his commentaries. He accepted a christological reading of Psalm 68 on the ground that to "lead captivity captive" is applied to Christ in Ephesians 4:8.[50] Theodore is often called the most learned scholar of the Antiochenes.

3. *John Chrysostom* (ca. 347-407) studied under Diodore with his friend and near contemporary Theodore, and felt an early call to the monastic life. He also served as presbyter in the church of Antioch, where his preaching made a special mark and earned him the name "golden tongue" *(Chrysostoma)*. Of particular note were his sermons "On the Statues" (387), which led to the imperial statues being overthrown. He regularly preached on the Bible, earning for many the title "the greatest expositor of Christendom," at least in the early Church. He was made patriarch (or archbishop) of

48. H. B. Swete, ed., *Theodori episcopi Mopsuestini In epistolas beati Pauli commentarii* (Cambridge: Cambridge University Press, 1880-82).

49. Zaharopoulos, *Theodore,* p. 106.

50. Theodore, *Commentary on the Psalms* 688; cf. Dudley Tyng, "Theodore at Mopsuestia as an Interpreter of the Old Testament," *Journal of Biblical Literature* 50 (1931): 301; cf. 298-303.

Constantinople in 398, against his own personal desire. He set about reforming the corruption of the imperial court, the clergy, and the whole church at Constantinople.

John Chrysostom was opposed to allegorical interpretation and condemned the teaching of Origen. His plain speaking made him enemies, especially Theophilus, patriarch (or archbishop) of Alexandria, and the empress Eudoxia. He was condemned, removed from his diocese, and formally deposed in 404. Although the Western Church and his own people supported him, he was forcibly moved to Pontus, and in effect killed. But in addition to more modern critical texts, his works fill six volumes of *The Nicene and Post-Nicene Fathers* (First Post-Nicene Series).[51]

Like his friend Theodore, Chrysostom depended wholly on the Septuagint as the Church's Old Testament. In his commentaries he expounds the genre and style of the biblical writer, as when he says Galatians "is full of a vehement and lofty spirit."[52] He comments on "gave himself for our sins" in Galatians 1:4: "The Law not only did not deliver us, but even condemned us."[53] On "not another gospel" (Gal. 1:6), he comments on the possibility of deception, and also on the unity of the four Gospels.[54] On "I conferred not with flesh and blood" (Gal. 1:16), he observes how absurd it would be "for one who has been taught by God afterwards to refer himself to men."[55]

Chrysostom's work on 1 Corinthians is formally called a "homily" but combines at first a succinct comment with an expository and applied homily. He catches the mood of 1 Corinthians at once: "Now here of him that calls is everything; of him that is called, nothing. . . . Nowhere in any other epistle does the name of Christ occur so constantly. But here it is, many times in a few verses."[56] When Paul asks that his readers "all speak the same thing," Chrysostom briefly discusses "that there be no schism . . . or division into many parts" *(schismata)* and no hint of doctrinal division.[57] On "the folly of the cross" (1 Cor. 1:18), Chrysostom comments, "It is nothing won-

---

51. Philip Schaff, ed., *A Select Library of the Nicene and Post-Nicene Fathers,* vols. 9-14, 1st ser. (1889-; reprint, Grand Rapids: Eerdmans, 1978-94).

52. John Chrysostom, *Commentary on Galatians,* on 1:1-3.

53. John Chrysostom, *Commentary on Galatians,* on 1:4.

54. John Chrysostom, *Commentary on Galatians,* on 1:7.

55. John Chrysostom, *Commentary on Galatians,* on 1:16.

56. John Chrysostom, *Epistles of Paul to the Corinthians,* hom. 1.1, and 2.7 (on 1 Cor. 1:1-5).

57. John Chrysostom, *Epistles of Paul to the Corinthians,* hom. 3.1 (on 1 Cor. 1:10).

derful, for it is a mark of those that perish not to recognise the things which lead to salvation."[58] He sees that it is almost a matter of what we might call today "internal grammar."

In the commentaries we find a model of sober, succinct exegesis, which takes account of the historical setting and looks at style and language. Even on the controversial passage in Galatians 4:22-31, he says of verse 24 that Paul "calls a type an allegory" and uses the word "type" until the end of the chapter.[59] In the homilies Chrysostom has a wider application, but this is usually sober and does not lead us wildly away from the text. He considers, for example, the purpose of parables in his *Homilies on Matthew* (Matt. 13:34, 35). He knows that the seed sown by the sower is the word of God, but this leads to an exhortation to ministers to study every book of the Bible.[60] In *Concerning the Statues* he retains an accurate exegesis about "the rich," but it is a short step to apply this to the pomp of the imperial statues.[61] His concern is always "to hear apostolic voices" or "a trumpet from heaven."[62] Unlike Clement of Alexandria, concealment means not mystery but *irresponsibility*.[63]

John Chrysostom declares, "The sacred writers even addressed themselves to the matter of immediate importance, whatever it might be at the time. . . . It is this writer's immediate object to declare that Christ was risen from the dead . . . that he was sent to God and came from God."[64] Hence the aim of the biblical writers remains primary, but allows for "application." Some have seen him as a mediating influence, close to his fellow Antiochenes, but not too far from the Alexandrians in understanding both exegesis and interpretation, and noting the difference.

4. *Theodoret of Cyrrhus* (ca. 393-460). Theodoret was born and educated in Antioch, where he entered the monastic life. Against his desire he was made bishop of Cyrrhus in Syria, some eighty miles east of Antioch, in 423. He fully engaged with the christological controversies of the time, and was a friend and adviser of Nestorius. This invited the hostility of Cyril of Alexandria, and Cyril's successor accused Theodoret of dividing Christ into *two* Sons of God. In view of this, only a portion of his writings has survived.

58. John Chrysostom, *Epistles of Paul to the Corinthians,* hom. 4.2.
59. John Chrysostom, *Commentary on Galatians,* on Gal. 4:24.
60. John Chrysostom, *Homilies on Matthew,* hom. 47.1-3.
61. John Chrysostom, *Concerning the Statues,* hom. 2.13.
62. John Chrysostom, *Concerning the Statues,* hom. 1.1.
63. John Chrysostom, *Concerning the Statues,* hom. 16.3.
64. John Chrysostom, *Commentary on the Acts of the Apostles,* hom. 1.1, 2.

Theodoret worked primarily as a biblical exegete. He quotes from Origen, Diodore, and Theodore of Mopsuestia. He wrote commentaries on the Pentateuch, Joshua and Judges, 1 and 2 Kings and 1 and 2 Chronicles. He knew Greek and Syriac, but it is debated whether he knew Hebrew. For example, he argues that *pneuma* or *ruach* in Genesis 1:2 means "wind" rather than "spirit." He comments on "God saw that it was good" (Gen. 1:18; 1:25) that it would be ungrateful to find fault with God's creation. The sentence "God knows that when you eat . . . you will be like God" (Gen. 3:5) is ironic.[65] We also possess fragments of Theodoret's commentaries on the Psalms, Jeremiah, Song of Songs, Luke, and the Epistles, and various sermons.

The exegesis of Theodoret remains mainly historical and "literal," but on the Song of Songs the lovers become Christ and the Church. He does not always reject a "fuller" meaning. He uses figurative or metaphorical language, typology, and sometimes allegory, but he criticizes any intrusion of an individual exegete's own ideas into the text.

4. The Bridge to the Middle Ages: Augustine and Gregory the Great

1. *Augustine of Hippo* (354-430) was born and educated in North Africa of a Christian mother, Monica, and a pagan father. He lived his early life as a pagan but was led to Christian faith by Monica's prayers and by the preaching of Ambrose of Milan. In 386 he was deeply moved by the hymns and canticles of the church at Milan. Influenced by the Manichees during his pagan period, he wrote, after returning to Africa in 388, *On Genesis* and *Against the Manichees*. In these he used allegorical interpretation. Following his conversion and subsequent ordination, he wrote a series of biblical commentaries, including those on Genesis, Matthew, Romans, and Galatians (all in 394), and a revision of his Romans (394-95).

Augustine's biblical commentaries reached a "high point" in his *On the Psalms* and *The Johannine Writings* in 414-17.[66] Augustine wrote many outstanding treatises on doctrine, including *On Christian Doctrine, On the Holy Trinity*, the *Enchiridion, On the Creed, Against the Manichees, Against the*

---

65. Theodoret, *Commentary on Genesis*, questions 8, 10, and 40.

66. Cf. Gerald Bonner, "Augustine as Biblical Scholar," in *The Cambridge History of the Bible*, ed. P. R. Ackroyd and C. F. Evans (Cambridge: Cambridge University Press, 1970), 1:543; cf. pp. 541-63.

Donatists, City of God, and moral treatises *On Marriage, On Widowhood,* and *On Continence.* Most famously he wrote his theological autobiography, *The Confessions.* We are not concerned primarily with all these, although together with his biblical homilies and commentaries they earned him ranking among the two or three greatest theologians of Christendom, or at least of the patristic Church. Of his biblical writings R. M. Grant writes, "Augustine is no simple traditionalist, yet he upholds the authority of the rule of faith. . . . The exegete must distinguish between literal and figurative statements. If he is still troubled, he should 'consult the rule of faith.' "[67] The understanding of Scripture is likely to come from the person who "aims at the enjoyment of God for his own sake."[68] Commands in Scripture are not figurative unless they seem to enjoin crime or vice. "Unless you eat the flesh of the Son of Man" (John 6:53) enjoins not literal cannibalism but a figurative meaning.

On Psalm 40:6 Augustine follows the Septuagint, but he understands God's preparing a "body" to include not only the "body" of the incarnation, but also the "body" of the Church, namely, "us." On the verse "Cast me not forth from before Thy face" (Ps. 51:11), he notes that this very prayer of confession "is the Holy Spirit . . . [so] you are joined to God."[69] On "the Word was made flesh" (John 1:14), Augustine writes, "By grace . . . the Word himself first chose to be born of man that you might be born of God unto salvation. . . . Not without reason did God wish for a 'human' birth, because he counted me (us) of some importance that he might make me immortal."[70] On "Blessed are they that mourn" (Matt. 5:4), Augustine comments, "Mourning is sorrow arising from the loss of things held dear."[71]

In many respects like John Chrysostom, Theodore and Augustine offer sober, succinct, historical exegesis, but not without "application." This is supported by a knowledge of "the rule of faith" and a strong view of sin and grace, as the Reformers recognized. James Wood writes, "The restless spirit of Augustine was not fully satisfied with allegory. His developing mind could not ignore the claims of the written word. Allegorical interpretation could be but one stage in a process."[72] Augustine writes, "Faith will totter if the author-

---

67. Robert M. Grant, *A Short History of the Interpretation of the Bible,* rev. ed. (London: Black, 1965), p. 87. See Augustine, *On Christian Doctrine* 3.2; cf. 3.5.

68. Augustine, *On Christian Doctrine* 3.10.16.

69. Augustine, *On the Psalms,* Ps. 51, section 16.

70. Augustine, *On the Gospel of John* 2.15.

71. Augustine, *On the Sermon on the Mount* 1.2.5.

72. Wood, *Interpretation of the Bible,* p. 65.

ity of Scripture begins to shake. Then, if faith totter, love itself will grow cold."[73] Sometimes, he admits, meanings seem obscure, but this helps to keep us from pride.[74] Academic rigor must be combined with love of God and for our neighbor. We do need education, including knowledge of history and philosophy, but also communion with God.[75] But this does not require massive learning but merely competence. The interpreter must also be honest.

Robert Markus offers an illuminating comparison of Augustine and Gregory of Rome. Both study and explore signs, but Augustine remains heir to a broad and mixed tradition of Greek and Christian thinking. Not until Ferdinand de Saussure did thinking about signs and signifiers in language become so sophisticated as that of Augustine. A hundred years later Gregory wrote out of a much narrower Church tradition. Markus writes, "Gregory had none of the hesitations that had led Augustine . . . to distrust allegory. . . . Quite the contrary. . . . With Gregory we are in a different world of exegesis."[76]

2. *Gregory the Great* (ca. 540-604) belongs to a different era, one in which one could afford to listen only to the Church. He gave away his wealth to support the poor, entered the monastic life, and in 585 became abbot of his former monastery. In due time he became archbishop of Rome, or pope. His writings tend to be practical, and his papacy is marked by the mission to England.

Alexandrian influence, especially through Origen and his Latin translator Rufinus, dominated this and much of the medieval period. Gregory stressed Origen's three levels of interpretation, especially in his *Morals in the Book of Job*. He also wrote reflections on Ezekiel and Kings, and some forty homilies on the Gospels. He saw Christ as the reference point for all the Scriptures, including the Old Testament. Hence he found a valuable tool in Origen's three levels of exegesis. He expounded Job on the historical level and then gave his "moral" or "mystical" interpretation. Robert Markus, as we saw, gave us a good reason for Gregory's different view of allegory from Augustine's.

It is often said that there is little originality in Gregory. But it is largely through him and his work that some of the biblical interpretation of the Church Fathers, especially Origen's, is mediated. Henri de Lubac tells us that

73. Augustine, *On Christian Doctrine* 1.37.
74. Augustine, *On Christian Doctrine* 2.6, 7.
75. Augustine, *On Christian Doctrine* 1.35, 36; 2.16.23; 2.28.42; and 2.40.60.
76. Robert Markus, *Signs and Meanings: World and Text in Ancient Christianity* (Liverpool: Liverpool University Press, 1996), p. 48.

a mingling of Gregory and Origen led to "spiritual understanding" being viewed as "the faith of Christ" combined with "mystery" or "the order of faith."[77] For most medieval exegetes, Lubac continues, Gregory is the first amongst masters, the homilist of the Church, and the clearest expositor of Holy Scripture. He is expert also in "the four senses." The influence of Gregory, in Lubac's view, accords with the prodigious praise he cites over two pages. Isidore of Seville, Bede of Jarrow, John of Salisbury, and many others up to Aquinas and other thinkers fall under his influence.

Some of these writers credit Gregory with the "Gregorian" fourfold sense of Scripture. It is well summed up by A. Dante (1265-1321), author of *The Divine Comedy,* in the following way. The literal focuses on sense experience of the world and is the foundation of all knowledge. "The allegorical level is at the centre of the *contemplative reason,* which sees the world around it as objective. . . . The moral, or third, level is that of the faith that transcends and yet also fulfils the reason, and the anagogic level is at the centre of the *beatific vision.*"[78] Another version reads: "The literal meaning teaches you what happened; the allegorical what you ought to believe; the moral what you should be doing about it; the anagogical what you may hope for (in the future life)."[79] Thus "Jerusalem" is the physical city at the literal level, the Church at the allegorical and moral levels, the Church triumphant or eschatological at the anagogical level. Sometimes the allegorical level is called the tropological level. Thus in his *Homilies on Ezekiel,* Gregory interprets the scroll "written on the inside and the outside" (Ezek. 2:10) as written on the inside through a spiritual understanding and on the outside through a literal sense.[80] It also promises heavenly, or invisible, things, which suggests an anagogical meaning.

5. The Middle Ages: Nine Figures from Bede to Nicholas of Lyra

1. *The Venerable Bede of Jarrow* (673-736) was a Benedictine monk in Northumbria at Monkwearmouth and Jarrow. He became a priest, but his

---

77. Henri de Lubac, *Medieval Exegesis,* vol. 2, *The Four Senses of Scripture,* trans. E. M. Maeierowski (Grand Rapids: Eerdmans; Edinburgh: T. & T. Clark, 2000), p. 118.

78. Northrop Frye, *The Great Code: The Bible and Literature* (New York and London: Harcourt Brace Jovanovich, 1982), p. 223.

79. James Atkinson, *Martin Luther and the Birth of Protestantism* (London: Penguin Books, 1968), p. 91.

80. Gregory, *Homilies on Ezekiel* 1.9.30.

popular title "Venerable" probably applies originally only to his bones in Durham Cathedral. He had an enormous output of books, of which the most famous is his *Ecclesiastical History of the English People*.

Bede knew patristic literature, and in his biblical commentaries used multiple senses and the allegorical method. In his appendix to the *Ecclesiastical History* he comments, "I spent all my life in this monastery, applying myself entirely to the study of Scriptures."[81] His commentaries treat Genesis 1–20, Exodus 24:12–30:21, Samuel, Kings, Song of Songs, Ezra, Nehemiah, Tobit, Mark, Luke, Acts, the Catholic Epistles, and Revelation. In his work on Luke he uses Jerome among others, but on the Old Testament his methods borrow from Philo and Origen. For example, at the beginning of Samuel, the Vulgate *"fuit vir unus"* (there was one man) is used to refer on the first level to Elkanah; on a second level it points to the unity of the elect; on the third, moral, level it points to a man who was not double-tongued; on a fourth level it refers to Christ. Thus we find four levels of meaning. Normally Bede offers a verse-by-verse commentary. He used Jerome and other patristic sources extensively, because he aimed to bring the English church fully into the patristic and Roman tradition.

2. *Alcuin of York* (ca. 735-804) was an educator. He compiled extracts from the Church Fathers for those students who had no direct access to patristic literature, and used these in his biblical commentaries. His second achievement was the standardization and correction of the biblical text, which he presented to the emperor Charlemagne on his coronation in 800.

3. *Bernard of Clairvaux* (1090-1153) was ordained in 1115, and became abbot of Clairvaux. His most influential biblical work was his *Sermons on the Song of Songs*, in which his method of exposition was to follow Origen and the Alexandrian allegorical tradition. The literal meaning concerned the marriage of Solomon; the allegorical meaning concerned Christ and the Church; the moral level of meaning concerned the practical life that stems from their union. As well as his Song of Songs, Henri de Lubac traces the profound influence of Origen, including his work on Lamentations. He is also known for his attacks on Abelard, his near contemporary. Bernard had a detailed knowledge of many biblical books, especially John and the Pauline Epistles. He expounded the Johannine theme of love, stressing that to love God because he is God is central to the Christian life.

4. *Hugh of St. Victor* (1096-1141) probably entered the Augustinian Ab-

---

81. Bede, *Ecclesiastical History* 5.24.

bey of St. Victor in Paris in about 1115, and wrote on grammar, geography, history, doctrine, and the Bible. In a telling comment on the three pairs of wings of the Septarium (Isa. 6:2), Hugh writes, "Scripture is understood in terms of history, allegory, and tropology. These points . . . are separate, because it separately kindles in souls the love of God and neighbour."[82] The *Noah's Ark Moralia* comes to us only as a fragment from a minor work, but it illuminates his exegetical method. The historical meaning includes explaining how things happened. However, many passages are likely to indicate how things will happen in the future.[83]

Hugh focused on the historical sense in his notes on the Psalms, Lamentations, Joel, and Obadiah. Exegetical tradition had tended to overlook the historical sense of these books. Also, in *On the Scriptures* he spoke of "the outward form of God's Word" that at first "may seem to you like dirt" but in fact merits "learning carefully what it tells you."[84] His outlook is reflected and developed by Andrew of St. Victor (d. 1175) and Richard of St. Victor (d. 1173).

5. *Peter Lombard* (ca. 1100-1161) was born in Lombardy, but went first to Reims and then in 1136 to Paris. He wrote commentaries on the Psalms and the Pauline Epistles. He became bishop of Paris in 1159. His chief work is *doctrinal,* including a book on the Trinity, a book on the incarnation, and a book on creation and sin. He quotes from the Latin Fathers, especially Augustine. He was influenced on the Bible by Hugh of St. Victor and the *Glossa Ordinaria,* which was the Vulgate with explanatory "glosses" *(Glossa)* by many authors. He did more than any in the twelfth century to develop a scholastic, rather than monastic, approach to the Bible.

Although he did not dispute the possibility of christological and moral meaning, Peter saw the Psalms in terms of *different types,* and classified those of the same type together. He was concerned about apparent textual discrepancies and looked at each psalm as a whole. On this basis his immediate aim was not devotional but doctrinal and ethical. He gave a more historical and literal interpretation of Paul than any other medieval writer, and viewed Paul's language about the silence of women in 1 Corinthians 14:34-36 as arising from a special contingent situation. The supposed preference for celi-

---

82. Hugh, *On Noah's Ark Moralia* 1.100.2; also Migne, *Patrologia Latina,* 221 vols. (Paris, 1844-64), 116:24.

83. Migne, *Patrologia Latina,* 176:994. Cf. Lubac, *Medieval Exegesis,* p. 100.

84. Hugh, *On the Scriptures* 5.13-15.

bacy in 1 Corinthians 7:1 was also dependent on contingent circumstances (here most modern commentators rightly see this as a quotation from some at Corinth).

Some criticized Peter Lombard for abandoning a more contemplative approach to the Bible in favor of a more "scientific" or technical approach. But this is precisely the point. In certain centers monasteries were giving way to universities, of which Paris and Oxford began to take shape in the later twelfth century. His *Book of Sentences* had an enormous influence. He asked questions about signs and signifiers in hermeneutics. Hugh of St. Victor and Abelard were particular influences.

6. *Stephen Langton* (ca. 1150-1228) assisted the barons of England against King John, and this ended with the Magna Carta. Stephen was consecrated archbishop of Canterbury, but John exiled him from England until 1213. Meanwhile he studied and taught the Bible in Paris. He related the Bible to doctrine and to pastoral care, and was associated with the founding of the University of Paris. He influenced biblical scholarship at Oxford and Cambridge. Like his predecessors, he taught *the fourfold sense* of Scripture: the literal, allegorical, moral, and anagogical.

7. *Bonaventura* (ca. 1217-84) had both a monastic and university background. He first entered a Franciscan monastery, but in 1235 he entered the University of Paris, and in 1243 entered its Faculty of Theology. He studied all biblical books and the work of Peter Lombard. His chief biblical writings were his commentary on Luke, in 1255-56, and works on Ecclesiastes and John. His exegetical method was most influenced by Hugh of St. Victor and Peter Lombard. His hermeneutics were deeply theological, focusing on the Trinity and the Holy Spirit. However, he recognized the distinctive function of legal books, historical books, Wisdom literature, and prophetic books. He saw Scripture as a single river, into which many different streams flowed. It is also a mirror and a ladder making doctrine possible. He spoke of the "multiplicity" of ways of understanding it, just as God is three in one.[85] He brought *doctrine and Scripture together,* and has been influential as a complement to Aquinas, even up to Vatican II.

8. *Thomas Aquinas* (1225-74) was the younger contemporary of Bonaventura, and the most respected and influential theologian of the Middle Ages in the Latin West. Many Roman Catholics still view his teaching as normative. He was a Dominican philosopher and theologian, born near

---

85. Bonaventura, prologue to *Breviloquium* 4.2.

Aquino in the region of Naples, Italy. As a child he was given to a Benedictine abbey but was then sent to the University of Naples and entered the Dominican Order. He next entered the universities of Paris and of Cologne (1248-51), and was strongly influenced by Albert the Great. As a lecturer in Paris he taught Isaiah and Jeremiah, and the *Sentences* of Peter Lombard. He returned to a Dominican house in Italy in 1259. In 1265 he was required in Rome, where he began his great work *Summa Theologiae,* which was a comprehensive systematic theology filling many volumes.

Thomas spoke of the Holy Spirit as the author of the Bible, but he also paid attention to its literary and linguistic diversity. He has sometimes been regarded as the first truly scientific commentator or expositor of the Bible. He regarded all theology as "scientific" but said theology was also based on the Bible. Indeed, he regarded the philosophy of Aristotle and his principle of fourfold causality as intensely relevant to theology, including the Bible and the sacraments. His view of transubstantiation depended on Aristotle's distinction between substance and "accidents" (what could be grasped by the senses).[86] On the Bible, final cause could reflect the purpose of God; while efficient cause represented the means used by the human writers.

Thomas adopted a fairly "commonsense" approach to the tradition of the fourfold sense, derived initially from Origen's threefold sense, and traditionally from Gregory. The literal sense was the foundation meaning. The other "senses" could not be used to prove *points of doctrine.* But the moral, spiritual or tropological, and anagogical or eschatological were not to be rejected. They had a part to play if they were relevant and not forced artificially.

Although the *Summa Theologiae* and *Summa contra Gentiles* are more widely known, a quarter of all his works were biblical commentaries. He wrote a commentary on the four Gospels, and his commentaries on John, Galatians, Ephesians, and the Epistle to the Hebrews are translated into English. On Ephesians 1:1, for example, we read, "The Apostle writes his letter to the Ephesians who were Asians from Asia Minor, which is part of Greece. . . . From Acts 19:1 [we know that] Paul found certain disciples."[87]

86. Thomas Aquinas, *Summa Theologiae,* Latin and English, Blackfriars edition, 60 vols. (London: Eyre and Spottiswood; New York: McGraw-Hill, 1963), vol. 58, qu. 75-77, pp. 53-195.

87. Thomas Aquinas, *Commentary on the Epistle of Paul to the Ephesians,* trans. F. R. Larcher, Aquinas Scripture Commentaries 2 (Albany, N.Y.: Magi Books, 1966), chapter 1, lecture I. Cf. also Aquinas, *Commentary on Paul's Epistle to the Galatians,* trans. F. R. Larcher (Albany, N.Y.: Magi Books, 1966), pp. 1-10; and Thomas G. Weinandy, Daniel Keating, and

Aquinas is interested in the historical situation of the writer and readers, as in a modern commentary. He sets out the genre of greeting, narrative, exhortation, and conclusion. The greeting "blessed be God" arises because the readers have been transformed by Christ.

Thomas carefully compares predestination and adoption in Romans, and assigns to final cause God's purpose and the glory of his grace (1:4, 5). Lecture 2 takes up the theme of being "pleasing to God" (1:6). He presents a verse-by-verse commentary in which the historical background and language are expounded as the literal sense.

The *Commentary on John* offers a similar kind of comment. Of the prologue Thomas comments that this was to show the divinity of the Son, as expounded by what Jesus did in the flesh (John 1:1-14). The preexistence of Christ relates to the logos in "the Philosopher" (Aristotle), but coheres with 1 Corinthians 10:4. The Gospel is not antirational. The Word differs from our own word in that it is perfect, it is God's act, and it is not the same nature as us. Word, rather than Son, avoids here the idea of generation.[88] Later, when the two disciples ask Jesus to teach them more, Jesus says, "Come and see" (John 1:39).

These are historical and explanatory comments of the kind found in a modern commentary. Thomas also uses the Fathers and often quotes Chrysostom, who is one of the best exegetes of the early Church. He has also written many other commentaries, including those on Job, Isaiah, Jeremiah and Lamentations, and doctrinal expositions of Matthew. Although the Council of Trent considered Aquinas authoritative, the Biblical Commission's document *The Interpretation of the Bible in the Church* (1994) broadly coheres with Protestant biblical interpretation.

9. *Nicholas of Lyra* (ca. 1270-1349) was a Franciscan who moved to Paris at about the age of thirty. He became a regent master in the University of Paris in 1309. He paid attention to the literal meaning of the biblical text. His verse-by-verse commentaries on the Bible show also a close knowledge of patristic and medieval sources. He has a rare knowledge of Hebrew and rabbinic exegesis. He looks to Hugh of St. Victor and Abelard, but is clearly of the new tradition of the universities. His *postilia moralis* carries on the tradi-

---

P. Yocum, eds., *Aquinas on Scripture: An Introduction to His Biblical Commentaries* (London: T. & T. Clark, 2005).

88. Thomas Aquinas, *Commentary on John*, trans. J. A. Weisheipl and F. R. Larcher, Aquinas Scripture Commentaries 3 and 4 (Albany, N.Y.: Magi Books, 1966, 1998), sections 23-25.

tion of a "spiritual" meaning, but within the context of theology or doctrine he gives priority to the literal or historical meaning. With his appropriation of Jewish exegesis, he did more than any of his time to bring methods of interpretation into the modern world. He showed careful judgment, which makes him a fitting conclusion to our survey of patristic and medieval exegesis. Henri de Lubac credits Nicholas with the quasi-scholastic aphorism: "The letter teaches events, allegory what you should believe; morality teaches what you should do, anagogy what mark you should be aiming for."[89] Gillian R. Evans sees Peter Lombard's commentaries as "standard works" on "the Road to Reformation."[90]

6. Recommended Initial Reading

Grant, Robert M., *A Short History of the Interpretation of the Bible,* 3rd ed. (London: Black, 1965; rev. ed., Philadelphia: Fortress, 1984), pp. 57-101 (1965 ed.) or 59-91 (1984 ed.).

Hanson, Richard P. C., *Allegory and Event: A Study of Sources and the Significance of Origen's Interpretation of Scripture* (London: SCM, 1959), pp. 133-61.

McKim, Donald K., ed., *Dictionary of Major Biblical Interpreters* (Downers Grove, Ill., and Nottingham: IVP, 2007), articles under the names discussed.

Smalley, Beryl, *The Study of the Bible in the Middle Ages* (Oxford: Blackwell, 1952, 1964), pp. 1-25, 83-106, and 281-92.

89. Lubac, *Medieval Exegesis,* 1:1.

90. Gillian R. Evans, *The Language and Logic of the Bible: The Road to the Reformation* (Cambridge: Cambridge University Press, 1965), p. 95.

CHAPTER VII

Reform, the Enlightenment, and the Rise of Biblical Criticism

This chapter raises some of the most difficult dilemmas for the theological scholar. Nicholas of Lyra and John Wycliffe lead us away from Origen and allegorizing, while not rejecting allegory altogether. The debate between Erasmus and Luther about the clarity of Scripture may give rise to misunderstanding. But the Enlightenment raises a genuine dilemma. On one side most biblical scholars will agree that one cannot address all hermeneutical questions by theology alone. To stress the need for faith will not determine in advance questions about history, language, or the individuality of each biblical writer. We need what became "The Introduction to the Old Testament or the New Testament." On the other side, however, writers such as J. S. Semler in biblical criticism were so eager to separate biblical exegesis and the canon from theology that often the authority and divine revelation of the Scriptures received only a theoretical nod of approval, and many (though not all) Enlightenment thinkers approached the Bible as secular literature or purely human writings.

Francis Watson and many others have exploded the myth of purely value-free inquiry. In this sense there was something naive about the Enlightenment attitude to tradition. Yet as Schleiermacher later agreed, hermeneutics is not an instrumental discipline used supposedly to endorse theological or Christian doctrinal conclusions at which some have already arrived. We are looking for "integrity" rather than Kant's "autonomy." But the issues are complex. Hence we need a chapter on the Reformers, the Enlightenment, and the varied attitudes embodied in the rise of biblical criticism.

1. Reform: Wycliffe, Luther, and Melanchthon

1. *John Wycliffe* (1328-84). Wycliffe studied at Baliol College, Oxford, became ordained, and was awarded a doctorate of divinity in 1372. He was elected master of Baliol College. King Edward III granted him the parish of Lutterworth in Leicestershire, which he held until his death. He sought to ground all his reforms in the authority of Scripture, arguing that it is the highest authority for every Christian. It provides the test of all Church councils and of the claims of religious experience.

Although we tend to date the beginning of the Reformation with Martin Luther, in his later writing Wycliffe urges the abolition of the papacy and rejects the doctrine of transubstantiation. He believed that this was in line with the truth of Scripture and the early Church, especially Augustine, Ambrose, and Anselm. In 1382 the archbishop of Canterbury prosecuted him for these views, and many at Oxford also condemned him. He then retired to pastoral work in his Lutterworth parish, before his death two years later. Wycliffe promoted a body of preachers who were given the name Lollards.[1]

In his inaugural lecture at Oxford, Wycliffe argued that the interpretation of Scripture must follow the intention of its divine author. To reach this required a moral attitude, or rightness of heart. It also assumed philosophical training and social virtue.[2] In 1377-78 he wrote and delivered at Oxford a series of lectures on the authority of the Bible, published as *On the Truth of the Holy Scripture*. He saw the Scriptures as God's Law, sufficient for the guidance of the Church as the Body of Christ.[3] Wycliffe was shocked at the ignorance of Scripture among the clergy. Hence he also wrote *The Pastoral Office,* in which he explained to them the emphasis of Luke-Acts upon poverty and self-discipline.[4] He stressed the literal or historical sense of Scripture but recognized that this might include metaphor (for example, in "the Lion of Judah" in Rev. 5:5). But he also allowed the moral sense, which could

---

1. John Wycliffe, *On the Eucharist,* trans. F. L. Battles, Library of Christian Classics, vol. 14 (London: SCM; Louisville: Westminster, 1963), 3.2, 1.1-2; pp. 61-62.

2. Beryl Smalley, *The Study of the Bible in the Middle Ages* (Oxford: Blackwell, 1964), p. 274.

3. John Wycliffe, *On the Truth of the Holy Scripture* (Kalamazoo, Mich.: Mediaeval Institute, and Western Michigan University, 2001), 1.55, 148, 245.

4. John Wycliffe, *The Pastoral Office,* trans. F. L. Battles, Library of Christian Classics, vol. 14 (London: SCM; Philadelphia: Westminster, 1963), 1.5, 15, and 2.1.1, especially pp. 36, 43, and 58.

be allegorical. Like Nicholas of Lyra, he drew attention to the various types and functions of biblical texts.

Wycliffe translated the New Testament into robust English and wrote commentaries on Job, Ecclesiastes, the Psalms, Song of Songs, Lamentations, and many of the prophets. He emphasized the truth, inspiration, authority, and sufficiency of Scripture. Thus he paved the way for the Reformation. He was especially concerned with the use of the Bible in preaching.

2. *Martin Luther* (1483-1546). Luther was born at Eisleben in Saxony, and gained entry to the University of Erfurt, southwest of Leipzig, at that time the most prestigious and among the most ancient universities of Germany. He studied grammar, rhetoric, and dialectic, which gave him skill with words. In theology, the greatest influence at Erfurt was Nicholas of Lyra.[5] At twenty-two, in 1505, Luther entered the Augustinian Order at Erfurt, and over the next two years became a monk, and was made deacon, and was ordained as priest. As well as studying Peter Lombard, he intensively studied the Bible. In 1508 Luther was called to the new University of Wittenberg to teach philosophy, but by 1509 he had returned to teaching the Bible. By 1512 he became professor of biblical studies. At Wittenberg he came under the influence of Staupitz, who encouraged him to study for his doctorate and advised him in his spiritual struggles.

The dawn of Reformation consciousness, James Atkinson argues, emerged as Luther was preparing his lectures on the Psalms, during April and May 1513.[6] He came to the verse "Deliver me in Thy righteousness" (Ps. 31:1). He recalled that at that time he "hated" both Paul and the whole idea of "righteousness," especially where the two come together, as in Romans 1:16-17. "In Thy righteousness deliver me" is repeated in Psalm 71:2. Luther wrote that his own "righteousness" was nothing, even as an obedient monk. He at first thought that the righteousness of God condemned him. But he came to realize that the righteousness of God meant not judgment, but the righteousness of Christ, which brought justification by grace alone. Humankind has only to appropriate this and to receive it as a gift.

E. G. Rupp and Benjamin Drewery describe Luther's "breakthrough" in his own words. Luther writes, "'The righteous shall live by faith.' There I began to understand that the righteousness of God is the righteousness in which a just man lives by the gift of God. . . . I felt myself straightaway born afresh and

---

5. Cf. James Atkinson, *Martin Luther and the Birth of Protestantism* (London: Penguin Books, 1968), pp. 32-33.

6. Atkinson, *Birth of Protestantism,* p. 76.

to have entered through the open gates into paradise itself."[7] It was akin to Barth's "strange new world of the Bible," which we consider in chapter X.

In his early writings (1517 to 1521) Luther emphasizes faith as the work of *God*. Luther writes, "Faith . . . is more the work of God than ours."[8] In the *Heidelberg Disputation* (1518) he writes further, "He deserves to be called a theologian who comprehends the visible things . . . of God seen through suffering and the cross. . . . The theologian of glory says bad is good and good is bad. The theologian of the cross calls them by their proper name."[9]

Catholic Christendom was at the time unpersuaded by Luther's interpretations of Scripture. But Germany and the Scandinavian countries looked to Wittenberg for their theologians. Luther argued that Erasmus the humanist gave insufficient place to Christ and the glory and grace of God. He accused Erasmus of being like "two persons in one."[10] Meanwhile, between 1516 and 1521 Luther lectured in the university on Romans, Galatians, and Hebrews, and twice on the Psalms.

Luther's early lectures on the Psalms followed the method of Nicholas of Lyra and Peter Lombard, and at that time included the medieval "fourfold sense." The literal sense conveyed the acts of God in history. Other senses recorded their appropriation by the community of believers. The anagogical sense arose because human understanding will be fulfilled by greater understanding in heaven. On Psalm 51 and Psalm 92 Luther wrote of the need to be distrustful of the self. Strength in weakness becomes a theme in his early commentary on Romans. On Romans 1:1 he writes, "We must wait for him (God) to reckon us as just and wise."[11] But he also accepted the concept of a christological meaning everywhere: "Every word of the Bible peals the name of Christ," he declares, or "The whole of Scripture deals with Christ throughout."[12]

7. E. G. Rupp and Benjamin Drewery, eds., *Martin Luther: Documents of Modern History* (London: Arnold, 1970), p. 6; Atkinson, *Birth of Protestantism*, p. 77.

8. Martin Luther, *Commentary on the Epistle to the Hebrews,* in *Luther's Early Theological Works,* ed. James Atkinson, Library of Christian Classics, vol. 16 (London: SCM, 1962), p. 201; cf. p. 25.

9. Martin Luther, *The Heidelberg Disputation* 20 and 21, in *Luther's Early Theological Works,* pp. 290 and 291. Cf. Luther, *Heidelberg Disputation* 23.

10. Atkinson, *Birth of Protestantism*, p. 89.

11. Gordon Rupp, *The Righteousness of God: Luther Studies* (London: Hodder and Stoughton, 1953), p. 134.

12. Atkinson, *Birth of Protestantism*, pp. 101 and 116.

Luther's *Commentary on Romans* (1516-17) reflects the care for detail with which he worked. It contains the more mature theology of the middle years, although it comes seven years before the Diet of Worms. He stated that the purpose of the epistle was "to tear down . . . all wisdom and righteousness as man understands them. . . . He [God] wants to save us by a righteousness and wisdom other than this . . . which does not come from ourselves . . . we must wait for the pure mercy of God."[13] He redefined "the power of God" in Romans 1:16 not as the power of force, but as what the world perceives as folly (cf. 1 Cor. 1:18-25). He writes that to be righteous and to be justified before God are the same thing (on Rom. 1:17 and Rom. 4:16-25). On Romans 4:7 he observes that "actual sin" is a "work," which will not save us. The error is akin to Pelagianism. He explores Paul's emphasis on human inability to fulfill the law. He makes this point especially on Romans 7:18, "To will is present with me, but how to perform the good I find not." Luther writes, "The entire man is flesh."[14]

This well engages with the "literal" message of Romans. Luther's *Commentary on Galatians* (1517) contains a larger proportion of material on the pope, but only as a way of distinguishing "works" from receiving grace from God through faith or appropriation. In the same year Luther produced his Ninety-five Theses. In 1518 Luther held a disputation with Cardinal Cajetan at Augsburg, of which he commented that Cajetan never produced one word of Scripture against him. In the same year he faced Eck at Leipzig, where again Luther triumphed through his use of Scripture. In 1521 Luther was called to appear before the emperor at the Diet of Worms. Luther bore testimony to the truth of his claims from Scripture, and eventually the emperor had him removed. Luther later recalled that all he did was to teach and preach God's Word: "I did nothing. . . . The Word did it all."[15]

After 1521 Luther wrote commentaries on Deuteronomy, the Minor Prophets, Ecclesiastes, 1 John, Titus, 1 Timothy, Isaiah, and Song of Songs (1531). Increasingly he resisted the allegorical or "spiritual" sense of Scripture, and multiple-meaning exegesis.[16] Many regard Luther's translation of

13. *Luther's Works,* ed. J. Pelikan, 56 vols. (St. Louis: Concordia, 1955-); in German, Weimarer Ausgabe (Weimar Edition; hereafter abbreviated WA), 56:157-59.

14. Luther, WA 56:343.

15. Cited often, including in Gordon Rupp, *Luther's Progress in the Diet of Worms, 1521* (London: SCM, 1951), p. 99, and Atkinson, *Birth of Protestantism,* p. 182.

16. A. Skevington Wood, *Captive to the Word: Martin Luther, Doctor of Sacred Scripture* (Exeter: Paternoster, 1969), p. 83.

the Bible into robust and accurate German as his greatest single work.[17] He had begun to translate certain passages in 1519, and did much during his confinement at Wartburg. It was published in 1534. Many view it as "a literary event of the first magnitude."[18] Luther believed that every believer should have access to the Bible, and his careful translation, based on the original languages, has become the standard translation in Germany.

Meanwhile Luther interpreted Scripture in one context in his prolonged battle with Rome. Rome had come heavily to rely on the Church Fathers and Aquinas virtually in place of the Bible. In a second context Luther battled with the fanatical left-wing reformers or the *Schwärmerei,* including Karlstadt and Münzer. In *The Babylonian Captivity of the Church* he argued against all theology not based on Scripture.

We have avoided covering again the ground discussed in *New Horizons in Hermeneutics.* However, we may perhaps repeat one point in summary. By arguing for the *clarity* of Scripture, Luther did not imply that commentaries were unnecessary, as we can see from his work. He was replying, in effect, to the claims of Erasmus that Scripture was so complex, and its arguments so many-sided, that we could never be committed to much more than *exploration.* Luther regarded this as amounting to a form of skepticism. The Bible, he insisted, is clear enough for *action.* The details of this argument on both sides are set out in *New Horizons.* I also argued in more detail there that Luther's reservations about allegory grew progressively.

3. *Philip Melanchthon* (1497-1560). Melanchthon was only fourteen years younger than Luther, and came to be known as Luther's friend, supporter, and assistant. He had qualities in his own right. He entered the University of Heidelberg in 1509, and by the time of his graduation had become known as a master of the Greek language. He studied further at the University of Tübingen, and learned Hebrew from the distinguished Hebraist J. Reuchlin. He published a Greek grammar, and in 1518 was appointed to teach classics at Wittenberg. There he met Luther.

Melanchthon supported Luther fully during the years of his earlier writings from 1518 to 1521. When Luther retreated temporarily to Wartburg Castle, Melanchthon took the lead in promoting his thought. In 1529, however, he showed what Luther saw as Zwinglian leanings on the Lord's Supper, or

17. For example, Wood, *Captive to the Word,* p. 95.
18. Kenelm Foster, in *The Cambridge History of the Bible,* vol. 3, ed. S. L. Greenslade (Cambridge: Cambridge University Press, 1963), p. 103.

the Eucharist. He was less antagonistic to Zwingli than was Luther.[19] Melanchthon was eager to preserve peace and unity among the Reformers. In 1530 he drew up the Augsburg Confession of Faith, which he presented to the emperor as an agreed doctrinal statement by all German Protestants. (This included Luther and Melanchthon, but left out the Swiss Reformer Zwingli.) This was the first Protestant confession of faith, and is today regarded as the statement of orthodox Lutheran doctrine.

While Luther was primarily writing commentaries, Melanchthon was producing a systematic theology. It was perhaps the first Protestant systematic theology based on the Bible. But Melanchthon also spent hours with Luther, in which he helped him with translation from Greek and Hebrew into German. He also returned to Wittenberg to lecture on Romans (1522) and on John (1523); he also published work on Matthew (1558). He used allegory on occasion but mainly adhered to the literal meaning of the biblical text. His methods reflect Luther's middle and later periods, but of the two he is perhaps the more critical and searching.

2. Further Reform: William Tyndale and John Calvin

1. *William Tyndale* (ca. 1494-1536) translated the first Bible from Greek and Hebrew into English between 1525 and 1535. This translation influenced the Authorized Version of James I in 1611, as well as the Coverdale Version of 1535-36. Tyndale was born in Gloucestershire, England, and educated at Magdalene Hall, Oxford. He completed his studies in divinity at Cambridge. He ministered at Little Sodbury, but on failing to gain the support of Bishop Tunstall of London he emigrated to Germany in 1524. He was greatly influenced by Luther's theology.

Tyndale promoted Luther's theology. In partial terms he anticipated what today we would call the speech-act, performative, or illocutionary function of some biblical texts (on performatives, see chapter XVII). The Bible, he wrote, conveys "promises of God"; "it maketh a man's heart glad"; it "nameth [us] to be heirs."[20] I have argued that within a dozen pages of his work he lists

---

19. Atkinson, *Birth of Protestantism*, pp. 273-74.

20. William Tyndale, *A Pathway into the Holy Scripture*, in Tyndale, *Doctrinal Treatises and Introductions to Holy Scripture* (Cambridge: Cambridge University Press, Parker Society, 1848), pp. 7-29.

and identifies no fewer than eighteen specific speech-acts performed by Scripture.[21] It names, appoints, promises, gives, condemns, kills, gives life, and so on. To him is credited the saying "If God spare my life, I will cause the boy that drives the plough to know more Scripture than you."[22] Tyndale was greatly indebted also to Erasmus's edition of the Greek Testament, as well as to the Latin Vulgate and Luther's German translation. His English, he claimed, was nearer to the Greek than the Latin was. Another aphorism attributed to Tyndale is the prayer "Lord, open the King of England's eyes."

2. *John Calvin* (1509-64). Calvin was born in Picardy, northern France, and educated in Paris. From 1528 he studied law at Orléans. He became an ardent advocate of the theology of the Reformation, and in 1535 was forced to flee from France and traveled to Basel (Basle) in Switzerland. He began to write *Institutes of the Christian Religion* (first edition) in 1536. En route to Strasbourg in the same year, he had to make a detour through Geneva. There W. Farel persuaded him to lead the city's rejection of the papacy. Calvin longed for peace and quiet for scriptural study but was persuaded to guide the Church, and to assist in reforming and governing the city. He wrote commentaries on virtually all the books of the Bible. His successive editions of the *Institutes* are comparable to the *Summa Theologiae* of Aquinas, to Schleiermacher's *Christian Faith,* or to Barth's *Church Dogmatics.* But he wished to produce a theology that was separate from his biblical commentaries. He has with justice been called the first "modern" commentator on the Bible. His exegetical writings tower over others.

Calvin's first commentary was on Romans, in 1540. In the preface he acknowledges the exegetical work of Philip Melanchthon and Martin Bucer, but he sees the need to go further. He observes that the chief virtue of an expositor lies in "lucid brevity" and in unfolding "the mind of the writer whom he has undertaken to expound."[23] He must not go outside these limits, adhering to "the meaning of the author."[24] Calvin owed something to his legal studies, which stressed the importance of the historical situation in which a law arose, as well as its practical application.

---

21. Anthony C. Thiselton, "Authority and Hermeneutics: Some Proposals for a More Creative Agenda," in *A Pathway with the Holy Scripture,* ed. Philip E. Satterthwaite and David F. Wright (Grand Rapids: Eerdmans, 1994), pp. 107-41, especially pp. 117-20.

22. Greenslade, *Cambridge History,* 3:141-42.

23. John Calvin, preface to *The Epistles of Paul to the Romans and the Thessalonians,* trans. R. Mackenzie, ed. T. F. Torrance (Edinburgh: Oliver and Boyd, 1964).

24. Calvin, preface to *The Epistles of Paul to the Romans and the Thessalonians.*

Calvin wrote the final edition of the *Institutes* four years before his death, in 1560. It was to serve as an interpretative key to theology and Scripture. In book 1, chapters 6 to 10, he set out the role of Scripture. Elderly persons, he observes, may need glasses to clarify what they see; even so Scripture and its interpretation give focus to a *vision of God*.[25] The Bible is derived from the Spirit of God (chapter 7). The credibility of Scripture is sufficiently proved as evident to reason (chapter 8). In the New Testament the first three Gospels provide a narrative in a modest style; John, however, "fulminates in majesty" and "strikes down more powerfully than any thunderbolt."[26] Fanatics, he writes, try in effect to subvert Scripture by private revelation, but they are wrong (chapter 9). His view is close to that of Irenaeus. Scripture directs us to the true God by rejecting other "gods" (chapter 10).

After his commentary on Romans, Calvin published a commentary on Genesis, a harmony of the Pentateuch from Exodus to Deuteronomy, and commentaries on Psalms, Isaiah, Jeremiah, Lamentations, Ezekiel, the Minor Prophets, Job, Samuel, and Joshua (1564). He wrote on all the books of the New Testament except 2 John, 3 John, and Revelation.[27] The Old Testament commentaries were mostly lectures; the New Testament commentaries were dictated at home. He did not spare himself, we are told, but worked much harder than his health and strength could bear. Calvin insisted on the "natural" or "literal" meaning of the text, in accordance with Erasmus and Renaissance humanism. Calvin declared, "Allegory was contrary to the humanistic canon of interpretation; and 'literalism,' that is the desire to get at an author's mind, was of the essence."[28] His primary concern was for "the honour of God," but he was constantly mindful of his fellow Protestant Christians who were suffering persecution in France and other areas.

T. H. L. Parker insists that Calvin's attacks on allegory "are not directed against the *sensus allegoricus,* but against an over-elaborated use of allegory in its general sense of extended metaphor."[29] On Daniel 10:5-6, Calvin observes: "I know that allegories are plausible; but when we reverently ponder

---

25. John Calvin, *Institutes of the Christian Religion,* trans. Henry Beveridge, 2 vols. (London: James Clarke, 1957), 1.6.1; vol. 1, p. 64.

26. Calvin, *Institutes* 1.8.11; vol. 1, p. 81.

27. Joseph Haroutunian and Louise Pettibone Smith, eds., *Calvin's Commentaries,* Library of Christian Classics, vol. 23 (London: SCM; Philadelphia: Westminster, 1958), p. 16.

28. Haroutunian and Smith, *Calvin's Commentaries,* p. 28.

29. T. H. L. Parker, *Calvin's Old Testament Commentaries* (Edinburgh: T. & T. Clark, 1986), p. 70.

what the Holy Spirit teaches, these speculations vanish away."[30] Genesis 15:11 comes close to allegory in Calvin's interpretation. He is cautious even about *typology*, although he can see God's providential ordering of events or persons in true typology. Christ and David, or the Passover and the paschal Lamb, provide such examples. In 1 Corinthians 10:1-6 he sees a providential parallel between the Church and Israel.

Both in his Old and New Testament commentaries Calvin shows a healthy respect for biblical history. But this is viewed in terms of divine providence and the continuity between two covenants. The bringing of the covenant of salvation was to prepare for Christ.[31] The law was given "to make transgressions obvious."[32] The book of Joshua witnesses to a low point in covenantal relationship but deals with the weakness and fallibility of God's people. On Genesis 25:1 he recognizes the fallibility of Abraham, and the metaphorical force of "dead" some thirty-eight years before death. On Genesis 6, after saying we need not delay on the structure of Noah's ark, he attempts to work out its historical detail. Calvin sees the thread of divine providence and covenantal promise as running through and linking these persons and events.

The anagogical sense, however, should not be dismissed. Calvin declares on Luke 12:50 that readers must reflect upon "the blessed and immortal rest of heaven." Hope will enable them to bear present suffering. He translates the Greek *eidos* in 2 Corinthians 5:7 as "sight" in "we walk by faith, not sight." "Now things hoped for are things hidden, as we read in Rom. 8:24."[33] Yet Calvin brings commentating into the modern era.

3. Protestant Orthodoxy, Pietism, and the Enlightenment

In the immediate wake of the Reformation, the sixteenth and seventeenth centuries saw a flowering of Protestant orthodoxy. John Henry Newman characterized the eighteenth century as one when "love grows cold." It witnessed the full impact of the Enlightenment and often "secular" thought,

---

30. Parker, *Calvin's Old Testament Commentaries*, p. 71.

31. John Calvin, *The Epistles of Paul to the Galatians, Ephesians, Philippians, and Colossians*, trans. T. H. L. Parker (Edinburgh: Oliver and Boyd, 1965), pp. 58-59.

32. Calvin, *Galatians, Ephesians*, p. 61.

33. John Calvin, *The Second Epistle of Paul to the Corinthians; The Epistles of Paul to Timothy, Titus, and Philemon*, trans. T. A. Smart (Edinburgh: St. Andrews Press, 1964), p. 69.

with crosscurrents of Pietism and less rationalist Christian devotion. Toward the second half of the eighteenth century and the beginning of the nineteenth, there followed the first phase of biblical criticism and the beginnings of Romanticism. We glance briefly, first, at Protestant orthodoxy.

1. *Matthias Flacius Illyricus* (1520-75) came to the University of Wittenberg in 1541, after coming under the influence of Erasmus and Renaissance humanism. He was appointed professor of Hebrew at Wittenberg, where he also lectured on Paul's epistles. He followed Luther and Melanchthon. Then, as professor at Jena, he wrote to defend Protestant orthodoxy against the Roman Catholic Church. Flacius wrote his main work on hermeneutics under the title *Clavis Scripturae Sacrae* in 1567, drawing on both Aristotle's rhetoric and exegesis from Origen up to his own time. The *Key* went through ten editions in the next hundred years, and was very influential. He argued that the "key" to all Scripture was Christ. He did not hesitate to use typological exegesis.

2. *Christian Wolff* (1679-1754) was a philosopher, not a biblical scholar. He came into contact with Pietism at Halle, and with Enlightenment philosophy. He was a prodigious author. He introduced into hermeneutics the multiplicity of author's intentions *(Absicht)*. For example, an author may recount different kinds of "history" with different intentions. This was an era when hermeneutics came into vogue, following the publication of J. C. Danhauer's *Hermeneutics* in 1654 at Strassburg. This seems to be the first use of the term "hermeneutics" from the Greek, rather than "theory of interpretation," which derived from the Latin. J. A. Turretin of Geneva is another example of Protestant orthodoxy in work published in 1728.

3. *J. M. Chladenius* (1710-59) produced his main book on hermeneutics in 1742. It was entitled *Introduction to the Correct Interpretation of Reasonable Discourses and Books,* and its most original contribution was a *perspectival* understanding of a "point of view" *(Sehe Punckt)* on the part of the author. In some respects it was the first recognition of a *historical* understanding. The interpreter "sees" the text from the point of view of a historical author and a historical interpreter, both conditioned and limited by their place in history. Often a given community will share the same given perspective.[34]

4. *The Early Pietists: Spener, Francke, and Bengel.* This group were ardent for renewal, reform, and mission. But, with the notable exception of Bengel,

---

34. Cf. Kurt Mueller-Vollmer, ed., *The Hermeneutics Reader* (Oxford: Blackwell, 1985), pp. 7-8 and 54-71, for a selection from his writings.

they tended to lack the intellectual concern and rigor of the Reformers. Philipp J. Spener (1635-1705) is usually credited with founding the movement. He stressed the importance of the Bible, which should be approached with study, prayer, openness to the Holy Spirit, and ideally as a community, not as a lone individual.

August H. Francke (1663-1727) stressed the centrality of the Bible, the need for renewal and conversion, and mission. Often this was to be accompanied by sorrow for past sin.[35] He founded a number of groups in the University of Halle, where Wolff encountered them. Although not formally a theologian, he wrote several works on hermeneutics. He claimed that the historical meaning of a biblical text was only its husk; the Word or "seed" was practical and spiritual. The Bible was interpreted in *community.*

Johann A. Bengel (1687-1752) was a New Testament scholar and textual critic. Many group him with the Pietists (as Erb does), but many also regard him as an orthodox Lutheran.[36] His work in 1734 is often regarded as the foundation work of textual criticism. In 1742 he wrote his *Gnomen Novi Testamenti,* which exists in a revised English translation. His work is succinct and is still useful today.

5. *The Later Pietists* include Friedrich C. Oetinger (1702-82), Nicholas Ludwig Count von Zinzendorf (1700-1760), and John and Charles Wesley (John, 1703-91; Charles, 1707-88). They span the eighteenth century and are concurrent with the Enlightenment and the beginnings of biblical criticism. They are virtually untouched in sympathy with both.

Friedrich Oetinger was attracted to Boehme, another Pietist, and was more concerned with practical life than with reason. Gadamer commends his pietism in contrast to Enlightenment rationalism. Understanding arises from the heart no less than the head. Count Zinzendorf was a radical Pietist, much influenced by Spener and Francke. In 1722 he heard of the plight of the Bohemian Brethren, or Moravians, followers of Huss. He offered them safety on his estate. In due course they bore the name *Herrnhut,* or the Lord's Watch.

Zinzendorf and the Moravians had an influence on the Wesleys, and initially on Schleiermacher. John Wesley first met the Moravians while en route to Georgia in America. Wesley's main influences included Luther's *Preface to*

---

35. See Peter C. Erb, *Pietists: Selected Writings* (London: SPCK; New York: Paulist, 1983), pp. 9 and 128-34.

36. Erb, *Pietists,* p. 23.

Romans, the Church of England, and the Moravians. From Luther's *Preface* he gained Luther's understanding of Romans 1:16-17. He writes, "I felt my heart strongly warmed. I felt I did trust in Christ, Christ alone, for salvation." Wesley came to believe that any unclear passage of the Bible was to be interpreted in the light of clearer ones. He used Bengel's Greek text, and wrote *Notes on the Bible.*

6. *The Enlightenment.* The term originated as a translation of the German term *Aufklärung* and is characteristic of much, if not most, eighteenth-century thought, with beginnings in the seventeenth century. Immanuel Kant (1724-1804) spoke of the Enlightenment of humankind from the tutelage of authorities being liberated to the mature autonomy and freedom of "modern" people, who could now think for themselves. The world, he said, long before Bonhoeffer, had come of age. In England the movement went back perhaps to John Locke (1632-1704), and certainly to David Hume (1711-76), Sir Isaac Newton (1642-1727), and the Deists (ca. 1624–ca. 1793). Many argue that the early seeds of the Enlightenment on the European Continent come from René Descartes (1596-1650) and Baruch (or Benedict) de Spinoza (1632-77). For the most part these are philosophers, but in biblical studies Johann Salomo Semler (1725-91) and Johann August Ernesti (1707-81) were crucial.

If we want to consult a recognized specialist work on this era, Henning Graf Reventlow's book *The Authority of the Bible and the Rise of the Modern World* traces changes from the Reformation, Erasmus, and Bucer, through the first Deists, to the rise of biblical criticism in the wake of the Enlightenment. After looking at the Reformation, he starts with the earliest of the Deists, Lord Herbert of Cherbury (1582-1648). He was English ambassador to the court of Louis XIII, after study at Oxford. He wrote to defend the central idea of "one natural religion, valid for all men," in contrast to the Christian God.[37] All men by nature are given the capacity for reasonable knowledge and judgment. They need not depend on some particular faith.

Reventlow next considers Thomas Hobbes (1585-1679). From 1640 to 1653 Hobbes was in exile, where he published *The Leviathan.* In his political philosophy he based ethics upon the natural capacities of humankind. "God" was unnecessary for ethics. Hobbes was a complex thinker.

The Latitudinarians in England, Reventlow argues, were heirs to the

---

37. Henning Graf Reventlow, *The Authority of the Bible and the Rise of the Modern World,* trans. John Bowden (London: SCM, 1984), p. 189.

Cambridge Platonists. With the Quakers, they were in tune with the laissez-faire ethos of 1688.[38] While they were nominally Anglican, they attacked all church doctrine as too narrowing. Human consciences are to be left free. Both movements hastened the drift away from any appeal to particular authorities. Allegedly they found roots in John Locke. But Locke believed in reasonableness, not in rationalism.

Reventlow next discusses the Deist debate. Here John Toland and his book *Christianity Not Mysterious* were influential. In his book Toland argued, like Descartes, "Reason is the only foundation of all Certitude. . . . Nothing Revealed . . . is exempted."[39] Next, Reventlow points out the effect of Sir Isaac Newton, even though Newton himself was a devout Christian or perhaps Unitarian. With his predecessors Robert Boyle and Francis Bacon, Newton left the idea that the world was like a machine created by God. The universe itself expressed God's total providence. There is no need for special interventions (miracles) to mend the perfect machine. In the heyday of Deism, God was seen as an absentee God who left the universe and humankind running "on their own." They had no need of a miraculous providence.

Deism and rationalism extended to the end of the seventeenth century and into the eighteenth. In 1698 Matthew Tindal (1653-1733) published *The Liberty of the Press* as a "Christian" Deist. He believed that the state should control the Church in matters of public communication. Anthony Collins (1676-1729) continued the Enlightenment and Deist approach by attacking arguments from miracle or prophecy in his *Discourse on Free Thinking* in 1713. Gottfried W. Leibniz (1646-1716) perpetuated Descartes's *rationalism* in his *Essays on Theodicy* (1710) and in *The Monadology* (1714). These aimed at a philosophy of self-identity and were individualistic. Christian Wolff accelerated the Enlightenment ethos in his *Rational Thoughts concerning God, the World, the Human Soul, and All Things* (1720). Tindal published his Deist *Christianity as Old as Creation* in 1730. Then Thomas Chubb (1679-1746) wrote *A Discourse concerning Reason* in 1731, in which he attacked prayer, prophecy, and miracle. In a similar but perhaps broader tradition, Joseph Butler (1692-1752) argued for the limits of reason in *The Analogy of Religion* (1736). Then David Hume published his *Treatise on Human Nature* in 1739-40, which was a skeptical work and also expressed doubt about miracles.

A further phase of Enlightenment thought began with Hume's later

---

38. Reventlow, *Authority*, p. 224; cf. pp. 223-85.
39. Reventlow, *Authority*, p. 297; cf. pp. 294-327.

works and Voltaire's *Philosophical Dictionary,* which spanned 1694-1778. It attacked the Church and questioned all authority. Jean-Jacques Rousseau (1712-78) published his *Social Contract* in 1762. This saw human "rights" as depending entirely on convention. The impact of the Enlightenment on biblical studies and theology can be seen in the work of G. E. Lessing, the anonymous *Wolfenbüttel Fragments,* later to be known as the work of Reimarus (1777-78). Most of all, the work of Johann S. Semler constituted a turning point. The three philosophical *Critiques* of Kant (second editions published in 1787, 1788, and 1790) had profound implications for theology. The climax was the French Revolution of 1789. Some might add the American Declaration of Independence in 1776, with its "self-evident" truths.

Kant defined the Enlightenment well, in 1784. It is the liberating "exodus from self-incurred immaturity, from inability to use one's understanding without the tutelage of another person." The Enlightenment person is self-sufficient, autonomous, and free. As we might expect, this had severe consequences for how one went about biblical interpretation. Many, but not all, saw freedom and objectivity as the key to biblical studies. Recently Mark Bowald has argued that this led to omitting in practice reference to God as the author of Scripture (see chapter XVII).[40] His general thesis is correct in its application to much, but not all, biblical criticism. The problem is more complex than his "solution" allows, but his general point is valid. I wish he had discussed Enlightenment thought and the rise of biblical criticism instead of focusing on philosophy and on Kant.

The Enlightenment did not submerge all Christian religion at the time. Pietism continued with William Law (1686-1761), John Wesley, and Jonathan Edwards (1703-58), among others. But they were in the minority, almost like protests. The next major step forward in hermeneutics was by Hegel and Schleiermacher in the nineteenth century.

4. The Rise of Biblical Criticism in the Eighteenth Century

The father of biblical criticism was arguably Johann S. Semler. But prior to his work two other candidates sometimes claim this title, although their contributions were by no means epoch making. Richard Simon (1638-1712)

---

40. Mark A. Bowald, *Rendering the Word in Theological Hermeneutics* (Aldershot and Burlington, Vt.: Ashgate, 2007), especially pp. 1-23 and 163-83.

was a loyal Catholic, a biblical scholar, and a member of the French oratory. He produced a work on the Pentateuch in 1678, arguing that two traditions in these books were so incompatible as to suggest that Moses could not have been their author. His aim was to undermine Protestant dependence on the Bible, but he was expelled from the French oratory for his views.

Jean Astruc (1684-1766) is the other candidate. He accepted Baruch Spinoza's contention that the books of the Bible were not necessarily a literary unity. In 1753 he applied this to Genesis and argued that two sources here had been conflated in a later edition. He called his book *Conjectures on the Original Material* and argued that Moses was the proto-author of one of the traditions before they were conflated. In particular, he noted the different names for God (*Elohim* in the "E" tradition; *Jahweh* in the "J" tradition). Thus he pioneered one axiom of much biblical criticism.

1. *J. S. Semler,* however, is the real founder of biblical criticism. Initially he was a Lutheran, and was appointed professor of theology in the University of Halle. He did not react well to Zinzendorf's Pietist groups at Halle. He argued that the text and canon of the Bible owed their origin entirely to *historical* factors and conditions, and disregarded arguments about divine inspiration or doctrine. Here is the direct effect of the Enlightenment. Certainly he argued against the extreme skepticism of G. E. Lessing and H. S. Reimarus. But his exegesis excluded theological factors, and in 1771-75 he published *A Treatise on the Free Investigation of the Canon* (in four volumes) arguing for *exclusively historical* factors in its formation.[41]

Predictably Semler rejected the fourfold sense of Scripture and the use of allegorical interpretation. He also rejected attempts to find allusions to Christ in the Psalms. He was close to what today is known as the history-of-religions perspective. He also pursued New Testament textual criticism ruthlessly to the exclusion of certain texts. In spite of his desire for "free" inquiry, he believed in some form of divine inspiration of the Bible but rejected "verbal" inspiration. He believed in the notion of "accommodation" of the Bible, or its revealed truth, to what ancient humankind could understand. He retained Lutheran doctrine in broad terms but argued that Lutheranism "leveled down" the variety and distinctive genre and traditions of the Bible. Semler emphasized in exegesis the understanding of the biblical writer in his historical situation and language in accordance with its "demonstrable use."

41. Johann S. Semler, *Abhandlung von freier Untersuchung des Canons,* 4 vols. (Halle: C. H. Hemmerde, 1771-75; 2nd ed. of vol. 1, 1776).

So committed was Semler to the historical meaning apart from theology that some thought he separated the Old Testament or the Hebrew Bible from the New Testament as the foundation for the Christian religion. He resisted the imposing of dogmatic theology on biblical exegesis and interpretation. Many have viewed Semler as a rationalist and a Deist, but he publicly criticized Deism and did assert the supernatural correlation of God in Christ. But as a *method of approach,* he emphasized historical factors alone, and thus decisively influenced biblical studies in what are called historical-critical methods.

2. *Johann August Ernesti* (1707-81) entered the University of Wittenberg and then moved to Leipzig. He became professor at Leipzig in 1756. He combined classics with the philosophy of Wolff, and stressed the grammatical and historical exegesis of the Bible. In his major book on the interpretation of the New Testament (1761) he argued that nonrational factors should be excluded. He argued for one single meaning of the text. He approached exegesis as a linguist and philologist, but in the distinct task of interpretation he argued that the Bible did not contradict itself. If it appears to do so, we must appeal to clearer passages.

Ernesti contributed to the supposed objectivity of biblical criticism but retained his theist faith. He had enormous influence on the eighteenth century, and is today remembered for his controversy with J. S. Bach. He reminds us of the pluriformity of methods in biblical criticism in his differences from Semler.

3. *Johann David Michaelis* (1717-91) was born into a Pietist family at Halle, and entered the University of Halle to study Hebrew, Aramaic, Arabic, and Ethiopic. In 1741 he traveled to England and formed a bridge between English and German scholarship. But his contact with English Deism led him to abandon Pietism in favor of the rationalist Protestant orthodoxy, which he found in Holland. In 1750 he became professor of Oriental languages at Göttingen. As also a privy councillor, he had much influence over the church and state of Hanover.

Michaelis attempted to shed light on the Bible through sources outside the Bible, especially Arabic material. He used not only cognate forms in the Arabic language but also Arabic customs to shed light on the literature of ancient Israel. In 1770-75 he wrote his *Commentaries on the Laws of Moses* in four volumes.[42] Michaelis argued, with the Deists in England, that these laws

---

42. Johann D. Michaelis, *Commentaries on the Laws of Moses,* trans. A. Smith, 4 vols. (Göttingen: Vandenhoeck & Ruprecht, 1814).

were not authoritative for all of life, but he defended their Mosaic author-ship. In his *Introduction to the Divine Scriptures of the New Testament* he re-jected the customary view of divine inspiration and the criterion of apos-tolic authorship for the New Testament canon. On the Gospels, for example, he believed that Matthew and John were apostolic but that Mark and Luke were not, although they still held a place within the Christian canon.

4. *Gotthold Ephraim Lessing* (1729-81) was a leading figure of the En-lightenment. He is mainly known today for overseeing the publication of H. S. Reimarus's *Wolfenbüttel Fragments,* which first appeared anonymously. In his book *Nathan the Wise* he portrayed religion as in effect man-made morality. In a now famous aphorism he argued that "The accidental truths of history can never become the proof of necessary truths of reason." In other words, he saw rational truth as eternal but historical truth as temporal and contingent. He placed "a broad ugly ditch" between the two, and dis-missed the historical claims of Christianity. On biblical studies, Lessing took up the notion that an Aramaic original lay behind Matthew, and that Mark and Luke supplemented it (1788).

Reimarus portrayed Jesus as a teacher of rational truths, which were dis-torted by apocalyptic expectations. But Jesus did require repentance. The simple teaching of Jesus was soon "corrupted" by doctrine (a theme Harnack and the liberals would later elaborate).[43] The Deists, Reimarus be-lieved, were right about natural religion and reason. "Jesus taught no new mysteries or articles of faith."[44] He believed that the Gospels contained seri-ous inconsistencies and that the disciples of Jesus were mistaken about the resurrection. Reimarus claimed there were no miracles or mysteries in Jesus' life; his death was a natural event; and his resurrection was falsified as his disciples tried to deceive the world into believing it.[45] Events were often con-trived to fit Old Testament prophecies. J. S. Semler wrote against these claims, which again demonstrates the plurality of biblical critical methods. But aspects of Lessing's thought are still promoted today.

5. *Johann Gottfried Eichhorn* (1752-1827). We might next have included Johann G. Herder (1744-1803), although Herder was not a rationalist but a Romanticist ahead of his time. He saw the teachings of Zoroaster as a sup-

---

43. *Reimarus: Fragments,* ed. Charles H. Tolbert, trans. R. S. Fraser (London: SCM, 1981), pp. 61-134 (sections 1-33).

44. *Reimarus,* p. 72.

45. *Reimarus,* pp. 240-69 (sections 55-60).

posed key to the New Testament and emphasized poetic literature within the Bible. J. G. Eichhorn is better known as one of the earliest writers on "introduction" to the Bible, including questions of the authorship, date, genre, and historical situation of its respective books. He succeeded Michaelis as professor at Göttingen in 1788.

At Göttingen Eichhorn taught Old and New Testament, Semitic languages, and the history of literature. He was a "neologist," or, in other words, he broadly accepted divine inspiration and revelation in the Bible but argued that plain reason was sufficient for interpreting it. He emphasized the "mythological" nature of the early chapters of Genesis. Like Herder, he understood these narratives as pictorial forms stemming from the childhood of humankind. Adam and Eve's flight from Eden was due to a thunderstorm, not to the intervention of God. A talking snake is a naive pictorial form, or myth. Eichhorn extended Michaelis's notion of a primitive Aramaic source lying behind Matthew, Mark, and Luke. He also derived from Jean Astruc the notion of sources lying behind the Genesis narrative.

6. *Johann Jakob Griesbach* (1748-1812) taught New Testament and church history at Jena. He was primarily a textual critic, initially following Bengel. He distinguished an Alexandrian, Western, and Byzantine tradition. He published a Greek Testament in which the *Textus Receptus* was abandoned in Germany for the first time. This text too uncritically followed Beza's early reading. He is most noted for his theory of the Synoptic Gospels that Mark was not the first Gospel; it followed Matthew and Luke. Most scholars today would dissent from this view, although it has been recently reviewed by W. R. Farmer. Again, Griesbach rejected interpretations of the Bible based on dogmatic theology rather than on historical interpretation of the text. But in his faith he seems to have remained an orthodox Christian.

7. *Johann P. Gabler* (1753-1826) concludes our survey of mainly eighteenth-century biblical critics. Gabler came under the influence of Eichhorn and Griesbach. He became professor of theology at Altdorf. He tried to establish "biblical theology" as a historical genre (after Semler), but one that forms the basis for dogmatic theology. Each biblical writer must be considered in relation to his time and place. Lessing's "ugly ditch" needs to be overcome. Doctrine is historically contingent on time and place. The theology of the Bible in its time and place is "true" *(wahr)* biblical theology; "pure" *(rein)* biblical theology is not conditioned by time and place, but is abstracted from "true" biblical theology. Gabler is perhaps furthest from the Enlightenment among the seven we have considered, but the idea of a "uni-

versal," pure biblical theology still derives from historical inquiry only. On specific biblical passages, there is still a tendency to exclude the so-called supernatural. Some accuse him of combining precritical and critical method. With Eichhorn, he is usually called a neologist. With Eichhorn he also developed a "mythical" approach to the Old Testament.[46]

5. Ten Leaders of Biblical Criticism in the Nineteenth Century

1. *Wilhelm M. L. De Wette* (1780-1849) deserves pride of place in founding a new epoch in biblical criticism in the nineteenth century. He was not the first to argue that the Pentateuch had origins much later than Moses. But he was the first to postulate an entirely new "critical" account of the development of Israel's history and religion by a careful reconstruction of Samuel and Kings.[47] He regarded Chronicles as secondary. He argued that Leviticus and Levitical practices were projected back from the postexilic period, and entirely recast the understanding of Israel's development and history.

De Wette dated the origin of Deuteronomy with Josiah's reform in 621 B.C. On the Psalms he stressed the variety of their genre and their respective settings. With Hermann Gunkel this would develop into the beginning of form criticism. He saw much of the priestly postexilic developments as a "decline" from the purity of prophetic religion. On the New Testament he distinguished three separate, sometimes conflicting theological traditions: the early Jewish-Christian, Pauline theology, and the Alexandrian represented by John and Hebrews. The book of Numbers is supposedly "mythical" or unhistorical.

De Wette was a colleague of Schleiermacher in the University of Berlin. But he left it to Schleiermacher to provide a milestone in hermeneutics. He had changed the face of biblical criticism. Once he came close to equating religion with morality, but he declared that the very variety of the biblical witness gave him new spiritual life and respect for Israel's identity as the people of God.[48] With the thinkers of the Enlightenment, he no longer saw history as the unfolding of the purposes of God.

---

46. John Rogerson, *Old Testament Criticism in the Nineteenth Century: England and Germany* (London: SPCK, 1984), p. 17.

47. Cf. Rogerson, *Old Testament Criticism,* pp. 29-30 and 34.

48. Cf. Rogerson, *Old Testament Criticism,* pp. 39-44.

2. *William Vatke* (1806-82) consciously drew on the view of historical development found in Hegel to sharpen De Wette's contrast, or antithesis, between a prophetic view of society and the cultic and liturgical system of postexile Judaism. His main critical influences were De Wette and Gesenius. He published his *Biblical Theology* in 1835, and collaborated also with David F. Strauss.

3. *Karl Lachmann* (1793-1851) was a philologist and textual critic. He became professor of classical and German philology in the University of Berlin, where he worked with Schleiermacher during his last years. He published two editions of the Greek Testament, in 1831 and 1842-50 (two volumes). Like Griesbach, he rejected the *Textus Receptus,* which followed Beza, but against Griesbach saw Mark as earliest of the first three Gospel writers.

4. *Opposition: Ernst Wilhelm Hengstenberg* (1802-69). We should not give the impression that biblical criticism swept the board without challenge, even in Germany. Hengstenberg became professor of biblical exegesis at the University of Berlin and attacked the theology of Schleiermacher and critical scholarship. Yet Rogerson comments, "Representatives of the 'new criticism' were not straightforwardly descended from the rationalists. . . . Confessional orthodox scholars were not straightforwardly descended from the supernaturalists. . . . Both had their roots in the Enlightenment."[49] Hengstenberg opposed the "critical school" with great learning and wrote a number of commentaries, which are still used by some today.

Hengstenberg had considerable influence, and the translation of his work into English awakened the English-speaking world to the controversy about biblical criticism. His best-known work is *The Christology of the Old Testament,* although his *Commentary on the Psalms* and other works are used today.[50] He argued that rationalism is the enemy of the Church.

5. *David Friedrich Strauss* (1808-74). In his earliest years Strauss was a disciple of Hegel and worked under F. C. Baur. In 1835 he became famous or notorious for his *Life of Jesus.*[51] As well as looking to Heyne, he borrowed Hegel's distinction between "representations" in religion and "critical concepts" *(Vorstellungen)* in philosophy. He argued that the Gospels were largely

---

49. Rogerson, *Old Testament Criticism,* p. 79.

50. Ernst W. Hengstenberg, *The Christology of the Old Testament* (Edinburgh: T. & T. Clark, 1854-58); Hengstenberg, *Commentary on the Psalms,* 2nd ed. (Edinburgh: T. & T. Clark, 1849-52).

51. David F. Strauss, *The Life of Jesus Critically Examined,* trans. and ed. P. C. Hodgson (Philadelphia: Fortress; London: SCM, 1973).

mythical, not historical. *Myths are ideas presented in the form of narrative.* Miracles and the supernatural are abandoned.[52] His quasi materialism in contrast to Hegel's view of "Spirit" *(Geist)* led to his being categorized with Feuerbach as a left-wing Hegelian.

Strauss produced further revised editions of his *Life of Jesus*. The third edition (1838-39) was followed by a fourth (1840), and a final fifth (1864). George Eliot translated the fourth edition into English. Eventually Strauss abandoned Christianity and attacked Schleiermacher for producing the supposedly last "churchly" theology. His book was criticized on all sides, even by Baur and Nietzsche, but was popular in its day. His denial of faith appeared in his *Old Faith and the New* in 1872.

6. *Ferdinand Christian Baur* (1792-1860). Baur wrote "The Party of Christ in the Church at Corinth: The Opposition between Petrine and Pauline Christianity" in 1831. He examined Paul's analysis of the *schismata* (divisions) in 1 Corinthians 1:11-13 and postulated a division in the early Church between the Petrine and Pauline "parties." Since that time J. Munck has shown that the *schismata* were not "parties" representing different doctrines, and some writers even regard the name involved as hypothetical. But Baur gave an account of development of the earliest Church on this basis.

In 1835 Baur expressed doubt about the Pauline authorship of the Pastoral Epistles and disputed the reliability of parts of Acts. Acts represented a "Catholic" attempt to smooth over differences between the Petrine and Pauline traditions. In 1853 he viewed only the four "major" Pauline Epistles as genuine (Romans, 1 and 2 Corinthians, and Galatians), and viewed Matthew as the first of the Gospels, and John as late. Although he attacked Strauss as a historian, Baur recognized only historical and sociological factors in the development of the New Testament Church.

7. *Benjamin Jowett* (1817-93). In England few perhaps lived up to the rigor of nineteenth-century German scholarship. There were two or three exceptions. Jowett was appointed Regius Professor of Greek in the University of Oxford in 1855. Although he had reservations about more radical biblical criticism, he contributed the essay "On the Interpretation of Scripture" to *Essays and Reviews* (1860), in which he argued that the Bible should be interpreted "like any other book." He became a central figure in the liberal "broad church" party in the Church of England.

---

52. Hans Frei, "David Friedrich Strauss," in *Nineteenth Century Religious Thought in the West,* ed. Ninian Smart et al. (Cambridge: Cambridge University Press, 1985), 1:215-60.

8. *Charles Gore* (1853-1932) became, successively, bishop of Worcester, Birmingham, and Oxford. He was educated at Oxford, mainly in Hebrew, and became highly influential. He represented liberal Anglo-Catholicism, and in 1889 edited *Lux Mundi,* which was meant to maintain High Church traditions while giving an approving nod in the direction of biblical criticism. Gore accepted the idea of development, or "progressive" revelation, and his work on the Holy Spirit and inspiration found a controversial reception. He viewed the history of the patriarchs as "idealized" and believed that Jesus was mistaken in some of his teaching.

9. *Julius Wellhausen* (1844-1918) was professor at Marburg in 1885. He remained a committed Christian, but he followed De Wette in his criticism of the Pentateuch. He is widely known for his classification of Priestly documents as "P," his close analysis of the Jahweh ("J") and Elohim ("E") traditions, and his recognition of the Deuteronomic as "D." This has remained the stock-in-trade of the Old Testament studies until recently. In the New Testament he held to the priority of Mark. He built largely on the work of De Wette.

10. *Brooke Foss Westcott* (1825-1901), *Joseph Barber Lightfoot* (1828-89), and *Fenton John Anthony Hort* (1828-92) are often grouped together as "the Cambridge Triumvirate."[53] Westcott went to Trinity College, Cambridge, where he became instructor to Lightfoot and Hort, and the three became lifelong friends. From 1870 to 1890 Westcott was Regius Professor of Divinity at Cambridge. In 1890 he succeeded Lightfoot as bishop of Durham. Lightfoot was appointed Hulsean Professor of Divinity (1861) in the University of Cambridge. In 1875 he became Lady Margaret's Professor of Divinity, and bishop of Durham in 1879. Hort became Hulsean Professor in 1878, and Lady Margaret's Professor. The three were clearly devout servants of the Church, and ordained members of the Church of England.

Westcott wrote commentaries on the Greek text of the Epistles and the Gospel of John. He addressed the minutest points of the construction and language of the text. He also seriously discussed the question of authorship, and the usual questions that come in an introduction. He also spent "many years of continuous labour" writing his commentary on Hebrews. He examined its textual, historical, linguistic, and theological details. He provided an excellent exposition of Christ as high priest and explored the Christology of the epistle.

---

53. William Baird, *History of New Testament Research,* 3 vols., vol. 2, *Jonathan Edwards to Rudolf Bultmann* (Minneapolis: Fortress, 2003), p. 60.

Lightfoot wrote several commentaries on the Pauline Epistles, again almost entirely on the Greek text. These included Galatians and Philippians, with extended notes on points of interest, including Paul's apostleship and his conversion in Galatians 1:15-17, and the ministry of the early Church in Philippians (1868). Against a more Catholic view Lightfoot insisted that every Christian is a priest of God. To Hort "the Triumvirate" assigned the Synoptic Gospels and Catholic Epistles. He produced fragments on 1 Peter, James, and Revelation, but he was dogged with poor health. Westcott and Hort also made significant contributions to New Testament textual criticism. In 1881 this culminated in the Revised Version.

Baird rightly states that these three were "giants in their own right — equal in stature to the tallest of the Germans. Moreover these British scholars were servants of the Church, dedicated to the advance of the Bible for faith and life."[54] They understood the importance of biblical research for Christian theology and refused to separate the two. Their important example prohibits any generalized comment about "biblical criticism," or "*the* historical-critical method," as if there were only one.

6. Recommended Initial Reading

Grant, Robert M., *A Short History of the Interpretation of the Bible,* rev. ed. (London: Black, 1965), pp. 102-32.

Greenslade, S. L., ed., *The Cambridge History of the Bible,* vol. 3, *The West from the Reformation to the Present Day* (Cambridge: Cambridge University Press, 1963), pp. 1-93 and 199-338.

McKim, Donald K., ed., *Dictionary of Major Biblical Interpreters* (Downers Grove, Ill., and Nottingham: IVP, 2007), articles on the names considered in this chapter.

---

54. Baird, *History,* 2:933.

CHAPTER VIII

Schleiermacher and Dilthey

Friedrich D. E. Schleiermacher (1768-1834) remains one of the greatest philo-sophical theologians of the nineteenth century, with Georg W. F. Hegel and perhaps Søren Kierkegaard. Schleiermacher has been called "the founder of modern hermeneutics" and "the father of modern Protestant theology."[1] He was born in Breslau, to a father who was pastor to the army in Prussia. His initial education was among the Moravians (or Pietists), first at Nierke and then at Barby near Halle, Germany. When he was sixteen he wrote, in accor-dance with his Pietism, of "Christ my Saviour." From the first, he wanted to become a preacher, as his "proper office."

Schleiermacher became chaplain to the Charité Hospital in Berlin in 1796. He next taught in the University of Halle as professor in 1804. He was heavily involved in the founding of the University of Berlin in 1810. He be-came professor of theology there, where he remained until his death, while serving as pastor with a ministry every Sunday at Trinity Church, Berlin, to which he was appointed in 1809. In his early years Schleiermacher longed for a broader education than he had received from the Pietist Moravians and at his theological college. With the reluctant agreement of his father, he entered the University of Halle. There he delighted in the scholarship of the Enlightenment. He neglected the Old Testament but read widely in philosophical theology and philosophy, especially Kant, Lessing, and Hume. He valued Kant's *transcendental* philosophy (not only

---

1. David E. Klemm, *Hermeneutical Inquiry*, vol. 1, *The Interpretation of Texts* (Atlanta: Scholars Press, 1986), p. 55, and Kurt Mueller-Vollmer, ed., *The Hermeneutics Reader* (Ox-ford: Blackwell, 1985), p. 72.

how we know, but also how knowledge is *possible* at all). He also valued Kant's work on the limits of reason and Kierkegaard's notion of "subjectivity" as personal involvement.

On one side, Barth wrote of Schleiermacher, "It is here [in preaching] that we must seek . . . the centre of his work. . . . Preaching to the congregation to awaken faith was by far the sweetest desire of his life."[2] Yet on the other side Schleiermacher hated the perceived narrowness of his conservative Pietist Moravian youth. He believed that no good could come from forcing one's ideas on other people.[3] Preaching a good sermon is like "striking up the music," or awaking "the slumbering spark."[4] He abandoned some of his more conservative beliefs but always insisted that "God-consciousness" and a personal, direct relationship with Jesus Christ are the essence of Christianity.[5] Hence he welcomed the Enlightenment and biblical criticism, and called himself a "Pietist of a Higher Order." In other words, he believed in utter dependence on God and personal relation with Christ, but he also welcomed exploring the *transcendental possibility* of theology, the Enlightenment, and biblical criticism.[6]

1. Influences, Career, and Major Works

Schleiermacher provides a great turning point in hermeneutics, comparable only with Gadamer's second great turning point in the second half of the twentieth century. Schleiermacher defines hermeneutics not as "rules of interpretation" but as "the art of understanding" or "the doctrine of understanding."[7]

2. Karl Barth, *The Theology of Schleiermacher: Lectures at Göttingen, 1923-24*, trans. G. W. Bromiley (Grand Rapids: Eerdmans, 1982), p. xiii. Cf. also Claude Welch, *Protestant Thought in the Nineteenth Century*, 2 vols. (New Haven and London: Yale University Press, 1972, 1985), 1:59-60.

3. Friedrich D. E. Schleiermacher, *On Religion: Speeches to Its Cultured Despisers*, trans. John Oman (reprint, New York: Harper and Row, 1959), p. 119.

4. Schleiermacher, *On Religion*, pp. 119-20.

5. Friedrich D. E. Schleiermacher, *The Christian Faith*, trans. H. R. Mackintosh and J. S. Stewart (Edinburgh: T. & T. Clark, 1931; reprint, 1989), pp. 355-475.

6. Schleiermacher, *The Christian Faith*, p. 12.

7. Friedrich D. E. Schleiermacher, *Hermeneutics: The Handwritten Manuscripts*, ed. Heinz Kimmerle, trans. James Duke and Jack Forstman (Missoula: Scholars Press, 1977), pp. 35-79 and 113.

1. Schleiermacher fell partly under the influence of the *Romanticist* movement. He stressed the "divinatory" *(divinatorisch)* and the "feminine" or suprarational in hermeneutics. He had strong reservations about "pure" Romanticism. On the other hand, he did not go all the way with Friedrich Schlegel in his Romanticism, although he shared rooms with him in Berlin around 1797. Rudolf Otto admittedly calls his work a "veritable manifesto of the Romantics," but Martin Redeker insists that we should not overestimate the influence of the Romantics.[8] Schleiermacher's Romanticism was strong but not decisive. Gadamer stresses his Romanticism when he criticizes Schleiermacher, as we see in chapter XI. Certainly Schleiermacher resisted "analysis," which is more scientific and often mechanistic as a way of explaining things. One can take a machine to bits and put it together again. But one cannot take a living butterfly to bits and put it back together as a living, organic entity.

In this respect Schleiermacher comes close to the English poet William Wordsworth. In 1798 Wordsworth wrote, "We murder to dissect." He also wrote, "Our meddling intellect mis-shapes the beauteous form of things." The *mechanistic* model of Deism and the rationalism of the eighteenth century were giving way to the *organic* model of the nineteenth century. Wordsworth claimed that analytic industry sees only difference, while we need a vision of the whole. Yet we also need scientific scholarship, which the Enlightenment seemed to promise. In this respect, Schleiermacher did not go the whole way with Romanticism.

2. Away from his theological college and in the University of Halle, Schleiermacher felt he could breathe and reach his own conclusions without constraint. Moravian piety, inherited from Count Zinzendorf, was hostile to the new biblical criticism. The German tradition was often called *Pietism;* while in England it was more readily associated with the Wesleys, or sometimes with the Quakers, who were not well disposed toward doctrine. At best it represented a religion of the heart, less one of the head. Schleiermacher welcomed its concern for a personal relationship with God through Christ, in spite of his greater concern for intellectual integrity, Kant, and biblical criticism.

Schleiermacher delighted in the intellectual, without wishing to renounce all his Pietism. G. P. Fisher and B. A. Gerrish therefore called him in

---

8. Martin Redeker, *Schleiermacher's Life and Thoughts* (Philadelphia: Fortress, 1973), p. 61.

modern terms "a liberal evangelical."[9] Whether he paid enough attention to human sin and to the Old Testament to merit the term "evangelical" may remain open to question. But Schleiermacher was "liberal" and certainly not Catholic. "Being in a relationship with God" always remained important to him.[10] Whereas the Enlightenment and Kant had defended human independence, and "autonomy" was the mark of human adulthood, Schleiermacher believed that the sense of utter dependence on God was the hallmark of all true religion.

3. The third important influence upon Schleiermacher was the philosophy of Immanuel Kant (1724-1804). Kant's critical philosophy formed a watershed in the history of philosophy. He moved beyond both rationalism and empiricism. In their place he expounded a *transcendental critical philosophy,* namely, thinking that addressed the very ground and very possibility of philosophy. Kant appreciated the difficulties that Leibniz faced and respected Hume's arguments, although he rejected his skepticism. Did they expect too much of human reason? What were the basis and limits of reason? In 1781 Kant published *The Critique of Pure Reason;* in 1788, *The Critique of Practical Reason;* and in 1790, *The Critique of Judgement.*[11] All addressed different aspects of this question.

Schleiermacher worked not only on theology but also on the possibility of theology; not only on hermeneutics but also on the possibility of understanding at all. Kant's philosophy required new thinking in theology. Kant had tried to define the very limits of reason; Schleiermacher put "immediacy" in the place of reason, or rather immediacy constituted the creative role of understanding, while reason provided a check on what immediate experience had understood or discovered. Kant argued that what the mind brings to it largely defines what we count as "experience." Schleiermacher agreed with this, but also added the missing factor of the immediacy of whatever we feel. It would not do him justice to reduce this to mere "feeling" in the psychological sense, rather than in a more ontological sense.[12]

4. In his *Speeches on Religion* in 1799, his very early work, Schleiermacher

---

9. B. A. Gerrish, *A Prince of the Church: Schleiermacher and the Beginning of Modern Theology* (London: SCM, 1984), pp. 18-20.

10. Schleiermacher, *The Christian Faith,* p. 12.

11. See Anthony C. Thiselton, *A Concise Encyclopaedia of the Philosophy of Religion* (Oxford: Oneworld, 2002; Grand Rapids: Baker Academic, 2003), pp. 155-59.

12. John Macquarrie, *Studies in Christian Existentialism* (London: SCM, 1965), pp. 31-44.

wrote that "true religion is sense and taste for the infinite."[13] He declared, "Piety cannot be an instinct craving for a mess of metaphysical and ethical crumbs."[14] At one extreme Schleiermacher almost identifies the Christian religion with culture; at the other extreme he berates the "cultural despisers" of religion for making judgments without consulting the "experts" in religion, namely, the pastors, priests, and theologians. "Yet religion is not knowledge and sciences."[15] He prepares the ground, in effect, for reconciling the Enlightenment with Reformation religion.

5. In 1800 Schleiermacher wrote his *Monologues (The Soliloquies)*, and in 1805 began his *Notes* on hermeneutics, which led in 1809-10 to his *Hermeneutics*, later edited by Heinz Kimmerle.[16] These became lecture notes delivered in the University of Berlin. Shortly afterward he published his delightful long essay *Christmas Eve: A Dialogue on the Incarnation*, in 1812. This contributes to his hermeneutics, explaining what he means by "the comparative (masculine)" and "the divinatory (feminine)."[17] Schleiermacher taught an impressive array of subjects: almost everything except the Old Testament. He was not primarily a biblical scholar, but believed wholeheartedly in the importance of the new discipline of "New Testament introduction," which he taught, and believed would fire students to new practical heights of preaching the New Testament. He had produced a book entitled *Philosophical Ethics*, and around 1811 produced his *Brief Outline on the Study of Theology* (published in 1830) as a new syllabus for students. Then in 1821 he published his greatest work, *The Christian Faith* (2nd ed. 1830-31). This is one of the classics of Christian theology, which has been compared even to Calvin's *Institutes* in importance for the history of thought.

Schleiermacher's great rival in the University of Berlin was Hegel. They held opposite views on the purpose of theology. Hegel saw theology as addressing intellectual curiosity; Schleiermacher saw it as training for professional clergy and for preaching.

Schleiermacher fell under the influence, then, of at least five factors: an

---

13. Schleiermacher, *On Religion*, p. 39.

14. Schleiermacher, *On Religion*, p. 31.

15. Schleiermacher, *On Religion*, p. 36.

16. Schleiermacher, *Hermeneutics*.

17. Schleiermacher, *Hermeneutics*, pp. 150-51; also Friedrich D. E. Schleiermacher, "Die Weihnachtsfeier: Ein Gespräch," in *Werke*, vol. 4 (Aalen: Scientia Verlag, 1967; from the 2nd ed., Leipzig, 1928), also *Christmas Eve: A Dialogue on the Incarnation*, trans. T. N. Tice (Richmond, Va.: John Knox, 1967), throughout.

upbringing among the devout Moravians; his Romanticism; openness to Enlightenment scholarship; the philosophy of Kant; and hermeneutics. But in each area he was not uncritical of what he inherited without modification or change. He strongly criticized the work of predecessors in all five fields. But his genius was not to reject them, but to think beyond them, and to combine them in creative ways.

2. Schleiermacher's New Conception of Hermeneutics

Hitherto, Schleiermacher claims, hermeneutics consisted of *"rules"* for the interpretation of Scripture. These rules were invoked largely *to support* understanding at which people had *already* arrived. They were not to create and initiate understanding. Schleiermacher writes, "Hermeneutics is part of the art of thinking."[18] This is the newer view of hermeneutics found in most modern universities, and becomes a turning point in the subject.

This immediately combines philosophical and biblical hermeneutics. On one side, Schleiermacher insists that in all texts, including biblical texts, "the art of understanding" needs to embrace how "the first readers could understand [the texts]" (p. 107). He insists, "Only historical interpretation can do justice to the rootedness of the New Testament authors in their time and place" (p. 104). But on the other hand, "Previous treatments of hermeneutics presuppose an ordinary level of understanding, an understanding that does not require art until it encounters something that does not make sense" (p. 49). Hermeneutics has therefore become also philosophical, not simply philological. The interpreter "should not begin solely with difficult passages, but should deal with easy ones" (p. 142; see also p. 97).

In his two *Academy Addresses* of 1829, Schleiermacher considers F. A. Wolf's hermeneutics and Ast's textbook on hermeneutics. He respects their philological work and recognizes that Friedrich Ast even reached a first, partial formulation of the hermeneutical circle, which we explained in chapter I, section 4. But Wolf and Ast still remain "scientific" (p. 179). They must also examine "the author's way of combining thoughts" (p. 188). They must "divine" the whole. This involves studying ideas. "In the sphere of artistic production," Schleiermacher insists, "I take this generally to include the poet

---

18. Schleiermacher, *Hermeneutics,* p. 97. Parenthetical page references in the following text are to this work.

and . . . even the philosopher as well as the artist" (p. 205). We must examine the author's "way of thinking" (p. 207). We must "be able to step out of one's own frame of view" (p. 42).

We are not just seeking "meaning." Although the point has not been widely noted, Schleiermacher insisted that the interpreter must also pay close attention to the *effects* of text, to what they set going, as well as "how a way of speaking originated" (p. 47). We must consider "the content of the text and its range of effects" (p. 151). This is sometimes called "the aim of the work" (p. 151). Schleiermacher distinguishes between the sense of a work and its "purport," in other words, what it does (p. 117). This distinction is not that of E. Hirsch's difference between meaning and significance.

Thus Palmer's notion that Schleiermacher's aim of historical reconstruction as "the reverse of composition" is helpful up to a point, but leaves much unsaid.[19] Palmer is virtually quoting Schleiermacher: "It [interpretation] is the reverse of composition."[20] But does this include the author's aim, which is more than historical reconstruction but has effects? Schleiermacher's concept of hermeneutics also includes what is common between the author and the reader. What is understood is what is held in common between the author and the reader. Understanding means "to put oneself in the position of an author."[21]

It may be difficult for us to realize that hermeneutics before Schleiermacher was so largely or even exclusively philological. To be sure, this was in part the effect of the Enlightenment. Patristic and Reformation interpretation was perhaps broader, but none had put the matter in quite the same way as Schleiermacher. Karl Barth was an opponent of his liberal emphasis on subjective experience, but he acknowledges, "He did not found a school, but an era," words originally used of Frederick the Great.[22] Barth makes the further comment: "He will in fact live for every age."[23]

---

19. Richard E. Palmer, *Hermeneutics: Interpretation Theory in Schleiermacher, Dilthey, Heidegger, and Gadamer,* Studies in Phenomenology and Existential Philosophy (Evanston, Ill.: Northwestern University Press, 1969), p. 86.

20. Schleiermacher, *Hermeneutics,* p. 69.

21. Schleiermacher, *Hermeneutics,* p. 113.

22. Karl Barth, *Protestant Theology in the Nineteenth Century* (London: SCM, 1972; Grand Rapids: Eerdmans, 2002), p. 425.

23. Barth, *Protestant Theology,* p. 428; cf. pp. 425-73.

3. Psychological and Grammatical Interpretation:
The Comparative and the Divinatory; The Hermeneutical Circle

Schleiermacher hoped that the relatively new discipline of New Testament introduction would bring the biblical texts *alive* for students. He wrote in his early *Notes* of 1805: "The interpreter must try to become the immediate reader of a text in order to understand its allusions, its atmosphere, and its special field of images."[24] One must consider multiple meanings, synonyms, and symbols (p. 51). Even then, interpretation demands attention to life: "Every child comes to understand the meanings of words only through hermeneutics" (p. 52). He says, "One must already know a man in order to understand what he says, and yet one first becomes acquainted with him by what he says" (p. 56). How do we explain this paradox? The "hermeneutical circle" gives part of the explanation. "The understanding of a given statement is always based on something prior, of two sorts — a preliminary knowledge of human beings, a preliminary knowledge of the subject-matter" (p. 59). These constitute "technical . . . grammatical interpretation. Therefore it is a cycle" (p. 61).

The hermeneutical circle is understood in two ways (pp. 99, 100, 110, and 112-27). The first stresses the relationship between the parts and the whole of a text or work. To understand the grammatical parts of a text, we need to understand the whole; but to understand the whole we need to understand the parts. Commentators work in this way. Every phrase or clause requires examination; but its understanding must be corrected in the light of what the whole sentence, paragraph, or book means. But our understanding of the book depends upon our understanding of the words, phrases, or parts. In the second place, every understanding is based on a provisional and preliminary understanding of what the text is about. As Bultmann expresses the matter, "to understand" a text of music or of mathematics, we need some idea of music or mathematics in the first place. This is a preliminary understanding, or what the Germans call pre-understanding *(Vorverständnis)*. Schleiermacher, Dilthey, Heidegger, Bultmann, and Gadamer use the term in both senses.[25] Schleiermacher writes, "Complete knowledge always involves

---

24. Schleiermacher, *Hermeneutics*, pp. 43 and 53. Parenthetical page references in the following text are to this work.

25. See Anthony C. Thiselton, "Hermeneutical Circle," in *Dictionary for Theological Interpretation of the Bible*, ed. Kevin J. Vanhoozer (London: SPCK; Grand Rapids: Baker Academic, 2005), pp. 281-82.

an apparent circle, that each part can be understood only out of the whole to which it belongs, and vice versa."[26] The hermeneutical circle is therefore perhaps better understood as a progressive hermeneutical spiral, as Grant Osborne well argues.[27]

This requires both the "comparative" and "divinatory" method. Schleiermacher explains these best in his ninety-two-page essay *The Celebration of Christmas, or Christmas Eve: A Dialogue on the Incarnation*. After they return from Christmas Mass or Christmas communion, the men and women of the household talk, and in effect each group celebrates the birth of Christ in its own way. The men discuss the conceptual difficulties of the incarnation. Their "masculine" principle is largely that of comparison and analysis. The women sing hymns to Jesus, whom they know intuitively, suprarationally, or through a more immediate relationship. Schleiermacher comments that the women are right, although in fact both the "feminine" divinatory principle and the "masculine" principle of analysis and comparison are complementary. Both are needed. But the "feminine" principle has been too neglected in the Church.

"The divinatory method seeks to gain an immediate comprehension of the author, as one individual. The comparative method proceeds by subsuming the author under a general type. . . . Divinatory knowledge is the feminine strength in knowing people; comparative knowledge, the masculine. Each method refers back to the other."[28] "Hermeneutics must begin with the whole."[29] What happens if we attend to only one of these methods? In an important statement Schleiermacher writes that if we follow only the divinatory method, we become *"nebulists"*; if we follow only the comparative, we risk *"pedantry."*[30]

Again, we may well be tempted to underestimate the novelty of Schleiermacher's approach. But is the "divinatory" method used in most biblical studies? Schleiermacher wrote that understanding a text of the New Testament is like understanding a friend. But even conservative colleges that I know have used the term "Bible analysis" for understanding passages of Scripture, as if personal understanding or suprarational or intuitive listening

---

26. Schleiermacher, *Hermeneutics*, p. 113.

27. Grant R. Osborne, *The Hermeneutical Spiral: A Comprehensive Introduction to Biblical Interpretation* (Downers Grove, Ill.: InterVarsity, 1991), pp. 1-16 and 366-96.

28. Schleiermacher, *Hermeneutics*, p. 150.

29. Schleiermacher, *Hermeneutics*, p. 166.

30. Schleiermacher, *Hermeneutics*, p. 205, italics mine.

had no place in this largely intellectual activity, even if "applications" are added.

A student once asked me whether Schleiermacher meant the same by "grammatical and psychological" as by "comparative and divinatory." I had to admit that I was not entirely certain. Schleiermacher seems to avoid a straight equation of this kind, and I have a complicated diagram in *New Horizons in Hermeneutics* that is intended to illustrate the difference.[31] "Grammatical" interpretation, however, is primarily linguistic, and involves the comparative method. "Psychological" interpretation involves understanding the author, and involves the divinatory. Yet Schleiermacher writes, "Every act of speaking is related to both the totality of the language and the totality of the speaker's thoughts."[32] Gadamer assimilates understanding into application (chapter XI), and the later Wittgenstein does likewise.

Before the advent of Heinz Kimmerle's edition of *Hermeneutics*, Lücke and Dilthey had left the impression that Schleiermacher's hermeneutics were heavily weighted toward the psychological. But Kimmerle presented language as of equal importance to psychology. Schleiermacher was interested in the particularities of an author, and yet also in the general or "universal" features of language. I argued in *New Horizons* that his emphasis on "language as a whole" came near to anticipating Ferdinand de Saussure's distinction between *la langue* (or the potential reservoir of language as a system) and *la parole*, word-use or language-in-action.[33] The grammatical and the psychological are convenient labels for describing different aspects of the hermeneutical task, both of which are necessary. But each shades into the other, for "Hermeneutics is part of the art of thinking, and is therefore philosophical. . . . A person thinks by means of speaking."[34] The decision about the two is merely one of practical strategy. Schleiermacher writes, "Psychological interpretation is higher when one regards the language exclusively as a means by which a person communicates his thoughts. The grammatical is employed only to clear away initial difficulties. Grammatical interpretation and language . . . are higher only when one regards the person and

---

31. Anthony C. Thiselton, *New Horizons in Hermeneutics: The Theory and Practice of Transforming Biblical Reading* (London: HarperCollins; Grand Rapids: Zondervan, 1992), p. 225.

32. Schleiermacher, *Hermeneutics*, pp. 97-98.

33. Thiselton, *New Horizons in Hermeneutics*, pp. 217-18.

34. Schleiermacher, *Hermeneutics*, p. 97.

his speaking exclusively as occasions for the language to reveal itself."[35] This says it all, on this subject.

4. Further Themes and an Assessment of Schleiermacher

1. Schleiermacher has no doubt that the process of interpretation is inexhaustible. The interpreter can continue to study language and the author until the interpreter improves his or her "linguistic competence" and aims at "complete knowledge of the person," so that the interpreter comes to understand "better than the author."[36] But can one understand "better than" the author? This question divides my classes every year.

When I read essays, I often say to the writer, "Did you really mean to say . . . ?" Essayists often acknowledge that I seem to have "a better understanding" of not only the subject matter but also their intentions. But what are we to say of Saint Paul? Is trinitarian theology new dogma that never occurred to Paul? What about such books as Gerd Theissen's *Psychological Aspects of Pauline Theology*?[37] Freud discovered the impact of the unconscious or subconscious in the modern world, yet would Paul have dismissed his findings on "the secrets of the heart," or Theissen's convincing explanation of glossolalia or of "speaking in tongues" as a lifting of the censor and welling up of the unconscious (cf. 1 Cor. 12:10 and 14:1-25)? Would he have said of the subconscious or of trinitarian theology, "Yes, this is what I meant to say"? Many in my hermeneutics classes said in the end, "It depends on what you mean by 'a better understanding' than the author": yes and no.

2. Schleiermacher is quite right to claim that hermeneutics overlaps with theories of knowledge, or epistemology. It cannot but involve the problem of understanding. Biblical hermeneutics and classical hermeneutics are philosophical as well as philological. Hermeneutics involves the divinatory, intuitive, suprarational, or "feminine" as well as the comparative and critical. Understanding a text is like understanding a friend. This transcendental insight draws both on pietism and Kant, and takes us further than the Enlightenment and the rise of biblical criticism. Moreover, authors like T. F.

---

35. Schleiermacher, *Hermeneutics*, p. 99.

36. Schleiermacher, *Hermeneutics*, pp. 100-101 and 112.

37. Gerd Theissen, *Psychological Aspects of Pauline Theology*, trans. J. P. Galwin (Philadelphia: Fortress; Edinburgh: T. & T. Clark, 1987), especially pp. 85-116 and 202-393.

Torrance speak of the need for faith, and Jens Zimmermann of communion with God.[38]

3. Schleiermacher is also right to argue that "understanding" a text in this way demands "the Communality of thought. . . . Every act of speaking is related both to the totality of the language and the totality of the speaker's thoughts."[39] For understanding is related to "life" and life in community. He saw the crucial difference between a "general" hermeneutics that asks about the nature of understanding and that which is intended to support, or argue for, something supposedly *already* understood.[40] Schleiermacher, as we have seen, rightly insists, "Hermeneutics is part of the art of thinking."[41] It involves "stepping out of one's own frame of mind" to understand "the other" (pp. 42 and 109).

4. Schleiermacher, like Dilthey, Heidegger, and Gadamer after him, accepted the limitations and opportunities for growth and expansion in a hermeneutical circle. Again, we refer to Grant Osborne on this point: it may be termed "hermeneutical spiral." Certainly understanding begins with a jump into "preliminary" understanding. This is like throwing the six that allows us to start going around the board. But by definition understanding is never definitive or perfect. Understanding is corrigible, provisional, and incomplete. As the later Wittgenstein would say, understanding does not have a sharp boundary. Schleiermacher observes that complete understanding is impossible; for "It would be necessary to have a complete knowledge of the language" as well as "a complete knowledge of the person who wrote the text. . . . In both cases complete knowledge is impossible" (p. 100). Hence, again, understanding is often, but not always, a slow process that takes time (like coming to faith often is).

5. None of this denies the activity of the Holy Spirit. The above point coheres with, and underlines, the Reformation doctrine of the fallibility of the Church. Even Vatican II borders on recognizing this, apart from formal promulgations of official Church doctrine. Schleiermacher writes, "The individuality of the writers was itself a product of their relationship to Christ. . . .

---

38. Thomas F. Torrance, *Divine Meaning: Studies in Patristic Hermeneutics* (Edinburgh: T. & T. Clark, 1995), and Jens Zimmermann, *Recovering Theological Hermeneutics: An Incarnational-Trinitarian Theory of Interpretation* (Grand Rapids: Baker Academic, 2004).

39. Schleiermacher, *Hermeneutics,* pp. 97-98.

40. Cf. Palmer, *Hermeneutics,* pp. 85-86.

41. Schleiermacher, *Hermeneutics,* p. 97. Parenthetical page references in the following text are to this work.

Change of mood and view [are a product of] the Holy Spirit" (p. 139). Schleiermacher acknowledges the changes of genre that can be found in the biblical writings, and stresses their positive importance for hermeneutics. They include "Paul as a dialectic writer and John as an historical writer" (p. 134). Sometimes this is insufficiently emphasized about Schleiermacher.

6. Schleiermacher anticipates Saussure's distinction between *la langue* as the potential language-system or reservoir of language and *la parole* as the activated word, or speech in action (p. 12). Furthermore, he distinguishes between the origin of the text (reaching "behind" a text), the content ("within" the text), and its effects ("in front of" the text). An interpreter must ask about each to recapture the text's "creativity" (pp. 108, 127, 151, 197, and 204).

7. Gadamer and others criticize Schleiermacher for not emphasizing the "historicality" (or historically conditioned status) of both text and interpreter. With regard to the former, this criticism may be overstated. Schleiermacher does stress that we have to understand what is "other" as "foreign" (p. 180). With regard to the latter, he speaks in several places of the need for the interpreter to step "out of his own frame of mind" (p. 42, aphorism 8). Moreover, while Hegel was his contemporary at the University of Berlin, he did not have the benefit of reading Gadamer and Heidegger. One can only speculate about his hypothetical thoughts on historicality today.

8. Meanwhile Schleiermacher was in other respects ahead of his time. He writes that the infinite significance of the Holy Scriptures does not contradict the limits of hermeneutics. His aim is to recapture their *creativity.* We had to wait many years before someone else emphasized the three dimensions of the setting, the content, and the effect of texts. Nevertheless, one other criticism, which concerns setting, has often been voiced against Schleiermacher.[42] Is his emphasis on *intention* due to his Romanticism and its concern with *origin?* Does he commit the "genetic" fallacy?

I reject this criticism on the ground that "intention" may be understood to denote the *author's aim.* To say that Paul "intentionally" expounded a theology of the cross and resurrection in 1 Corinthians is not to make claims about Paul's inaccessible "inner mental processes," but to say something about Paul's conscious aims. Schleiermacher does not commit "the genetic fallacy," as this has been called. Paul Ricoeur has three excellent chapters on this in *Oneself as Another,* and Nicholas Wolterstorff goes even further than

---

42. See Randolph W. Tate, *Biblical Interpretation: An Integrated Approach* (Peabody, Mass.: Hendrickson, 1991), throughout.

Ricoeur in showing how indispensable this concept remains for hermeneutics and for notions of divine discourse.[43]

9. Nevertheless, Schleiermacher's theology does focus on the subjective experience of the individual. This does not invalidate his hermeneutics, but it alerts us to possible weaknesses in his theology. Perhaps in this respect Gadamer and Ricoeur offer correctives, but we may doubt whether they could have reached their positions without at least many of Schleiermacher's insights into hermeneutics.

5. The Hermeneutics of Wilhelm Dilthey

Wilhelm Dilthey (1833-1911) is widely recognized as Schleiermacher's successor in hermeneutics. He is also his biographer, writing his *Life of Schleiermacher.* He was born in Wiesbaden, the son of a theologian of the Calvinist tradition. He studied in the universities of Heidelberg and Berlin, reading theology, philosophy, and history. After a further period of philology, he prepared his *Habilitation* (the German qualification for university teaching, usually taken after the Ph.D.). He became professor at Basel in 1866, and then at Berlin in 1882. He is best known for his attempts to make hermeneutics a basis for the *Geisteswissenschaften* (the "human sciences," or humanities, letters, and social sciences). He was one of the first to apply hermeneutics to the social sciences, and was an ardent admirer of Schleiermacher, who inspired his studies. His "complete writings" run to twenty-six German volumes, although at the time of this writing few of them have been translated into English.[44]

43. Paul Ricoeur, *Oneself as Another,* trans. Kathleen Blamey (Chicago and London: University of Chicago Press, 1992), pp. 88-168, and Nicholas Wolterstorff, *Divine Discourse: Philosophical Reflections on the Claim That God Speaks* (Cambridge: Cambridge University Press, 1995), pp. 130-71.

44. Wilhelm Dilthey, *Gesammelte Schriften,* 26 vols. (Göttingen: Vandenhoeck & Ruprecht, 1914-2005), especially vol. 5, *Die geistige Welt: Einleitung in das Philosophie des Lebens,* 1924; vol. 7, *Der Aufbau der geschichtlichen Welt in den Geisteswissenschaften,* 1927; vol. 12, *Zur Preussischen Geschichte. Schleiermachers politische Gesinnung und Wirksamkeit,* 1936; and vols. 13 and 14, *Leben Schleiermachers,* 1966 and 1970. Some selections are in English, including *Wilhelm Dilthey: Selected Works,* ed. Rudolf A. Makreel and Frithjof Rodi, 6 vols.: vol. 1, *Introduction to the Human Sciences* (Princeton: Princeton University Press, 1989), unedited; vol. 3, *The Formation of the Historical World in the Human Sciences;* vol. 4, *Hermeneutics and the Study of History* (projected); and vol. 6, *Philosophy and Life* (unpublished but projected);

Dilthey came to see in hermeneutics the foundation of the *Geistes-wissenschaften*. He traces the tradition in philosophy of seeking previous groundings of theories. But none, Dilthey believes, has given sufficient attention to how *historically conditioned* both the subject matter and the interpreter are. He rejects the positivism of Auguste Comte as naive, and he rejects the evolutionary ethics of Herbert Spencer as overstated. He combines a radically historical approach with the search for system. With Herder and especially Schleiermacher, he seeks to replace Hegel's emphasis on Spirit or Mind *(Geist)* with Life *(Leben)*.

Dilthey had great ambition. He recognized that Bacon had done much to found the natural sciences. But what Bacon had done for physical sciences, and what Kant and Hegel had done for philosophy, he hoped to do for the "human sciences." "Science" is simply a coherent complex of propositions, whose propositions are well grounded. But propositions about human life, he insisted, are distinctive over against propositions about the natural world. Human self-consciousness includes a moral, historical, and spiritual dimension that must be recognized. *Lived experiences* lie behind human society. We must take seriously mental processes and inner life. Hence to analyze the causal nexus of nature is insufficient for the *Geisteswissenschaften*. The human being knows himself only in *history*.

Dilthey argued that "in the veins of 'the knowing subject' (for example of Descartes, Locke, Hume, and even Kant) *no real blood flows*."[45] In contrast to them and to Hegel, Dilthey established "life" *(Leben)* or *"lived experience"* *(Erlebnis)* as the key category of the human being. "Life" is a shared flow of human activities and experiences, in both social diversity and the individual's experience. Yet there is a "nexus" or interweaving that *binds together* disparate individuals. This "connectedness" *(Zusammen-hang)* finds expression in a common language of signs, symbols, speech, and writing, and in human practices and institutions such as laws. "Expressions" *(Lebensäusserungen)* of this kind objectify the subjective experi-

---

Wilhelm Dilthey, *Introduction to the Human Sciences*, trans. R. J. Betanzos (Detroit: Wayne State University Press, 1988); and the best known are Wilhelm Dilthey, *Selected Writings*, ed. H. P. Rickman (Cambridge: Cambridge University Press, 1976), and H. A. Hodges, "Selected Passages from Dilthey," in *Wilhelm Dilthey: An Introduction* (London: Oxford University Press, 1944), pp. 109-56; Wilhelm Dilthey, "The Rise of Hermeneutics," trans. Frederick Jameson, *New Literary History 3* (1972): 229-441, and *Gesammelte Schriften*, 5:317-31.

45. Wilhelm Dilthey, *Gesammelte Schriften*, vol. 5, *Die geistliche Welt. Einleitung in das Philosophie des Lebens* (Leipzig and Berlin: Teubner, 1927), p. 4.

ence of human life. They thus contain "more . . . than any introspection can discover."[46]

Dilthey thus contributed three things to hermeneutics. First, he *extended* hermeneutics to include law, social sciences, and all human institutions beyond language. If it applies to language, hermeneutics applies to all human society and its concrete institutions. Second, Dilthey insisted that both interpretation and objects of interpretation are radically conditioned by their *place in history,* or *historicality.* Here he stands between Hegel and Heidegger, and receives credit for this from Gadamer. Third, he uses *"life"* as the common medium between objects of interpretation and the interpreter. The interpreter is to *"relive" (nacherleben)* the other's experience by stepping out of his or her shoes and exercising "sympathy" *(Hineinversetzen)* or "transposition."[47]

Strangely, at about this time the first bishop of Southwell and Nottingham, Bishop George Ridding, was preparing a litany of remembrance for his clergy in which, exactly like Dilthey, he formulated the notion of stepping sensitively into the shoes of the other, in order to think and feel as the other felt and thought. But both writers stressed feeling the *differences* of the self from others as well as "measuring their feelings by our own."[48] Ernst Fuchs and Manfred Metzger insist that we can never "relive" the experiences of another, because each individual is unique. Nevertheless, this remains a worthy *aim,* underlined by Dilthey. Dilthey, as we have said, is aware of historical distance and difference, as his interpretation of Luther shows. He writes, "Understanding (German, *Verstehen*) is a rediscovery of the 'I' in the 'You.' . . . We may ask how much this contributes to solving the general problem of epistemology."[49]

Gadamer applauds Dilthey's efforts to move away from introspection and self-consciousness to seeing humankind as historically situated within the flow of human life. Dilthey also adopted the hermeneutical circle found then in Schleiermacher, and more recently in Heidegger, Bultmann, Fuchs, and Gadamer. He says, "The whole must be understood in terms of its indi-

---

46. Wilhelm Dilthey, *Gesammelte Schriften,* vol. 7, *Der Aufbau der geschichtlichen Welt in den Geisteswissenschaften* (Leipzig and Berlin, 1927), p. 206; Dilthey, *Selected Writings,* p. 219.

47. Dilthey, *Gesammelte Schriften,* 7:213-17; *Selected Writings,* pp. 226-27.

48. Bishop George Ridding, *A Litany of Remembrance: Compiled for Retreats and Quiet Days for His Clergy* (reprint, London: Allen and Unwin, 1959), p. 7.

49. Dilthey, *Gesammelte Schriften,* 7:191; or *Selected Writings,* p. 208.

vidual parts; individual parts in terms of the whole."[50] But Gadamer strongly disapproves of the next step that Dilthey takes. Dilthey has a more positive view of "science," or coherent, general thought, than Gadamer. He traces a "connectedness" (Zusammenhang) or pattern of correspondence or generality, as well as the particular and the distinctive, in human life. Thus he attempts a "science" of human language and institutions, which Gadamer believes betrays human particularity. Life expressions are, in effect, general "deposits" left by the "lives" of individual human beings, as the Romantics, led by Herder, tended to think. But Gadamer rejects this. The criticism may be overstated, and is not uncontroversial, even in hermeneutics. But Gadamer has a point.

It is not surprising that social science takes up Dilthey's work as one of its options. Dilthey, we have seen, extended hermeneutics to include all human institutions. He turns hermeneutics into a special kind of "science." Heidegger and Gadamer reject this, but it leads to the discussion of "life-world" and system found in Jürgen Habermas, and Emilio Betti also attempts this approach, which is more "objective" than Gadamer's. It is impossible to escape the shadow of Dilthey today. "Lived experience" includes also works of art. Dilthey rightly expanded the scope of hermeneutics, and he did give due attention to time and to history. "Putting oneself in someone's place" as a way of understanding may not be entirely possible, but it is a profoundly Christian aim in expressing concern for the other. It is also true, as Dilthey maintained, that "One has to wait till the end of history" fully to understand.[51] We reach fuller understanding only at the end of life. As Jesus said to Peter, "What I am doing now you do not understand; but later you will understand" (John 13:7).

6. Recommended Initial Reading

Bauman, Zygmunt, Hermeneutics and Social Science: Approaches to Understanding (London: Hutchinson, 1978), pp. 27-41.

Mueller-Vollmer, Kurt, ed., The Hermeneutics Reader (Oxford: Blackwell, 1985), pp. 148-64.

---

50. Dilthey, Gesammelte Schriften, 5:336; Selected Writings, p. 262.

51. Cf. Zygmunt Bauman, Hermeneutics and Social Science: Approaches to Understanding (London: Hutchinson, 1978), p. 41.

Palmer, Richard E., *Hermeneutics: Interpretation Theory in Schleiermacher, Dilthey, Heidegger, and Gadamer,* Studies in Phenomenology and Existential Philosophy (Evanston, Ill.: Northwestern University Press, 1969), pp. 75-123.

Schleiermacher, Friedrich, *Hermeneutics: The Handwritten Manuscripts,* edited by Heinz Kimmerle, translated by James Duke and Jack Forstman (Missoula: Scholars Press, 1977), pp. 95-151.

Thiselton, Anthony C., *New Horizons in Hermeneutics: The Theory and Practice of Transforming Biblical Reading* (London: HarperCollins; Grand Rapids: Zondervan, 1992), pp. 204-53.

CHAPTER IX

Rudolf Bultmann and Demythologizing the New Testament

Rudolf Bultmann (1884-1976) is one of the most prestigious names in New Testament twentieth-century scholarship. He was born in Wiefelstede, Germany, the son of a Lutheran pastor, and after a distinguished school career entered the University of Tübingen, and then the University of Berlin. Jülicher and Krüger featured among his teachers. He submitted his *Habilitation* thesis (postdoctoral work) on Paul the apostle, and became a lecturer in New Testament studies. In 1910 he published work on Paul's diatribe style, and in 1921 *The History of the Synoptic Tradition.* The same year (1921) he became professor of New Testament at Marburg University. From 1923 to 1928 he consulted with Martin Heidegger in philosophy and with Hans Jonas on Gnosticism, and shared seminars with them. He remained at Marburg for most of his life.

1. Influences and Earlier Concerns

Bultmann is of major significance for hermeneutics. He and Heidegger agreed that *de-objectifying* texts was a major way of understanding religious texts and exposing their importance for today. He also built solidly on Dilthey, and on the hermeneutical tradition of preliminary understanding, or pre-understanding, which Schleiermacher, Dilthey, and Heidegger had already formulated. In 1950 he expounded this principle of all hermeneutics with particular reference to Dilthey. According to Dilthey, he wrote, this is the "technique of understanding expressions of life set in written form."[1]

---

1. Rudolf Bultmann, "The Problem of Hermeneutics," *Zeitschrift für Theologie und*

This makes the individual human being genuinely a historical entity. But do we have a means of attaining to this historical knowledge? This is "the problem of hermeneutics."

Bultmann acknowledges that to understand a text necessitates examining linguistic usage, but he also sees the New Testament authors as "historically conditioned."[2] He agrees with the Enlightenment's emphasis on philosophy and language, and also with Schleiermacher's insistence that hermeneutics involves the art of understanding rather than mere hermeneutical "rules." Dilthey, he argues, appropriates these ideas, but both Schleiermacher and Dilthey, he claims, are also one-sided.

Bultmann insists that the interpreter needs "an interest which is based in the life of the inquirer," if he or she is to ask productive questions of the text. The presupposition for understanding *"is the interpreter's relationship in his life to the subject which is . . . expressed in the text."*[3] His most famous exposition of this principle comes in an essay collected in *Existence and Faith.*[4] He declares, "I only understand a text of music if and in so far as I have a relationship to music. . . . I only understand a mathematical text if I have a relationship to mathematics."[5] What is rejected is an "objective," value-neutral observation of the text. This is useless, but is encouraged by many of Bultmann's former teachers.

Among the subjects and texts examined are poetry, art, and the New Testament. Some credit for this insight is given to J. J. Winckelmann. But the decisive influence is Martin Heidegger. We can no longer aim at "objectivity" in interpretation. Bultmann writes, "To demand that the interpreter must silence his subjectivity and extinguish his individuality . . . is therefore the most absurd one that can be imagined."[6] This applies to the biblical writings, where *existentiell* knowledge of God is required in some form, whether it is asking questions about salvation or asking even about happiness. But Bultmann does not mean pre-understanding in any Barthian sense.

Kirche 47 (1950): 47-69; reprinted in Bultmann, *Essays Philosophical and Theological* (London: SCM, 1955), p. 234; cf. pp. 234-61.

2. Bultmann, *Essays Philosophical and Theological,* p. 236.

3. Bultmann, *Essays Philosophical and Theological,* p. 241, italics in original.

4. Rudolf Bultmann, "Is Exegesis without Presuppositions Possible?" in *Existence and Faith: Shorter Writings of Rudolf Bultmann,* ed. S. M. Ogden (London: Collins, 1964), pp. 342-52.

5. Bultmann, *Essays Philosophical and Theological,* pp. 242-43.

6. Bultmann, *Essays Philosophical and Theological,* p. 255.

Bultmann's hermeneutics, we saw, naturally built upon the influence of Schleiermacher, Dilthey, and Heidegger. Yet equally momentous influences also lie behind his specific program of demythologizing the New Testament. I have tried to trace these in *The Two Horizons*.[7] Bultmann fell under the influence of the neo-Kantian thought of his day. Hermann Cohen (1842-1918) and Paul Natorp (1854-1924) were leading neo-Kantians. They argued, as Kant had, that we cannot think or speak of an object as if it preceded thought. We know an object *(Gegenstand)* only insofar as it is already an object of our thought. Cohen challenged Kant's assumption that these objects were somehow or in some sense "given." This extension of Kant was important. The leading scientists of the day, Hermann von Helmholtz, Heinrich Hertz, and Ludwig Boltzmann, argued for the subjectivity of sensory qualities. Space itself depends on the human constitution. The central idea in Hertz's approach was that we can produce only "models" *(Bilder)* or "representations" *(Darstellungen)* of reality. (Today DNA is often explained in terms of "models.")

For Bultmann this meant a radical devaluing of "describing objects" as a way of encountering reality. In fact, the New Testament writers did not intend to *describe reality,* he claimed, but to *confess their faith.* Bultmann then linked his neo-Kantian epistemology (or theory of knowledge) to his distinctive nineteenth-century Lutheran theology. According to the principle of *law,* thinking "objectifies" *(objektivieren)* data. In Johnson's words, "To know is to objectify in accordance with the principle of law."[8] The law becomes associated with "works," "description," and "report," while "grace" becomes associated (in Bultmann's view) with address and testimony. It need hardly be said that this is not Luther, but nineteenth-century Lutheranism.

Two influences combine here. One is Bultmann's close contact in 1923-28 with Heidegger and Hans Jonas. Jonas insists that the Gnostics did not think of planets and planetary guardians as "objective" entities at all, but as ways of expressing the experience of spiritual ascent. Bultmann concluded that for the New Testament writers, too, the supposedly "objective" language was merely its *mythological form* of expression. The "real" New Testament thought behind the myth was *"kerygma,"* preaching, or testimony.

The second, further influence came from Bultmann's own form criticism.

7. Anthony C. Thiselton, *The Two Horizons: New Testament Hermeneutics and Philosophical Description with Special Reference to Heidegger, Bultmann, Gadamer, and Wittgenstein* (Grand Rapids: Eerdmans; Exeter: Paternoster, 1980), pp. 205-92.

8. Roger A. Johnson, *The Origins of Demythologizing: Philosophy and Historiography in the Theology of Rudolf Bultmann* (Leiden: Brill, 1974), pp. 49-50.

He formulated this in 1921 in the *History of the Synoptic Tradition.* Here the real purpose of Synoptic Gospel language was testimony or address, not description or report. The best way of putting this at its most positive is to say that it is always *practical,* and is address *from* God, not "objective" or value-neutral truth *about* God. The worst way, as we shall see, is to argue that language is *either* descriptive *or* nondescriptive, not a mixture or overlapping of both.

Meanwhile Bultmann writes, "Our radical attempt to demythologize the New Testament is in fact a perfect parallel to St. Paul and Luther's doctrine of justification by faith alone apart from the works of the law. Or rather, it carries this doctrine to its logical conclusion in the field of epistemology [theory of knowledge]. Like the doctrine of justification it destroys every false security. . . . Security can be found only by abandoning all security."[9] When conservative colleagues were "defending" the reliability of the New Testament, Bultmann saw it as his calling to "let the fires of scepticism burn" (like his teacher, Krüger) so that people did not place their trust in the wrong thing. His historical skepticism, then, *cohered* with his program of demythologizing. He had little interest in "historical facts." Any life-of-Jesus theology is mistaken. It leads to "Christ after the flesh."[10]

For Bultmann God is therefore outside the realm of cognitive knowledge. "God would not be objectively given" *(Da ware Gott eine Gegebenheit),* and God is beyond "a system of cognitions" *(Erkenntnissen).*[11] Even to believe in the cross of Christ, he writes, "does not mean to concern ourselves with an objective event [*ein objektiv anschaubares Ereignis*] . . . but to undergo crucifixion with him."[12] He writes further, "If we follow the objectifying representations of the New Testament, the cross is indeed understood as a mythical event. . . . But even within the New Testament it does not at all say what it is supposed to say."[13]

9. Rudolf Bultmann, "Bultmann Replies to His Critics," in *Kerygma and Myth,* ed. Hans-Werner Bartsch, trans. R. H. Fuller, 2 vols. (London: SPCK, 1962, 1964), 1:210-11.

10. Rudolf Bultmann, *Faith and Understanding,* vol. 1 (London: SCM, 1969), p. 132.

11. Rudolf Bultmann, "What Does It Mean to Speak of God?" in Bultmann, *Faith and Understanding,* 1:60 (German ed., p. 32).

12. Rudolf Bultmann, "New Testament and Mythology," in *Kerygma and Myth: A Theological Debate,* ed. Hans-Werner Bartsch, 2 vols. (London: SCM, 1953), 1:86 (German, vol. 1, p. 46); retranslated in Bultmann, *New Testament Mythology and Other Basic Writings,* selected, edited, and translated by Schubert M. Ogden (Philadelphia: Fortress, 1984), pp. 35-36.

13. Bultmann, "New Testament and Mythology," in *New Testament Mythology,* pp. 33-34; cf. Bartsch, ed., *Kerygma and Myth,* 1:35-36.

Not only do we find Albrecht Ritschl (1822-89) and Wilhelm Herrmann (1846-1922) behind this, but also Søren Kierkegaard and Martin Heidegger. Faith is not directed toward pseudo-objective statements about Christ, or about God, but to the bare word of God himself. It is not past history *(Historie)* that is the object of faith, but participation in living history *(Geschichte)*. Bultmann further draws from Kierkegaard the idea that "subjectivity is truth." Kierkegaard writes, "*The objective accent falls on WHAT is said, the subjective accent on HOW it is said.* . . . Objectively the interest is focussed merely on the thought-content, subjectively on the inwardness . . . the passion of the infinite, and the passion of the infinite is truth. . . . This subjectivity becomes the truth."[14]

Rudolf Bultmann was thus influenced by philosophy, by biblical studies, and by theology. In philosophy he was profoundly influenced by neo-Kantian theories of knowledge and the "new" science of Hertz, Helmholtz, and Boltzmann, as well as by Kierkegaard and Heidegger. In biblical studies he was strongly influenced by the "history of religions school" and especially by form criticism as originally pioneered by Hermann Gunkel on the Psalms. In theology he was heavily influenced by Ritschl and Herrmann on faith, and especially by nineteenth-century Lutheranism, which was rather different from, as well as exhibiting similarities to, Luther's own theology.

Thus Bultmann approached de-objectifying or demythologizing the New Testament with the best of intentions to be faithful to its witness. But does his program bear out these positive intentions?

2. Bultmann's Notions of "Myth"

Bultmann, we have seen, is concerned with de-objectifying language about God, or rather, address from God. But unfortunately this is only one of three largely incompatible definitions of "myth" that he gives.

To be sure, Bultmann defines myth as functioning to convey human attitudes, but looking at face value as if it described objective events. Thus near the beginning of his famous 1941 essay in *Kerygma and Myth*, Bultmann writes, "The real purpose of myth is not to present an objective picture of the world as it is, but to express man's understanding of himself in the world

---

14. Søren Kierkegaard, *Concluding Unscientific Postscript to the Philosophical Fragments* (Princeton: Princeton University Press, 1941), p. 181, italics and capitals in original.

in which he lives. Myth should be *interpreted* not cosmologically, but anthropologically, or, better still, existentially."[15] Mythology, Bultmann argues, expresses the "otherworldly" in terms of this world, as for example in God's "sending" his Son. Transcendence is expressed as spatial distance. Hans Jonas expressed this understanding of myth in his Marburg dissertation of 1928.[16]

The problem is that elsewhere Bultmann explicitly defines "myth" almost identically with *analogy*. It looks anthropomorphic, yet it seeks to avoid anthropomorphism. Bultmann writes, "Myth is here used in the sense popularized by the 'History of Religions' School. Myth is the use of imagery *(die Vorstellungsweise)* to express the other worldly in terms of this world, the divine in terms of human life."[17] Helmut Thielicke and many others ask how demythologizing could be possible at all if myth is like analogy. Thielicke writes that all religious language inevitably uses this-worldly language, for there is no other that we can use. "It affects the very foundations of the Church."[18] He criticizes "a non-Biblical principle derived from contemporary secular thought [being] applied to the interpretations of the Bible."[19]

Bultmann anticipates this criticism. He attempts not a formal definition of myth, but one in terms of an outdated worldview. Myth, he argues, explains unusual or surprising phenomena in terms of the invasion of supernatural forces. Here we encounter his famous definition of myth as supporting the notion of a "three-decker" universe. "The world is viewed as a three-storied structure, with the earth in the centre, the heaven above, and the underworld beneath. Heaven is the abode of God and of celestial beings — the angels. The underworld is hell. . . . These supernatural forces intervene in the course of nature and in all that men think and will and do. . . . Miracles are by no means rare. . . . Man is not in control of his own life."[20] This helps to

---

15. Bultmann, "New Testament and Mythology," in *Kerygma and Myth,* 1:10; cf. Bultmann, *New Testament Mythology,* p. 9.

16. Hans Jonas, *Gnosis und spätantiker Geist II, 1: Von der Mythologie zur mystischen Philosophie* (Göttingen: Vandenhoeck & Ruprecht, 1954), pp. 3-4. James Robinson takes this up in *Interpretation* 20:70-71.

17. Bultmann, "New Testament and Mythology," in *Kerygma and Myth,* 1:10 n. 2; cf. Bultmann, *New Testament Mythology,* p. 42 n. 5.

18. Helmut Thielicke, "The Restatement of the New Testament Mythology," in *Kerygma and Myth,* 1:138; cf. pp. 138-74.

19. Thielicke, "The Restatement," 1:149.

20. Bultmann, "New Testament and Mythology," in *Kerygma and Myth,* 1:1; cf. Bultmann, *New Testament Mythology,* p. 1.

explain why myth needs to be interpreted and demythologized, but it is at radical variance with a formal definition of myth.

R. W. Hepburn, who was at the time professor of philosophy at Nottingham University, England, makes the point that in terms of definition Bultmann cannot have it both ways. One definition of myth, if it is right, suggests demythologizing; the other suggests the impossibility of demythologizing.[21] One concerns form of mode of myth; the other concerns its content. Now, nearly seventy years on, we may wonder whether it is "mythological" to suggest that humankind is not "in control" of its own destiny. Postmodern writers often pose this question. Moreover, John Macquarrie targets Bultmann's outmoded view of miracle for criticism. Bultmann writes, "It is impossible to use electric light and the wireless and to avail ourselves of modern medical and surgical discoveries, and at the same time to believe in the New Testament world of spirits and miracles."[22] Macquarrie, however, writes: "To the educated Christian nowadays, a miracle is not an event which constitutes a break in the course of nature, but an event in which God reveals himself for faith. 'Miracle' is a religious concept."[23] In his book *An Existentialist Theology*, Macquarrie went further. He wrote that Bultmann propagated "a pseudo-scientific view of a closed universe that was popular half a century ago."[24]

Walter Schmithals, Friedrich Gogarten, and Schubert Ogden try to defend Bultmann at this point. They argue that Bultmann's concerns about "science" and "modern man" rest not on an interpretation of the world that we can dispense with, but take account of reality as it is.[25] Ogden argues that however much the results of scientific inquiry may change, the method and worldview remain constant.

Nevertheless, is it the case, for example, that to use modern medicine

21. R. W. Hepburn, "Demythologizing and the Problem of Validity," in *New Essays in Philosophical Theology*, ed. A. Flew and A. MacIntyre (London: SCM, 1955), pp. 227-42.

22. Bultmann, "New Testament and Mythology," in *Kerygma and Myth*, 1:5; cf. Bultmann, *New Testament Mythology*, p. 4.

23. John Macquarrie, *The Scope of Demythologizing: Bultmann and His Critics* (London: SCM, 1962), p. 237.

24. John Macquarrie, *An Existentialist Theology: A Comparison of Heidegger and Bultmann* (London: SCM, 1955), p. 168.

25. Walter Schmithals, *An Introduction to the Theology of Rudolf Bultmann*, trans. John Bowden (London: SCM, 1968), pp. 27-95 and especially pp. 232-72, and Schubert Ogden, *Christ without Myth: A Study Based on the Theology of Rudolf Bultmann* (New York: Harper and Row, 1961), pp. 38-39.

and to believe in miracles are exclusive alternatives? Bultmann risks confusing de-objectification and his claims about justification with "what is acceptable to modern man." The root cause of this is an incompatible three-fold definition of "myth" in terms of form and content. A. Boyce Gibson represents a more sophisticated view of miracle when he comments, "If, as Hume supposes, laws of nature are founded in experience, there is no question of violation, because laws are only progress reports. Anything may happen later. . . . Anything that happens for the first time is to be discredited [according to Hume and Bultmann]."[26] Such a view was also held nearly a thousand years ago. Thomas Aquinas long ago defined "miracle" not as *contra naturam* (against nature) but as *praeter naturam* (beyond nature). In the twentieth century G. J. Warnock the philosopher and David Cairns the theologian wrote that what we "experience" as causation is only a constant conjunction of events.[27] We may therefore question Bultmann's assumption that the idea of miracle has become "impossible" for people today, at least on these grounds.

3. Existential Interpretation and Demythologizing: Specific Examples

Bultmann insists that demythologizing is demanded by the New Testament itself. The descriptive *appearance* of New Testament language, he argues, impedes and obscures its true intention and content. "Myth" provides an additional and unnecessary stumbling block to modern man, which is not part of the New Testament message. This is *kerygma*, or proclamation, not myth, which should be interpreted. Bultmann writes, "To insist on retaining faith in primitive mythology demands nowadays a sacrifice of intellect which man in New Testament times was not asked to make. It is an additional stumbling-block."[28] There is a difference between rejecting Scripture and "rejecting the world-view of scripture," which is largely derived from apocalyptic.[29]

26. A. Boyce Gibson, *Theism and Empiricism* (London: SCM, 1970), p. 268.

27. J. G. Warnock, "Every Event Has a Cause," in *Logic and Language,* ed. A. G. W. Flew, 2nd ser. (Oxford: Blackwell, 1966), 1:95-111, and David Cairns, *A Gospel without Myth? Bultmann's Challenge to the Preacher* (London: SCM, 1960), pp. 123-25.

28. Rudolf Bultmann, *Jesus Christ and Mythology* (London: SCM, 1960), p. 36; cf. Ogden, *Christ without Myth,* p. 63, and Schmithals, *Introduction,* pp. 255-57.

29. Bultmann, *Jesus Christ and Mythology,* pp. 35-36.

It is valuable that Bultmann's aim is to remove false stumbling blocks to faith, in order to highlight the offense of the cross. Too often it is the subcultural baggage of Christians that puts people off the gospel. Bultmann strongly dissociates himself from old-fashioned liberalism, which seeks to remove unpalatable truths from the gospel to make it easier to believe. His gospel has to do with *kerygma,* or address, not with mere teaching. Yet when we look at specific examples of demythologizing, clearly an insufficient amount of the original material remains.

1. On the *cross* itself, which is so important to him, Bultmann includes within its "mythical character" the notion of "the victim whose blood atones for our sins. He bears vicariously the sins of the world."[30] It is half true that when we consider the cross, it is mythical to concern ourselves with a "process wrought outside of us and our world, with an objective event."[31] The cross involves participation in Christ, not an event wholly "outside us," in which we remain utterly uninvolved. But Bultmann writes, "Christ is crucified 'for us,' not in the sense of any theory of sacrifice or satisfaction."[32] Some would argue that Bultmann can say this only because he replaces the Old Testament by existentialist philosophy as the pre-understanding for the New Testament. He rightly wants to say that we must "make the cross our own"; but are these mutually exclusive alternatives?

2. The case with the *resurrection* is no easier; indeed, it is exactly the same. Bultmann writes, *"Faith in the resurrection is really the same thing as faith in the saving efficacy of the cross."*[33] Bultmann explicitly declares, "Christ the crucified and risen one encounters us in the word of proclamation and nowhere else."[34] Although it is perhaps cheap, there is truth in the jibe that for Bultmann and his followers the resurrection occurs only at 11 A.M. on Sunday mornings, when the word of God is preached. Bultmann is right that understanding and believing in the resurrection mean "being raised with Christ," but John Macquarrie is right to ask how it can make

30. Bultmann, "New Testament and Mythology," in *Kerygma and Myth,* 1:35; cf. Bultmann, *New Testament Mythology,* p. 36.

31. Bultmann, in *Kerygma and Myth,* 1:36; cf. Bultmann, *New Testament Mythology,* p. 35.

32. Bultmann, "New Testament and Mythology," in *Kerygma and Myth,* 1:37.

33. Bultmann, "New Testament and Mythology," in *Kerygma and Myth,* 1:41, italics in original; cf. pp. 38-43; cf. Bultmann, *New Testament and Mythology,* p. 39; cf. pp. 36-41.

34. Bultmann, "New Testament and Mythology," in *New Testament Mythology,* p. 39; cf. Bultmann, in *Kerygma and Myth,* 1:41.

sense to speak of being raised with Christ unless Christ actually died and was raised.[35]

3. Bultmann's third specific example, namely, his approach to *Christology*, is illuminating. On one side, he is right that there is a practical dimension to Christology in the New Testament. As Johannes Weiss observed, the currency and meaning of "Christ is Lord" (the earliest Christian confession) are seen best in what it means for me to be Christ's slave. Charismatic congregations mean this when they sing, "We build him a throne." But is this all that it means to call Christ "Lord"? Christ "was declared to be Son of God with power . . . by the resurrection from the dead . . . Jesus our Lord" (Rom. 1:4). His Lordship does not depend on the Church, or the individual, but upon *God.* This is the burden of Karl Barth's criticism of Bultmann. Bultmann both disables any integration between New Testament exegesis and systematic theology, and empties the *kerygma* of its basis in acts of God.[36]

In 1951 the World Council of Churches invited Bultmann to pronounce on the debate about whether it was right to limit membership to those who acknowledged "Jesus Christ as God and Saviour." His answer is famously contained in his *Essays Philosophical and Theological* (German, *Glauben und Verstehen,* vol. 2, 1955). Bultmann first points out that Jesus Christ is called "God" explicitly only in John 20:28, the confession of Thomas. But, he continues, "The decisive question might now be this: whether and how far titles at any time intend to tell us something about the nature of Jesus — how far is a Christological pronouncement about him also a pronouncement about me? Does he help me because he is God's Son, or is he the Son of God because he helps me?"[37]

The traditional proposition does mean something for Bultmann, however. It affirms, Bultmann writes, "that God is to be encountered in him (Christ) and only in him."[38] Nevertheless, he continues, this is very different from reciting the Nicene Creed: "very God of very God." The Greeks were interested in objective "nature," but the Hebrews adopted an existential ap-

---

35. John Macquarrie, "Philosophy and Theology in Bultmann's Thought," in *The Theology of Rudolf Bultmann,* ed. Charles W. Kegley (London: SCM, 1966), p. 141.

36. Karl Barth, "Rudolf Bultmann — an Attempt to Understand Him," in *Kerygma and Myth,* 2:83-132, especially pp. 84-85 and 91-102.

37. Bultmann, "The Christological Confession," in *Essays Philosophical and Theological,* p. 280.

38. Bultmann, "The Christological Confession," p. 284.

proach. Bultmann concludes, "The formula 'Christ is God' is false in every sense in which God is understood as an entity which can be objectivised. . . . It is correct if 'God' is understood as the event of God's acting."[39] Once again, what Bultmann wants to assert about self-involvement is correct; but what he denies is incorrect. Indeed, self-involvement, as J. L. Austin notes, is often valid on the basis of what is the state of affairs.[40] I have repeatedly argued for this in *Thiselton on Hermeneutics*.[41]

4. Clearly what Bultmann has said about Christology, the cross, and the resurrection applies to God himself. "It is not permitted to understand God's act as a phenomenon within the world that can be perceived apart from an existentiell encounter with it. . . . To speak of God's act means to speak at the same time of my own existence."[42] Even God's act seems to be limited to his addressing persons. For Bultmann insists on pressing the Lutheran insight that apart from faith God is hidden. But there is none of the care and subtlety that we find in E. Jüngel's exposition of this question. For Bultmann everything is an either/or, hardly ever "both . . . and . . ."

5. We may initially sympathize with Bultmann's pronouncements about *eschatology*. Heaven is not primarily a spatial entity. It is not in heaven that we find God, preachers sometimes say, but in God that we find heaven. If he were emphasizing the analogical or symbolic character of much of its imagery, it might be possible to agree. But his category of "myth" takes us too far. Bultmann insists, "We can no longer look for the return of the Son of Man on the clouds of heaven, or hope that the faithful will meet him in the air" (1 Thess. 4:15). Worse, in *Jesus Christ and Mythology* he argues that the whole eschatological drama is borrowed from apocalyptic. "The *parousia* of Christ never took place as the New Testament expected. History did not come to an end."[43] Here he depends on the interpretation of the New Testament fashionable in his day and led by such scholars as Albert Schweitzer. Today scholars such as G. B. Caird and N. T. Wright have questioned this interpretation of the evidence, largely on the basis of a better understanding of metaphor.

39. Bultmann, "The Christological Confession," p. 287.

40. As in Anthony C. Thiselton, "More on Christology: Christology in Luke; Speech-Acts-Theory and the Problem of Dualism in Christology," in *Thiselton on Hermeneutics: Collective Works with New Essays* (Grand Rapids: Eerdmans; Aldershot: Ashgate, 2006), pp. 99-116.

41. *Thiselton on Hermeneutics*, pp. 51-150.

42. Bultmann, "Bultmann Replies," 1:196.

43. Bultmann, *Jesus Christ and Mythology*, p. 14; cf. pp. 11-17.

Bultmann maintains that the very concept of "kingdom of God," clearly attested in earlier sources, is part of "the eschatological drama" of apocalyptic. It becomes confused, he argues, with the primitive mythology of "the three-storey universe," in which the world is enslaved by demonic forces. The Holy Spirit is a genuine entity or person. In Bultmann's view, however, the Spirit is only "the possibility of a new life. . . . The Spirit does not work like a supernatural force."[44]

Yet the specific examples of demythologizing should not blind us to the problem that Bultmann wants to address and to solve. He does not wish to eliminate "the Christ occurrence." He further explains, "What critics have occasionally objected is that I interpret the New Testament with the categories of Heidegger's philosophy of existence. I fear that they have missed the real problem. What ought to alarm them is that philosophy all by itself sees what the New Testament says."[45] The "real problem" is that in Bultmann's view the New Testament speaks not about abstract entities. It does not "describe"; it addresses humankind much as Heidegger's *Dasein,* who is a participant, not a spectator. Such a person is justified not by "works" of historical belief, but by grace and participation in the Christ event.

For John Macquarrie, therefore, in spite of his criticisms elsewhere, Bultmann has the merit of putting the (right) question *(Fragestellung)* and using the right conceptual scheme or conceptuality *(Begrifflichkeit).*[46] He puts to the New Testament text questions that we ought to ask. Moreover, he avoids imposing the category of substance on everything that he finds there. For example, he rightly does not look for language about "the soul" as an entity, but first looks for "modes of being." Bultmann writes, "Heidegger's analysis of the ontological structure of being would seem to be no more than a secularized philosophical version of the New Testament view of human life."[47]

By "philosophy" Bultmann and Macquarrie mean here primarily Heidegger's philosophy, which had enormous influence in Germany between the two wars. We reserve most of our discussion of Heidegger to the chapter on Gadamer, although some readers may wish to anticipate this dis-

---

44. Bultmann, "New Testament and Mythology," in *Kerygma and Myth,* 1:22; cf. Bultmann, *New Testament Mythology,* p. 20.

45. Bultmann, *New Testament Mythology,* p. 23; cf. Bultmann, "New Testament and Mythology," in *Kerygma and Myth,* 1:25.

46. Macquarrie, *An Existentialist Theology,* pp. 13-14; cf. pp. 3-26.

47. Bultmann, in *Kerygma and Myth,* 1:25.

cussion. In England writers such as Gilbert Ryle objected to radical weaknesses in Heidegger's philosophy, as we note below. But Heidegger rejects what he calls "the Greek interpretation of being" and substitutes a more "historical" and "subjective" (or subject-related) understanding. Heidegger writes that "Being" is a reality that is close to hand, not an abstract "concept." Human beings encounter it as *Dasein*, being-there, or in their historical, concrete existence here and now. "The understanding of oneself which leads along this way we call 'existential.'"[48] Further, Heidegger declares, "Whenever *Dasein* tacitly understands and interprets something like Being, it does so with *time* as its standpoint."[49] The philosophical history of inquiries about "Being" must therefore be destroyed. Phenomenology and interpretation must take the place of more traditional categories. We begin with ways for *Dasein* to be, which may be authentic or inauthentic.

4. Criticisms of Bultmann's Program as a Whole

Bultmann's program, as Giovanni Miegge points out, depends on a sharp polarization between *kerygma* and myth. *Kerygma,* Miegge argues, is the content, while "the 'myth' provides the 'framework.'"[50] Moreover, according to Bultmann's form criticism, even the *kerygma* arose only from the faith of the primitive community. Miegge continues to declare, "Faith in the risen Jesus projects itself retrospectively onto the Jesus of history. . . . Above all, what is derived from the Hellenistic community is the new understanding of Christ as *Kyrios,* Lord, and as Son of God. . . . The Gnostic myth, then, offered to Christian faith (is) . . . an appropriate framework of concepts and pictorial forms."[51]

David Cairns similarly points out that there is "a radical pulling apart of faith from the historical."[52] We must distinguish Bultmann's historical skepticism, he says, from his flight from the historical. It is the former, however,

48. Martin Heidegger, *Being and Time,* trans. John Macquarrie and Edward Robinson (Oxford: Blackwell, 1962), pp. 32-33.

49. Heidegger, *Being and Time,* p. 39, italics in original.

50. Giovanni Miegge, *Gospel and Myth in the Thought of Rudolf Bultmann,* trans. Stephen Neill (London: Lutterworth, 1960), p. 20.

51. Miegge, *Gospel and Myth,* pp. 26, 29, and 31.

52. David Cairns, *A Gospel without Myth? Bultmann's Challenge to the Preacher* (London: SCM, 1960), p. 141.

that makes the latter possible. His nineteenth-century version of Lutheranism, too, makes this plausible, turning a defense of the reliability of the New Testament into a historical and epistemological "work." His neo-Kantianism places "description" and "report" on one side of a dualism, and "grace," "address," and "hearing" on the other. But Graham Stanton and N. J. Young have asked whether the New Testament authors were allegedly indifferent to "facts" about Jesus of Nazareth.[53] We are not denying that the Synoptic Gospels were as much to be an influence on the present as to give historical reports, but the two are not mutually exclusive alternatives.

In *Jesus Christ and Mythology* Bultmann suggests that Paul begins to replace the "myth" of apocalyptic expectation with the existential language of being united with Christ. John demythologizes eschatological or cosmic conflict into notions of "false teachers." Bultmann writes, "The way for demythologizing was already paved" (2 Cor. 5:17; John 5:26; 1 John 4:16).[54] But if Paul and John wished to express truth in this latter way, why did they not do so consistently? There is an element here of "Heads, I win; tails, you lose." Moreover, there is no linear chronological sequence in Paul, in spite of C. H. Dodd's claim, from future to "realized" (present) eschatology, even if Bultmann attempts an unconvincing answer in his *History and Eschatology*.[55]

We have discussed Bultmann's view of history. His view of miracles is connected with this but distinct from it. Wolfhart Pannenberg refers to this relegating of belief in the miraculous to the category of myth. "The acceptance of divine intervention in the course of events . . . is fundamental to every religious understanding of the world, including one which is not mythical."[56] "Eschatology does not display mythical features."[57] We take the point that Bultmann does not wish to be associated with earlier liberals such as Harnack and Jülicher. He does not advocate "a few basic principles of religion and ethics" that are easy for "modern man" to accept. For then the *kerygma*

53. Graham N. Stanton, *Jesus of Nazareth in New Testament Preaching,* Society for New Testament Studies Monograph Series, no. 27 (Cambridge: Cambridge University Press, 1974), throughout; cf. Norman J. Young, *History and Existential Theology: The Role of History in the Thought of Rudolf Bultmann* (Philadelphia: Westminster, 1969).

54. Bultmann, in *Kerygma and Myth,* 1:208.

55. Rudolf Bultmann, *History and Eschatology* (Edinburgh: Edinburgh University Press, 1957), chapters 3 and 4.

56. Wolfhart Pannenberg, "Myth in Biblical and Christian Tradition," in Pannenberg, *Basic Questions in Theology,* trans. R. A. Wilson (London: SCM, 1970-73), 3:14.

57. Pannenberg, *Basic Questions in Theology,* 3:68; cf. pp. 71-74.

ceases to be *kerygma*. But can there be any *kerygma* without history, without acts of God in the world? Bultmann works with an outmoded view of language, in which language is *either* descriptive *or* address. But for such a view he relies on Karl Bühler and a given but mistaken tradition about language. We now know from Wittgenstein, Austin, Searle, Recanati, and others, not to mention the "politeness theory" of Brown, that language overlaps in function and speech-acts may depend on states of affairs.[58] On top of this, Bultmann's very concept of myth is deeply self-contradictory and self-defeating.

Bultmann's program proves itself to be profoundly old-fashioned, as we should expect a view first formulated in 1941 to be. Many obvious criticisms remain unanswered. Yet in many ways Bultmann seeks to expose "the true stumbling block of the cross." He is right that the true intent of language about the last judgment is a call to accountability now, but he is wrong to deny all future or referential meaning concerning the last judgment. Otherwise the *kerygma* becomes little more than a bluff. This kind of example puts in a clear light why the so-called Bultmann School has split largely into left-wing and right-wing critics. Christology, his right-wing critics claim, has been dissolved into soteriology. This becomes clear in his discussion of John, and some claim in John 6. From a Catholic perspective, Josef Blank observes, "What stimulates too little discussion in Bultmann is that this discourse on bread [in John 6] is basically *Christology*."[59] We may add that his "Hellenistic" and "gnostic" view of John's concepts is severely dated, not least in the light of Qumran, where dualisms are not infrequent in first-century Jewish writings. René Marlé also expresses regret that although he is not quite "Marcionite," more attention should have been given to the content of the Old Testament.[60]

5. The Subsequent Course of the Debate: Left-Wing and Right-Wing Critics

Some critics of his program believed that Bultmann did not go far enough. If much of the language of the New Testament is either mythological or sym-

58. *Thiselton on Hermeneutics*, pp. 51-150.

59. Josef Blank, in *Rudolf Bultmann in Catholic Thought*, ed. Thomas F. O'Meara and Donald M. Weisser (New York: Herder and Herder, 1968), p. 105, italics in original; cf. pp. 78-109.

60. René Marlé, "Bultmann and the Old Testament," in *Rudolf Bultmann in Catholic Thought*, pp. 110-24.

bolic, why stop with the uniqueness of the cross? Herbert Braun, Karl Jaspers, Fritz Buri, and to a degree Schubert Ogden defend this view, and have come to be known as Bultmann's "left-wing" critics.

Herbert Braun was born in 1903 and educated at the universities of Königsburg and Tübingen. He is best known in Germany for his work on the New Testament and Qumran, although outside Germany he is also well known for his radical existential interpretation whereby even "God" becomes a myth or symbol for self-understanding.[61] Jesus and God are symbols that ever seek to serve as ways of understanding humanity. Braun argues with Bultmann that a God who objectively intervenes in the world is no longer credible. Why regard Jesus or God as entities at all? Protestant theology since Schleiermacher, Braun believes, has been moving toward recognizing that we are dealing only with ways of expressing our experience, to which we give the names "Christ" and "God." But we can manage without even these names. They, too, can belong to the great program of demythologizing and de-objectifying. Braun offers a more popular version of this in "Vom Verstehen der Neuen Testamentes" ("On the Understanding of the New Testament").[62]

Many have responded vigorously to Braun, but none more strongly than Helmut Gollwitzer.[63] Braun, he argues, simply rejects "theism." Theism requires some sort of metaphysics or ontology by definition. Moreover, Braun is too skeptical of first-century worldviews. Pannenberg, Macquarrie, Hepburn, and others criticize the confusions embodied in Bultmann's use of "myth," put forward by Bultmann and by Braun. "God," Gollwitzer argues, is a personal God, and his name is "irreplaceable and unsurrenderable."[64] He concludes, "The theistic way of speaking as a way of expressing Christian faith cannot be outgrown by another."[65]

Karl Jaspers (1883-1969) writes primarily as a psychiatrist and philoso-

61. Herbert Braun, "Der Sinn der neotestamentlichen Christologie," *Zeitschrift für Theologie und Kirche* 54 (1957): 341-77; cf. Braun, *Qumran und das Neue Testament* (Tübingen: Mohr, 1966).

62. Herbert Braun, "Vom Verstehen der Neuen Testamentes," *Neue deutsche Hefte*, November 1957, pp. 697-709; reprinted in Braun, *Gesammelte Studien zum Neuen Testament und Umwelt* (Tübingen, 1962), pp. 243-309.

63. Helmut Gollwitzer, *The Existence of God as Confessed by Faith,* trans. James W. Leitch (London: SCM, 1965), pp. 35-45.

64. Gollwitzer, *Existence of God,* p. 42.

65. Gollwitzer, *Existence of God,* p. 44.

pher, not a theologian. He first studied law and medicine, and became a lecturer in psychology at Heidelberg University. At the age of forty he turned to existentialist philosophy, and became professor of philosophy at the University of Basel, Switzerland. In psychology he addressed especially the problems of paranoia and illusion, and in philosophy he was profoundly influenced by Kierkegaard and Nietzsche. He emphasized a philosophy of existence, and the freedom of the individual.

Religion could, for Jaspers, perform a positive role in the discovery of truth, but it must not be an exclusivist religion, and it must be true *for the inquirer.* Different inquirers discover *"transcendence"* in different ways and forms. Existential analysis could discover "religion" rather than Christianity. Jaspers is distinctly pluralistic in his approach. In his essay in *Kerygma and Myth* he confesses to feeling like a traveler in a foreign country. But he describes Bultmann's approach as "in effect altogether orthodox and illiberal, despite his liberality as a man and a historian."[66] In his *Philosophy* he argues that when an individual reaches the limits of science or empiricism, he or she can either relapse into despair or choose by a leap of faith to believe in some kind of transcendence or self-transcendence. But *transcendence* does not necessarily imply a personal God. Something lies "beyond" the world, but not a personal God.

Bultmann replies to Jaspers that he has not abandoned a philosophy of existence. He follows Heidegger, who goes beyond the traditional subject-object schema or conceptual scheme. Jaspers fails to understand the predicament that the interpreter faces. The real problem, for Bultmann, concerns Jaspers's philosophy, but how to interpret the Bible. Bultmann insists on the uniqueness of the New Testament. The answer, he writes, is in the end, "Lord, to whom shall we go? Thou hast the words of eternal life (John 6:68)."[67]

Few scholars stand midway between right and left, endorsing Bultmann's view. But probably the most notable are Friedrich Gogarten (1887-1967), Hans-Werner Bartsch (b. 1915), and Walter Schmithals (b. 1923). Gogarten was professor of theology at the University of Jena from 1927 and at Göttingen from 1933. He expands Bultmann's program in *Demythologizing and History.*[68] Walter Schmithals studied at Marburg and Münster. He

---

66. Karl Jaspers, "Myth and Religion," in *Kerygma and Myth,* 2:174.

67. Rudolf Bultmann, "A Case for Demythologizing," in *Kerygma and Myth,* 2:194.

68. Gogarten's best-known works include *Christ the Crisis* (London: SCM, 1978) and *Demythologizing and History* (London: SCM, 1955).

lectured at Marburg and became professor of New Testament in the University of Berlin. He wrote *An Introduction to the Theology of Rudolf Bultmann* and also wrote on Gnosticism and Corinth, and many other books. He also argues for a view of politics that is not distinctively Christian.

The majority of scholars, however, fall into the category of "right-wing" critics. Helmut Thielicke (1908-86), Karl Barth (1886-1968), and Julius Schniewind (1883-1948) stand among the earliest critics of Bultmann's program. Thielicke attacks his account of worldview, but also points out that if we follow his definition of myth we deny the truth of *creatio ex nihilo*.[69] He writes, "The question is not whether the New Testament can be emancipated from myth, but whether human thought can. . . . Space, time, and causation are not objective categories."[70] Thielicke questions many aspects of Bultmann's proposals.

In their early days there were certain similarities between the approaches of Barth and Bultmann. In their shared dialectical theology both rejected the supposed value-neutrality of the New Testament, as Bultmann's early support for Barth's *Commentary on the Epistle to the Romans* showed. But Barth became increasingly uneasy with Bultmann's view of history, ontology, and much else. He agrees that we do not extract theoretical propositions from the New Testament. Here Bultmann is right. He recognizes that we cannot call Bultmann a "liberal" of the same order as Adolf Harnack, Wilhelm Bousset, or Adolf Jülicher. The *kerygma* concerns God's act, not human subjective experience. Moreover, God's saving action is based upon Christology, and in Bultmann we find a soteriology that is derived from Christology. He does not give enough attention to what occurred "on the third day." Bultmann owes too much to a supposed Lutheranism.[71]

Schniewind is no less robust than Barth in his attack on Bultmann. "We cannot reject *Historie* because it is not vitally present for us, and accept *Geschichte* because it is."[72] Eschatology, he argues, is future history, and Christology is vital. "Either Caesar in all his glory is Lord and Saviour . . . or else Jesus of Nazareth is."[73] Many others might be mentioned, from Ernst Kinder to W. Künneth. In Britain we may include Ian Henderson, John Macquarrie, and David Cairns, among others. Meanwhile Bultmann insists

69. Thielicke, "The Restatement," 1:144-45; cf. pp. 138-74.
70. Thielicke, "The Restatement," 1:158.
71. Barth, "Bultmann," 2:121-23.
72. Julius Schniewind, "A Reply to Bultmann," in *Kerygma and Myth*, 1:83; cf. pp. 45-101.
73. Schniewind, "A Reply to Bultmann," 1:91.

that he learned from Heidegger not what the New Testament says, but how to say it. Not everyone is convinced. Ian Henderson argues that interpreting the New Testament is more like interpreting a masterpiece than explaining a code.[74] No one would be foolish enough to throw away the original. In spite of their seriously dated excesses, Bultmann's proposals deserve a critical hearing for some positive insights they contain.

6. Recommended Initial Reading

Bultmann, Rudolf, "New Testament and Mythology," in *Kerygma and Myth: A Theological Debate,* edited by Hans-Werner Bartsch, 2 vols. (London: SCM, 1953), 1:1-44; retranslated in Bultmann, *New Testament Mythology and Other Basic Writings,* selected, edited, and translated by Schubert M. Ogden (Philadelphia: Fortress, 1984), pp. 1-44.

Jensen, Alexander, *Theological Hermeneutics,* SCM Core Text (London: SCM, 2007), pp. 115-34.

Thiselton, Anthony C., *The Two Horizons: New Testament Hermeneutics and Philosophical Description with Special Reference to Heidegger, Bultmann, Gadamer, and Wittgenstein* (Grand Rapids: Eerdmans; Exeter: Paternoster, 1980), pp. 227-92.

74. Ian Henderson, *Myth in the New Testament* (London: SCM, 1952), p. 31.

CHAPTER X

Some Mid-Twentieth-Century Approaches: Barth, the New Hermeneutic, Structuralism, Post-Structuralism, and Barr's Semantics

1. Karl Barth's Earlier and Later Hermeneutics

1. *Barth's Background and Career.* Karl Barth (1886-1968) was born at Basel in Switzerland, of a Calvinist family. He studied first at Berne, Switzerland, and then at Berlin, Tübingen, and Marburg in Germany. Among his teachers were Wilhelm Hermann, Adolf Jülicher, and Adolf von Harnack, whose liberalism Barth came later to oppose. From 1911 Barth was pastor at Safenwil in Switzerland.

From 1915 to 1918 Barth produced *The Resurrection of the Dead*, on 1 Corinthians, and most of the essays in *The Word of God and the Word of Man*, which contained his programmatic essay "The Strange New World within the Bible."[1] These stress a discontinuity between "natural religion" and the Christian gospel. Barth stressed "Let no man glory in men" (1 Cor. 3:21), and argued that the main defect at Corinth was "the boldness, assurance, and enthusiasm with which they believe not in God, but in their own belief in God and in particular leaders and heroes."[2] In "The Strange New World within the Bible" Barth wrote, "A new world projects itself into our ordinary world. . . . It is not right human thoughts about God which form the content of the Bible, but right divine thoughts about men."[3]

The motivation of such an outlook was the early failure of his hitherto

---

1. Karl Barth, *The Resurrection of the Dead*, trans. H. J. Stenning (London: Hodder and Stoughton, 1933; German, 1915-16); and Barth, *The Word of God and the Word of Man*, trans. D. Horton (London: Hodder and Stoughton, 1928).

2. Barth, *Resurrection*, p. 17.

3. Barth, *The Word of God*, pp. 37 and 43.

liberal theology, which he learned from his teachers, to cut any ice in Safenwil. Largely ignoring the biblical criticism of his former teachers, he wrote his *Commentary on the Epistle to the Romans* in 1918, and produced a second edition in 1922, in which he attacked the method of his former teachers.[4] In 1925 he was appointed professor at the University of Göttingen, and in 1930 he was appointed professor at Bonn. In 1934 he was the main author of the Confessing Church's Barmen Declaration against the Nazis, which proclaimed the sole Lordship of Christ. Predictably he was then dismissed from his chair in 1935, and became professor at Basel, where he remained until his formal retirement in 1962. From 1932 he worked on his magisterial *Church Dogmatics,* which was still in progress when he died in 1968. His commentary on Romans would alone have assured him an international reputation, but his *Church Dogmatics* became one of the most influential works of Christian writing ever, and in English translation runs to fourteen large volumes.[5]

2. *Barth's Earlier Approach to Hermeneutics.* The early period of Barth's theology up to the second edition of *Romans* (1915-22) may be called the period of dialectical theology, or theology of crisis, in which he stressed God's transcendence or holy otherness, and the distance between an infinite and holy God and the finitude and fallenness of humanity. Because we cannot speak directly or univocally of such a God, divine revelation addresses us with both a yes of grace and a no of judgment, crisis, or otherness, in dialectical form.

In his commentary on Romans (second edition of 1922) Barth writes that if he has a "system" at all, it springs from what Kierkegaard called the "infinite qualitative distinction" between human time and God's eternity: "God is in heaven and thou art on earth."[6] Barth continues, "The relation between such a God and such a man . . . is for me the theme of the Bible and the essence of philosophy. Philosophers name this KRISIS of human perception — the Prime Mover; the Bible beholds at the same cross-roads — the figure of Jesus Christ."[7] For him in his earlier period, therefore, the twofold significance of biblical hermeneutics is, first, that we must use "the analogy

---

4. Karl Barth, *The Epistle to the Romans,* trans. E. C. Hoskyns (Oxford and London: Oxford University Press, 1933).

5. Karl Barth, *Church Dogmatics,* ed. G. W. Bromiley, T. F. Torrance, and others, 14 vols. (Edinburgh: T. & T. Clark, 1957-75).

6. Barth, *Romans,* p. 10 (2nd ed., German, 1922).

7. Barth, *Romans,* p. 10.

of faith" to be able to speak to, or to listen to, God indirectly or dialectically, and second, this language must be christocentric, for a theology of "crisis" points to Christ.

Barth's commentary has little time for the human sciences *(Geisteswissenschaften)*, or for general hermeneutics as their possible basis (with Dilthey). He writes, "Disillusioned with psychology and history we turn ourselves to the Bible."[8] But then this brings the danger of making even the Bible an "idol" in place of the living God (Rom. 12:3). Romans 8:5-9 shows that "the mind of the flesh" can be an enemy of the Spirit, and can seek a counterfeit "peace." Yet Barth also writes in his preface: "My sole aim is to interpret Scripture. . . . No one can of course bring out *(auslegen)* the meaning of a text without at the same time adding something to it *(einlegen)*."[9] Thus Barth aims at theological exegesis for his own times. The reader must hear the word of God afresh in faith and obedience. The theological content is vital. Some at Corinth failed to believe in the resurrection of 1 Corinthians 15 because "Some have not the knowledge of God" (1 Cor. 15:34).[10] The Bible is the "other," a "new, greater world."[11]

Barth and his liberal former teachers were equally shocked at the stance of the other. Hermann, Jülicher, and Harnack were shocked that Barth had discarded a value-neutral approach and seemed to bypass much biblical criticism, or at least to regard it as no more than the preliminary stage of exegesis. Barth, for his part, believed that their approach was bankrupt for the contemporary reader. Liberalism, he insisted, was not "modern" at all, but cast the *kerygma* of Jesus and Paul into an insipid "teaching," which was not *kerygma* (proclamation) at all. To the surprise of many, Rudolf Bultmann at first supported the early Barth, agreeing that the New Testament presents *"kerygma"* rather than banal "teaching."[12] Only later did he come to regard Barth's theology as too mythological, and parted company with his early theology. Yet both men stressed the transcendence (or "otherness") of God,

---

8. Barth, *Romans*, p. 431.
9. Barth, *Romans*, p. ix.
10. Barth, *Resurrection*, p. 190.
11. Barth, *The Word of God*, p. 42.
12. Cf. James M. Robinson, "Hermeneutics since Barth," in *New Frontiers in Theology*, vol. 2, *The New Hermeneutic*, ed. James M. Robinson and John B. Cobb, Jr. (New York and London: Harper and Row, 1964), pp. 1-77, and Francis Watson, *Text, Church, and World: Biblical Interpretation in Theological Perspective* (Edinburgh: T. & T. Clark, 1994), pp. 1-14, 226-40, and 243-45.

and both emphasized the indirect or analogical nature of Christian language that tried to express divine revelation.

3. *Barth's Later Hermeneutics.* As the Second World War and Nazism became an increasing threat, Barth reflected more deeply on the nature of analogy, and his christocentric perspective became also more trinitarian. On the former subject he broke with his close colleague Emil Brunner, who stressed the ordinances of marriage and the state, and the possibility of repentance, as pointing to the analogy of being *(analogia entis)* expounded by Thomas Aquinas. For Barth, only the analogy of faith *(analogia fidei)* could adequately safeguard the transcendence or otherness of God. The subject is complex and subtle, and much can be said on both sides.[13]

Much of Karl Barth's middle or later thought on the subject comes in the nearly 400 pages of sections 19-21 of his *Church Dogmatics* I/2 (English, 1956).[14] His previous sections cover humankind as doer of the Word of God, the love of God, and the praises of God. Now he continues the theme that humankind recognizes the distinctiveness of the Bible because through it the Holy Spirit makes possible human obedience to Christ as Lord of the Church, and response to the word spoken by Moses and the prophets, and to the word spoken by the Evangelists and the apostles.[15] The revelation, however, finds expression in the Bible as *witness* to God's revelation, and it is a witness to "the lordship of the triune God."[16] In the Bible we encounter "human words written in human speech," which witness to revelation.[17]

Barth further emphasizes that the Word of God is "for the Church." Hence in sections 20 and 21 he speaks of the nature of the Church as recipient of this Word and the significance of this for the doctrine of the Trinity. Hence: "Biblical hermeneutics cannot let itself be dictated to by a general hermeneutics."[18] But we are still addressed by a human word, in all its historical particularity. This is also "divine revelation," and as such "the

13. Cf. Alan J. Torrance, *Persons in Communion: An Essay on Trinitarian Description and Human Participation with Special Reference to Volume One of Karl Barth's "Church Dogmatics"* (Edinburgh: T. & T. Clark, 1996).

14. Barth, *Church Dogmatics* I/2 (Edinburgh: T. & T. Clark, 1956), pp. 457-740 (German, pp. 505-990).

15. Barth, *Church Dogmatics* I/2, section 19.1, p. 457.

16. Barth, *Church Dogmatics* I/2, section 19.1, p. 458 (cf. German, p. 512).

17. Barth, *Church Dogmatics* I/2, section 19.1, p. 463.

18. Otto Weber, *Karl Barth's "Church Dogmatics": An Introductory Report*, trans. A. C. Cochrane (London: Lutterworth, 1953), p. 58.

analogia Fidei . . . is drawn into the darkness and light of its mystery."[19] To be understood by us (i.e., in interpretation) it lays hold on us; it is not we who master it. The Church confirms or establishes this witness on the part of Scripture. "Holy Scripture is the Word of God to the Church and for the Church."[20] It is, however, also no more than a *"witness"* to revelation, while the biblical canon is *recognized* (not created) by the Church. The Old and New Testaments belong to the canon. The Bible also witnesses not only to revelation, but through the prophets and the apostles to the Church.

In section 20 Barth argues that the Church does not claim "direct, absolute and material authority for itself," but mediates "the authority of Holy Scripture."[21] The Church is not absolutely preserved from human error. But in matters of revelation the decisive event is the resurrection of Christ. Barth also quotes the standard biblical texts concerning the authority of the Bible in 2 Timothy 3:14-17 ("You have known the sacred writings from childhood. . . . All scripture is inspired by God and is useful . . .") and 2 Peter 1:19-21 ("Men and women moved by the Holy Spirit spoke from God"). The Church may see itself as self-sufficient; or it can be an "obedient" Church. In the latter case, it may "confess" its faith, as in the Barmen Declaration of the Confessing Church against Hitler and Nazism. It is "under" the Word of God.

Barth shows that this has a trinitarian dimension. The obedience of the Church, "under" Scripture, is a response to the Holy Spirit, who makes it possible, and an acknowledgment of the lordship of God, Father and Son. The sections on Scripture (sections 19-21 of the *Church Dogmatics*) lead on first through "The Freedom of the Word" (section 21) to "The Proclamation of the Church" in its mission doctrine, and ethics (section 22), and "Dogmatics as a Function of the Hearing Church" (section 23). This section completes the second half of part I on the Word of God. Hermeneutics is to serve this end. The Trinity plays a vital part; so also do analogy and the Church.

4. *Assessment.* It is understandable that the paths of Barth and of Bultmann radically diverge. They agree that language about the transcendent God is analogical, but Barth sees a more radical discontinuity between God and humanity than most others. He presents hermeneutics as part of his theology of God as Father, Son, and Holy Spirit, "from above." He emphasizes

---

19. Barth, *Church Dogmatics* I/2, section 19.1, p. 472.
20. Barth, *Church Dogmatics* I/2, section 19.2, p. 475.
21. Barth, *Church Dogmatics* I/2, section 20, p. 538.

that the Bible is by human authors, and is no more than a "witness" to christocentric revelation. He stresses that hermeneutical understanding demands obedience. He gives a place to the role of the Church and the canon, as Hans Frei and Brevard Childs do after him. We cannot do without Barth's insights, but they are part of his theological thought. Barth says relatively little about the everyday problems of hermeneutics, but it is good to bear in mind his theological perspective. Recently Mark A. Bowald has called for an account of divine agency in hermeneutics, and Barth gives this emphasis.[22]

It is sometimes said that Barth moved from a christological to a trinitarian perspective, but he did not leave the former behind. His home background anchored him to a love of the Bible, and his powerful reaction against historical-critical methods ensured that biblical criticism should not be followed blindly, nor with a value-neutral pretense.[23] He rightly urged that Jesus of Nazareth did more than "teach" moral truths or general maxims. In his early work he made good use of Kierkegaard.

Barth described his *Anselm: Fides Quaerens Intellectum* (1930) as a "vital key" to the *Church Dogmatics*. He saw "belief" as a process initiated by God. Many would argue that he went too far in writing "No" to Brunner in 1934, but this was written out of a special situation in Rome. He is strong on the need for self-criticism in Christian theology. He believes that "God may speak to us through Russian communism, a flute concerto, or a dead dog."[24] But God speaks "where and when God . . . fulfilling the word of the Bible . . . lets it become true."[25] God's word is above all a word of promise, which is actualized in the present as a transforming event. Whatever the practicalities of hermeneutics, this broader perspective remains true. In Barth's view "God can be known only through God." "Understanding" comes from God.

2. The So-Called New Hermeneutic of Fuchs and Ebeling

As we observed in the chapter on the parables of Jesus, we have deliberately made this discussion shorter than some, because we have written at length

---

22. Mark Alan Bowald, *Rendering the Word in Theological Hermeneutics* (Aldershot and Burlington, Vt.: Ashgate, 2007).

23. Cf. Telford Work, *Living and Active: Scripture in the Economy of Salvation* (Grand Rapids: Eerdmans, 2002), pp. 67-100.

24. Barth, *Church Dogmatics* I/1, section 3, p. 55.

25. Barth, *Church Dogmatics* I/1, section 4, p. 120.

several times on this subject elsewhere. Not many developments have occurred since I wrote, and the subject, which was important in the early 1960s, has generally lost much of its attention and interest, especially since its Heideggerian notion of language has been recognized as one-sided and its overgeneralized concept of "speech-event" does not fully match the more sophisticated theory of J. L. Austin, John Searle, F. Recanati, and others.

Ernst Fuchs (1903-83) and Gerhard Ebeling (1912-2001) are generally regarded as the founders of the so-called "new" hermeneutic, and its chief exponents. Fuchs was a former pupil of Bultmann, and like him a Lutheran. He was educated at the universities of Bonn, Berlin, Tübingen, and Marburg. Like Ebeling, together with G. Bornkamm and Ernst Käsemann, he criticized Bultmann for going too far in his reductive view of history, and founded the "New Quest" of the historical Jesus. He wrote *Christ und der Geist bei Paulus* (1932), *Hermeneutik* (1954), and *Marburger Hermeneutik* (1968).[26] He seeks to conflate existential hermeneutics with his particular view of texts, especially those that concern the parables of Jesus. To date, probably only *Studies in Historical Jesus* has appeared in English.

Gerhard Ebeling taught at Tübingen, but then at Zürich, Switzerland. In 1960 he published *Word and Faith,* a volume of essays on various subjects, but worked mainly in church history.[27] He also wrote *The Word of God and Tradition, An Introduction to a Theological Theory of Language,*[28] *The Nature of Faith, Theology and Proclamation, Luther,* and *The Study of Theology.* Both Fuchs and Ebeling have written several articles on the new hermeneutic in English translation, including one by each in a volume edited by James Robinson and J. L. Cobb, Jr., *New Frontiers in Theology,* volume 2, *The New Hermeneutic* (1964).[29]

Fuchs believes that the New Testament *kerygma* (proclamation) creates, rather than assumes, faith. Like Barth, Fuchs and Ebeling urge that the Holy

26. Ernst Fuchs, *Hermeneutik,* 4th ed. (Tübingen: Mohr, 1970) and *Marburger Hermeneutik* (Tübingen: Mohr, 1968).

27. E.g., Gerhard Ebeling, *Word and Faith,* trans. J. W. Leitch (Philadelphia: Fortress; London: SCM, 1963).

28. Gerhard Ebeling, *The Word of God and Tradition,* trans. S. H. Hooke (London: Collins, 1968), and Ebeling, *An Introduction to a Theological Theory of Language* (London: Collins, 1973).

29. Ernst Fuchs, "The New Testament and the Hermeneutical Problem," in *New Frontiers in Theology,* vol. 2, *The New Hermeneutic;* cf. G. Ebeling, "Word of God and Hermeneutic," in *New Frontiers in Theology,* 2:78-110.

Spirit and the Word of God have power to create this faith (Heb. 4:12-13). They both insist that the text itself is meant *to live*. But they also argue that in a changed situation "The *same* word can be said to another time only by being said differently."[30] Fuchs and Ebeling also follow Dilthey, Heidegger, and Bultmann in insisting on the important role of preliminary understanding, or pre-understanding.

This living Word encounters the hearers or readers as a "language event." Fuchs uses the word *Sprachereignis* (language event); Ebeling prefers *Wortgeschehen* (literally, word event, or more broadly, speech event).[31] A language event, Fuchs argues, does not arise merely from processes of cognitive thought. The text itself directs and shapes the reader. The event of language thereby brings about fresh understanding. It produces "empathy" or "common agreement" or "mutual understanding" *(Einverständnis)* between how God himself sees things and the vantage point or horizon of the readers. The text is therefore more than an object or an instrument. Language-event and empathy, or common understanding, both lie at the heart of the new hermeneutic. Ebeling declares, "The basic structure of word is therefore not statement."[32]

Fuchs and Ebeling agree with Bultmann in seeing the New Testament writings not as descriptions, reports, or cognitive statements, but as address and "indirect" discourse. Like Bultmann, they separate these two modes of discourse and allow not even an overlap. Here both Bultmann and the new hermeneutic are too heavily influenced by Heidegger. The existential appeal to personal "experience" runs too high here. Fuchs writes, "We should accept as true only that which we acknowledge as valid for our own person."[33] Ebeling insists that hermeneutics is not the understanding *of* language, "but understanding THROUGH language."[34]

Yet both Fuchs and Ebeling stress the application and transforming action of the Word, in contrast to examining or describing its content. It is not a matter of theory and talk; the Word of God through the indirect language

---

30. Gerhard Ebeling, "Time and Word," in *The Future of Our Religious Past: Essays in Honour of Rudolf Bultmann*, ed. James M. Robinson (London: SCM, 1971), p. 265; translated from *Zeit und Geschichte* (1964).

31. Fuchs, *Marburger Hermeneutik*, pp. 243-45, and *Studies of the Historical Jesus* (London: SCM, 1964), pp. 196-212; cf. Ebeling, *Word and Faith*, pp. 325-32.

32. Ebeling, "Word of God," p. 103.

33. Fuchs, "The New Testament," p. 117.

34. Ebeling, "Word of God," p. 93.

of the Bible *masters* and *shapes* the reader. In many of his writings Fuchs argues that this reflects the love of Jesus and the sovereignty of grace. The parables of Jesus lead to eternal life, and the Beatitudes give and enact blessing rather than merely talk about it. To put a mouse in front of a cat is like seeing the language event of the text in operation. Jesus, especially in the parables, stands alongside the hearer. As we saw in chapter III, on the parables, love does not just "blurt out," but provides in advance a place of meeting. This often takes the form of providing the "world" of the text, in which a "common understanding" is reached. Parables offer the *pledge* and promise of Jesus, which amount to "God's kindness."[35]

1. Fuchs and Ebeling do bring a *creative* dimension to those passages they handle. If they were not under the spell of Heidegger and Bultmann, much of their program might be compared with D. D. Evans, *The Logic of Self-Involvement,* in Anglo-American philosophy, even though their speech-acts are not what Austin and Evans call true "illocutionary" performatives. Admittedly Fuchs says, "One cannot treasure too highly the empirical."[36] Simply to consider an engineering construction, he says, demonstrates this. But he then alludes to Bultmann's program of demythologizing the New Testament, in which the existential gives us "more" than "the facts," and description or report falls from view. Only what is self-involving has the character of truth. In a review of my work on the new hermeneutic written in 1973-74 but published in 1977, Stephen Neill complains that my essay first gave a very favorable impression of the new hermeneutic but then "pulled it all apart."[37] But this faithfully reflects the nature of the new hermeneutic. Much is attractive, but much is also false. It has generated considerable controversy. Yet why must we accept all or nothing? It uses the notions of language event, "world," and "common understanding" creatively. Yet Fuchs insists that the resurrection of Jesus Christ is a "linguistic event" rather than one of "objective" history. May it not be *both* self-involving *and* "factual"?

2. Fuchs and Ebeling also tend to use biblical texts selectively. Fuchs implies that critical study may "first strike the text dead." Yet their attempt to "let the text strike home" *(treffen)* has little of the subtlety of Ricoeur's

---

35. Fuchs, *Historical Jesus,* pp. 33-37.

36. Fuchs, "The New Testament," p. 115.

37. Anthony C. Thiselton, "The New Hermeneutic," in *New Testament Interpretation,* ed. I. H. Marshall (Exeter: Paternoster, 1972), pp. 308-33; cf. Neill's review in *Church of England Newspaper,* 18 November 1977, p. 20.

"post-critical naïveté."[38] (See below.) They tend to focus on such genres as hymns, poems, or metaphors and parables at the expense of more discursive discourse. 1 Corinthians 13 and Philippians 2:5-11, discussed in *Hermeneutik* and elsewhere, receive more attention than some parts of the Epistles. Their strength lies in what they say about "indirect" language. But 1 Corinthians 15:3-6 or 3-8 equally demands the attention of the interpreter.

3. Fuchs and Ebeling have a view of language that remains rooted in elements drawn from Heidegger, but they ignore a broader linguistic tradition. Although Fuchs explicitly disclaims the influence of the later Heidegger, Ebeling's words about "language poisoning" and "fragmentation" in the *Nature of Theological Language* seem to owe much to the later Heidegger's claim that humankind has "fallen out of being." Indeed, there is almost a hint of word magic in their notion of the power of the word, as I have previously argued.

Yet it is possible to understand these pronouncements about language in a more charitable and positive way. Where both Fuchs and Ebeling speak of creative, authentic language as "gathering," they also have in mind that the language of the home can bind together our common understanding. This applies to the Church. In this sense, sharing right language and interpretation can bind into one a scattered church.

4. Best of all, the new hermeneutic seeks to draw attention to "the rights of the text," as that which is *master,* and not servant, of the interpreter, congregation, or community of readers. We are not in the business of merely manipulating concepts when we seek to interpret the New Testament. Ebeling writes, "The Word of God . . . is only given in the constantly renewed interpretation of Holy Scripture."[39] Fuchs comments, *"The truth has ourselves as its object,"* and "The texts must translate us before we can translate them."[40]

Yet Fuchs and Ebeling belong to the Bultmann school of interpretation, and press biblical criticism as far as they can. They urge mythological and existential interpretation based on "experience." On the one hand they urge listening and obedience, and see the Church as serving the Word of God; on the other hand the movement has tended to peter out today, partly because

---

38. Fuchs, *Historical Jesus,* pp. 196-98 and 202.

39. Ebeling, *The Word of God,* p. 26.

40. Fuchs, "The New Testament," p. 143, italics in original, and in *Zeit und Geschichte,* p. 277.

existential interpretation and Heidegger are no longer fashionable, partly because they show internal contradictions. They have influenced Robert Funk and several writers in America. But Amos Wilder asserts that in the end, largely because of their view of language and history, "Fuchs refuses to define the content of faith. He is afraid of the loss of immediacy. . . . Revelation, as it were, reveals nothing!"[41] Paul Achtemeier concludes a study of the new hermeneutic with a similar conclusion. The very success of early Christian proclamation depends upon its being *historically true* in content.[42] But contrary to Stephen Neill's comment, this does not prevent our learning something from the new hermeneutic. It is, however, no longer "new," if it ever was. At its peak it was probably overrated.

3. Structuralism and Its Application to Biblical Studies

Structuralism may mean various things, depending upon whether we are thinking of structuralism in linguistics or in social anthropology or in psychology. In *linguistics* it derives ultimately from the work of the linguistics scholar Ferdinand de Saussure (1857-1913), who saw language *(la langue)* as a general system or structure from which particular words or acts of speaking *(la parole)* were selected.[43] Within the system or structure the internal relations between words, especially relations of contrast, were crucial. They were paradigmatic, as when we select "pint" in contrast to "quart" of milk, or syntagmatic, as when we select "pint" or "quart" functions in relationship with "milk." "Kingdom" stands in "syntagmatic" (linear) relation to "of God"; the "hiddenness" of God stands in "paradigmatic" relation to the "manifestation" of God.

In biblical studies this had two later effects. First, it was taken to imply that language was autonomous and generated meaning *internally* rather than by its relation to history or to life. Second, it was initially welcomed as an "objective" science of language. Many reacted against the subjectivity of existentialism and of existential interpretation. It appeared that language

---

41. Amos Wilder, "The Word as Address and the Word as Meaning," in *New Frontiers in Theology,* 2:213; cf. pp. 198-216.

42. Paul J. Achtemeier, *An Introduction to the New Hermeneutic* (Philadelphia: Westminster, 1969), pp. 156-57; cf. pp. 149-65.

43. Ferdinand de Saussure, *Course in General Linguistics,* ed. C. Bally and A. Sechehaye, trans. R. Harris (London: Duckworth, 1983).

functioned as a system or structure, independently of human attitudes or experience.

Structuralism also found a place in *social anthropology*. Here Claude Lévi-Strauss in particular argued that kinship terms, for example, depended for their meaning on a contrast or *difference* within an implied structure or system. Thus "brother" differed from "sister" or "wife" because of its place in whole systems of relations. Similarly, Jacques Lacan later worked out a structuralist system in *psychology*.

Of these three approaches, the first is most influential in biblical structuralism. In contrast to existential interpretation, François Bovon wrote in 1978 (he has since then perhaps modified his view), "Some today rightly propose to read the text first in itself, understood for itself, apart from all reference to an author, to a history or to a reader. . . . A text does not have a single door nor a single key."[44] Saussure's linguistics led to Jost Trier's formulation of field semantics. Trier wrote, "Only as part of a whole . . . does a text yield a meaning, and only within a field *(nur im Feld gibt es Bedeutung)*."[45] In a "field" of meaning, the semantic scope of *red* and *yellow*, for example, depends on whether *orange* plays a part in the field:

Red	Yellow

Red	Orange	Yellow

Trier was not far from what Lévi-Strauss would claim for "fields" in social anthropology, for he included food and kinship terms in his semantic analysis.

Numerous writers in linguistics and semantics have endorsed and developed the approach of Saussure and Trier. Stephen Ullmann, John Lyons, and Eugene A. Nida develop this insight, and it is applied to biblical lexicography by John Sawyer, Erhardt Guttgemanns, Kenneth L. Burner, and Nida himself.[46] Because each word functions within a field or domain, Nida (with

44. François Bovon, introduction to *Exegesis: Problems of Method and Exegesis in Reading (Genesis 22 and Luke 15)*, ed. François Bovon and Grégoire Rauiller, trans. D. G. Miller (Pittsburgh: Pickwick, 1978), p. 1; cf. pp. 1-9.

45. J. Trier, *Der deutsche Wortschatz im Sinnbezirk des Verstandes: Die Geschichte eines sprachlichen Feldes* (Heidelberg: Winter, 1931).

46. John Lyons, *Introduction to Theoretical Linguistics* (Cambridge: Cambridge University Press, 1968), and Lyons, *Semantics*, 2 vols. (Cambridge: Cambridge University Press, 1977); and John F. A. Sawyer, *Semantics in Biblical Research* (London: SCM, 1972).

James Barr) concludes, "Words do not carry with them all the meanings which they may have in other sets of co-occurrences."[47]

In literature this principle was taken up in Russian formalism by Vladimir Propp and later developed in France by A. J. Greimas. They produced a "narrative grammar." A binary system of hero and villain is essential to most stories or folktales. These were supplemented usually by a helper for the hero, by a task that was set him, by opponents who opposed him, and sometimes by some such reward for victory as the hand of the king's daughter. Propp (1895-1970), who wrote *The Morphology of the Folktale* in 1928, was born and educated in St. Petersburg, and significantly influenced Lévi-Strauss and Roland Barthes. He argued that the narrative generated a system, within which he identified thirty-one narratemes, relating to the characters and actions of the story as a standardized "grammar." For example, the hero leaves home; an interdiction is addressed to him; the villain enters the story; the hero is deceived; the hero and villain engage in combat; the villain is defeated; the villain is exposed; the hero marries the princess, and perhaps ascends to the throne. Thirty-one such events are postulated.

Algárdas J. Greimas (1917-92) was born and educated in Lithuania, but after three years in France he returned in 1944. There he worked with Lévi-Strauss and especially with Barthes. Following Propp, he sought the "deep structure" that, he believed, underlay all narrative. Meaning is generated by the relation between signs *(semiotics)* within a linguistic system. Like Saussure, he saw the relation between language and the world as arbitrary, and the product of convention. In narrative a character may serve as active subject or as passive object, that is, as "sender" or "receiver." To subject and object, sender and receiver, he adds "helper" and "opponent." In a folktale this may be a dragon or a witch. In 1966 he proposed calling these "actantial models."[48] The axes are largely psychological: desire, power, and knowledge play their part in the story. The sender initiates the action; the opponent and helper may intervene. The narrative ends with victory and reward for the hero. There may be subcategories of actant. Greimas reduces Propp's thirty-one narratives to twenty or fewer.

Roland Barthes (1915-80) is an acknowledged leader in the area of

47. Cf. E. A. Nida and Johannes P. Louw, *Greek-English Lexicon of the New Testament Based on Semantic Domains,* 2 vols. (New York: United Bible Societies, 1988, 1989), and Erhardt Guttgemanns, *Forum Theologie Linguisticae* (Philadelphia: Pickwick, 1973).

48. A. J. Greimas, *Sémantique Structurale: recherche de méthode* (Paris: Larousse, 1966; reprint, Paris: Presses Universitaires, 1986).

structuralism. Barthes grew up in Paris and graduated from the Sorbonne in 1939. He gained his licentiate to teach grammar and philosophy after a period of illness. In 1953 he wrote *Writing Degree Zero,* and in 1957, *Mythologies.* He turned to structuralism and semiotics, writing *The Death of the Author* in 1967 and in 1970 his book on Balzac, entitled *S/Z.* During the late 1960s and the 1970s he collaborated with Jacques Derrida and worked on post-structuralism and Marxism.

The easiest work of Barthes to read is his *Mythologies,* which is a collection of essays designed to show the "deep" structure that underlies modern myths. One well-known myth is a wrestling match as a staged performance.[49] It acts out society's notions of good and evil, and suffering, defeat, and justice. It draws on exaggerated stereotypes. Another is the picture of young black men in military uniform. This looks like an innocent portrayal but in fact serves to convey the notion of the glories of the French empire, which has black soldiers serving under its flag.[50]

In his later book *Elements of Semiology* (French, 1964), Barthes expounds *system* in Ferdinand de Saussure with particular reference to garment systems, food systems, and even furniture systems. It may appear innocently that the choice of a short skirt, a long skirt, or trousers depends on the weather or on their respective availability. But most often the choice projects a "deeper" meaning: that of how we wish people to perceive us. The same is true of choices of furniture. The surface meaning of what we have chosen for sheer comfort hides the deeper meaning of our social aspiration.[51] I have used Barthes's examples in *New Horizons in Hermeneutics.*

Even the early *Writing Degree Zero* (1953) heralded aspects of structuralism. For "zero" represents a writing without style, although "natural" or totally "style-less" writing is impossible. Everything shows an underlying disguised agenda of social class or of power. But from around 1967 onward, Barthes saw that even the "differences" within the linguistic system were contrived rather than "natural," and the focus on structuralism moved to a focus on *post*-structuralism and *post*modernism, especially in collaboration with Jacques Derrida. (See chapter XVI.)

If a linguistic sign signifies something only by virtue of the differential

---

49. Roland Barthes, *Mythologies* (London: Jonathan Cape, 1972), pp. 15-19.

50. Barthes, *Mythologies,* p. 116.

51. Roland Barthes, *Elements of Semiology* (London: Jonathan Cape, 1967), pp. 25-30 and 58-66.

gap that arises from the language system, it is not surprising that many attempted to apply structural analysis to the Bible, especially to biblical narrative. Saussure's notion of a systematic relation of *difference* or absence seemed to promise a new method of approach to the text of the Bible.[52] Daniel Patte provides a structural reading of Galatians 1:1-10, in which he sees God and humanity in binary opposition. Yet God is "sender" who enacts reconciliation with the receiver through Christ as mediator.[53] Dan Otto Via provides a structuralist analysis of the parable of the unjust judge. The narrative moves from a state of deficiency (a lack of justice) through opposition (the judge refuses to hear the widow) toward well-being and reward (the judge vindicates her). God gives a mandate to the judge (as sender); the judge is to communicate justice as subject, although at first the principle is rejected or violated when the widow becomes subject. Via develops the *actants* of Propp and Greimas.[54]

In the late 1970s this kind of structuralist analysis of biblical texts was all the rage in the journal *Semeia,* which bore the subtitle *An Experimental Journal for Biblical Criticism.* This applies to volume 9 (1977), among others, in which Mary Ann Tolbert, Dan Otto Via, Jr., Bernard Scott, Susan Wittig, and John Dominic Crossan write on the parables of Jesus. Tolbert explored the parable of the son (Luke 15:11-32) with reference to psychoanalysis. She argues that the parable "represents a wish-fulfilment dream," and the two sons "elements of a complex unity."[55] Like Barthes, she believes in the validity of multiple interpretation. The elder son reflects rigid morality like the super-ego of Freud; the father represents a unifying center; the younger son desires unity and wholeness. Via considers the same parable from a Jungian perspective. Again he sees opposition, deficiency, condemnation, and welcome. Scott offers a wholly structuralist perspective on Luke 15:11-32. He rejects an allegorical understanding of the elder son as not representing the Pharisees. He identifies the father as subject, the two sons as object, but the two sons in

52. Cf. Jean-Marie Benoist, *The Structural Revolution* (London: Wiedenfeld and Nicholson, 1978), pp. 3-4.

53. Daniel Patte, *What Is Structural Exegesis?* (Philadelphia: Fortress, 1976), pp. 59-76.

54. Dan Otto Via, "The Parable of the Unjust Judge: A Metaphor of the Unrealised Self," in *Semiology and the Parables: An Exploration of the Possibilities Offered in Structuralism for Exegesis,* ed. Daniel Patte (Pittsburgh: Pickwick, 1976), pp. 1-32.

55. Mary Ann Tolbert, "The Prodigal Son: An Essay in Literary Criticism from a Psycho-Analytic Perspective," *Semeia* 9 (1977): 7; cf. pp. 1-20; cf. also Mary Ann Tolbert, *Perspectives on the Parables* (Philadelphia: Fortress, 1979).

conflict as constituting opponents to the father's plan. The parable, he concludes, is not myth but its opposite, a subversion of values.

Wittig also defends the notion of multiple meanings. A parable, contrary to Dodd and Jeremias, is pluriform or polyvalent.[56] She alludes to Charles Morris's theory of signs, or his semiotics. A parable and a text, she argues, have multiple "codes" that generate meaning. These may be geographical, cosmological, kinship terms, or economic. But more than one system can operate at one time. Hence a commutative system may imply certain truths or values that are unstated. The receiver of the signs may not know the interpretive "code" intended, and decode the sign in a different way from that intended.[57] We explore her approach in more detail in our chapter on reader-response theory (chapter XV).

Barthes offers a structuralist analysis of Acts 10–11, in which the Gentile centurion, Cornelius, and the apostle Peter receive visions pointing to the reception of Gentiles in the Church. Although Barthes is a nontheist, the inclusion of people hitherto excluded from the new Church is congenial to his politics. He looks for the "code" of the passage.[58] The "code" makes possible the discovery of underlying and sometimes disguised meaning. For example, he argues elsewhere that Balzac projects an elitist picture of French middle-class intellectuals. In Acts 10 he examines the narrative code "There was in Caesarea a man named Cornelius, a centurion of the Italian cohort." Here a historical code overlaps with the "semic" code, "a devout man," and a further chronological code. Looking to Propp and Greimas, he identifies a code of actions. A further sequence follows with Peter's question and its answer. The account of the visions is summarized and repeated in this relatively short passage. He concludes that the mainspring of the text is communication, not quest.

Other similar examples might be cited. Jean Calloud looks at the narrative of the temptations.[59] The Spirit gives a mandate to Jesus as receiver, to whom the devil as sender sends texts, for which the Word of God is helper. Here Calloud in effect replicates Propp or Greimas. Edmund Leach offers an

---

56. Susan Wittig, "A Theory of Multiple Meaning," *Semeia* 7 (1977): 75-103.

57. Wittig, "Theory of Multiple Meaning," p. 91.

58. Roland Barthes, "A Structural Analysis of a Narrative from Acts X–XI," in *Structuralism and Biblical Hermeneutics: A Collection of Essays*, ed. and trans. Alfred M. Johnson (Pittsburgh: Pickwick, 1979), p. 117; cf. pp. 109-39.

59. Jean Calloud, *Structural Analysis of Narrative* (Philadelphia and Missoula: Scholars Press, 1976), pp. 47-108.

analysis more on the lines of Claude Lévi-Strauss when he looks at the birth narratives, in which he notes contrasts between Elizabeth and Mary, and between John the Baptist and Jesus.[60] Barthes also considers Jacob's wrestling with the angel (Gen. 28:10-17). But we do not wish to repeat what we have written elsewhere.[61]

Structuralism began to collapse as three factors were taken more into account. (1) It became clear from the later work of Barthes, together with Foucault, Derrida, and others, that the so-called structures were just as arbitrary as other aspects of language. This recognition of relativity led to *post-structuralism,* in which the radical pluriformity of meaning was still further emphasized. (2) Many queried whether structuralism shed much light on "meaning" at all. J. L. Crenshaw was invited to offer a "response" to Via's structuralist treatment on the unjust judge. He responded, surely rightly, that he doubted whether Via's structural reading "contributes anything substantial to our understanding of the story. I confess to further uneasiness over the lack of objective criteria in the assignment of actantial roles."[62] (3) The whole movement disengages the text from *history or human life.* It is traditional in biblical studies to examine the *Sitz im Leben,* or historical setting and context, as well as the literary genre of a text.

Nevertheless, Barthes's early approach, along with that of others, does aim at finding a "deep" structure behind disguises. We shall consider this further in Paul Ricoeur's hermeneutic of suspicion. We might mention also Habermas's emphasis on "interest" and his critique of Gadamer, both of which remain relevant. It is also true that, as Saussure and Trier have stressed, meaning emerges from "differences" within a larger whole. Nevertheless, hermeneutics requires that we study both history and language, and where appropriate, also theology.

4. Post-Structuralism and Semantics as Applied to the Bible

Post-structuralism has partly been covered under structuralism. But, as Sturrock observes, whereas Lévi-Strauss and Jacques Lacan are both "uni-

---

60. Edmund Leach, "Structuralism and Anthropology," in *Structuralism: An Introduction,* ed. David Robey (Oxford: Oxford University Press, 1973), pp. 37-56.

61. Anthony C. Thiselton, "Structuralism and Biblical Studies: Method or Ideology?" *Expository Times* 89 (1978): 329-35.

62. J. L. Crenshaw, "Response to Dan O. Via," in *Semiology and the Parables,* p. 54.

versalists" (i.e., they believe that structures are innate or "objective"), "Derrida . . . like Barthes and Foucault, is a bitter opponent of transcendent systems of thought, which purport to offer their adherents systems of dominance."[63] If Lévi-Strauss and Lacan are "universalists," then the later Barthes, Foucault, and Derrida are relativists, and they promote post-structuralism. A "code," or the channel through which the content of a text is communicated, is as "arbitrary" as Saussure claimed for language as a signifier. It entirely reflects subjective attitudes of race, class, or other interests.

Barthes increasingly stressed this approach from the mid-1960s. Because the text is relative to people's interest, meaning is not objective, and is "postponed." In his book *The Pleasure of the Text* (1973), he speaks of the text as undoing "nomination" (or naming in language). The use of multiple codes may appear to allow multiple perspectives and to generate multiple meanings. But to mean all things in general may imply meaning nothing in particular, and aiding the *dissolution* of the text. The subject and the content become undone.

The dissolution becomes a major theme of Kevin J. Vanhoozer's book *Is There a Meaning in This Text?*[64] His three main chapters in part 1 are called "Undoing the Author," "Undoing the Book," and "Undoing the Reader."[65] He declares that Barthes refuses to assign a fixed meaning to any text. This, argues Vanhoozer, "liberates an activity we may call counter theological. . . . To those who refuse to halt meaning is finally to refuse God."[66] On the same page, Vanhoozer quotes Derrida's comment, "Deconstruction is the death of God put into writing." Yet Vanhoozer shows how deconstruction is almost synonymous with post-structuralism. Although it is sometimes claimed that deconstruction is a positive and serious philosophy, this movement remains but a short step from postmodernism. The postmodernism of Derrida, and perhaps of Richard Rorty and Stanley Fish, is hardly "mid-twentieth-century," and we therefore postpone further consideration of this trend until we discuss postmodernism in chapter XVI. We shall then also consider Foucault and François Lyotard.

---

63. John Sturrock, ed., *Structuralism and Since: From Lévi-Strauss to Derrida* (Oxford: Oxford University Press, 1979), p. 4.

64. Kevin J. Vanhoozer, *Is There a Meaning in This Text? The Bible, the Reader, and the Morality of Literary Knowledge* (Grand Rapids: Zondervan, 1998).

65. Vanhoozer, *Is There a Meaning?* pp. 37-196.

66. Vanhoozer, *Is There a Meaning?* p. 30; cf. Roland Barthes, "Death of Author," in *The Rustle of Language*, trans. R. Howard (New York: Hill and Wang, 1986), p. 54.

We may conclude this chapter, however, by considering an influential study in semantics by James Barr (1924-2006) of Edinburgh, Manchester, and Oxford. In 1961 he published *The Semantics of Biblical Language.*[67] He, too, drew on the general linguistics of Saussure, but in the direction of linguistics rather than of structuralism. He emphasized Saussure's distinction between synchronic (at the present moment) and diachronic (historical) studies of language. The latter was often a study not of word meaning, but of word history. As an Old Testament scholar, Barr ruthlessly attacked any confusion between these, and the tendency to use this mistake to defend the notion of a contrast between "Hebrew" and "Greek" ways of thinking. He argued that *Theological Dictionary of the New Testament,* edited by G. Kittel, Thorlief Boman's *Hebrew Thought Compared with Greek,* and J. Pedersen's *Israel: Its Life and Culture* were serious culprits of this error.[68]

Barr also argued that linguistic work on the Bible often depended on overselective examples, and ignored accepted methods in general linguistics. The notion, for example, that Hebrew is "more concrete" than Greek depends on such selected examples as "a man of strength," or "words of truth."[69] Pedersen is in error here, especially in regarding the Hebrew language as "primitive." Many also assume that linguistic structure and thought structure reflect each other, when Saussure showed that the relation was arbitrary and rested only on convention. Word studies by Pedersen, Boman, and many others show ignorance or neglect of linguistics. Barr writes, "Grammatical gender, then, is a prime example of a linguistic structure which cannot be taken to reflect a thought structure."[70] The notion that Hebrew is more "dynamic" than Greek depends on the same error.

Barr also attacks on the basis of linguistics the dubious practice of "etymologizing." Etymology appears to provide "the essence" of a meaning, but this is "a dubious homiletical trick," for diachronic analysis shows that

---

67. James Barr, *The Semantics of Biblical Language* (Oxford: Oxford University Press, 1961).

68. Gerhard Kittel and Gerhard Friedrich, eds., *Theological Dictionary of the New Testament,* trans. G. W. Bromiley, 10 vols. (Grand Rapids: Eerdmans, 1964-76; German from 1933); T. Boman, *Hebrew Thought Compared with Greek* (London: SCM, 1960); and Johannes Pedersen, *Israel: Its Life and Culture,* 2 vols. (Oxford: Oxford University Press, 1926, 1940; 2nd ed., vol. 2, 1963).

68. Barr, *Semantics,* p. 40.

69. Barr, *Semantics,* pp. 29-30.

70. Barr, *Semantics,* p. 40.

word history is not its meaning.[71] The principles behind the earlier volumes of G. Kittel's *Theological Dictionary* come in for special attack. Barr criticizes what he calls "illegitimate totality transfer," by which the meanings of a word derived from a variety of passages are read as contributing to the meaning of the word wherever it occurs.[72] He concludes by suggesting sounder methods for "biblical theology."

Barr's *Semantics of Biblical Language* sheds a flood of light on the use of linguistics in biblical interpretation. It is a valuable contribution to hermeneutics. Some of his later work is more negative, but this does not detract from his semantics, even if some claim that here and there he verges toward overstatement.

5. Recommended Initial Reading

1. ON BARTH'S HERMENEUTICS

Barth, Karl, "Holy Scripture," in *Church Dogmatics* I/2, edited by G. W. Bromiley and T. F. Torrance (Edinburgh: T. & T. Clark, 1956), sect. 19, pp. 457-83.
————, "The Strange New World within the Bible," in Barth, *The Word of God and the Word of Man,* translated by D. Horton (London: Hodder and Stoughton, 1928), pp. 28-50.
Torrance, T. F., *Karl Barth: An Introduction to His Early Theology, 1910-1931* (London: SCM, 1962), pp. 63-95 and especially pp. 95-105 and 118-132.
Weber, Otto, *Karl Barth's "Church Dogmatics": An Introductory Report,* translated by A. C. Cochrane (London: Lutterworth, 1953), pp. 57-72.
Work, Telford, *Living and Active: Scripture in the Economy of Salvation* (Grand Rapids: Eerdmans, 2002), pp. 67-100.

2. ON THE NEW HERMENEUTIC

Achtemeier, Paul J., *An Introduction to the New Hermeneutic* (Philadelphia: Westminster, 1969), pp. 116-32 and 149-65.
Ebeling, Gerhard, "Word of God and Hermeneutic," in *New Frontiers in Theol-*

---

71. Barr, *Semantics*, pp. 114-60.
72. Barr, *Semantics*, pp. 218 and 222; cf. pp. 206-62 on Kittel.

ogy, vol. 2, *The New Hermeneutic,* edited by James M. Robinson and J. B. Cobb, Jr. (New York: Harper and Row, 1964), pp. 78-110.

Fuchs, Ernst, "The New Testament and the Hermeneutical Problem," in *New Frontiers in Theology,* vol. 2, *The New Hermeneutic,* edited by James M. Robinson and John B. Cobb, Jr. (New York and London: Harper and Row, 1964), pp. 111-163.

————, *Studies of the Historical Jesus,* translated by A. Scobie (London: SCM, 1964), pp. 194-206.

Thiselton, Anthony C., "The New Hermeneutic," in *New Testament Interpretation,* edited by I. H. Marshall (Exeter: Paternoster, 1972), pp. 308-33.

3. STRUCTURALISM AND POST-STRUCTURALISM

Barthes, Roland, François Bovon, and others, *Structural Analysis and Biblical Exegesis,* translated by A. M. Johnson (Pittsburgh: Pickwick, 1974), pp. 1-33.

Johnson, Alfred M., ed., *Structuralism and Biblical Hermeneutics: A Collection of Essays* (Pittsburgh: Pickwick, 1979), pp. 1-28 and 109-44.

Sturrock, John, ed., *Structuralism and Since: From Lévi-Strauss to Derrida* (Oxford: Oxford University Press, 1979), pp. 1-15 and 52-79.

Vanhoozer, Kevin J., *Is There a Meaning in This Text? The Bible, the Reader, and the Morality of Literary Knowledge* (Grand Rapids: Zondervan, 1998), pp. 15-32.

4. THE SEMANTICS OF JAMES BARR

Barr, James, *The Semantics of Biblical Language* (Oxford: Oxford University Press, 1961), pp. 21-45 and 206-46.

Thiselton, Anthony C., "Semantics and New Testament Interpretation," in *New Testament Interpretation,* edited by I. Howard Marshall (Exeter: Paternoster, 1977), pp. 75-88 (part of the essay).

CHAPTER XI

Hans-Georg Gadamer's Hermeneutics:
The Second Turning Point

We saw that hermeneutics was never the same after the first great turning point that was the work of Schleiermacher. Gadamer offers a second turning point for the twentieth century. He offers a hermeneutic divorced from Enlightenment rationalism, and yet "historical" in a new sense, going further even than Hegel and Dilthey, and influenced by Heidegger. Gadamer repudiates value-neutral "science," at least as applied to hermeneutics.

1. Background, Influences, and Early Life

Hans-Georg Gadamer (1900-2002) was born in Marburg. His mother died when he was only four, but Gadamer held that he nevertheless inherited from her a vaguely "religious disposition."[1] Gadamer's father, Johannes, was orientated toward the sciences. He hoped Hans-Georg would follow in the sciences, and was scathing about the "chattering professors" *(Schwätz-professoren)* of the humanities and literature.[2] Nevertheless, when Hans-Georg entered university, he gave him freedom to make a choice in the matter.

Gadamer attended a good school and wrote essays on literature and Plato's philosophy, his life interest. He entered the University of Breslau, where he studied a range of literature and languages with philosophy. He

1. Jean Grondin, *Hans-Georg Gadamer: A Biography,* trans. Joel C. Weinsheimer (New Haven and London: Yale University Press, 2003), p. 21.

2. Hans-Georg Gadamer, "Reflections on My Philosophical Journey," in *The Philosophy of Hans-Georg Gadamer,* ed. Lewis Edwin Hahn (Chicago and La Salle, Ill.: Open Court, 1997), p. 3; cf. pp. 3-63.

read especially Lessing, Kant, and Kierkegaard. He then transferred to the University of Marburg, where he read philosophy under the neo-Kantian Paul Natorp and under Nicholai Hartmann. He was thoroughly aware of debates about the nature and limits of reason, and its relation to science. In the summer of 1919 he attended Richard Hönigswald's lectures on the philosophy of science, which marked his further introduction to neo-Kantianism, with its ambivalence about the limits of reason yet the importance of science. This was intensified by his entry to the University of Marburg later the same year to study with Natorp, as well as with Hartmann.

Meanwhile Gadamer continued his studies of art history, until in 1922 he produced a dissertation entitled "The Nature of Pleasure according to Plato's Dialogues." The same year he fell victim to polio. The year 1922 also witnessed the beginnings of Gadamer's crucial distinction between "problems," which are "fixed" abstractions, and concrete, moving questions, which arise out of specific situations. This becomes a key in his great book on hermeneutics, *Truth and Method*.[3] Gadamer asserts in *Truth and Method*, "Problems are not real questions that arise of themselves, and hence acquire the pattern of their answer from the genesis of their meaning, but are alternatives that can only be accepted in themselves."[4] Kant's "problems" exist only as fixed points "like stars in the sky."[5]

The next year (April-July 1923) Gadamer came to Freiburg and met Martin Heidegger (1889-1976), whose disciples called him "the secret king" of philosophy and "the great Heidegger." At first Gadamer was disappointed. But Heidegger was shortly called to Marburg, and he began to work out a "historical" theory of knowledge in contrast to the more abstract "system" of the Roman Catholic Church and Thomism. Heidegger recognized that extraphilosophical influences were at work in his thinking. On one side he explored "historicity" and historical reason; on the other, he wrote, "Accompanying me in the search were the young Luther and the model of Aristotle. . . . Kierkegaard added impetus, and Husserl gave me eyes."[6] Gadamer

3. Hans-Georg Gadamer, *Truth and Method*, 2nd English ed. (London: Sheed and Ward, 1989), p. 376; German, *Wahrheit und Methode: Grundzüge einer philosophischen Hermeneutik* (1960; 2nd German ed. 1965, 5th German ed. 1986).

4. Grondin, *Hans-Georg Gadamer*, p. 84.

5. Gadamer, *Truth and Method*, p. 377.

6. Martin Heidegger, *Phänomenologische Interpretationen ausgewählter Abhandlungen des Aristoteles zur Ontologie und Logik* (reprint, Frankfurt: Klostermann, 2005), 63:5, cited by Grondin.

warmed to Heidegger's emphasis on "historicality" (that everything is conditioned by its given place in history), but not the subjectivity of the consciousness of the individual, as the way into phenomenology.

At Marburg University from 1923 to 1927, the year of *Being and Time,* Heidegger worked with Rudolf Bultmann, and with Hartmann and Natorp as philosophical colleagues, and also with Gadamer, Hannah Arendt, and Hans Jonas. In 1928 Heidegger returned to Freiburg, to succeed the great Edmund Husserl as professor. These were the years of devastating inflation in Germany, and Gadamer records how he received practical help from Heidegger. (The German mark rose four trillion dollars on 15 November 1923. People could buy hardly anything.) During these years Heidegger, with Gadamer, studied Wilhelm Dilthey, and Schleiermacher on "the art of understanding." Dilthey suggested that hermeneutics constituted a distinctive methodology for the human sciences, or *Geisteswissenschaften.*

Heidegger also held seminars on Aristotle's ethics. In the years that led to *Being and Time,* Heidegger abandoned more abstract concepts and explored how the Greeks experienced "Being" primordially and in temporal terms, in contrast to the "Latinization" of Scholasticism in the Middle Ages. He emphasized the power of the poetic. Gadamer appreciated these aspects of Heidegger's work, especially his work on art. By 1928 he completed his *Habilitation* thesis on Plato's dialectical ethics, especially Plato's *Philebus.* Heidegger remained his mentor and was one of his examiners. Gadamer became *Privatdozent* and, later, assistant to Karl Löwith in the University of Marburg.

All this prepared for Gadamer's later statement that *phronēsis* and Plato were more important to him than *Truth and Method* and hermeneutics.[7] Yet this early meeting with Heidegger profoundly influenced his hermeneutics. First, Heidegger's *Dasein* (a concrete being-there) influenced his contrast between abstract problems and questions that arose from concrete historically conditioned human life. Second, both came to reject Husserl's starting point with individual consciousness. Third, both saw wisdom as different from instrumental reason in Kant or Aristotle. In fact, "wisdom" led to the rebirth of a new Aristotle. Fourth, Heidegger believed in the centrality of interpretation. In *Being and Time* he wrote: "In interpretation . . . we 'see' it [what is to hand] *as* a table, a door, a carriage. . . ."[8] The "circle" in under-

---

7. Gadamer, "My Philosophical Journey," pp. 9-10.

8. Martin Heidegger, *Being and Time,* trans. John Macquarrie and Edward Robinson (Oxford: Blackwell, 1962), p. 188 (German, p. 148; cf. pp. 188-95).

standing belongs to the structure of meaning. *"If we see this circle as a vicious one, and look for ways of avoiding it . . . then the act of understanding has been misunderstood from the ground up."*[9] In other words, for Heidegger and for Gadamer understanding and interpretation are *provisional, historical, and temporal,* resting on *pre-understanding* unavoidably. This stands at the heart of *Truth and Method,* where *"method"* looks back disparagingly to the *rationalism* of René Descartes, the Enlightenment, and human consciousness as providing a neutral starting point.

Gadamer and Heidegger see this approach as relatively conducive to progress in science and technology, but not for life. Life is not value-neutral. The starting point for Heidegger and for Bultmann is more existential. Heidegger defines things in terms of a "towards which." The "ready-to-hand" is not grasped theoretically. Thus a hammer is for hitting things in, not (in this sense) wood and metal if it is ready-to-hand *(zuhandenheit).*[10] A practical relation perceives it as equipment or a tool *for* something. Gilbert Ryle believed that the ability to abstract is a sign of superior culture, and criticized Heidegger on this ground. But Heidegger, like the later Ludwig Wittgenstein, and with Gadamer, believes not that man *cannot* abstract, but that this is not the way to reach the heart of meaning and truth.[11]

Gadamer was profoundly influenced by Heidegger's and Kierkegaard's view that Being and truth could not be approached in terms of objectification and generalization. He rejected what the later Wittgenstein called "the craving for generality" that is "the method of science."[12] With Bultmann they agreed on the need for "de-objectification." Hans Jonas found this among the gnostics, whose cosmology was primarily existential. Heidegger writes, "The relational reality of this signifying we call 'significance.' This is what makes up the structure of the world."[13] By contrast, Descartes sees the *extension* as basically definitive ontologically for the world. In Descartes's sense, the world is a spatiotemporal reality "out there." For

---

9. Heidegger, *Being and Time,* p. 194 (German, p. 153), italics in original.

10. Heidegger, *Being and Time,* p. 98 (German, p. 69).

11. Gilbert Ryle, *Collected Papers,* 2 vols. (London: Hutchinson, 1971), 1:268 (from his review of *Being and Time*). Cf. Anthony C. Thiselton, *The Two Horizons: New Testament Hermeneutics and Philosophical Description with Special Reference to Heidegger, Bultmann, Gadamer, and Wittgenstein* (Grand Rapids: Eerdmans; Exeter: Paternoster, 1980), p. 198 n. 139.

12. Ludwig Wittgenstein, *The Blue and Brown Books: Preliminary Studies for the "Philosophical Investigations"* (Oxford: Blackwell, 1969), p. 18.

13. Heidegger, *Being and Time,* p. 120 (German, p. 88).

Heidegger and Gadamer "world" is not spatial, but constructed by historic human beings in time. When Gadamer places "Truth" and "Method" in ironic opposition, he refers to Descartes's rationalist notion of "Method." Heidegger also selects Descartes for attack. He begins with *Dasein,* or *Being-there.* "A stone's throw" or "as long as it takes to smoke a pipe" is a more "real" expression of measurement than "two miles" or "a hundred yards."[14]

Understanding, both Heidegger and Gadamer say, comes before statement. The assertion of a judgment is for Heidegger a "derivative" mode of interpretation.[15] For Gadamer "statements" can be used for various purposes, especially for propaganda. The purposes are often more important than the statement, and the statement itself offers no guarantee of objectivity. Wolfhart Pannenberg and others regard this undervaluing of cognitive propositions as the Achilles' heel of Heidegger's and Gadamer's thought. Heidegger asserts, "Communication is never anything like the conveying of experiences, such as opinions or wishes."[16] But is this the case always? The later Wittgenstein expresses the point with more caution: "What we call 'descriptions' are instruments for particular uses."[17] We must make "a radical break with the idea that language always functions in one way, always serves the same purpose — to convey thoughts — which may be about houses, pains, good and evil, or anything else you please."[18] This is why he constantly distinguishes between meaning and application.

In the 1930s Gadamer read more widely still in the poets, Kierkegaard, and Plato. In 1934 Heidegger was involved with the Nazis, and became rector of Freiburg University, but later the same year he became disillusioned by their anti-Semitism. That year Gadamer became professor at Kiel. In 1935 his application to become professor at Marburg was rejected by the state, probably because of his help to Jews. In 1936 he lectured on "Art and History," which later became a key theme in *Truth and Method.* He attended Heidegger's lectures entitled "The Origin of the Work of Art." Finally in 1937 Gadamer became, first, extraordinary professor at Marburg, and then "ordinary" (officially recognized) professor there, before moving to Leipzig.

In the University of Leipzig Gadamer pursued interests that would

14. Heidegger, *Being and Time,* p. 140 (German, p. 105).
15. Heidegger, *Being and Time,* p. 195 (German, p. 154).
16. Heidegger, *Being and Time,* p. 205 (German, p. 162).
17. Ludwig Wittgenstein, *Philosophical Investigations,* German and English, English text trans. G. E. M. Anscombe (Oxford: Blackwell, 1967), section 291.
18. Wittgenstein, *Philosophical Investigations,* section 304.

emerge in *Truth and Method:* he lectured on art and history, and on Hegel and Plato. He also taught Kant, Romanticism, Aristotle, Rilke's poetry, and the pre-Socratic philosophers. Meanwhile Heidegger's philosophy was changing, and moving from his earlier existentialism to poetry and language in his later thought after the "turn" *(Kehre)* in his thought. The later Heidegger came to believe that humankind had "fallen out of Being."[19] His path increasingly diverged from Gadamer's, except for their shared belief in the importance and revelatory power of art, the creative power of poetry, their attempted rejection of dualism, and the hermeneutical circle. Gadamer comments, "My mission was different from Heidegger's . . . who was searching for a more appropriate language than that of Catholicism."[20] At Heidegger's funeral service in 1976, Gadamer spoke of Being in Heidegger as something like "God," although many will disagree with this identification.

It has been necessary to contextualize Gadamer. Nevertheless, as Pannenberg once commented orally, it was a pity that one single man, namely, Heidegger, held such great influence over so many. Heidegger acknowledges the change in thinking, but calls it a "turn" *(Kehre),* not a reversal. In *On the Way to Language* he writes: "I have left an earlier standpoint, not in order to exchange it for another one, but because even the former standpoint was merely a way-station along the way. The lasting element . . . is the way."[21]

2. *Truth and Method* Part I:
Critique of "Method" and the "World" of Art and Play

We have seen how Gadamer distinguishes between the "technical reason" of René Descartes (1596-1650) and the rationalists, and the wisdom *(phronēsis)* needed in life and in hermeneutics. In *Truth and Method* Gadamer begins by distinguishing between "method," or the rationalism of Descartes, and the "historical" tradition of Giambattista Vico (1668-1744) and the *sensus communis* of the Romans. This in effect virtually turns Western philosophy upside down, for Vico's tradition was virtually buried underground between the secular Enlightenment and the rationalism and empiricism that fol-

---

19. Martin Heidegger, *Introduction to Metaphysics* (New Haven: Yale University Press, 1959), p. 37. On the later Heidegger, cf. Thiselton, *The Two Horizons,* pp. 327-42.

20. Grondin, *Hans-Georg Gadamer,* p. 24.

21. Martin Heidegger, *On the Way to Language* (New York: Harper and Row, 1972), p. 7.

lowed it, and until Hegel and Dilthey. In his early thought Gadamer had learned from Plato the importance of asking fruitful questions.

What is to be put in the place of reason as Descartes understands it? Gadamer points out that studies of hermeneutics begin "from the experience of art and historical tradition."[22] Part I is called "The Question of Truth as It Emerges in the Experiences of Art." What is the role of "method," Gadamer asks, for the *Geisteswissenschaften,* or humanities, literature, and social science? It is all very well, perhaps, for the sciences, as Droysen, Mill, or even Dilthey conceived of "science." The humanities, or *Geisteswissenschaften,* however, are based on *Bildung,* or formative culture. For Gadamer, *Bildung* entails more than culture; it is involved in human formation and is almost ethical. It certainly addresses education, and above all keeps "oneself open to what is other."[23]

Vico preserves the wisdom or *prudentia* of the ancients, in contrast to the Sophists. He develops "this" communal sense, which is of decisive importance for practical life. This is not unconnected with "common sense" in Thomas Reid and in Scottish philosophy, and with humor and wit in Shaftesbury. Eventually it is represented in Pietism, with its emphasis on the heart, of which Oetinger is representative on the continent of Europe. Oetinger attacked Wolff's hermeneutics as too exclusively rationalist, preferring a "fuller sense" of Scripture. The German Enlightenment and Kant, however, led people away from this tradition.

Gadamer gives a number of pages to Kant on human judgment. Kant, like Descartes, is an individualist who virtually ignores community, tradition, and history. He relegates the communal to matters of taste. But taste is not knowledge and truth: "We will have to proceed with the problems of *aesthetics.*"[24] Kant's legacy is the subjectivizing of aesthetics, "where beauty is in the eye of the beholder."[25] But aesthetics is not art; it is the conceptualization of art. Hegel relates both more directly to "historical" experience *(Erlebnis).* "*Erleben* means primarily to be still alive when something happens."[26] In 1905 Dilthey gave precedence to life experience and to poetry. Schleier-

22. Gadamer, *Truth and Method,* p. xxiii.

23. Gadamer, *Truth and Method,* p. 17.

24. Gadamer, *Truth and Method,* p. 41, italics in original; cf. pp. 30-42.

25. Gadamer, *Truth and Method,* pp. 42-55. Cf. I. Kant, *Critique of Judgement,* trans. Werner Pluhar (Indianapolis: Hackett, 1987).

26. Gadamer, *Truth and Method,* p. 61. Parenthetical page references in the following text are to this work.

macher, Hegel, Dilthey, and Stefan George all shared a philosophy that rejected "the mechanization of life in contemporary mass society" (p. 63). *Erlebnis* becomes epistemological. Symbol is seen to have a metaphysical background, and there is a renewed use of allegory.

All the same, *abstraction* remains part of aesthetic consciousness. "Kierkegaard seems to me to have been the first to show that this position is untenable. In many writers aesthetics became a history of worldviews." But, Gadamer writes, "*All encounters with the language of art is an encounter with an unfinished event, and is itself part of this event*" (p. 99, italics in original). This is reminiscent of the later Heidegger.

In the second part of part I Gadamer moves to the ontology of the work of art and its significance for hermeneutics. He introduces his notion of "play," in which "Play fulfils its purpose only if the player loses himself in play" (p. 102). "It is the game that is played — it is irrelevant whether or not there is a subject who plays it" (p. 103). The "rules" of the game exist regardless of who plays it. "*The primacy of play over the consciousness of the player* is fundamentally acknowledged" (p. 104, italics in original). Players lose themselves in the game; its "rules" determine how they act, and the "world" in which they live. This is quite different from the attitude of the spectator. "Every game presents the man who plays it with a task" (p. 107). A child gives himself or herself to the game; for the adult it is more serious still. Each becomes absorbed. "Play draws him into its domain" (p. 109).

Gadamer now applies this to art. "My thesis, then, is that the being of art cannot be defined as an object of an aesthetic consciousness. . . . *It is part of the event of being that occurs in presentation,* and belongs essentially to play as play" (p. 116, italics in original). The ontological consequences are that a new objectivity is found in the play or in art, not in the human consciousness, as it was in Descartes. Each "presentation" (or performance) may vary from the previous one, but the presentations are united in the nature of the game or the work of art. The actual reality of the play or of a work of art cannot be detached from its presentation. The same is true of a festival, which *exists in* its celebration. Reality or ontology looks toward a historical and temporal event. A festival exists only in being celebrated. In Lutheran theology, Gadamer writes, the sermon performs this function as a living word. Gadamer's commentator Joel Weinsheimer has a particularly helpful section on this in his book, with various examples.[27]

---

27. Joel C. Weinsheimer, *Gadamer's Hermeneutics: A Reading of "Truth and Method"*

This is the heart of part I. We do not access reality through the consciousness of an individual, as in Descartes, but by becoming a participant in it and experiencing its formative presence. Like games, festivals, and concerts, it may not be replicated in exactly the same form, but may reflect what Wittgenstein calls "family resemblances." They may perhaps be likened to "the score" in the example of music. Gadamer concludes part I with a discussion of picture *(Bild)*, the original *(Ur-bild)*, play *(Spiel)*, representation, signs, and time. Finally he compares Schleiermacher's hermeneutics of reconstruction, which he regards as inadequate and partly mistaken, with Hegel's hermeneutics of integration, of which he approves.

Gadamer questions whether Schleiermacher provided an adequate approach. He prefers to follow Hegel. Schleiermacher, he believes, was obsessed by the *original* meaning of texts. Gadamer accepts his circular relationship between the whole and the parts, although he insists that this is not new. Schleiermacher has his own theological agenda, unlike Semler. Dilthey later discarded any dogmatic purpose. But F. A. Wolf, F. Ast, and Schleiermacher (and even Dilthey) try to equate hermeneutics too closely with "technical" reason, or a technique. They try to serve the art of understanding, but "Schleiermacher, it is true, calls his hermeneutics a technique."[28] He is still dominated by Romanticism, Gadamer claims, and is not yet sufficiently open to the culture of the Enlightenment. He gives him credit for his emphasis on the *community*, and his view that *Verständnis* (understanding) is near to *Einverständnis* (common understanding or shared agreement). But he neglects the content of what there is understanding or agreement *about*, in order to focus on human consciousness. What about the common subject matter?

"Historical interpretation in Schleiermacher's sense," Gadamer concludes, "is too subjectivist. Question and answer receive minimal attention. In the end he falls victim to the eighteenth century."[29] Dilthey looked at the problem differently. Gadamer appreciates Schleiermacher's "brilliant comments" on grammatical interpretation, but criticizes his reliance on dogmat-

---

(New Haven: Yale University Press, 1985), p. 111; cf. also Georgia Warnke, *Gadamer: Hermeneutics, Tradition, and Reason* (Cambridge: Polity Press, 1987), and Anthony C. Thiselton, *New Horizons in Hermeneutics: The Theory and Practice of Transforming Biblical Reading* (London: HarperCollins; Grand Rapids: Zondervan, 1992), pp. 313-30.

28. Gadamer, *Truth and Method*, p. 178.
29. Gadamer, *Truth and Method*, p. 185.

ics, when he turns to content.[30] This, Gadamer claims, constitutes an isolating of understanding.

Does Gadamer overstate these criticisms? Arguably Gadamer does, because he is thinking primarily of artistic thought and works of art. On this subject he regards Schleiermacher as too strongly influenced by Kant. Schleiermacher does ask what a text sets going, as we have seen. Moreover, the "rootedness" of the biblical text in concrete situations remains important. He speaks also of, "as it were, transforming oneself into the other" as too "psychological" or "subjectivist." Indeed, Georgia Warnke claims that in Gadamer's view Schleiermacher remains tied to "Cartesian certainty," method, and human consciousness.[31]

Gadamer calls Schleiermacher a leading voice of historical romanticism. Although he defined hermeneutics as "the art of avoiding misunderstanding," he verges on the "scientific." His talk of "the other" merely rests on intersubjectivity and Christian dogma. Schleiermacher unwittingly "collapses the distinction between interpreter and authors."[32] He goes little further than philology. Are some of these stronger statements entirely fair to Schleiermacher? What is true is that Gadamer lacks Schleiermacher's emphasis on criteria. We shall see in the next chapter that Ricoeur remedies this. It is understandable that Gadamer criticizes his subjectivity and emphasis on human consciousness. But Gadamer also believes that Schleiermacher led astray Ranke, Droysen, and Dilthey. "Historical interpretation," however, is found "in methodologist terms neither in Ranke nor in . . . Droysen, but for the first time in Dilthey, who consciously takes up Romanticist hermeneutics, and expands it into a historical method."[33]

3. *Truth and Method* Part II: Truth and Understanding in the Human Sciences

We have already said that in criticizing Schleiermacher, Gadamer prefers partly to follow the approach of his near contemporary rival Georg Hegel.

30. Gadamer, *Truth and Method,* pp. 186-87.
31. Warnke, *Gadamer,* p. 6.
32. Gadamer, *Truth and Method,* p. 193.
33. Gadamer, *Truth and Method,* p. 198.

Hegel acknowledges the importance of "historical" reason whereby the interpreter and subject matter are both conditioned by this place in history. He also pays attention to the historical situation of the interpreter, which may be very different from that of the author. Moreover, he believed in universal world history. Meanwhile, Dilthey sees historical reason as "pure reason." He remains concerned for "experimental knowledge" and "verifiable discoveries" in history.[34] This is part of Dilthey's concern with "life" *(Leben)*. Dilthey retains a concern for "consciousness," as his admiration for Husserl shows. Dilthey tries to use Hegel's historical reason, but his other concerns mean that this amounts to relatively little. "Historical consciousness appropriates what seemed specially reserved to art, religion and philosophy."[35] But Hegel conceived of historical consciousness as constantly altering and being subject to inexhaustible "Being."

Dilthey wrestled constantly with the questions left by Hegel, especially the issue of how history transforms persons. But he was enough of a child of the secular Enlightenment to seek in historical reason a *method* distinctively for the *Geisteswissenschaften,* or the human sciences. But hermeneutics aims at transformation, as Hegel saw, not replication. Art is always "more" than the life expression, historical institution, or text. Dilthey believed he was legitimating the "human sciences" epistemologically; but he was unwittingly betraying their deepest aspects. He provides a "half-rejection, half-affirmation of Hegel's philosophy."[36] His hermeneutics is more of a "deciphering" than a historical experience *(Erfahrung)*.

Gadamer next turns to Husserl and to Count (Graf) Yorck. He concludes that they did not solve the problem of hermeneutics. With Heidegger, Gadamer was disillusioned with Husserl's *Logical Investigation.* Edmund Husserl tried to draw subjectively from research on ontology, but failed. He was insufficiently "historical" in his account of consciousness, and remained too abstract. His main contribution was to introduce the concept of *horizon,* which is crucial for hermeneutics. This also paves the way for, or even implies, the historicality and finitude of the human viewpoint. Moreover, the horizon is not something fixed and static, but moves with us as we advance. Husserl did not fully realize the importance of "horizon" as a concept, but he also explored the notion of *life-world.* Here he reaches the edge of historical

34. Gadamer, *Truth and Method,* p. 221.
35. Gadamer, *Truth and Method,* p. 229.
36. Gadamer, *Truth and Method,* p. 241.

experience. The life-world is the "world" of persons. But Husserl is flawed, Gadamer believes, by transcendental idealism. "Life" in the end becomes subjectivity. "Life" is no different from what it is for Dilthey. The same in principle applies to Yorck. The project of "hermeneutics phenomenology" reaches relative success only in Heidegger.

Heidegger provided a basis on which to proceed. Everything is to be understood only within the horizon of time and history. Heidegger abandoned a fundamental ontology, at least as a starting point, beginning instead with the concrete human *Dasein,* or being-there. He saw being as an event, not a "thing," and went beyond previous philosophies. Rightly, Heidegger looked to the ancient Greeks. The "turn" was not a new departure from *Being and Time,* but a fulfillment of Heidegger's earlier aims. Heidegger rightly saw, however, that he wrestled with a hitherto unresolved problem. He was right to begin first with *Dasein's* historicity, Gadamer argues, and then to try to move on toward an ontology. This transcended previous metaphysics and certainly the philosophy of Descartes. Understanding was no longer a methodological concept. "A person who 'understands' a text . . . has not only projected himself understandingly toward a meaning . . . but the accomplished understanding constitutes a new state of intellectual freedom."[37] This is why Heidegger's advance over Dilthey is so pivotal. Understanding is, in effect, cumulative and embedded in the flow of time; it is not geared to individual subjectivity, like a timeless snapshot.

Gadamer has some questions about "care" in *Being and Time,* and about the later Heidegger after the "turn." The emphasis on care is not wrong, but will not achieve all that Heidegger hopes. Nevertheless, Gadamer broadly approves of the analysis of "temporality" *(Zeitlichkeit)* in part II of *Being and Time.* This is not "time," but the transcendental ground for the possibility of time. Gadamer and Heidegger also have differences about "tradition": Heidegger is more pessimistic; Gadamer, more optimistic. But both stress "presence" in different ways, and both point to the importance of art as providing a key example of "presence."

Now that Gadamer has traced the hermeneutical tradition from Schleiermacher to Heidegger, we come to his important "theory of hermeneutical experience." He first addresses the problem of presupposition, "prejudice," or "prejudgment" *(Vorurteile).* "The fundamental prejudice (or pre-judgment) of the Enlightenment is the prejudice against preju-

---

37. Gadamer, *Truth and Method,* p. 260.

dice itself; which denies tradition 'its power.'"[38] This concept gains a negative power, and too much in life is considered to be value-free.

In his *Kleine Schriften* Gadamer alludes to the excellent example of statistics. Statistics appear to be objective and neutral, but they are seldom that in practice. Everything depends on their purpose and presentation. But this brings us back to the role of "prejudice." Gadamer writes, *"It is not so much our judgements as it is our 'prejudices' (or 'pre-judgements,' Vorurteile) that constitute our being."*[39] He declares, "What is established by statistics seems to be the language of facts, but which questions these facts answer and which facts would begin to speak if other questions were asked are hermeneutical questions."[40] Everything is hermeneutical. "No assertion is possible that cannot be understood as an answer to a question."[41] Everything for the Enlightenment must be free from superstition. But its thinkers failed to recognize that everything is driven by tradition, history, and interpretation, and they nurtured the "nonsensical tradition" of pure, neutral "consciousness."[42] Gadamer observes, "Self-reflection and biography — Dilthey's starting points — are not primary." They are not an adequate basis for the hermeneutical problem. In fact, he continues, "History does not belong to us: we belong to it."[43] Gadamer reaches his grand conclusion: *"The prejudices (pre-judgements, Vorurteile), of the individual, far more than his judgements, constitute the historical reality of his being."*[44]

Grondin argues that when Gadamer says "history does not belong to us; we belong to it," we ought to recall how part of the "givenness," historical finitude, or what Heidegger also calls our "thrownness" *(Geworfenheit)* arose.[45] In 1918-19 Gadamer experienced the defeat of Germany and victory of the allies; in 1919 the Russian revolution; in 1922 the devastating attack of polio; in 1923 his fateful meeting with Heidegger; in 1923-24 the crippling effects of inflation in Germany; and above all, in 1933 the rise of Nazism, Hit-

---

38. Gadamer, *Truth and Method*, p. 270.

39. Hans-Georg Gadamer, *Philosophical Hermeneutics*, trans. David Linge (Berkeley: University of California Press, 1976), p. 9, italics mine; cf. pp. 3-17.

40. Gadamer, *Philosophical Hermeneutics*, p. 11.

41. Gadamer, *Philosophical Hermeneutics*, p. 11.

42. Gadamer, *Truth and Method*, p. 275.

43. Gadamer, *Truth and Method*, p. 276.

44. Gadamer, *Truth and Method*, pp. 276-77, italics mine.

45. Grondin, *Hans-Georg Gadamer*, p. 57; Heidegger, *Being and Time*, pp. 172-79 (German, pp. 134-40), section 29.

ler, and the Third Reich. Historical finitude, or "thrownness," meant for Heidegger *Dasein,* Being-in-the-world, Being-toward-death, and fallenness. Gadamer and Heidegger lived through almost the same tumultuous and uncontrollable events. Yet most German professors between 1914 and 1933 shared a kind of common faith that the solution to all problems would come by science or technological advance. It was the attitude of the Enlightenment. Gadamer's radical dissent from this approach may have begun as early as 1912 with the sinking of the *Titanic.*

Hence Gadamer explores "the rehabilitation of authority and tradition."[46] Authority does not mean *blind* obedience, but, he writes, "It rests on acknowledgement and hence on an act of reason itself which, aware of its own limitations, trusts in the better insight of others."[47] The Enlightenment never recognized this. Nor did Romanticism. There is an "antithesis" between tradition and historical research. Gadamer appeals to the example of the classical, taken up in America by the Roman Catholic theologian David Tracy.[48] The fruit of insight into tradition should not be dismissed as the thought merely of a past historical era, nor made into a "suprahistorical" truth.

This leads Gadamer to consider temporal distance and *effective history* or the *history of effects (Wirkungsgeschichte).* In spite of talk about "the fusion of horizons," those of the past and present never completely come together, and historical and temporal distance must be respected. We must find *"the right questions to ask"* of a historical text or situation. Gadamer assimilates Husserl's and Heidegger's notion of "horizon," which "includes everything that can be seen from a particular vantage point."[49] It is "something into which we move and that moves with us. Horizons change for a person who is moving. Thus the horizon of the past . . . is always in motion."[50] Reading texts

46. Gadamer, *Truth and Method,* pp. 277-85.

47. Gadamer, *Truth and Method,* p. 279.

48. David Tracy of the so-called Chicago School has written *Blessed Rage for Order: The New Pluralism in Theology* (New York: Seabury Press, 1971), in which he largely discusses the nature of theology and the place it gives to *Verstehen* (understanding); cf. David Tracy, *The Analogical Imagination: Christian Theology and the Culture of Pluralism* (London: SCM, 1981), and Tracy, *Plurality and Ambiguity: Hermeneutics, Religion, and Hope* (London: SCM, 1987). The second work takes up the notion of "the classics." Cf. also my discussion of these three major works in Anthony C. Thiselton, *The Hermeneutics of Doctrine* (Grand Rapids: Eerdmans, 2007), pp. 104-15.

49. Gadamer, *Truth and Method,* p. 302.

50. Gadamer, *Truth and Method,* p. 304.

in this way gives rise to historical consciousness. "If we put ourselves in someone else's shoes, for example, then we will understand him — i.e. become aware of the otherness . . . — by putting *ourselves* in his position."[51]

The last part of part II is entitled "The Recovery of the Hermeneutical Problem." Gadamer writes, "Understanding always involves something like applying the text to be understood to the interpreter's present situation."[52] This leads beyond Romanticist hermeneutics but does not return to pietism. For "application" is not a separate "third thing," but integral to understanding. Gadamer views Betti as failing in this respect.

Gadamer illustrates his claim from music, drama, and legal hermeneutics, although it is a pity that he does not discuss the later Wittgenstein at length. Understanding, Wittgenstein argues, depends upon receiving training. It is no good looking for meaning "independently of experience," or as if "the engine were idling."[53] The later Wittgenstein writes, "The language-game in which they are to be applied is missing."[54] "We talk about it as we do about the pieces in chess when we are stating the rules of the game, not describing their physical properties."[55] "The same thing can come before our minds when we hear the word and the application *(seine Anwendung)* still is different."[56] "The application *(Anwendung)* is still a criterion of understanding."[57] In legal hermeneutics, we "understand" when we see how a law is applied. Application, Gadamer insists, is "the central problem of hermeneutics."[58]

Even Aristotle, Gadamer writes, distinguishes moral wisdom from technical reason. Understanding involves the former. Similarly the legal historian may call upon *technē*, but "the jurist understands the meaning of the law from the present case."[59] Understanding a text cannot be simply a scientific or scholarly exploration of its meaning. Bultmann, he argues, presumes that in theology or biblical interpretation we need "a living relationship" between the interpreter and the text. Science alone is not enough.

51. Gadamer, *Truth and Method*, p. 305.
52. Gadamer, *Truth and Method*, p. 308.
53. Wittgenstein, *Philosophical Investigations*, sections 88 and 92.
54. Wittgenstein, *Philosophical Investigations*, section 96.
55. Wittgenstein, *Philosophical Investigations*, section 10.
56. Wittgenstein, *Philosophical Investigations*, section 140.
57. Wittgenstein, *Philosophical Investigations*, section 146; cf. sections 151-78.
58. Gadamer, *Truth and Method*, p. 315.
59. Gadamer, *Truth and Method*, p. 325.

Gadamer now examines historically affected (in many translations historically effective) consciousness. Hegel was right about the connection between history and truth. History suggests that in seeking understanding "someone already favours something."[60] Hence we build up an expectation, or have it thwarted. It may be that we learn through suffering. This is to experience one's own historicity. Hans Robert Jauss takes up these reflections. In this situation or experience, there is something creative when we engage the "other," whether this is a tradition or a person. The "other" really has something to say to us, if we are genuinely "open" to the other. "Openness to the other, then, involves recognizing that I must accept some things that are against me, even though no one else forces me to do so."[61]

This makes us aware of dialectic, as Socrates and Plato insist. It makes us aware also of "*the priority of the question* in all knowledge and discourse."[62] This leads to his "logic of question and answer," and especially to H. G. Collingwood. Collingwood remains, in Gadamer's view, the only person who has developed this logic of question and answer. He does not appear to consider Mikhail Bakhtin.[63] Collingwood insisted that we can understand a text only if we understand what questions it answers. Questioning opens up possibilities of meaning. Gadamer comments, "The logic of question and answer that Collingwood elaborated puts an end to talk about permanent *problems*."[64] "Problems" belong to rhetoric, not to philosophy. Problems are, as it were, fixed and self-contained. The notion is derived from Kant. Hermeneutics by contrast is concerned with historical or contingent "questions that arise." Hence, Gadamer writes, "Reflection on the hermeneutical experience transforms questions back to questions that arise, and derive their sense from their motivation."[65] This ends part II of *Truth and Method*.

60. Gadamer, *Truth and Method*, p. 355.

61. Gadamer, *Truth and Method*, p. 361.

62. Gadamer, *Truth and Method*, p. 363, italics in original.

63. Mikhail Bakhtin, *Problems of Dostoevsky's Poetics*, trans. Caryl Emerson (Minneapolis: University of Minnesota Press, 1984).

64. Gadamer, *Truth and Method*, p. 375, italics in original.

65. Gadamer, *Truth and Method*, p. 377; cf. Thiselton, *The Hermeneutics of Doctrine*, pp. 3-8, and Brook W. R. Pearson, *Corresponding Sense: Paul, Dialectic, and Gadamer* (Leiden, Boston, and Cologne: Brill, 2001), pp. 93-97.

4. *Truth and Method* Part III:
Ontological Hermeneutics and Language, with Assessments

1. It is predictable that in part III of *Truth and Method* Gadamer would turn to the subject of language. Parts I and II are perhaps most distinctive, and at least outside Germany have made the most impact. Language, Gadamer writes, is the medium of hermeneutical experience. He rightly begins with the phenomenon of the *conversation,* pointing out that in a linguistic "medium of understanding" fresh insights "may arise," which could not have been predicted.[66] No one knows in advance what will "come out" of a conversation. The more the conversation partner is "other," the more creative will be the points that emerge. Conversation, including that between a text and its interpreter, bridges a gulf, and allows fresh points to arise.

2. Gadamer also considers translation. He writes that translation is like all interpretation. A translator is painfully aware of where he or she falls short of the original, but it is vital to put material into his or her own "world." He or she is to bring the two horizons together. In this we see a model of interpretation, in which "the historicality of interpretation is the *concretion of historically-effected consciousness.*"[67] This so far is not greatly controversial, and is useful and well argued. But we proceed to a point that can be readily contested.

3. Gadamer is too ready, in my view, to divorce language from life, even if he claims that it remains historically conditioned. He claims that tradition is essentially verbal in character, especially when it is written. Language alone is the medium of understanding, and it presents and ensures the priority of the question. History becomes, in effect, a presupposition of language. Gadamer speaks of what "linguistics teaches," and of "the concept of language that modern linguistics and philosophy of language take as their starting point."[68] But here he speaks of Ernst Cassirer and ignores Ferdinand de Saussure and the greatest exponents of linguistics or the philosophy of language. Elsewhere Gadamer speaks of "the convergence of my concept of game with the concept of language-games in the later Wittgenstein."[69] But

---

66. Gadamer, *Truth and Method,* pp. 384-85.
67. Gadamer, *Truth and Method,* p. 389, italics in original.
68. Gadamer, *Truth and Method,* pp. 402-3.
69. Gadamer, "My Philosophical Journey," p. 42.

Wittgenstein writes explicitly: "I shall also call the whole, consisting of language and the actions into which it is woven, the 'language-game.'"[70] He rightly also observes, "Here the term 'language-game' is meant to bring into prominence the fact that the *speaking* of language is part of an activity, or of a form of life."[71] Gadamer restricts himself largely to writers on language in the German tradition.

Furthermore, there is too much discussion of language as "names" in Gadamer, and frankly old-fashioned discussions of language. One might argue that in 1960 or earlier he did not have access to writers like John Searle. But Wittgenstein had rejected in the early 1950s the notion of language as naming, and such "superquestions" as "What is language?"[72] Language as a phenomenon divorced from life has too much dominance in the later Heidegger, as well as in the literary theory of the 1950s, and in Ernst Fuchs and Gerhard Ebeling. Moreover, it conflicts with Gadamer's rightful emphasis on the incarnation. Perhaps we should say that at least Gadamer is ambiguous about this question.

4. Later in his part III on language Gadamer seems to concede that the Greeks and Plato, or at least the traditional understanding of them, were wrong, and Christian theology right, about the enfleshment of the Word: "the Word became flesh" (John 1:14).[73] The lengthy discussion of Plato's *Cratylus* ends by rejecting the notion of language as a second-class imitation of reality, and accepting convention rather than nature as the basis of language. Augustine and Christian scholastics alluded to "the word of the heart," and thereby avoided Plato's problem.[74] For Gadamer the word in the world (Saussure's *la parole*) is a matter of *actualizing* the potential *(la langue),* and this harmonizes with Saussure.

5. The further point is not ambivalent, nor is it controversial. Gadamer, like the later Wittgenstein, believes that concept formation is primarily a matter of language, and that language itself is not primarily instrumental but can reveal new truth. Language can enable us to see the world in a new way. "Concept-formation . . . occurs in language."[75] Wittgenstein makes this abundantly clear. He writes, for example: "When language-games change,

---

70. Wittgenstein, *Philosophical Investigations,* section 7.

71. Wittgenstein, *Philosophical Investigations,* section 23.

72. Wittgenstein, *Philosophical Investigations,* sections 38, 40-43, 47-49, 50, 66, 81, 88-92.

73. Gadamer, *Truth and Method,* pp. 418-28, especially pp. 419 and 429.

74. Gadamer, *Truth and Method,* p. 420.

75. Gadamer, *Truth and Method,* p. 428; cf. pp. 428-38.

then there is a change in concepts, and with the concepts the meanings of words change."[76]

6. The next point is more controversial, but in the way that Gadamer intends it, not as controversial as the third point. It is the noninstrumental, creative use of language. Gadamer rejects the "sign" theory of language. We participate, he insists, in language. Language and words have primordial power. He is entirely right that language functions are to be distinguished from mere language forms. He draws from John and from Christian theology that language has saving power. In this sense language is an encompassing medium, not a mere tool. However, in another sense language and words are also tools. Gadamer falls into the typical Germanic trap of seeing the matter as an either/or rather than as a both/and. In Wittgenstein and in Paul Ricoeur, language can open up a "world." As we have already cited from him, Wittgenstein urges, "Think of tools in a toolbox. . . . The functions of words are as diverse as the functions of these objects."[77]

Gadamer, however, views language more like a poet than as an exponent of linguistics or an Anglo-American philosopher. He chooses to enter into dialogue with Wilhelm von Humboldt, Aristotle, Hegel, and Plato, rather than with Saussure and Saussure's successors. Gadamer is still under the spell of Heidegger, where the "presence" of a world has more to do with architecture and poetry in his later work than with ordinary everyday life. Yet Gadamer is right that in some circles the creative power of language is taken seriously. The emphasis found in Gadamer and Heidegger on "disclosure" is right. Palmer writes, "Gadamer chooses the concept of disclosure. . . . Language discloses our world — not our environmental scientific world or universe, but our life-world."[78] Like Heidegger, he speaks of Hölderlin and poetry. Here we are subject to the play of language itself. For hermeneutics is universal in the sense that everything is hermeneutical, and "there is no understanding that is free of all prejudice. . . . We encounter discipline of questioning and inquiry, a discipline that guarantees truth."[79]

---

76. Ludwig Wittgenstein, *On Certainty,* German and English (Oxford: Blackwell, 1969), section 65.

77. Wittgenstein, *Philosophical Investigations,* section 11; cf. section 23.

78. Richard E. Palmer, *Hermeneutics: Interpretation Theory in Schleiermacher, Dilthey, Heidegger, and Gadamer,* Studies in Phenomenology and Existential Philosophy (Evanston, Ill.: Northwestern University Press, 1969), p. 205.

79. Gadamer, *Truth and Method,* pp. 490-91.

5. Further Assessments of the Three Parts of *Truth and Method*

1. We saw from Gadamer's biographical background that his influences included the early Greeks, Kant, Hegel, Kierkegaard, Dilthey, and above all Heidegger. For Plato and Kant, reality was split into two parts, the phenomenal and the "noumenal" or ideal. For Kierkegaard truth was subjective, in the sense of requiring participation and involvement. The latter provides an enrichment of hermeneutics, except for the devaluing of assertions or propositions, which Gadamer sees as capable of becoming used for propaganda, Robert Sullivan argues, and as closing off questions.[80] Hegel, Dilthey, and Heidegger attack the Enlightenment's way of assuming that reason held the key to all inquiry, irrespective of history and the historical conditioning of the inquirer. In effect, all reality is hermeneutical. Much of this is positive for hermeneutics, especially the emphasis on "historicality" from Hegel to Heidegger. Although Kantian dualism is unfortunate, Gadamer firmly puts "technical reason" in its place. No knowledge is value-neutral, and the sciences will take us only part of the way.

2. Second, as Brook Pearson and others emphasize, Gadamer firmly gives priority *to how questions arise* rather than to "problems" as fixed, isolated entities. Husserl's notion of the *horizon* or perspective is developed as that which is moving, or moves with us. We see differently as we advance, and this may apply publicly to tradition. Gadamer rejects the individualism of Descartes and of the empiricists, and rejects the starting point of "individual consciousness."

3. Third, Gadamer's paradigm of the experiencing of *a game* or a festival or art is more than suggestive for hermeneutics. It provides an understanding that is a needed corrective to more traditional philosophical perspectives. Gilbert Ryle's criticism of Heidegger about abstraction is only partly right. There are moments and questions for which abstraction is not the answer, but involvement is needed. As I have urged elsewhere, Gadamer writes, "Hermeneutics is above all a practice. . . . In it what one has to exercise above all is the ear, the sensitivity for perceiving prior determinations, anticipations, and imprints that reside in concepts."[81] This is a key point, which influences entirely our approach to listening to Scripture.

80. Robert R. Sullivan, *Political Hermeneutics: The Early Thinking of Hans-Georg Gadamer* (University Park and London: Pennsylvania State University Press, 1980), pp. 26-27.
81. Gadamer, "My Philosophical Journey," p. 17.

4. Fourth, Gadamer's concept of *"effective history" (Wirkungsgeschichte)* is both valid and fruitful. Historical finitude means *the limits of self-consciousness*, but the interpreter listens to the prejudices, or the prejudgments, of himself or herself, and their community. Gadamer has made us look at Hegel's "historical reason" more carefully again.

5. Of course, we may question certain conclusions as controversial. First, many point out that Gadamer allows no "final answer" to any question. Like a work of art, questions are inexhaustible. Gadamer does not seem to think that in the end we can produce *"criteria"* of meaning, except for "application." Certainly there would not be conformity with the original author. Life moves on, and for Gadamer hermeneutics is never replication. As Joel Weinsheimer makes clear, "answers" are as variable as different performances. There is a missing ingredient in Gadamer's hermeneutics that Paul Ricoeur seeks to rectify. Gadamer rejects the "explanatory" axis that Schleiermacher, Apel, and Ricoeur retain.

Second, one might initially welcome Gadamer's fusion of understanding and *application*. But if there is no difference at all, are we not led back inevitably to our previous problem? Where is the role of criteria?

Third, is it possible that Gadamer himself has shifted in his account of *language?* Part III of *Truth and Method* seems to locate Gadamer too near to Heidegger.[82] Gadamer replies to Schmidt that the ethics of language features in his more recent correspondence with Heidegger. But this presupposes some human agency, and thus points to a relation between language and life that is more than a "presupposition." We have seen how Wittgenstein, let alone John Searle and advocates of "politeness theory," would differ from Gadamer here. Paul Ricoeur gives greater prominence to human agency.[83] Moreover, his own onetime pupil, Hans Robert Jauss, speaks of the historically successive readings of texts that belong to reception history. Jauss complains that his concept of the classical also has limits.

6. Nevertheless, Gadamer has done more than anyone to dethrone Descartes and the Enlightenment as arbiters of meaning and truth. We can never put the clock back before *Truth and Method*. Everything is hermeneutical; everything requires interpretation.

---

82. Dennis J. Schmidt, "Putting Oneself in Words . . . ," in *The Philosophy of Hans-Georg Gadamer,* p. 484; cf. pp. 483-95.

83. Paul Ricoeur, *Oneself as Another,* trans. Kathleen Blamey (Chicago and London: University of Chicago Press, 1992), pp. 40-168.

6. Recommended Initial Reading

Gadamer, Hans-Georg, "Reflections on My Philosophical Journey," in *The Philosophy of Hans-Georg Gadamer*, edited by Lewis Edwin Hahn (Chicago and La Salle, Ill.: Open Court, 1997), pp. 3-63.

———, *Truth and Method*, 2nd English ed. (London: Sheed and Ward, 1989), pp. 3-30 and 277-379.

Jensen, Alexander, *Theological Hermeneutics*, SCM Core Text (London: SCM, 2007), pp. 135-44.

Palmer, Richard E., *Hermeneutics: Interpretation Theory in Schleiermacher, Dilthey, Heidegger, and Gadamer*, Studies in Phenomenology and Existential Philosophy (Evanston, Ill.: Northwestern University Press, 1969), pp. 162-217.

Thiselton, Anthony C., *New Horizons in Hermeneutics: The Theory and Practice of Transforming Biblical Reading* (London: HarperCollins; Grand Rapids: Zondervan, 1992), pp. 313-31.

Weinsheimer, Joel C., *Gadamer's Hermeneutics: A Reading of "Truth and Method"* (New Haven: Yale University Press, 1985), pp. 63-213.

CHAPTER XII

The Hermeneutics of Paul Ricoeur

1. Background, Early Life, Influences, and Significance

Paul Ricoeur and Hans-Georg Gadamer rank as the two most significant theorists of hermeneutics of the twentieth century. But although much of his theological work remains implicit rather than explicit, Ricoeur will have a lasting impact on the future of Christian theology perhaps even more than Gadamer.

1. Paul Ricoeur (1913-2005) was born at Valence, in France, of a devout Protestant family.[1] His father died in the First World War when Paul was only two. His mother also died, and Paul grew up under the care of his paternal grandparents and an aunt at Rennes. Paul graduated from the University of Rennes in 1932 and studied philosophy at Sorbonne in Paris in 1934. Here he came under the influence of the Catholic existentialist philosopher Gabriel Marcel (1889-1973). Marcel taught that human beings were unique individuals, not to be categorized as a mere number or a case. His influence on Paul is apparent, and Paul took his master's degree in 1935. But in 1939 the Second World War interrupted Ricoeur's further studies. He joined the army, and his unit was captured in 1940.

2. During his years as a prisoner of war, Ricoeur studied German philosophy, especially that of the psychiatrist-philosopher and existentialist thinker Karl Jaspers; the phenomenology of Edmund Husserl; and the philosophy of Martin Heidegger, including his notion of *existence, historicality,*

---

1. Paul Ricoeur, "Intellectual Biography," in *The Philosophy of Paul Ricoeur,* ed. Lewis E. Hahn (Chicago: Open Court, 1995), p. 5.

possibility, and humans as *Dasein,* which became crucial for Ricoeur. After the war he taught at the University of Strasbourg (1948-54), the only French university with a Protestant faculty of theology. Ricoeur was awarded his doctorate in 1950. In 1949 he published *Le Voluntaire et l'Involuntaire.*[2]

In 1956 he became professor of philosophy at the Sorbonne and wrote *Fallible Man* and *The Symbolism of Evil,* both published in French in 1960 (English 1965 and 1967).[3] *Fallible Man* was originally planned as the second volume of a tripartite work on the human will and finitude, and betrays the influence not only of Marcel but also of the Jewish existentialist philosopher Martin Buber. Human subjectivity is important. There is more to human life than empirical causality, observation, or reality, as we find in many "sciences."

3. In 1965 Ricoeur produced his book *Freud and Philosophy,* in which he rejected Freud's worldview as positivistic but accepted his emphasis on the need for *interpretation,* or hermeneutics.[4] However, unlike Gadamer, he saw both "explanation" *(Erklärung)* and understanding *(Verstehen)* as vital to interpretation. Explanation alone can be reductive, but it also offers the critical dimension that makes understanding possible. Only through "explanation" can we reach the "post-critical naïveté" of understanding. Ricoeur wrote, "Hermeneutics seems to me to be animated by this double motivation: willingness to suspect, willingness to listen; vow of rigor, vow of obedience. In our time we have not finished doing away with *idols* and we have barely begun to listen to *symbols.*"[5]

4. During some of these years Jacques Derrida became Ricoeur's assistant. But in 1965 Ricoeur left the more traditionalist Sorbonne to work with an experiment in "progressive" education at Nanberre University. Then in 1968 Ricoeur moved to the Catholic university of Louvain in Belgium. Here he published a book of essays, *The Conflict of Interpretations* (1969), which betrayed his pluralism in hermeneutics. Finally Ricoeur moved to the Uni-

---

2. Paul Ricoeur, *Freedom and Nature: The Voluntary and Involuntary* (Evanston, Ill.: Northwestern University Press, 1966), from French *Le Voluntaire et L'Involuntaire* (Paris: Aubier, 1949).

3. Paul Ricoeur, *Fallible Man,* rev. and trans. Charles A. Kelbley (New York: Fordham University Press, 1985, 1st Eng. ed. 1965); Ricoeur, *The Symbolism of Evil* (Boston: Beacon Press, 1969; 1st Eng. ed. 1967).

4. Paul Ricoeur, *Freud and Philosophy: An Essay on Interpretation,* trans. Denis Savage (New Haven and London: Yale University Press, 1970), from the French, *De l'interprétation: Essai sur Freud* (1965).

5. Ricoeur, *Freud and Philosophy,* p. 27, italics in original.

versity of Chicago in 1970, where he served as professor of philosophy until 1985. He published *The Rule of Metaphor* in 1975 and *Interpretation Theory* in 1976.[6]

5. The stage was now set for his two greatest works, preceded by books of essays, *Essays on Biblical Interpretation* (essays from 1969 to 1980) and *Hermeneutics and the Human Sciences* (essays from 1971 to 1980).[7] The first of Ricoeur's greatest works was *Time and Narrative,* published in three volumes between 1983 and 1985 (English translation 1984-88). The French title, *Temps et Récit,* means perhaps, according to Vanhoozer, "time and telling."[8] Here Ricoeur explores the temporal logic of plot, or emplotment. He draws on both Augustine's notion of extended time and Aristotle's unifying notion of temporal emplotment. The "telling" of the plot depends on an organizing principle of narrative-plot and narrative-time. The second of Ricoeur's greatest major works is his book *Oneself as Another.*[9] Here he returns, as in *Fallible Man,* to the problem of the human self, with the importance of human agency, action, relationship with others, and moral accountability. The self is not the lone individual self of Descartes, nor even the bodily self of P. F. Strawson, but a being of whom ethics cannot be left out of account.

6. After his monumental book *Oneself as Another,* Ricoeur wrote on religion, the Bible, and narrative in his *Figuring the Sacred* (English 1995), and on specific biblical passages in *Thinking Biblically: Exegetical and Hermeneutical Studies* (1998).[10] He then turned increasingly to ethical questions in *The*

6. Paul Ricoeur, *The Rule of Metaphor: Multi-Disciplinary Studies of the Creation of Meaning in Language,* trans. Robert Czerny with Kathleen McLaughlin (London: Routledge and Kegan Paul, 1977), and Ricoeur, *Interpretation Theory: Discourse and the Surplus of Meaning* (Fort Worth: Texas Christian University Press, 1976).

7. Paul Ricoeur, *Essays on Biblical Interpretation,* ed. Lewis S. Mudge (Philadelphia: Fortress, 1980; London: SPCK, 1981), and Ricoeur, *Hermeneutics and the Human Sciences: Essays on Language Action and Interpretation,* ed. and trans. John B. Thompson (Cambridge: Cambridge University Press, 1981; French 1981).

8. Paul Ricoeur, *Time and Narrative,* trans. Kathleen Blamey and David Pellauer, 3 vols. (Chicago and London: University of Chicago Press, 1984, 1985, 1988); French, *Temps et Récit* (Paris: Editions du Seuil, 1983, 1984, 1985); cf. Kevin J. Vanhoozer, *Biblical Narrative in the Philosophy of Paul Ricoeur: A Study in Hermeneutics* (Cambridge: Cambridge University Press, 1990), p. x.

9. Paul Ricoeur, *Oneself as Another,* trans. Kathleen Blamey (Chicago and London: University of Chicago Press, 1992); French, *Soi-même comme un autre* (Paris: Editions de Seuil, 1990).

10. Paul Ricoeur, *Figuring the Sacred: Religion, Narrative, and Imagination,* trans. David Pellauer and Mark I. Wallace (Philadelphia: Augsburg Fortress, 1995); Paul Ricoeur and

Just (2000) and *Reflections on the Just* (French 2001, and English two years after his death, in 2007).[11] In these last volumes he seeks to combine ethical virtue as promoted by Aristotle and others with the more absolute and universal morality of the will found in Kant.

Ricoeur gives a very brief account of the development of his earlier thought as an appendix to *The Rule of Metaphor.* First he addressed the problem of human finitude and guilt in both *Fallible Man* and *The Symbolism of Evil.* Existential philosophers of the 1940s, 1950s, and early 1960s had addressed the philosophy of the will, emphasizing human guilt, bondage, alienation, or what in religious language amounts to sin. In Heidegger and in Bultmann this condition was called *inauthentic* existence. In Jaspers it related to boundary situations, and in Marcel, to despair. Marcel had already in 1932-33 published an article on Jaspers and Jaspers's limit-situations, which influenced Ricoeur. In 1947 Ricoeur undertook a comparative study of Marcel and Jaspers.

Ricoeur's use of existential phenomenology at that time owed something to his reading of Edmund Husserl and to his discovery of Maurice Merleau-Ponty. Merleau-Ponty resisted the usual interpretation of phenomenology in his *Phenomenology of Perception.* Ricoeur contrasts Jean-Paul Sartre's *Being and Nothingness* (1943), which, he says, produced in him only distant admiration but no conviction. He also studied further Jaspers's notion of transcendence. Where Jaspers had spoken of "ciphers of transcendence," however, Ricoeur saw that "deciphering" could be a model of *hermeneutics.* Indeed, his criticism of Rudolf Bultmann was that language operated in more multiple modes than Bultmann allowed.[12] He came to see that the discovery of varied meanings in language was perhaps more vital even than phenomenology. In accordance with the spirit of the times, Ricoeur was losing interest in some versions of phenomenology, and turning to linguistics and the philosophy of action. He saw that issues of language were involved in the problem of evil, where symbolic language used metaphor such as estrangement, burden, and bondage as primary symbols, even if embedded in a narrative.

André LaCocque, *Thinking Biblically: Exegetical and Hermeneutical Studies,* trans. David Pellauer (Chicago and London: University of Chicago Press, 1998).

11. Paul Ricoeur, *The Just,* trans. David Pellauer (Chicago and London: University of Chicago Press, 2000); Ricoeur, *Reflections on the Just,* trans. David Pellauer (Chicago and London: University of Chicago Press, 2007).

12. Paul Ricoeur, "Preface to Bultmann," in *Essays on Biblical Interpretation,* pp. 52-53; cf. pp. 49-72.

In *The Symbolism of Evil* Ricoeur followed phenomenology and Dilthey in considering the "lived experience" of humanity, but found that he had to introduce a hermeneutical dimension into reflective thought. For symbols involve "double meaning expressions." Words such as "bondage" or "burden" come from everyday life, but the empirical, everyday meaning is conjoined, even if in tension, with a moral or spiritual realm, as Max Black argued about metaphor. Some metaphors, he acknowledges, are merely didactic, illustrative, or ornamental. But the truly creative metaphor is *interactive* between two domains of meaning. Ricoeur speaks here of "layers" of meaning, or of multiple meaning, or of "split reference."[13] He draws on the resources of Max Black and Roman Jakobson.

Symbols, however, also often become "buried" in narrative. These are usually narratives of myths, or what Childs and Caird call "broken myth." Thus Ricoeur drew on both the Hebrew and Greek background to sin, using both the story of Adam in the Bible and the Orphic tragic myth. He also drew on the well-known work of Mircea Eliade in religious studies. He seeks to interpret the biblical narrative but regards it as inappropriately a narrative of the fall in the technical or doctrinal sense, but as a narrative of *wisdom*. Ricoeur's autobiographical comments suggest that 1965-1970 marked the end of an era for him and for paradigms in French philosophy. The stage was set for his central work in hermeneutics and his return from language to a philosophy of action and the will.

2. The Middle Period: The Interpretation of Freud, *The Conflict of Interpretations,* and Metaphor

1. Ricoeur recalls that at about this time, with Heidegger's earlier "turn," interest shifted to the dynamics of *language* and to creative *poiēsis*. This newer interest violently opposed humanism, phenomenology, and hermeneutics. Claude Lévi-Strauss led the way from 1955 to 1964 with structuralism, allegedly based on Ferdinand de Saussure's *General Linguistics* (1913) and Lévi-Strauss's research into cultural anthropology culminating in *Mythologies: I,* in 1964. Together with this new move to structuralism came a Marxist interpretation with Louis Althusser and the psychologist Jacques Lacan's Marxist reading of Freud. Ricoeur's careful response was "to dissociate structuralism

13. Ricoeur, *The Rule of Metaphor,* p. 6.

as a universal model," but nevertheless to use this approach only where it could be appropriately applied to specific cases.[14]

Ricoeur's great book on psychoanalysis, *Freud and Philosophy* (French 1965; English 1970), was a classic on the need for the dimension of "explanation" in contrast to "understanding," although both are fully involved in hermeneutics. He recognized the validity of psychoanalysis in explaining causally the psychological devices of self-deception without for a moment surrendering to Freud's mechanistic and materialist worldview. Freud's work, Ricoeur believed, was a classic of hermeneutics because he did not accept the recounted "text" of the self at face value, but probed into that superficial and deceptive text to see the true "text" of reality that lay buried underneath it. Ricoeur saw this as a true model of hermeneutics because it probed behind the alleged "text" to the real, genuine text of life.

This "probing underneath the classical and projected text" led to the formulation of Ricoeur's "hermeneutics of suspicion," which remains the interpreter's weapon against what Habermas calls "interest"; or our desires, concerns, and vested interests, which may distort our understanding of the text. Ricoeur writes, "Freud invites us to look to dreams themselves for the various relations between desire and language. First it is not the dream as dreamed that can be interpreted, but rather the text of the dream account."[15] Freudian analysis seeks to recover the true underlying "text" beneath what is said. This opens up desire and double meaning.

Freud's mistake was to reduce everything to "forces" that were ultimately physical or material only. He missed the richness or "overdetermination" of meaning in his patients' language. Aristotle saw that to interpret a sentence yields more than the sum of its individual words. A noun, for example, on its own has no reference to time, as he saw. Even Nietzsche saw that interpretation involves the whole of philosophy. Hence we repeat Ricoeur's famous words about his hermeneutic of suspicion, to which we earlier referred: "Hermeneutics seem to me to be animated by this double motivation: willingness to suspect, willingness to listen; vow of rigor, vow of obedience" (p. 27). As we have seen, he seeks the destruction of what we have made in our own image, and the capacity to hear transforming or creative language.

14. Ricoeur, "Intellectual Biography," p. 19.
15. Ricoeur, *Freud and Philosophy*, p. 5. Parenthetical page numbers in the text that follows are to this work.

Ricoeur then speaks equally of "post-critical faith" or "a second naïveté" (pp. 28-29). This is a rational faith, for it has passed through critical inquiry and explanation. Ricoeur accepts the need for archaeology of explanation, but this is not the whole story; it remains empty without "understanding."

In his section entitled "Interpretation as Exercise of Suspicion," Ricoeur calls "the three great destroyers" Marx, Nietzsche, and Freud "masters of suspicion." All three clear the horizon, Ricoeur comments, for a more authentic word. He finds in Freudian analysis that the symbol is vital but equivocal. Symbolic logic cuts across hermeneutics, with its concern only for precision and singleness of meaning. In the eyes of the logician, hermeneutics will seem content with ambivalent meaning. But this is not a weak substitute for definition. It is the result of wider reflective thought. We must destroy the idols, to listen to symbols.

Ricoeur reads Freud in further detail. First, he shows that without hermeneutics the 1895 project is wholly "scientific," and attempts to explain everything in terms of mechanistic "forces" (pp. 69-86). But Freud's book *The Interpretation of Dreams* shows advances, including a place for the emotional as well as the "psychical." Ideas, thoughts, and reason find a place, and Ricoeur introduces "figurative" interpretation. The dream has a meaning *(Sinn)*. The dream-*as-dreamed* ("the dream-*thought*") is not the dream as remembered and *recounted*. It is changed by "condensation" and displacement, or in other words abbreviated and scrambled resulting in overdetermination (p. 93). *Overdetermination* means that, with more than one level of meaning, dreams can be variously interpreted. Freud suggested that often infantile scenes were presented as recent experience. They may be hallucinatory. We interpret to locate the dream-thoughts behind or underneath the account. This often takes the form of wish-fulfillment revealed in sleep but repressed by consciousness.

Freud is realistic about the *id*. Ricoeur speaks of the universal narcissism of man and man's self-love. Yet he tells us this work on Freud was not well received in France, because many of the French intellectuals of the day were preoccupied with Lacan. But although Lacan addressed linguistic issues, Ricoeur found more immediate relevance to humanities in Freud's work on intelligibility, disguise, and interpretation or meaning.

2. *The Conflict of Interpretations* is a book of essays on various topics.[16]

---

16. Paul Ricoeur, *The Conflict of Interpretations: Essays in Hermeneutics*, trans. D. Ihde (Evanston, Ill.: Northwestern University Press, 1974); French (Paris: Éditions du Seuil, 1969).

Ricoeur considers Descartes and consciousness, structuralism and double-meaning, psychoanalysis and Freud, and symbols, religions, and faith. Many essays elaborate *The Symbolism of Evil* and *Freud and Philosophy,* but hermeneutics remains the main theme, and there is a greater engagement with philosophy of language as well as the foundation of the human or social sciences.

Although structuralism looks back to Saussure, Ricoeur rightly considers the speech-act and recent studies of Ludwig Wittgenstein, of J. L. Austin, and of P. F. Strawson. The unit of meaning is not the word, but the sentence, or discourse. He writes primarily "to shed light on the debate about structuralism and its value."[17] He concedes that it sheds explanatory light on *la langue,* on language as a storehouse of possibilities actualized in *la parole.* From this is excluded the human agent and his or her history. It is therefore purely semantic rather than hermeneutical. This level of analysis is entirely empirical. It involves synchronic rather than diachronic (historical) linguistics. This presupposes a closed system, as Trier, and before him Saussure, argued. This system is an *autonomous* entity of *internal* relations.

This signals the triumph of so-called scientific enterprise. But it excludes the act of speaking. As Humboldt and especially the French linguistics scholar Émilio Benveniste (1902-76) emphasized, communication cannot be wholly explained in behaviorist or stimulus-response terms, for language is grounded in life. The work of Roland Barthes, A. J. Greimas, and Gérard Genette remains useful up to a point, but is not comprehensive. We must see the relation between system and the human act, or between the structure and the event. In a previous essay in *The Conflict of Interpretations,* Ricoeur discusses "double meaning" as a hermeneutical problem. The part played by such structuralists as Greimas is comparable to the part played by Freud in the subsequent essays on psychoanalysis. They explain some features, but not all, of language and discourse. Ricoeur includes further essays on phenomenology and on symbolism, and one on Heidegger.

3. *The Rule of Metaphor* (1975) again calls attention to the multilayered richness of language. It seeks to develop further some of the themes in *The Conflict of Interpretations. What symbol is to word, metaphor is to sentence.* Again Benveniste remains influential, but especially the notion of interactive domains in Max Black. As Mary Hesse and Janet Martin Sorkice have also urged, metaphors of a creative kind do not merely constitute illustrations or ornaments, nor do they substitute for other analogies, but they may convey

---

17. Ricoeur, "Structure, Word, Event," in *The Conflict of Interpretations,* p. 79.

cognitive truth. They also add heuristic power, or power to discover, as Ricoeur argues in "Metaphor and Reference." He takes up Aristotle's definition of metaphor. Metaphor "consists in giving the thing a name that belongs to something else . . . on grounds of analogy."[18] It thus involves change and movement, and transposition. Metaphors allow two semantic domains to interact creatively.

This book is a virtual encyclopedia of metaphor from Aristotle onward. Metaphor is independent of simile. Creative metaphor gives new insights, as do also "models" in the sciences. It can perform at the level of the sentence what *mythos* (perhaps in English, plot) achieves for a poem. Within metaphor we can find "the family of metaphors," namely, tropes, figures, and allegories. Ricoeur discusses predication and identity with reference to P. F. Strawson's *Individuals,* and semantics and rhetoric of metaphor.

Ricoeur dedicates his essay "Metaphor and the New Rhetoric" to A. J. Greimas. The essay begins with a discussion of Josef Trier and his notion of "semantic fields." This is fundamental to any structuralist account of language. Again Ricoeur mentions Gérard Genette and Max Black as important dialogue partners. Greimas's "grammar" of semiotics leaves much out of account. Synecdoche and metaphor, for example, may operate with a specificity and what he calls "semantic impertinence." General rules do not allow for, or predict, their creativity. The remaining essays contain discussions of major figures in the history of metaphor, including Roman Jakobson. Interestingly, "Metaphor and Philosophical Discourse" is inscribed, "For Jean Ladrière," who has done much to illuminate pragmatics or language events in liturgy.[19] Ricoeur rightly subtitles this whole book "Multi-Disciplinary Studies of the Creation of Meaning in Language." He looks at the extralinguistic features of language and begins his explanation of "refiguration" in a creative reading of texts.

3. The Later Period: *Time and Narrative*

Ricoeur's two classic works are the magisterial *Time and Narrative* (three volumes, first published in French in 1983-85) and *Oneself as Another* (1990; English 1992). Ricoeur tells us the ground was prepared in part by his read-

18. Ricoeur, *The Rule of Metaphor,* p. 13.
19. Ricoeur, *The Rule of Metaphor,* pp. 257-313.

ing of Dilthey, and by his insistence on exploring both explanation and understanding. He also tells us of his prior move to America. These remain "primary" sources for hermeneutics.

Ricoeur also tells us that his essay "What Is a Text? Explanation and Understanding" (1970) was first written for a volume in honor of Hans-Georg Gadamer, and this also prepared the way.[20] In this essay he acknowledges that the emancipation of the text from oral language raised a great upheaval. Ricoeur notes how Dilthey saw the inner life as expressed in external signs, which are signs of another mental life. Dilthey also saw the need for both explanation and understanding in hermeneutics. He concludes his essay with a new concept of interpretation as appropriation in the present.

Time was the philosophical theme that most governed *Time and Narrative.* This was due in part to four different factors. It was (1) partly a result of a dialogue with Heidegger and Greimas; (2) partly to develop and to correct earlier lectures on time; (3) partly a result of seeing the importance of history; and (4) partly because he was impressed by the work of the Old Testament scholar Gerhard von Rad. Ricoeur was thoroughly familiar with Heidegger's historicality and temporality (*Zeitlichkeit,* the transcendent ground for the possibility of time).

1. In volume 1 of *Time and Narrative* Ricoeur begins with Augustine and especially with book 11 of Augustine's *Confessions* on the "discordance," or extension, of time as past, present, and future. He addressed the difficulties of temporal experience as noted and described by Augustine. Augustine sees the experience of a future as *expectation;* present experience as a matter of *attention;* and past experience as a matter of *memory.* Ricoeur comments, "Through the experience of human time (memory, attention, and hope) we come to understand the world, its objects, and our own present."[21] Augustine considers these a series of disparate "moments." As a whole they are part of creation, and true of the whole history of humankind. Of themselves these experiences convey a "discordance," but God (or history) holds them together "in the direction of eternity." Augustine believes that time was created *with* the world. The dialectic of time and eternity produces a hierarchy of levels of temporalization. This is shaped by how close or how far a given experience approaches, or moves away from, this pole of eternity. A dialectic of *intentio* and *distentio* becomes anchored in eternity and time, looking to

20. Ricoeur, *Hermeneutics,* pp. 145-64.
21. Ricoeur, *Time and Narrative,* 1:16.

the future in hope. Too often we wrongly regard narratives as a matter of mere flat logic and report.

2. Aristotle's *Poetics* is regarded as complementary with Augustine on time. Ricoeur tells us that in his concept of "emplotment" *(mythos)* we find the opposite point to that found in Augustine. The poetic act yields *"concordance"* or coherence in the temporal logic of *emplotment. Mythos,* or emplotment, becomes "the organization of the events."[22] In this "organization" the operative character of the participants in it becomes known in their actions. In this sense the whole makes *Verstehen* (understanding) possible.

3. In the third main chapter of part I of volume 1 Ricoeur discusses the dynamic of the emplotment that follows. He argues that "refiguration" comes through the reception of the work. The whole is grounded in a pre-understanding of the world of action. But it is still characterized by "temporality" *(Zeitlichkeit)* that gives unity to character and person. Thus the plot is "made present" in hermeneutics. We have arrived at "narrative understanding." Ricoeur will speak more of this unity in volume 2. There is always a coherent synthesis of the heterogeneous, which may take the form of a *dramatization.* Other writers also trace the drama of Christian doctrine and narrative.[23]

4. In the second half of volume 1 Ricoeur turns his attention to the relation between *narrative and history.* Surprisingly, he does not seem to mention Hans Frei, whose writing has received enormous attention in the Anglo-American world. But he would probably not be content with Frei's "history-like" narrative. He allows for "historical intentionality" and argues for an "indirect" relation between narrative and history, which would address epistemological questions that perhaps Frei does not fully answer.

The historical researcher will not find that "raw" historical events are necessarily always present in the emplotment that narrative presents. For example, in narrative-time the Gospel of Mark speeds up the early events of the life of Jesus, gains a medium speed after Peter's confession of faith, but slows down greatly in the passion narrative to show that it is to this that early events are leading. Ricoeur explains that the historical event has not been

---

22. Ricoeur, *Time and Narrative,* 1:33; Aristotle, *Poetics* 50a.15.

23. Cf. Hans Urs von Balthasar, *Theo-Drama: Theological Dramatic Theory,* trans. G. Harrison, 5 vols. (San Francisco: Ignatius, 1988-98); Kevin J. Vanhoozer, *The Drama of Doctrine: A Canonical Linguistic Approach to Christian Theology* (Louisville: Westminster John Knox, 2005); and Anthony C. Thiselton, *The Hermeneutics of Doctrine* (Grand Rapids: Eerdmans, 2007), pp. 62-80.

eliminated in every respect; but as "revelation-as-event things are totally accounted for."[24] There is also an "event" for the reader in the present. This event is generated both by God and by the plot of the narrative. Later he speaks of the "quasi event."

5. Volume 2 gives us part III of *Time and Narrative.* This particularly addresses the configuration (or change) of time in fictional narrative. The term *mimēsis,* used by Plato, Aristotle, and Erich Auerbach, distinguishes this form of narrative from purely historical accounts, and may include folktale, epic, tragedy, comedy, and the fictional novel. Here Ricoeur seeks to broaden and deepen how emplotment often works. Hence he discusses, for example, Gérard Genette's analysis of order, duration, and frequency in narrative-time, including *prolepses,* or flash-forwards to the end, which incidentally shed light on the narratives of the four Gospels, as well as the format of standard detective stories.[25] Much is occupied with theories of literature, and applied to such writers or works as Virginia Woolf's *Mrs. Dalloway,* Thomas Mann's *Magic Mountain,* and Marcel Proust's *Remembrance of Things Past.*

6. Volume 3, like volume 1, consists of two main parts. In section 1 Ricoeur addresses the relation between the human experience of time (which may include narrative-time) and the cosmological, astronomical, or chronological time that clocks or the solar system measures. I have discussed this in *The Promise of Hermeneutics.*[26] Ricoeur introduces this by looking again at Husserl's phenomenology. For Husserl the present "now" is not contracted into a mere point, but is related to intentionality. Kant ascribed all time, along with space and causality, to the "inner" categories imposed by the mind, and Ricoeur sets himself the task of discovering why and how Kant reached this conclusion. His transcendental aesthetic, he concludes, has to "hide" phenomenology. Some examples are correct, as when we say "the time comes," but Kant overlooks the *double* experience of time as both human time and clock time.

In chapter 3 of the first part of volume 3, Ricoeur turns to the relation between time and Heidegger's "historicality." Heidegger primarily looks at how *Dasein* experiences time in a subjective way, but admits the validity of chronological or cosmological time. Care captures the "authentic" structure

24. Ricoeur, *Time and Narrative,* 1:222-23.

25. Ricoeur, *Time and Narrative,* 2:83-88.

26. Anthony C. Thiselton (with R. Lundin and C. Walhout), *The Promise of Hermeneutics* (Grand Rapids: Eerdmans; Carlisle: Paternoster, 1999), pp. 183-209.

of time, but this is not the only way of looking at it. Time, as perceived by *Dasein*, is "narrated time." To have flashbacks, flash-forwards, and variations in the perceived speed of time is not an exception to clock time, but reaches the heart of human experience. Anticipation or expectation is more "authentic" for people than bare futurity. Yet temporality has a unity beyond this. Dilthey saw this "connectedness" *(Zusammenheit)* of life, and it gives meaning to historicality. Humankind is "within" time, as narrative and interpretation confirm.

7. The last part of *Time and Narrative* consists of the seven chapters that form section two of the third volume. Ricoeur begins again with the relation between *"lived* time" and *historical* time. History can usually creatively refigure natural time, through such devices as the calendar. We speak about contemporaries, predecessors, and successors. Thereby we connect together the network of history, as Dilthey argued. Thus there is a third form of time, which Ricoeur sometimes calls "mythic time," presumably in the sense of an emplotment of the raw succession of events.

We discover that this usually contains "a founding event," such as the birth of Jesus Christ or Pentecost, which occurs at regular intervals. Calendar time therefore borrows from physical time a continuum of events. Benveniste has rightly drawn attention to this. We may also see the influence of Gerhard von Rad behind Ricoeur's approach. Ricoeur points out that historians are guided by their own themes and agendas. A connection therefore comes from the historians' practice. Historians borrow the phrase "the significance of the trace" from Emmanuel Lévinas. The existential and the empirical once again overlap.

Ricoeur turns again to fictional narrative and *imagination,* referring back to volume 2. Here we see further the split between *lived* time and *world* time, but in a varied form. I used for example in the *Promise of Hermeneutics* the model of an employee *waiting* in time for the director or manager, where time becomes a marker of social or economic status. As patients, we *wait* in the surgery for the doctor. Fiction and life are full of such examples.

Ricoeur thus returns to the "troubling" question of the reality of past events in narration.[27] He seems to be more "troubled" than Hans Frei about what it means to say that something "really" or literally happened. At times Ricoeur seems to approach the Romanticist notion that past events have a "trace," which is perhaps the best a text can recover. Some Cambridge theo-

---

27. Ricoeur, *Time and Narrative,* 3:142; cf. pp. 142-56.

logians in the 1960s spoke of a "loose fit" between events in history and their theological meaning. Ricoeur discusses whether we can speak of "the same" event in history and the present. Reenactment, he argues, is a sign of "the same" in the present. For if the past is not "the same" in the present, does it encounter us as "other"? History may seem to be an affirmation of otherness, because the past is also different from the present.

8. This relation may best be described in terms of the "world" of the text and the "world" of the reader, in contrast to a vocabulary of reference. This notion of "world" is explicitly close to Gadamer's. Ricoeur writes, "Application is not a contingent appendix added on to understanding and explanation, but an organic part of every hermeneutic project."[28] Elsewhere Ricoeur also calls this "application," but comments that this is not a simple concept. As in *The Rule of Metaphor,* he insists that we cannot bypass the experience of "seeing as." In reading, the text yields the world of the reader.[29]

9. The next chapter returns to develop a related theme: the interweaving of *history and fiction.* Phenomenology gives this commensurability. Fiction is usually "quasi-historical."[30] But in chapter 9 of volume 3 Ricoeur asks whether Hegel has not turned a historian's history into a philosopher's history. Universal history becomes "world-history." We must therefore leave Hegel behind, in spite of his notion of historical reason. We must avoid *abstracting* the future and the past. The term "the horizon of expectation," Ricoeur argues, could not have been better chosen. It is used by Gadamer's former pupil, Hans Robert Jauss. It illustrates the genuineness of how we experience futurity: it is a *future-becoming-present,* not an *abstraction,* as in Hegel. *Geschichte* is closer to what we experience than *Historie,* because the past must live in the present.

10. Ricoeur concludes with an examination of *tradition.* He is more cautious than Gadamer about its authority and legitimacy. In this respect the critique of ideology has something to say. Every judgment and every prejudgment or prejudice remains fallible. Admittedly, however, a succession of readings speaks of "lived time" and deserves being listened to. We ourselves are part of a tradition. But the present must equally be challenged. On one side Ricoeur rejects "the icy demon of objectivity"; but on the other hand he insists that we must heed the realities of experience and intersubjective life.

28. Ricoeur, *Time and Narrative,* 3:158.

29. Ricoeur, *Time and Narrative,* 3:159-60; cf. pp. 166-79.

30. Ricoeur, *Time and Narrative,* 3:191.

Ricoeur concludes that what he has argued about *time* squares with the mediation of the indirect discourse of *narrative*. He wishes to allow the refiguration of time by narrative. We must also keep in view the difference between cosmological and phenomenological perspective, and the *aporias* (multilayered ambiguities) of time. This leads to the question of narrative identity, which Ricoeur will take up in *Oneself as Another*. In turn, this leads to responses to *characters*, which means assuming an *ethical ethos*, or exploring *responsibility*. This, too, forms part of the major agenda in *Oneself as Another*. We are given "a version of the world that is never ethically neutral."[31] Narrative shows the connectedness of things, as Dilthey saw. Nevertheless, Ricoeur recognizes that there are also limits to narrative. For example, we cannot move beyond the duality between phenomenology and cosmology, and there is always the temptation to assign a single fixed meaning to narrative for all generations. This does not abolish the need for narrative, with its ethical and political implications.

4. *Oneself as Another:* The Identity of the Self, "Otherness," and Narrative

In 1990 Ricoeur produced *Soi-même comme un autre* (English, *Oneself as Another*, University of Chicago Press, 1992). This book is largely on selfhood and the identity of self, with its implications for narrative and for ethics. The identity of the stable self implies otherness.

1. The self of Descartes gives knowledge of *"what"* I am, but the stability of the self for Descartes depends upon God. This was attacked by Nietzsche, who urged the deceptiveness of all language. The so-called autonomy of the self, moreover, is bound up with solicitude for one's neighbor. The first study in *Oneself as Another* is on identity reference and considers especially P. F. Strawson's *Individuals*. Ricoeur shows the limitations of this position, including its avoidance of the "I-You" relation.

2. In the second study Ricoeur considers the "I" as a *speaking subject*. F. Recanati, J. L. Austin, and John Searle take the discussion forward but fail to address adequately to whom the subject speaks. From where does action come? Ricoeur also considers deictic terms, that is, those like "here" or "there," "I" or "you," which combine a location with the perspective of a speaker.

---

31. Ricoeur, *Time and Narrative,* 3:249.

3. The third study looks at the philosophy of action without agents, with reference partly to G. E. M. Anscombe. The grammar of "wanting" takes us further, but there is still no adequate answer to the question *"Who?"* Anscombe rescues "intention" after a fashion, but doing something "intentionally" (as an adverb only) still leaves unanswered questions. Donald Davidson produces useful material on action, but even he does not answer Ricoeur's questions fully.

4. We progress further with the agent of study four. Descartes, Kant, and Hegel refer to the self as agent. But problems abound still. H. L. A. Hart shows the complexity of ascription. "Ascribing" remains only a partial solution to the problem of selfhood.

5. The turning point of Ricoeur's argument comes in the fifth and sixth studies, on personal identity and narrative identity.[32] The greatest gap in previous considerations was temporality. The problem of the self is caused by changes within the person, so we must address the temporal dimension. Hence we must look at human time and narrative, to understand the dialectic between sameness and selfhood. Fiction may stimulate the imagination here. Narrative tells us about the connectedness of human life, but the continuity of the self is fundamental. *Keeping one's word in a promise is a basic sign of this* continuity and stability. Ricoeur writes of "keeping one's word in faithfulness to the word that has been given."[33] But *promising* is *ethical;* and if it is faithfulness to the word of God, it is also *religious,* even if it reveals constancy and stability on the part of the self.

6. Predictably, Ricoeur turns to John Locke for further details, analogies, and parables of self-identity. Locke considered the role of memory. But as David Hume pointed out, this is not enough. We cannot superimpose sameness on successive perceptions. Ricoeur is happier with Derek Parfit's attack on Hume's identity criteria in *Reasons and Persons.* But in the end it is only as a "moral subject" with belief and in-relation-to-others that Ricoeur is comfortable. We have to make sense of the unity of our life by asking moral questions.

This requires that we consider the interconnectedness of events through narrative and emplotment. Dilthey, again, saw this. This takes us out of the realm of the merely contingent, as Kant saw. Ricoeur writes, "The category of character is therefore a narrative category as well."[34] Even for Propp and

---

32. Ricoeur, *Oneself as Another,* pp. 113-39 and 140-48.
33. Ricoeur, *Oneself as Another,* p. 123.
34. Ricoeur, *Oneself as Another,* p. 143.

Greimas (the classic structuralists of narrative), nevertheless, character, role, and action find an essential place. Plot requires this. It requires a person who is accountable for his or her acts. It gives them ethical identity. This is necessary for the question "Who am I?"

5. *Oneself as Another:* Implications for Ethics; Other Later Works

1. The remainder of Ricoeur's studies — seven, eight, and nine — are on ethical implications. The seventh and eighth studies are complementary. In the seventh Ricoeur considers "the ethical aim" of the self with particular reference to Aristotle and the virtues. The Aristotelian perspective was that the self has purpose. "Good" is teleological: the good life of the self aims at positive virtue. This does allow for rational deliberation. Ricoeur considers Alasdair MacIntyre's later thought in this context. The good life, he argues, is *"with and for others in just institutions."*[35] It cannot be solitary. Merleau-Ponty's "I can" denotes the capacity for ethical action toward others. Friendship, Aristotle insists, is part of this. Friendship works toward establishing relations of goodness.

Christians will interpret this virtue in terms of love *(agapē).* The Jewish philosopher Emmanuel Lévinas (1906-95) would agree that there can be no stable self without "another" who summons it to responsibility. For Aristotle it remains the ethics of reciprocity. It relates to giving and receiving. Lévinas speaks here of "the face" of the other. Not to be able to give oneself constitutes a violation of the integrity of the self. The self must be able to give compassion or sympathy to the other. This is the supreme test of *solicitude.* This self can "receive" also from a friend's weakness. This is irreplaceably being "myself." This in turn gives rise to judicial systems of constraint, and to political discussion and action.

2. In the complementary eighth study Ricoeur agrees with MacIntyre that the problem remains of "Whose Justice?" Hence he turns to the morality expounded by Kant (1724-1804). MacIntyre argues that we have largely "lost our comprehension . . . of morality"; namely, "the contrast between manipulative and non-manipulative social relations" has largely disappeared.[36] Mac-

---

35. Ricoeur, *Oneself as Another,* p. 180, italics in original.

36. Alasdair MacIntyre, *After Virtue: A Study in Moral Theory,* 2nd ed. (London: Duckworth, 1985), pp. 2 and 26.

Intyre also argues that we can never recover this unless we ask, "Of what story or stories do I find myself a part?"[37] Ricoeur, in effect, agrees with this. But if we want to speak of "good" without qualification, we must also speak of *moral obligation*. As Kant declared, "Morally good" means "good" without qualification. This leads us to Kant's problem of universality. His answer depended on the absolute or categorical imperative of the human will and human "autonomy." Kant declared, "Act only on that maxim through which you can at the same time will that it should become a universal law."[38]

There are indeed well-known replies to Kant. To Friedrich Schiller is ascribed an ironic response to Kant's emphasis upon duty as struggle: "Willingly serve I my friends, but I do it, alas! With gladness. Hence I am cursed with the doubt that virtue I have not attained!" Nevertheless, Kant's "categorical imperative" did universalize moral obligation as an absolute. Obligation further provides *motivation*. This requires freedom and autonomy in Kant's view, but Ricoeur notes how these relate to heteronomy. Autonomy alone would be opposed to the heteronomy of the arbitrator. Respect for the other and self-esteem are involved, even if evil is radical.

Ricoeur at first seems to combine Aristotle's call for virtue with Kant's call for response to moral obligation, and to find this especially in solicitude and love. He writes, "The commandment we read in Leviticus 19:18 . . . is repeated in Matthew 22:39: 'Love your neighbour as yourself.'"[39] Yet Ricoeur also writes that love and hate are subjective principles that do not fully constitute objective universals. So Kant's intention remains in doubt. The principle of *autonomy* seems to eliminate all "otherness." Thus an internal tension exists in Kant. He is right that the only "good" without qualification is the good will. Utilitarianism is not fully morality. Deontological virtue is to be retained. Socially we require a theory of justice.

For this Ricoeur at first considers John Rawls. But Rawls's theory rests upon a pre-understanding of what is unjust and just. It risks circularity. Ricoeur bases his theory of justice on *practical wisdom*. He then compares the morality of tragedy. What are we to make, for example, of Antigone's concept of justice? What Antigone believes to be her duty *conflicts* with what Creon considers *his* duty. Hence Ricoeur is not wholly satisfied with the wis-

---

37. MacIntyre, *After Virtue*, p. 216.

38. Immanuel Kant, *Groundwork for the Metaphysics of Morals*, trans. A. W. Wood (New Haven and London: Yale University Press, 2002; German 1805).

39. Ricoeur, *Oneself as Another*, p. 219.

dom of tragedy. We must aim between universalism and contextualism, to look for such key concepts within the good life as those that concern "the other," namely, "security," "prosperity," "liberty," "equality," and "solidarity." These are important for social and political discussion. Each invites rational deliberation. Moreover, each has symbolic resonances that transcend a single meaning, and each carries with it *solicitude* for the other. They may even reflect Heidegger's *solicitude*. With Hegel, we observe both historical situations with their contexts and morality, but with Aristotle we resort to an inadequate "practical wisdom" *(phronēsis)*.

3. Do not then maxims pass the test of constituting *universals?* Practical wisdom will help us to deploy these same maxims *as situations determine.* Always *respect for fellow human beings* is enjoined. There may be degrees of responsibility and a "minimal" autonomy. But *solicitude* always involves respect for the *"otherness" of the other person,* even in novel situations. Morality will involve conflict, if not struggle; but this does not invalidate the universal need for practical wisdom.

Kant's demand for "autonomy" is historically conditioned by the context of the Enlightenment, where he sees humankind as liberated from the tutelage of uncritical tradition. But this remains a "dialogic" concept, not an absolute one. We need therefore a reinterpretation of Kant, namely, one that looks at the universal, and another that takes Habermas and "interest" into account. In his two-volume work *The Theory of Communicative Action,* Jürgen Habermas (b. 1929) takes account of "interest" and of "life-world," and also how far language and communication impinge on ethics.[40] Aristotle's *phronēsis* combines with Kant's morality and Hegel's *Sittlichkeit* (a morality in which *historicality and universality* are recognized).

4. The tenth study concerns *ontology.* Ricoeur's emphasis on action and selfhood queries a substance-centered ontology, but not a substantial stability of the self-in-interaction-with-otherness. He considers Heidegger's *Dasein* among modes of being. Ricoeur writes, "What matters to me more than any other idea is the idea toward which the preceding discussion of Aristotle's *energeia* (power) was directed. . . . Otherness is not added on to selfhood . . . but belongs to the ontological constitution of selfhood."[41] It designates the self-constancy of "myself" *(ipse)* and involves intersubjectivity.

---

40. Jürgen Habermas, *The Theory of Communicative Action,* trans. Thomas McCarthy, 2 vols. (Cambridge: Polity Press, 1984-87); and Ricoeur, *Oneself as Another,* pp. 280-83.

41. Ricoeur, *Oneself as Another,* pp. 316-17.

The biblical qualities of "self-constancy" and "continuity of development" stand at the heart of everything. Even suffering becomes a part of ontology, which is otherwise neglected, and narrative takes its due place. Ricoeur writes, "To say 'I am' is to say 'I want, I move, I do.'"[42] *Existing is also resisting.* "I can" remains central to the issue, as we have seen. We need temporality and "the otherness" of other people.

This, in effect, concludes *Oneself as Another.* But Ricoeur has not finished his writing. Twenty-one papers are collected in Ricoeur's *Figuring the Sacred* (English 1995).[43] These take up various topics. Religious language, Kant, Rosenzweig, Lévinas, biblical themes, and imagination are among them. Next Ricoeur published *Thinking Biblically* with André LaCocque.[44] They consider Genesis 1 and 2, with particular reference to Gerhard von Rad, Claus Westermann, Edmond Jacob, Karl Barth, and others on the doctrine of creation; part of the Ten Commandments (Exod. 20:13); resurrection or raising to life (Ezek. 37:1-14); the cup of desolation from the cross (Ps. 22); and other passages mainly from the Old Testament. LaCocque's exegesis is followed by Ricoeur's hermeneutical reflections.

In the first few years of the new millennium and in the previous years, Ricoeur turned his attention to ethics, publishing *The Just* in 2000 (French 1995) and *Reflections on the Just* (French 2001; English 2007).[45] The latter consists of studies, readings, and exercises. *The Just* reflects lectures delivered in various places. Ricoeur refers back to studies seven and eight of *Oneself as Another,* where he looks at Aristotle on virtue and Kant on moral obligation. He provides a needed teleology and a needed deontology. But the crucial study is perhaps that on practical wisdom.[46] Ricoeur also considers "rights" (lecture 1) and "responsibility" (lecture 2). The question of rights raises all the old questions about selfhood ("Who?" "What?" "Can I?") and the institutional structure of questions about rights. The second involves a conceptual analysis of responsibility. One declares "the other" responsible, but always there is the "interhuman." The concept of responsibility must be extended.

In other lectures Ricoeur considers John Rawls's theory of justice, concluding that Rawls leaves us with ambiguity unless we are open to the kinds

---

42. Ricoeur, *Oneself as Another,* p. 321.
43. See n. 10 above.
44. See n. 10 above.
45. See n. 11 above.
46. Ricoeur, *The Just,* pp. xxi-xxii.

of correctives that J. Habermas and K. O. Apel have made. Ricoeur shows in the essay "After Rawls' Theory of Justice" that neither a sense of "fairness" nor consensus is adequate. The remaining essays address plurality, argumentation, and judgment. *Reflections on the Just* pursues the same themes, with the same emphasis on virtue, but perhaps more on "a respect for the dignity of the other that is equal to the respect one has for oneself."[47]

6. Five Assessments: Text, Author's Intention, and Creativity

Because Ricoeur covers such a huge sweep of topics, he leaves room for a variety of judgments in many areas. We have considered Ricoeur's theory of symbol and metaphor; his use of Freud; explanation and understanding; understanding and appropriation; the text and the author; emplotment in narrative; his concept of fiction, its relation to history; the use of imagination; different biblical genres; the special importance of Wisdom literature; his notion of *mimēsis;* the relation between truth and history; historical reason in Hegel and Dilthey, and historicality in Heidegger; prescriptive law, love, and justice; the identity of the self and otherness; and the wider contribution he makes to religion and to ethics. How can any simple evaluation address all these? We restrict our attention primarily to Ricoeur's hermeneutic, even if this indirectly involves all these topics.

1. One of the finest studies of Ricoeur up to 1990 is Kevin Vanhoozer's book *Biblical Narrative in the Philosophy of Paul Ricoeur.*[48] He rightly says, "Ricoeur refuses to follow the historical critics in the reduction of the text to its constituent traditions, or to confine its meaning to the original situation and its reference to '*what actually happened.*'"[49] At the same time, he will not countenance a purely structuralist approach that reduces a text's sense to its imminent relations and cuts it off from any extreme linguistic reference. This is broadly right, although some would dissent from such a reductionist view of history. Some compare him with Frei at this point.

Ricoeur values "possibility" so highly that he tends to see all historical report as refigured in the interests of present actualization. Vanhoozer speaks of an "ugly ditch" between history and fiction. In Aristotle's view the historian

---

47. Ricoeur, *Reflections on the Just,* p. 3.
48. See n. 8 above.
49. Vanhoozer, *Biblical Narrative,* p. 12, italics mine.

merely describes what was the case; the poet what might be. Ricoeur applies this to the Bible, which serves the Bible to shape life creatively.

However, the relation between truth, narrative, and history is more complex in Ricoeur. *Mimēsis* operates at various levels. Ricoeur acknowledges that this relation between narrative and history is "troubling."[50] Certainly fiction stimulates imagination. But Ricoeur also believes in "historical intentionality," and the reality of "founding events" such as the birth of Jesus Christ. He does not wish the event eliminated in every respect. He acknowledges the reality of the past, but he follows Gerhard von Rad and Rudolf Bultmann as seeing the past only as of present significance *(Geschichte,* not *Historie),* as if we had to choose between a "dead" past and a tradition that is alive and still speaks today. So although it suffers from some overstatement and perhaps oversimplification, Vanhoozer's verdict points in a valid direction. Ricoeur cannot both have his cake and eat it, but too often he tries to say yes to both sides. Ricoeur is right to stress "reenactment" or actualization in the present, but he is wrong to appear to reduce examples of historical report to something else. He argues rightly that historical report is not always the right focus. But Luke makes it clear that he, for example, seeks to be both historically accurate and alive to the present.[51] Vanhoozer makes it clear at several points that he does not object to Ricoeur's main point, but rejects his generalizing tendency here.

2. A striking feature of Ricoeur's difference from Gadamer and similarity with the critique of Habermas arises from his right resolve that *explanation and understanding* are *each* crucial to hermeneutics. Dan R. Stiver makes it clear that this is bound up with his early work on *Fallible Man* and *Freedom and Nature: The Voluntary and Involuntary.*[52] Since all human judgments about interpretation remain fallible, we must have a checking device

---

50. Ricoeur, *Time and Narrative,* 3:142; cf. pp. 142-47.

51. Anthony C. Thiselton, "'Reading Luke' as Interpretation, Reflection, and Formation," in *Reading Luke: Interpretation, Reflection, Formation,* ed. Craig G. Bartholomew, Joel B. Green, and Anthony C. Thiselton (Grand Rapids: Zondervan; Carlisle: Paternoster, 2005), pp. 3-63; and the essays by David Wenham and Joel Green, pp. 55-78 and 79-103.

52. Dan R. Stiver, *Theology after Ricoeur: New Directions in Hermeneutical Theology* (Louisville and London: Westminster John Knox, 2001), pp. 100-160, esp. 100-104; Ricoeur, "Hermeneutics and the Critique of Ideology" and "Metaphor and the Central Problem of Hermeneutics," in *Hermeneutics and the Human Sciences,* pp. 63-100 and 165-81; Ricoeur, *Freud and Philosophy,* throughout; Ricoeur, *The Rule of Metaphor,* pp. 66-333; Ricoeur, *Interpretation Theory,* pp. 71-88; and Ricoeur, *Time and Narrative,* 1:111-28 and 155-74.

in our hermeneutics. This cannot be ignored, whether the focus is on psychoanalysis of the human mind, on semiotics or structuralism in language, or on the referential or literal dimension of metaphor.

Ricoeur takes seriously from the beginning all those "involuntary" features in hermeneutics that distort meaning to our advantage, including the "interest" of desires yet unconscious. Ricoeur, Stiver writes correctly, found that prosaic phenomenological description was inadequate to express all the dimensions of human life. This becomes even more critical in the multiform interpretation of symbol and metaphor. *The Symbolism of Evil* addresses human "fault," including the symbols of stain, defilement, sin, and guilt. These may be called "symbolic," if thereby the meaning is "polyvalent." Symbol, like the Bible itself, is also *inexhaustible*. Ricoeur develops Kant's thought that "the symbol gives rise to thought."[53]

A more radical expression of fallibility comes in *Freud and Philosophy,* where desire is so repressed as to issue in disguised interests from the unconscious. This emphasis accords with a biblical stress on the deceitfulness of the heart, and even the unreliability of conscience as a guide to good conduct (Jer. 17:9; 1 Cor. 4:1-5). As for the interpreter, he or she must first lose his or her ego "in the desert of criticism" and then find it again in "post-critical naïveté."[54] Werner Jeanrond also stresses "suspicion and retrieval," and writes, "Ricoeur has stressed the need for a theory of interpretation which would allow the interpreter to deal critically with the ambiguous nature of all linguistic events."[55]

The Enlightenment, positivism, and some biblical criticism are admittedly wrong to imagine that a text is approached wholly as a value-neutral object, without the interpreter's being influenced by his or her interests and desires. Ricoeur saw that *explanation* may prevent distortion or illusion in understanding. Even semiotics and structuralism may sometimes help to perform this role. We cannot claim, moreover, that Ricoeur failed to understand Gadamer in this respect. He looked especially to Habermas and Apel on communication. He also advocated looking to the three masters of suspicion, Nietzsche, Marx, and Freud. Ricoeur concluded that Gadamer's approach to hermeneutics was too uncritical, and that "different perspectives"

---

53. Ricoeur, *The Symbolism of Evil,* pp. 347-57.

54. Stiver, *Theology after Ricoeur,* p. 147; Mark Wallace, *The Second Naïveté: Barth, Ricoeur, and the New Yale Theology* (Macon, Ga.: Mercer University Press, 1990).

55. Werner G. Jeanrond, *Theological Hermeneutics: Development and Significance* (London: Macmillan, 1991), p. 71.

from different traditions were simply inadequate for the task of criticism. Gadamer does not address the issues of ethics, power, and domination with adequacy. This theme coheres with Ricoeur's Protestantism within a largely Catholic country, although his emphasis on the ambiguity of so many texts may be rejected by many. Luther and Calvin argued that biblical texts were clear and of a single meaning; but they would have agreed about deception, self-interest, and the fallibility even of the Church.

3. When we turn to *textuality* in Ricoeur, we find that John B. Thompson, one of his early commentators and critics, argues that Ricoeur "does not produce a compelling case for his distinction between modes of discourse, nor does he offer a satisfactory defence for his conception of action as a text. . . . The work of Ricoeur does not yield a coherent account of the relation between action and structure."[56] J. L. Austin, Gilbert Ryle, and the later Wittgenstein focus on the surrounding circumstances of language. First-person utterances are often *performative* or illocutionary. Wittgenstein also takes account of the temporal character of utterances. Following him, Peter Winch is concerned with history and social change. Phenomenology studies human actions, and Ricoeur follows this approach. Texts and actions are seen as objectified consciousness. Descriptive discourse is thus laden with human value. The interpretation of human texts and action cannot be "scientific," even when they relate to economic or political spheres. The text becomes for Ricoeur a model of human action and an object to be understood. Thompson views this as unsatisfactory.

Thompson argues that Habermas makes a more significant contribution to the subject at every level. Labor is governed by technical rules formulated in literal language, and ideologies can distort communication systematically. Ricoeur supposedly neglects the place of *context* and social change in context. Semiology and structuralism are no real substitutes for this. Ricoeur and Habermas both recognize the place of power and ideology or interest, but his indebtedness to Heidegger leads Ricoeur to oppose this to scientific analysis. Ricoeur's notion of action does have limitations. Thompson attempts to situate action within a wider social context. He is right that ordinary language philosophy in Austin, Ryle, and the later Wittgenstein proves the importance of looking at the "surroundings" for language.

Yet Ricoeur's *Essays on Biblical Interpretation* shows that he carefully

---

56. John B. Thompson, *Critical Hermeneutics: A Study in the Thought of Paul Ricoeur and Jürgen Habermas* (Cambridge: Cambridge University Press, 1981, 1983), p. 115.

distinguishes between modes of discourse in a way overlooked by Thompson. Since these essays did not appear, at least in English, until 1981, Thompson could not take account of them. Indeed, it is only in his earlier work that Ricoeur is vulnerable to all of Thompson's criticisms, and Thompson does write primarily with sympathy for Habermas. Ricoeur distinguishes carefully between at least six modes of biblical discourses: the prescriptive, or law; the psalmic, or hymnic, which addresses God; the didactic, such as the epistles; the prophetic; Wisdom literature, which, we have said, makes its point as exploration, or indirectly "from behind" the reader; and above all, narrative, which perhaps forms the bulk of biblical material. Ricoeur points out rightly that the Church and its preachers tend to assimilate diverse genres as prophetic discourse (as in Jer. 2:1), where the prophet speaks in the name of God, and revelation becomes largely "Thus saith the Lord." But narrative passes on traditions as a *Credo:* "My father was a wandering Aramean. . . . We called on Yahweh the God of our fathers . . ." (Deut. 26:5-10). Ricoeur asserts, "What is essential in the case of narrative discourse is the emphasis on the founding event or events as the imprint, mark, or trace of God's act. Confession takes place through narration."[57]

There is also "prescriptive discourse" corresponding to "the will of God," and practical life. The Law constitutes one aspect of this, and is also part of the human response to covenant. Jesus stressed "the law and the prophets" (Matt. 7:12). Wisdom discourse is different again, and its themes include the "limit situations" spoken of by Karl Jaspers as the annihilation of the human and the incomprehensibility of God. It also speaks of suffering, especially in Job 42:1-6, and functions as indirect revelation. Sometimes Job and Ecclesiastes "correct" the overpressing of Deuteronomic option. Finally, hymnic discourse, exemplified especially by the Psalms, invokes God in first-person address. This, too, is part of revelation, and yet is perhaps the least "preached upon." It is often from a first person to a first person.

4. Nicholas Wolterstorff approves of Ricoeur's attention to language, but too often surrenders to the "pluralistic, polysemic, and at most analogical" in revelation of God.[58] Ricoeur's theology of God moves in a Barthian direction, in which revelation is always mediated, and would allow little room for

---

57. Ricoeur, *Essays on Biblical Interpretation*, p. 79.

58. Nicholas Wolterstorff, *Divine Discourse: Philosophical Reflections on the Claim That God Speaks* (Cambridge: Cambridge University Press, 1995), p. 59; cf. pp. 58-63 and 130-52; and Ricoeur, *Essays on Biblical Hermeneutics*, pp. 74-75.

Wolterstorff's approach. But perhaps his more detailed criticism is that Ricoeur in effect rejects "authorial-discourse," interpretation and intention of the writer. Certainly Ricoeur seems to give the reader a more active role than the text. Wolterstorff quotes Ricoeur: "The text is mute. . . . The text is like a musical score, and the reader like the orchestra conductor."[59] *La langue* is the code; *la parole* is the discourse. Speech is always actualization. But Wolterstorff is concerned with the "noematic," or broadly cognitive truth-content, of the text.

Sometimes a text will report, or even presuppose, a state of affairs. Here the intention of the author is decisive. One might claim this for large sections of perhaps Luke, or certainly 1 Corinthians and Galatians. Sometimes this may not be so crucial, as with the book of Jonah or many of the Psalms. The question, though, still has some role in determining "responsible" interpretation. Otherwise, however the reader interprets the text is "right."[60]

Wolterstorff seems to be saying that Ricoeur is not wholly consistent here. For he appeals to dialogic texts, which Ricoeur acknowledges. The author's place is part of the temporality of the text, and its "I's" and "You's" are important. Wolterstorff asks, "How could Ricoeur give central importance to authorial discourse in his philosophy of language, and then, in his theory of text interpretation acknowledge only textual sense interpretation?"[61] He wishes to avoid Romanticism, but surprisingly this is a rare place where he avoids his customary inclusive approach. More account needs to be taken of the specificity of given texts.

5. When all has been said, however, Ricoeur does focus on the creativity of language, on what a text sets going, and in the historicality of both text and reader. In his very brief treatment Jensen seems to imply this, noting the transformative power of texts in Ricoeur.[62] David Klemm tries to go with both Ricoeur and some critics when he says that Ricoeur deciphers "hidden meaning in unfolding levels of meaning implied in the literal meaning."[63] To this may be added his stress on temporality and narrativity. In his work of

59. Wolterstorff, *Divine Discourse*, p. 133; Ricoeur, *Interpretation Theory*, p. 75.

60. Anthony C. Thiselton, *Can the Bible Mean Whatever We Want It to Mean?* (Chester, U.K.: Chester Academic Press, 2005), throughout.

61. Wolterstorff, *Divine Discourse*, p. 149.

62. Alexander Jensen, *Theological Hermeneutics*, SCM Core Text (London: SCM, 2007), pp. 144-50.

63. David E. Klemm, *Hermeneutical Inquiry*, 2 vols. (Atlanta: Scholars Press, 1986), p. 192.

metaphor Ricoeur tries to show how language undergoes creative mutation and transformation. One of his chief concerns is to transmute "clock time" into "human time."

This creativity finds expression in Ricoeur's turn to ethics, for which the basis is human freedom, and the belief that "I can." In spite of *The Symbolism of Evil* and *Freud and Philosophy*, Ricoeur is ambivalent here. He recognizes the place of evil, the unconscious, and the involuntary and deceptive; but he is perhaps too uncritical of Kant on *autonomy*. The Christian has only derivative autonomy, if it is appropriate to speak of autonomy at all. He or she is "under sin" even when he or she is redeemed.[64] In combining his hermeneutics, his understanding of selfhood, and his understanding of narrative with ethical questions about the self and the world, he opens up what John Wall calls the theme of "moral creativity."[65] Wall sees this "poetics of possibility," or "poetics of the will," as part of the classic conception of the need for faith in some larger movement of grace. For "I can," which comes from the Beyond, creates a world of possibility, which speaks of love and the transformation of society. But Ricoeur is reluctant to make his theology too explicit.

7. Recommended Initial Reading

Jenson, Alexander, *Theological Hermeneutics*, SCM Core Text (London: SCM, 2007), pp. 144-51.

Ricoeur, Paul, *Essays on Biblical Interpretation*, edited by Lewis S. Mudge (Philadelphia: Fortress, 1980; London: SPCK, 1981), pp. 23-95.

————, *Freud and Philosophy: An Essay on Interpretation*, translated by Denis Savage (New Haven: Yale University Press, 1970), pp. 3-36.

————, *Time and Narrative*, translated by Kathleen Blamey and David Pellauer, 3 vols. (Chicago and London: University of Chicago Press, 1984, 1985, 1988), 1:3-51, 3:80-96.

Thiselton, Anthony C., *New Horizons in Hermeneutics: The Theory and Practice of Transforming Biblical Reading* (London: HarperCollins; Grand Rapids: Zondervan, 1992), pp. 344-78.

64. Anthony C. Thiselton, *Systematic Theology*, trans. G. W. Bromiley, 3 vols. (Edinburgh: T. & T. Clark; Grand Rapids: Eerdmans, 1991, 1994, 1998), 2:1, 179, 224, 265; see pp. 231-76.

65. John Wall, *Moral Creativity: Paul Ricoeur and the Poetics of Possibility* (Oxford: Oxford University Press, 2005), pp. 9, 31, and throughout.

CHAPTER XIII

The Hermeneutics of Liberation Theologies and Postcolonial Hermeneutics

1. Definition, Origins, Development, and Biblical Themes

The term "liberation hermeneutics" generally refers to the use of the Bible in the liberation theologies developed especially in Latin America toward the end of the 1960s and throughout the 1970s. But it still has a presence in Latin America and perhaps in parts of Africa and India, although often in the different form of postcolonial hermeneutics. It has also influenced some versions of feminist hermeneutics. It is tempting to date the movement from 1968 when Gustavo Gutiérrez (b. 1928), a Dominican priest, produced an agenda for the Second Conference of Latin American Bishops at Medellín, Colombia. This Peruvian theologian later developed his thought in his book *The Theology of Liberation* (Lima, Peru, 1971; Salamanca, Spain, 1972; English, London, 1973).[1]

The movement, however, has a much longer history. This is chronicled by Enrique Dussel and Phillip Berryman, among others. Dussel traces the initial impetus to Bartolomé de Las Casas (1474-1566), whom he questionably and controversially calls the greatest theologian of the sixteenth century.[2] Las Casas condemned what he called the enslavement and forced Christianization of the Indians, arguing that God gave the Law only to Israel, not even to Abraham as an individual. Christ is crucified again, he argued, in

---

1. Gustavo Gutiérrez, O.P., *A Theology of Liberation: History, Politics, and Salvation*, trans. Sister Caridad Inda and John Eagleson (London: SCM, 1974; Maryknoll, N.Y.: Orbis, 1973; Lima, Peru, 1971).

2. Enrique Dussel, ed., *The Church in Latin America, 1492-1992* (London: Burns and Oates; New York: Orbis, 1992), especially pp. 43-48; cf. pp. 1-184.

the extermination of the Indians by the Spanish in the name of Christ. Vasco de Quiroga (1470-1565), bishop of Michoacán, Mexico, supported this complaint.

Berryman concentrates on the origins of the movement in Central America, rather than South America. He examines Guatemala, El Salvador, Honduras, Nicaragua, and Costa Rica, beginning with laws emanating from the Spanish Crown in 1542.[3] Berryman insists that Central America is "based on an act of conquest and domination, with thousands of Indians being killed. . . . In this conquest the church was a key factor. Missionaries were the only force denouncing the cruelties and attempting to moderate the effects of the conquest. Despite heroic exceptions, however, the church normally acted as an integral element of the overall enterprise of conquest and domination."[4] This era of conquest, followed by the colonial period and the "development" in the 1960s and early 1970s, contributed, Berryman argues, to the crisis of revolution today.

In 1821 Central America became formally independent of Mexico, but became split apart by conservative and liberal politics. By 1838 Central America split into five republics. The liberals placed their confidence in the production of coffee and other goods and its economic "development," but lands and sources of production were seized by the educated and elite. Peasant revolts toward the end of the nineteenth century were abortive. The military was upgraded, especially in Guatemala and El Salvador. The five states in Central America began to confiscate church property and to wage war on the Catholic Church and its monopolies. The Church lost its earlier authority and was widely perceived as an agent of European domination. Protestant missionaries were encouraged to enter Latin America.

In 1932 the Great Depression saw a drastic fall in coffee prices. By the 1950s the policy of "development" was in ruins, as far as the poorest were concerned. By the 1970s peasants and the landless suffered further economic decline, while land was used by expert groups.

Biblical themes, which became the stock-in-trade of liberation theology, began to emerge early on. In the sixteenth century Pedro de Córdobo compared the oppression of the Indians with that of Israel in Egypt; the Jesuit

---

3. Phillip Berryman, *The Religious Roots of Rebellion: Christians in the Central American Revolutions* (London: SCM, 1984), especially pp. 13-38; cf. Ralph Woodward, *Central America: A Nation Divided* (New York: Oxford University Press, 1976), pp. 23-47.

4. Berryman, *Religious Roots of Rebellion*, pp. 35-36.

Manuel Lacunza (1731-1801), originally from Chile, argued that oppression in the books of Daniel and Revelation, and Israel's liberation from Egypt, or from Babylon, could inspire the struggle for freedom in Mexico. He was, however, expelled from the Catholic Church. Azarias H. Pallais, a priest and poet of Nicaragua (1884-1956), saw the exodus motif as central for liberation theology. But not all relied upon biblical themes and texts. Priests from Brazil formed a revolution in 1817 and 1824 under the influence of the French Enlightenment. They attacked all authority and promoted the use of individual reason.

If the sixteenth and seventeenth centuries constituted eras of colonialism, 1807 stands as the date of emancipation from the governments of Spain and Portugal in some countries, although the influence of the European governments remained strong. Brazil finally became a republic in 1889, and Argentina in 1853. The Puerto Rican state remained Spanish until 1898, but then effective control passed to the USA. During this period, "development" became the catchword to close the economic gap between rich European nations and poor Latin American former colonies. But many Latin Americans saw "revolution" as a better alternative, looking at the relative prosperity of Cuba by comparison.

For many years the main response of the Church was to reinforce traditional values. Catholic mission was joined by Protestants in the seventeenth century, and England had been heavily involved in the Caribbean from 1625. But within the Catholic Church the movement known as Catholic Action grew from its beginnings in the 1930s to become influential in support of native Latin America in the 1950s and 1960s. A first Conference of Catholic Bishops was held in 1955, and the New Catholic Left emerged at about that time, or indeed much earlier. A polarization emerged between those who sought economic aid from the Western powers and those who placed their hopes on revolution. They compared the relative prosperity and freedom of the people in Cuba with repressive military regimes. Cuba was reached by Christopher Columbus in 1492. Its current population of some eleven million was originally a mixture of Spanish and African slaves (with the original Taino people, who were largely exterminated).

In the nineteenth century there were slave revolts (1812). Independence came in 1898, but Spanish patronage ensured that key positions in the church remained Spanish. Meanwhile a sense of national identity became stronger, especially when the United States entered war against Spain and set up its naval base at Guantánamo (1934). Owing largely to Catholic Action,

Spanish patronage came to an end. By 1990 the largest Protestant church was Iglesia Evangélica Pentecostal de Cuba, with 56,000 members. Forty-one percent of Cubans were Catholic. Revolution came on 1 January 1959 with Fidel Castro, who established a one-party communist or Marxist state. In 1961 the government closed the Catholic university, nationalized Catholic schools, and expelled 136 priests. Protestant churches shrank in numbers, although there was a surge in 1994-95. With the retirement of Castro from the presidency in 2008, it is hoped that the regime will become more relaxed.

Much of the inspiration for revolution came from the "Paris Manuscripts," or early writings, of Karl Marx (1818-83), not from the later atheistic writings of Marx, or from Leninist or Stalinist Marxism. Between 1838 and 1843 Marx focused on the French Revolution, with its theoretical ideals of liberty, equality, and brotherly fraternity.[5] He believed that economic forces of production were the underlying reason for inequality and division among people. Capitalism contained the seeds of its own destruction. To other Latin American peoples the growing economic prosperity of Cuba, its independence, and its nationalization of power and resources seemed the answer to a divided society of rich and poor. However, in his later writings Marx developed a semideterminist and materialist theory of history, which left no room for Christian faith. In 1844 he published *Die Deutsch-Französchichen Jahrbucher* and met Friedrich Engels. In 1845-46 they wrote *The German Ideology*, which assimilates Feuerbach's atheistic critique of religion. In 1848 they wrote *The Communist Manifesto*. In London Marx wrote the three volumes of *Das Kapital.* In these later works Marx's "left-wing Hegelianism" and antitheist materialism are dominant as a theory of history, as well as his theme of the exploitation of labor. These later writings inspired Vladimir I. Lenin (1870-1924) and Joseph Stalin (1879-1953) in Russia, and birthed Marxism-Leninism. It is also known as "dialectical materialism." Just as the capitalist stage had overcome feudalism, so state socialism would oust capitalism. Then would come the era of communism, when each would receive according to his or her need, and each would work according to his or her ability.

Unjust land ownership posed a problem in many countries of South America. In Brazil large holdings represented 43 percent of the ownership of the land, yet only 3 percent of all agricultural workers held land. Holdings of less than twenty-five acres made up 52 percent of all landholdings. In addi-

---

5. J. Andrew Kirk, *Theology Encounters Revolution* (Leicester: Inter-Varsity, 1980), pp. 27-30.

tion to this there were millions of landless people. Brazil has a land area slightly smaller than that of the United States. Argentina published a constitution in 1853, but experienced confusion and at times chaos in subsequent years. After a period of growth, it suffered economically in the Depression, until the first presidency of Juan Perón (1946-55). Military coups took place in 1955, 1962, 1966, and 1976. In 1983 democracy was restored, but again there was a gap between rich and poor. Chile owes much to the production of nitrate by Britain, and has a strong middle class. But in 1973 a military coup overthrew Salvador Allende, with help from the United States, and General Augusto Pinochet took control of the state, which he headed until 1990. Bolivia declared freedom of belief in 1906. However, it suffers from the cocaine trade; it grows about half the world's supply. Colombia is the fourth-largest state in South America (after Brazil, Argentina, and Peru). Its government has suffered instability for over a century. It engaged in civil war from 1948 to 1958. Large landowners have cooperated with military forces to preserve the economic status quo. The murder of workers, students, intellectuals, and opposition to the dominant regime occurred from 1986 to 1988. Finally, Peru, the second-largest South American state, has witnessed an autocratic government by military regimes and dictators, as well as guerrilla warfare. In 2003 it was said that 54 percent of the people lived below the poverty line. Between 1985 and 1990 foreign debt increased to $20 million, and the country suffered hyperinflation.

It is not surprising that the initial formal birth of liberation theology came from Peru in 1968, with the work of Gustavo Gutiérrez. But before this we must note the influence of the Second Vatican Council (1962-65) in preparing the way. In the early 1960s a small group of Roman Catholic and Protestant theologians met to discuss the plight of the poor in Latin America. They presented their findings in Petrópolis, Brazil, in 1964 as "a critical reflection on praxis." The Second Vatican Council backed their concern. *Apostolicam actuositatem* encouraged justice as a source of theology; and they encouraged Catholic Action and ecclesial "base" communities, emphasizing the place of love and justice for the poor. The poor were to work primarily *to change social structures.* The Council decreed: "All men are endowed with a rational soul and are created in God's image. . . . There is a basic equality between all men, and it must be given greater recognition."[6]

---

6. Austin P. Flannery, O.P., ed., *Documents of Vatican II* (Grand Rapids: Eerdmans, 1975), p. 929.

In 1964 Dom Helder Camara became archbishop of Recife in northeast Brazil. Camara called the oppression of the poor "a second violence" inflicted upon "countless human beings who suffer restrictions, humiliations, injustices, who are without prospects, without hope, their condition that of slaves."[7] He later took up *Populorum Progressio* (par. 31) from Vatican II concerning a just war on behalf of the oppressed. Northeast Brazil was probably the area of greatest poverty in the country.

From northeast Brazil before this, Paulo Freire also began his mission of "awareness making" or "consciousness raising" *(concientización)*. The poor, he argued, needed to become aware of their condition, just as Moses was commanded to do for the slaves in Egypt (Exod. 4:31). Freire instigated literacy classes to do this and to teach the people how to liberate themselves from their domination by oppressive structures. In April 1964, however, a military coup took place in Brazil, which was a blow to expectations encouraged by Freire. Meanwhile he continued this work first in Brazil and later in Argentina.

Many Catholic religious thinkers began to turn to earlier Marxism as a way of achieving structural change. They also found at this time rapport with the earlier work of Jürgen Moltmann, with his emphasis on hope, promise, transformation, and eschatology, and similarly with J. I. Metz, both from Germany. In the face of military coups in Brazil, Argentina, Paraguay, and Bolivia, Camilo Torres was one of many who explicitly urged that Catholics should participate in revolution.

2. Gustavo Gutiérrez and the Birth of Liberation Theology

In 1968 Gustavo Gutiérrez (b. 1928) introduced the term "liberation theology" to characterize the debate and provided the agenda a few months later for the Conference of Catholic Bishops held at Medellín, Colombia. The bishops sought help from him and his Peruvian colleagues in preparing a program of social reform, mindful of the new emphasis of Vatican II. In particular Gutiérrez spoke of, and urged, *solidarity with the poor* as his key theme. He later expounded and published his contributions in *A Theology of Liberation.*[8]

7. Cf. J. Andrew Kirk, *Liberation Theology: An Evangelical View from the Third World* (London: Marshall, Morgan and Scott, 1979), p. 31.

8. Gustavo Gutiérrez, O.P., *A Theology of Liberation: History, Politics, and Salvation,* trans. Sister Caridad Inda and John Eagleson (London: SCM, 1974; Maryknoll, N.Y.: Orbis, 1973; Lima, Peru, 1971).

1. Gutiérrez saw theology as a *critical reflection on praxis.*[9] This is heavily influenced by earlier Marxist thought and by biblical eschatology. He says Jürgen Moltmann is promising a new way to formulate theology. Moltmann also draws on the promissory theology of Gerhard von Rad and the philosophy of hope of Ernst Bloch.

"Praxis," Berryman urges, is not merely "practice" in opposition to theory, but theory and practical conduct based on theory.[10] The term is often misused to mean merely "practice" in Christian circles, and its philosophical and technical origins in Aristotle, Hegel, Feuerbach, Marx, and Sartre are often forgotten. Richard Bernstein helps us to put the record straight.[11] Marx uses the term when he observes in his eleventh thesis on Feuerbach: "The philosophers have only *interpreted* the world in various ways; the point is to *change* it" (italics in original). In practice this involves a going out of oneself and a commitment to God and our neighbor.

2. Second, Gutiérrez refers back to the *Bandung Conference* of 1955, when *African and Asian* countries united with Latin America as a "Third World." While he welcomes their awareness of underdevelopment, he questions whether "development" can ever turn around "a total social process."[12] The term "development" marked the aspirations of the poor "during the last few decades," but its agenda and advantage are always shared with "the rich countries" (pp. 25-26). The poorer countries must become master of their own destiny in freedom. He writes, "Marx deepened and renewed this line of thought in his unique way" (p. 29). He sought the transformation of the world. Gutiérrez also sees Freud and Marcuse carrying this forward. "The goal is not only better living conditions [but] a radical change of structures, a social revolution" (p. 32). This accords with the biblical message "For freedom — Christ has set us free" (Gal. 5:1). This is the meaning of *liberation.*

3. The next category is *theological.* Gutiérrez is dissatisfied with the concept of "Christendom," or where Christendom has reached, and seeks *"a new Christendom"* to mark a new stage in the life of the Church. This recognizes "the autonomy of the world" and honors "the rise and development of an adult laity" (pp. 54-57 and 63-67). Like the Enlightenment, it seeks the libera-

---

9. Gutiérrez, *A Theology of Liberation,* pp. 6-15, especially pp. 6 and 13.

10. Phillip Berryman, *Liberation Theology* (London: Tauris, 1987), p. 85.

11. Richard J. Bernstein, *Praxis and Action* (Philadelphia: University of Pennsylvania Press, 1971; London: Duckworth, 1972), p. xi and throughout.

12. Gutiérrez, *A Theology of Liberation,* pp. 23-24. Parenthetical page references in the following text are to this work.

tion of the secular from the tutelage of religion, and rejects any antithesis between the Church and the world. It holds to the Pauline theme of the *universal Lordship* of Christ. Salvation and creation are a single process.

One must not rest content with an economic diagnosis only of the divide between rich and poor. One must take account of Helder Camara's "spiral of violence" and of Paulo Freire's "pedagogy of the oppressed" (pp. 89 and 91).[13] In the "new Christendom" the Church must no longer support the economically powerful group, but be committed "to revolutionary political groups" (p. 103). This involves "active participation" with the oppressed and the rejection of "paternalism" (p. 113). Revolution eclipses "development." This is the meaning of faith. The center of God's design for the world is Christ, who transforms us by his death and resurrection.

4. A further theme is *hermeneutical and eschatological.* The Bible establishes a link between creation and salvation especially in the exodus. Second Isaiah is emphatic on this (Isa. 51:9-10). The symbolism of destroying Rahab and deliverance from Egypt applies to us and to Latin America (Pss. 74:13-14; 89:10; Isa. 51:9; Deut. 4:20; 26:8). "Egypt" is the land of oppression and slavery (Exod. 13:3; 20:2; Deut. 5:6; cf. Exod. 3:7-10; 14:11-12; 19:4-6). Gutiérrez writes, "The God of the Exodus is the God of history and of politics . . . the *Go'el* [Redeemer] of Israel" (p. 157). He brings new creation.

God is therefore the God of eschatological promises, and this is a gift accepted in faith. The journey of Abraham demonstrates this (Gen. 12:1; 15:1-16; Rom. 4:12; Gal. 3:16-29). As Ricoeur might say, this promise becomes fuller and more definitive. Here Gutiérrez refers to Gerhard von Rad on salvation history. God is leading ahead of his people, temporally. This temporal progress finds fulfillment in Christ. The covenant forms an important place and means of meeting.

5. From this premise Gutiérrez infers that *to honor God is to do justice to the neighbor* (Prov. 14:20; Deut. 24:14-15; Jer. 31:34). Here he cites 1 John (4:7-8); the verdict at the judgment (Matt. 25:45); the Magnificat (Luke 1:47-49). History thus offers hope to the oppressed, and we are "saved in hope" (Rom. 8:24). Again he cites the work of Paulo Freire, and also Ernst Bloch and Jürgen Moltmann on hope. This is why eschatology is political theology. Like Ricoeur, he has been "through" the critical to emerge at the postcritical level. Even the life of Jesus has political resonances. The empirical is part of an incarnational theology. "To evangelise . . . is to incarnate the Gospel in

---

13. Cf. Paulo Friere, *Pedagogy of the Oppressed* (New York: Herder and Herder, 1970).

time" (p. 271). Hence we look for a new Christian community and for a new society. "The class struggle is a part of our economic . . . and religious reality" (p. 273; cf. pp. 273-79). We look for Christian brotherhood, and for freedom from oppression and slavery, in solidarity with the poor.

It would not be accurate to assume that this critical survey merely recapitulates ground covered in *New Horizons in Hermeneutics*. Although it happens that there I have also extracted themes from Gutiérrez's work, they do not necessarily correspond, and I have reread the entire work of Gutiérrez, independently of what I have written in *New Horizons*. I shall reserve my assessment of this work until later, except to point out that as with Schleiermacher and his tradition, "liberals" usually begin with human experiences while conservatives seek to begin with revelation. Gutiérrez sees Christian faith as "on the move" rather than "once for all," but seeks to set up a reciprocal dialectic between the Bible and human experience. Whether this has been entirely successful, readers may judge. His work, however, must be assessed in the context of its times, and the social dimension was (or is still) urgent.

3. The Second Stage: "Base Communities" and José Porfirio Miranda in the 1970s

Exponents of liberation theology, especially Carlos Mestos and Rubem Alves, are insistent that "base communities" primarily represent a lay-led movement or network not contrived by academic theologians. Lay-led communities also reveal most about liberation hermeneutics.

Base communities are grassroots groups, mainly of laypeople, ranging from a dozen to around thirty or so in number. Tape-recorded transcripts have been made available that illustrate their use of the Bible. The best-known is *The Gospel in Solentiname*.[14] The community lives on the southern edge of Lake Nicaragua, near to the Costa Rican border. It is different from many base communities for its leader was Ernesto Cardenal (b. 1919), who founded the community with a group of friends in January 1966 and transcribed the record of their contemplative reflections on the Bible between 1971 and 1976. Ernesto Cardenal was a Catholic priest who was made bishop

---

14. Ernesto Cardenal, *The Gospel in Solentiname* (Maryknoll, N.Y.: Orbis, 1982); cf. also the extraction in Berryman, *Religious Roots of Rebellion*, pp. 9-21.

by Pope Pius XII in 1952, and archbishop by Pope Paul VI in 1957. He is currently archbishop emeritus of Mexico.

Thus, understanding "communist" as implying equality within the community and "Marxist" as reflecting the humanism of the early Marx, the community's reflection on the Magnificat (Luke 1:68-79) is transcribed as follows by Ernesto Cardenal: "What would Herod have said about Mary?" "Rosita replies, 'That she was a communist.' Another responds: 'The point [is] . . . she was a communist. . . . That [the Magnificat] is Revolution. The rich person or the mighty is brought down, and the poor person, the one who was down, is raised up.'" One of the young people says: "She spoke for the future, it seems to me, because we are just barely beginning to see the liberation she announces."[15] Mary is in the end described as a "Marxist," without a sense of anachronism. The disciples, too, were seen as poor, as those who "abandoned their belongings," says Natalia. Elvis comments, "The importance of the truth of Christ is that it was the birth of the Revolution, right?" One of the community observes, "God is in all of us who love each other."[16]

José Porfirio Miranda (1924-2001) wrote eleven books, of which his second was *Marx and the Bible* (1971; English 1974) and his fifth was *Being and the Messiah* (1973; English 1977). Both are classics of liberation theology and liberation hermeneutics.[17] He wrote out of his context in Mexico, both as a philosopher and biblical scholar, and in 1995 also wrote on the necessity of scientific research. His aim in *Marx and the Bible* is "the necessity of building a classless society . . . a society free of classes."[18]

Miranda is less interested in supposed parallels between Marx and the Bible than in new understandings of the Bible. He believes that this new understanding matches much in Marx. He draws especially on philosophies of power, including the work of Emmanuel Levinas. He begins with the current economic situation in Mexico and elsewhere in Latin America, where the workers produced the product but "violence prevented them from exercising it; a violence that is institutional, legal, juristical" (p. 11). The biblical writings,

15. Cardenal, *The Gospel in Solentiname* (Study on the Magnificat, 1).

16. Cardenal, *The Gospel in Solentiname*, vol. 3; p. 103; reprinted in Berryman, *Religious Roots of Rebellion*, pp. 14-17.

17. José Porfirio Miranda, *Marx and the Bible: A Critique of the Philosophy of Oppression* (Maryknoll, N.Y.: Orbis, 1974; London: SCM, 1977), and *Being and the Messiah: The Message of St. John*, trans. John Eagleson (Maryknoll, N.Y.: Orbis; London: SCM, 1977).

18. Miranda, *Marx and the Bible*, p. xiii. Parenthetical page references in the following text are to this work.

however, demand justice. He appeals to Proverbs 10:2, Daniel 4:27, Job 42:10, and Matthew 6:12. Justice involves almsgiving (Ps. 112:3, 9). In fact, he challenges the legitimacy of the wage system, supported by the Vatican.

In the second chapter of his book Miranda turns to the Bible in more detail. He writes of hermeneutics and exegesis: "Once we have established the possibility of different 'meanings,' each as acceptable as any other, then the scripture cannot challenge the West" (p. 36). Academic scholarship too easily allows whatever "meaning" of the text we like to choose. Often, he argues, the past burdens us with "interpretations" that are not true or relevant. To begin with, the prohibition of images (Exod. 20:4-6; Deut. 5:8-10) abolishes the dualism of a "spiritual" and material world. So does Romans 1:18, with its emphasis on injustice (Rom. 1:18-25). Knowing God involves respecting justice (Jer. 22:13-16; Hos. 4:1-2; 6:4-6; Isa. 11:9). Amos speaks of the priority of justice over culture (Amos 5:21-25; cf. Isa. 1:11-17). 1 John speaks of knowing God and showing love (1 John 3:17-18; 4:7; cf. Matt. 22:39-40) (pp. 61-63). This is related to *praxis* (Deut. 10:12–11:17).

We need not trace Miranda's agreement through *Marx and the Bible* in every detail. In chapter 3 he speaks of God's intervention in history, especially as the God of the exodus, where he stresses Exodus 6:2-8 and its resonance in the prophets (Hos. 13:4; Isa. 40:27; 41:17; 45:15, 21; 61:3; Ezek. 34:27). It is God's plan to bring justice and liberation to the world (Ps. 82:3-4). This is so from the period of the judges to Paul and Jesus. Laws, he argues, like Luther, are for the defense of the weak (pp. 137-60). He refers especially to Gerhard von Rad on the Old Testament and the prophets.

The most creative and distinctive part of the book is what Miranda calls "the true meaning of Romans," where justification is seen not as *individualist* "putting right," but as a *corporate and communal* "putting right" in justice for the oppressed (pp. 169-99). Paul attacks *adikia* in Romans (Rom. 1:15–3:20). He addresses the "structural" importance of a new relationship with God on a different basis. Miranda cites Otto Michel as commenting, "[The] justice of God is at the same time judicial sentence and eschatological salvation" (p. 173). Eberhard Jüngel and Rudolf Bultmann also see *dikaiosunē ek Theou* (righteousness from or of God) as the central issue here. The so-called "new look" on Paul does not invalidate this. In Britain the conservative evangelical writer Tom Holland confirms this "corporate" understanding of Paul.[19] Both Miranda and Holland defend their "corporate" reading

19. Tom Holland, *Contours of Pauline Theology: A Radical New Survey of the Influences*

of Paul by his close relation to the Old Testament. Romans 9–11 bears out this reading. Käsemann, Müller, Stuhlmacher, and Kertelge also in effect support it. Romans 7 should certainly not be understood in an individualistic, autobiographical way, as Bultmann and Kümmel rightly insist. Romans 9–11 represents the same theme, not a mysterious change of subject. The concern for "putting things right" in no way contradicts Paul's belief that the law has failed (Rom. 5:20).[20]

Miranda now relates this to the kind of worldview found in Marcuse, Sartre, and Bloch. Paul places "the wisdom of the world" under judgment. Faith is submission to the judgment of God, not a special kind of "work."[21] Faith is directed toward Christ and his resurrection. Putting on Christ is entering a new order of existence (Rom. 4:17). Of this Paul is "not ashamed," and hope does not deceive. Miranda calls this "the dialectics of faith."[22] The new community is under the new covenant, which we may call "knowing Yahweh" in love and in justice.

The other book by Miranda that most influenced liberation hermeneutics is *Being and the Messiah,* which largely concerns the Gospel of John. But he begins with a critique of oppression and exchange-value as "a mode of existence." He believes that the plight of the poor is not solved by a revolution and assault on power alone; the arbitrariness of exchange-value is the ultimate cause of unjust division. We must begin with human concerns, as Kierkegaard, Heidegger, and Sartre did.[23] Karl Marx saw that exchange-value does not correspond with material reality, but is the result of manipulation. The labor of the proletariat is bought cheaply through this mental construct. But it is based solely on the desire for personal gain.[24] This aspect is silenced, but it profoundly militates against the New Testament (Rom. 5:19, 21; 1:18-32). This is why "reformist palliatives" do not solve the problem, but merely hide it.[25]

We cannot defend the way "Christianity" has connived in this, Miranda argues, by speaking of an "ethical God." We must return to the God of the

---

on *Paul's Biblical Writings* (Fearn, Scotland: Christian Focus, 2004), throughout, especially pp. 141-56 and 287-92.

20. Miranda, *Marx and the Bible,* pp. 187-92.
21. Miranda, *Marx and the Bible,* pp. 201-10.
22. Miranda, *Marx and the Bible,* pp. 229-92.
23. Miranda, *Being and the Messiah,* pp. 2-7 and 15-17.
24. Miranda, *Being and the Messiah,* pp. 7-14.
25. Miranda, *Being and the Messiah,* p. 21.

Bible; this is the God who named himself "I will be," not "I am" (Exod. 3:12-14; Hebrew imperfect with future meaning, not LXX, or Greek, with present). Humankind's contempt for the one who is brother (Gen. 4:1-11) brings a curse upon humanity. Yet God promises to release humankind from this slavery (Exod. 6:6, 12; 14:11-12; 15:25-26), and not by some merely "inner" or "spiritual" redemption. History advances without some mythological "return"; Yahweh rejects culture in favor of ethical justice (Amos 5:21-25). For God is the God of the future, and "to know" him is to love justice for one's fellow.

Being can be understood only in relation to time. This was Heidegger's contribution. Thus the Bible looks for the eschaton. The Beatitudes of Matthew 5:1-10 speak of what *will* be given to those who are blessed (as in Ps. 37:2-20). Abraham looks in trust to the future (Rom. 4:13 and Heb. 11). *Paul* speaks of "paradise" (2 Cor. 12:4). *Matthew* speaks of the last judgment (Matt. 25:31-46). History is moving toward its telos. This has ethical significance. *John* does not give an account of "timeless" being, or of realized eschatology. He does indeed speak of those who have already passed from death to life (John 5:24; 1 John 3:14). But this has a christological content. John's vision is both contingent and future-directed. There is double emphasis in John: on "this world" in the present, and on "the hour" of Jesus' death and resurrection.

The "Word" is important in John. The word gives life, and is essentially in John the word of love (John 1:4; 14:23-24). The word of life also features in 1 John (1 John 1:1; 2:5) as the word of love. 1 John is not merely concerned with Docetism, but with perceiving Christ as the Christ who requires love. Bultmann is inadequate here. What is needed is transformation of the self, as Kierkegaard saw. The West too easily dismisses the historical Jesus, and does not understand him. Through the Spirit, the Paraclete, transformation becomes possible, and Christians can "keep my Word" (John 14:15).[26]

4. The Second Stage Continued: Juan Luis Segundo, J. Severino Croatto, Leonardo Boff, and Others

José Porfirio Miranda (1924-2001) was probably among the earliest of those who published in the 1970s. Gustavo Gutiérrez, we have noted, was born in

---

26. Miranda, *Being and the Messiah*, p. 213; cf. pp. 203-22.

1928. Perhaps next in time and in influence comes Juan Luis Segundo (b. 1925, of Uruguay), then perhaps Severino Croatto (b. 1930, of Argentina). Hugo Assmann (b. 1933, of Brazil) writes more on systematic theology than on the Bible. Leonardo Boff (b. 1938), a Franciscan of Brazil, began to publish at the end of the 1970s, and continues to write, as does his brother Clodovis Boff. All are Catholic except Rubem A. Alves (b. 1933), who undertook doctoral work at Union, New York, and Princeton Theological Seminary, and the Arentinian Methodist José Míguez Bonino. Mention should also be made of Jon Sobrino (b. 1938), initially of Barcelona, Spain, but then of El Salvador.

1. *Juan Luis Segundo of Uruguay* places *the hermeneutical circle* and hermeneutics at the center of his influential book *The Liberation of Theology*.[27] He insists that "Christianity is a *biblical* religion" (italics in original), but the church must listen to the Bible in the light of the nature of society today (p. 7). He insists that the liberation theologian must allow his preunderstanding to be shaped both by sociology and by an active involvement in society. He attacks academic theology for often missing this dimension; abstract theology can never liberate. But Max Weber comes in for the same criticism. Weber explains the causes of class division, but he remains at the level of "science" or descriptive analysis. Hence he fails to change the world. Segundo is partly inspired here by Hugo Assmann. Evil and injustice are structural, as Marx saw. But even Marx seems concerned to promote happiness rather than justice. The hermeneutical circle "proves that a theology is alive" (p. 23). Black theology and the work of James Cone provide a positive example in this respect, as does some feminist hermeneutics, many will add.

Segundo further argues that if the Church presents an "unchanging" theology, this merely offers a reason for unbelief or even idolatry. Vatican II hints in this direction. Sociology ought to help, but it is impeded by abstraction and by a fragmentation into "scientific" accounts of pieces of "everyday" problems. It no longer offers a world-changing, structural solution. It does not even do full justice to Marx's dialectical materialism, but oversimplifies it. Even the work of Max Weber stops short of a sufficiently full and detailed account.

Most seriously of all, a split emerges between sociology and politics. It is

27. Juan Luis Segundo, *The Liberation of Theology*, trans. John Drury (Dublin: Gill and MacMillan, 1977), pp. 7-38 and throughout. Parenthetical page references in the following text are to this work.

as if first-century "almsgiving" is a good enough political solution to the division between rich and poor today. This is tantamount to using the method of the Pharisees (Mark 3:1-3). They do not know how to interpret the signs of the times (Matt. 16:2-3), but rely on repeating the demands of ancient texts literally in a changed situation.

In all this "commitment" is the first step. We must announce the gospel *"from within a commitment to liberation"* (p. 83, italics in original). Jesus acted in the context of political struggle, but generally European scholarship, Segundo maintains, has lost sight of the historical Jesus. Today we must follow Assmann's argument about ideologies, as well as Bultmann's argument about the hermeneutical circle. How capable is the Church of living out the needed dialectic? Here Segundo explicates some pastoral issues about the Catholic and Protestant churches, especially in the light of eschatology. Jesus did not spell out the exact kind of mutual love that followers had to display. Christians were to use their responsible imagination, and to do so creatively. It is in order to appeal to "the people" to make revolutions on this basis. Segundo's de-ideologizing has some parallel with Bultmann's program of demythologizing. Finally, Juan Luis Segundo urges that a hermeneutic of suspicion must also guide the church. This is a vital part of the hermeneutical circle (p. 231; cf. pp. 228-40).

2. *J. Severino Croatto of Argentina,* together with Segundo, shows very great concern for *hermeneutics.* In 1978 he published *Exodus: A Hermeneutics of Freedom* in Spanish.[28] Croatto begins with Paul Ricoeur's hermeneutics and quickly proceeds to consider Hans-Georg Gadamer. Like Segundo, he also appeals to the hermeneutical circle. He writes, "Social practices always signify . . . an appropriation of meaning" (p. 3; cf. pp. 1-3). He considers the Exodus narratives in the light of effective history in Gadamer, surplus of meaning in Ricoeur, and "signs of the times" in the use of the hermeneutical circle. "My hermeneutical moment is different from that of one or another reader. . . . I do not first carry out an exegesis . . . and subsequently relate it to the facts of our world. . . . The facts must be prior to my interpretation to the biblical Word" (p. 11).

The exodus is a reservoir of meaning, a "locus" of meaning for today. It

28. J. Severino Croatto, *Exodus: A Hermeneutics of Freedom,* trans. Salvator Attanasio (Maryknoll, N.Y.: Orbis, 1981). Cf. Hugo Assmann, *A Practical Theology of Liberation,* trans. Paul Burns, introduction by Gustavo Gutiérrez (London: Search Press, 1975); and also Kirk, *Liberation Theology,* pp. 46-48. Parenthetical page references in the following text are to Croatto's *Exodus.*

is not merely the bald happening of the thirteenth century B.C., but projects what has been reflected upon by faith, and says "more" than a historical report. Here both Gadamer and Ricoeur lie behind the point. Moses had first to make the Israelites *aware* that they were oppressed (Exod. 6:9) in a way parallel to Paul Freire's *concientización,* or consciousness raising. *Then* came the word of liberation. Moses needed them to confront the powers. The hermeneutical circle runs both backward to the archetypal event and forward to the existential present.

Humankind was created for freedom. The passages in Genesis make this clear (Gen. 1:26-28; 4:17-22; 5:3). The image of God in humankind has become distorted; secularization means "paganization" (pp. 36-38). Therefore the world needs the prophet as "conscientizer" of alienated humanity (Jer. 5:26; 7:5). Christ speaks first as the Suffering Servant (Isa. 41–53; Mark 8:29-30), then as Liberator. As such he confronts the Pharisees. Croatto writes, "Jesus addresses himself to all marginalized people . . . oppressed by egoism . . . and by the 'religious' structure" (p. 51; cf. pp. 55-66). Finally, Paul is the "radical human liberation" who delivers humankind from sin, death, and the law. Here is a parallel to the liberation in the exodus (Exod. 19:4; cf. Rom. 7:12-16).

Severino Croatto continues his concern for hermeneutics in *Biblical Hermeneutics: Toward a Theory of Reading as the Production of Meaning* (Maryknoll, N.Y.: Orbis, 1987).

3. Meanwhile *Leonardo Boff* (b. 1938) of Brazil published *Jesus Christ Liberator* in Portuguese in 1972, and in English in 1978.[29] *Jon Sobrino* (b. 1938), who ministered mainly in El Salvador, published *Christology at the Crossroads* (English 1978).[30] Boff begins with a section on biblical criticism and the identification of Christ, and writes, "Each generation must answer within the context of its own understanding of the world, of this person, and of God" (p. 1). Christology is "not a doctrine . . . but an announcement, a call of faith" (p. 9). It is going beyond the historical Jesus, the presence of a new reality. The radical call of Jesus is to love.

For Boff this brings us to the heart of hermeneutics. He considers the hermeneutics of historical criticism, which includes form criticism and re-

---

29. Leonardo Boff, *Jesus Christ Liberator: A Critical Christology of Our Time,* trans. Patrick Hughes (Maryknoll, N.Y: Orbis, 1978; London: SPCK, 1980). Parenthetical page references in the following text are to this work.

30. Jon Sobrino, *Christology at the Crossroads: A Latin American Approach,* trans. John Drury (Maryknoll, N.Y.: Orbis; London: SCM, 1978).

duction criticism. He then expounds *existential hermeneutics, the hermeneutical circle,* and the *hermeneutics of salvation history* (pp. 38-43). Above all, we must look to the priority of criticism over dogmatics. From the confession of the Church we may move to Jesus' demand for the absolute meaning of the world. This is the kingdom or rule of God. *Jesus is liberator* of the human condition. This requires "a revolution in our thinking and acting" (p. 64; cf. pp. 64-79). He brings creative imagination and originality, although he is also "the one who disconcerts, and is condemned. He loved to the end."

We have seen that most of these writers make much of commitment to justice, solidarity with the poor, and hermeneutics or the hermeneutical circle in particular. How does this movement develop beyond the 1970s and 1980s to the present day?

5. The Third Stage: Postcolonial Hermeneutics from the 1980s to the Present

Books and papers on liberation theology seemed to abound in the 1980s. Norman K. Gottwald edited *The Bible and Liberation* in 1983, with contributions from Gerd Theissen, George Pixley, Walter Brueggemann, Elisabeth Schüssler Fiorenza, himself, and others.[31] Leonardo Boff collaborated with his brother Clodovis to produce *Introducing Liberation Theology,* published in Brazil in 1986.[32] Phillip Berryman, as we have seen, published *The Religious Roots of Rebellion* in 1984. E. Dussel wrote his history of the movement in 1985. Clodovis Boff published *Theologie und Praxis* in 1986. Severino Croatto wrote his book on biblical hermeneutics in 1984. José Porfirio Miranda published *Communism in the Bible* in 1982. Chris Rowland and Mark Corner wrote their book *Liberating Exegesis* in 1989. Juan Luis Segundo published *The Historical Jesus of the Synoptics* in 1985. Many stressed that the Bible belongs to the people, rather than to scholars.

No truly new dominant theme emerges, and the emphasis on the hermeneutical circle remains virtually the same. Consultation with several

31. Norman K. Gottwald, ed., *The Bible and Liberation: Political and Social Hermeneutics* (Maryknoll, N.Y.: Orbis, 1983).

32. Leonardo Boff and Clodovis Boff, eds., *Introducing Liberation Theology* (London: Burns and Oates, 1987).

bishops of Latin America, including Gregory Venables, Anglican primate of the Southern Cone, has suggested that the movement is now at best patchy, but still derives its inspiration mainly from the communities and writings of the 1970s, other than where economic and political situations give it fresh impetus. Thomas L. Schubeck, S.J., admits, "The euphoria initially felt by theologians, pastoral workers, and the people, began to diminish as they encountered opposition to programs of liberation within the church."[33] In many parts of Latin America, Schubeck continues, military governments made arbitrary arrests and thereby aroused left-wing politicians. Brazil, Guatemala, Haiti, Nicaragua, and Paraguay offer examples.

Meanwhile a third conference of Latin American bishops was held in 1979 at Puebla, Mexico, which included some opposition to liberation theology, at least by those whom many might regard as more extreme in their views. Nevertheless, they explicitly favored some of the Medellin recommendations, speaking of a "preferential option" for the poor. Liberation theology began to widen its focus to include feminism and the churches outside Latin America, especially of India and Africa. Women theologians came forward in other places, including Elsa Tamaz of Costa Rica, Ivone Gebara of Brazil, and Maria Pilar Aquino of Mexico.[34] Similarly Mercy Amba Oduyoye of Ghana explored the same area, especially with reference to the plight of single mothers. They resisted violence against women, especially in times of war. We discuss this movement in the next chapter, especially under "Womanist Hermeneutics." But critics of any sort of extremism have included the present Pope Benedict, better known for his criticism formerly as Joseph Cardinal Ratzinger. Michael Novak and James Gustafson of the United States have also voiced criticisms of liberation theology, arguing that it often reduces Christian faith to secular politics.

Liberation theology has also shown concern for the environment. Indeed, some characterize its fourth stage (1993 to the 2008) as that of *ecology and globalization*. Others prefer to use the term *"postcolonial"* hermeneutics. They react strongly against the borrowing of theological and biblical method from Europe and the United States. They demand a stronger focus

---

33. Thomas L. Schubeck, S.J., "Liberation Theology," in *The Encyclopedia of Christianity*, ed. Erwin Fahlbusch, Jan Milič Lochman, et al., trans. G. W. Bromiley, 5 vols. (Grand Rapids: Eerdmans, 1999-2008), 3:260; cf. pp. 258-65.

34. Elsa Tamez, "Cultural Violence against Women in Latin America," in *Women Resisting Violence*, ed. Mary John Mananzan et al. (Maryknoll, N.Y.: Orbis, 1996), and Maria Pilar Aquino and D. Mieth, eds., *The Return of the Just War* (London: Search Press, 2001).

on the nations of the Southern Hemisphere, urging the cancellation of debt for Argentina, Brazil, and Mexico, and in many parts of Africa.

Exponents of postcolonial hermeneutics urge the abandonment of methods of reading used by the former colonial powers. Even the notion of a "literary canon" is regarded as centered often on Europe, with Shakespeare and Dickens its core. The Bible has been perceived as a European export. Even some from the "settler colonies" of Canada, the United States, Australia, New Zealand, and South Africa sometimes voice these criticisms. By contrast, exponents look to native America, to Aborigines in Australia, and to Maoris in New Zealand for much of their inspiration. Perhaps, some argue, associated with this is an anti-Israeli "Canaanite" reading of the wilderness wanderings and the conquest of the Holy Land.

In Ghana Mercy Amba Oduyoye represents the postcolonial approach.[35] She stresses that the church did not originate in Europe. In 1989 she founded the Circle of Concerned African Women Theologians to encourage African women to publish on culture and religion from their own point of view. In their consultation at Johannesburg in 2005, the Circle claimed six hundred members. In 2002 they met to consider HIV and AIDS.[36] In 2006 they planned for the next stage of research.

Black South African theology began to look for a distinctive identity with black students and black consciousness under Steve Biko in 1969, and later Desmond Tutu urged that his theology transcended both white and black communities. Bonganjalo Goba and especially Itumeleng Mosala combine black theology with sociology and Marxism.[37] Allan Boesak looked for resonances between the narrative of Cain and Abel (Gen. 4:1-16) and landless people in South Africa.[38] His hermeneutics is similar to that of Severino Croatto, where the starting point is the "cry" of oppressed people

---

35. Mercy Amba Oduyoye, *Hearing and Knowing: Theological Reflections on Christianity in Africa* (1993; reprint, Eugene, Oreg.: Wipf and Stock, 2004), and Oduyoye, *Introducing African Women's Theology* (reprint, Sheffield and New York: Continuum, 2004).

36. Mercy Amba Oduyoye and Elizabeth Amoah, eds., *People of Faith and the Challenge of HIV/AIDS* (Ibadan: Sefer, 2005). Cf. John Parratt, *An Introduction to Third World Theologies* (Cambridge: Cambridge University Press, 2004).

37. Bonganjalo Goba, *An Agenda for Black Theology: Hermeneutics for Social Change* (Johannesburg: Skotaville, 1988), and Itumeleng J. Mosala, *Biblical Hermeneutics and Black Theology in South Africa* (Grand Rapids: Eerdmans, 1989).

38. Allan Boesak, *Black and Reformed: Apartheid, Liberation, and the Calvinist Tradition* (Maryknoll, N.Y.: Orbis, 1984).

(Exod. 3:7, 9). Almost all writers writing after 1985 refer to the *Kairos Document* of that year, which challenged the Church to new attitudes to the poor.

Mosala writes in a materialist and "postcolonial" vein, appealing to the Marxism of Norman Gottwald and others. He finds in the Old Testament ruling-class sources, which he rejects, turning Boesak's interpretation of Genesis 4:1-16 virtually upside down. Even the concept of "Messiah" is too "royal" for Mosala, the construction of a Zion-based elite. He views the Latin American liberation movement, including José Porfirio Miranda, as insufficiently radical. He looks for ideology behind the Old and New Testaments, just as some feminists seek to de-ideologize what they see as patriarchal assumptions drawn from an outmoded culture rather than from theology.

In the Indian subcontinent a radically pluralist hermeneutics associated with Archie C. C. Lee advocated a cross-culturalism. But more distinctively postcolonial hermeneutics operates with a more explicit hermeneutic of suspicion and stresses the role of the marginalized in rightly reading texts out of their own situation. R. S. Sugirtharajah is a leader in this approach.[39] He has written at least five books and edited nine, and is currently professor of biblical hermeneutics at Birmingham University in the U.K., where he gained the Ph.D. He earlier studied at Serampore. In *The Bible and the Third World* Sugirtharajah begins by considering India, China, and Africa, then looks at the legacy of colonialism, while in part III he considers the "vernacular hermeneutics" of the indigenous peoples.[40] He gives some identity-specific readings of the Bible, and considers the outcome of liberation hermeneutics.[41]

R. S. Sugirtharajah is also board editor of *Semeia* 75 (1996), which is entitled *Post-colonialism and Scriptural Reading*. Susan VanZanten Gallagher speaks of the complicity of the Christian missionary enterprise with the structure of colonial oppression, and Sugirtharajah calls for more voices of protest.[42] Laura Donaldson writes that too often the Great Commission (Matt. 28:19-20) confuses the Word with European conquest. Jon Berquist

39. R. S. Sugirtharajah, ed., *Asian Faces of Jesus* (Maryknoll, N.Y.: Orbis; London: SCM, 1993); Sugirtharajah, ed., *Voices from the Margins: Interpreting the Bible in the Third World* (Maryknoll, N.Y.: Orbis; London: SPCK, 1989, 2006); Sugirtharajah, *The Bible and the Third World* (Cambridge: Cambridge University Press, 2001); Sugirtharajah, *The Bible and the Empire: Postcolonial Explorations* (Cambridge: Cambridge University Press, 2005).

40. Sugirtharajah, *Bible and the Third World*, pp. 175-202.

41. Sugirtharajah, *Bible and the Third World*, pp. 259-65.

42. Laura E. Donaldson, in *Semeia* 75 (1996): *Post-colonialism and Scriptural Reading*, pp. 3 and 5-6.

argues that one advantage for interpretation is to see how imperial powers used texts to validate their enterprise.[43] Musa W. Dube also expounds an imperial mind-set with reference to John 4:1-42. Kimberly Rae Connor argues that the spirituals anticipated postcolonial hermeneutics with their cry for justice and Afro-American sensitivities.

It is not easy to know where to draw a line in postcolonial biblical interpretation. Sugirtharajah argues that many concepts are derived from Hindu, Buddhist, and Confucian cultures and societies. Along with himself, he includes Fernando Segovia and Stephen Moore. Segovia is a Cuban American who now teaches at Vanderbilt University in America. It is unclear how much of his Catholic and Christian heritage Moore rejects, but many infer that his central approach is that of postmodernism. In any case, he teaches in the U.K. In contrast to liberation theology, Sugirtharajah claims that postcolonial hermeneutics not only challenges ideological interpretation (as liberation hermeneutics does) but also challenges "the position and prerogative given to the Bible itself."[44]

First, liberation hermeneutics does seek to remain broadly *biblical,* although many would argue that its appeal to "experience" prevents it from ever hearing anything that might be uncongenial to it. It sees gaps and ambiguities embedded within the Bible. *Second,* liberation hermeneutics gives privilege *selectively* to *certain parts of the Bible,* for example, to the Exodus narrative and to Romans 1:16. Postcolonial hermeneutics resists doing this. *Third,* liberation hermeneutics has *a restrictive notion of the poor,* whereas postcolonial hermeneutics has a wider plurality of focus. *Finally,* liberation theology, according to Sugirtharajah, is more *christocentric* than postcolonial hermeneutics. The latter has a more hospitable approach to other religions with supposedly common elements.

In 2004 the *Global Bible Commentary* appeared, with some seventy contributors paying attention to their own diverse backgrounds.[45] They were to attend to their "life-context."[46] Chris Rowland, although English, writes superbly on Revelation from a background in Brazil and liberation theology. Gerald West writes as a gifted biblical scholar who took his doctorate in En-

43. Jon L. Berquist, "Post-colonialism and Imperial Motives for Colonization," *Semeia* 75 (1996): 15-35.

44. R. S. Sugirtharajah, in David F. Ford (with Rachel Muers), *The Modern Theologians,* 3rd ed. (Oxford: Blackwell, 2005), p. 546.

45. Daniel Patte, ed., *Global Bible Commentary* (Nashville: Abingdon, 2004).

46. Patte, *Global Bible Commentary,* p. xxiv.

gland but teaches in South Africa. He writes on 1 and 2 Samuel, finding twenty-six points of resonance between 1 Samuel and Africa.[47] J. Severino Croatto writes on Isaiah 40–55, and Khiok-Khing Yeo of China, on 1 Thessalonians. Some would perhaps claim that many contributions, however, do not reach this high standard of scholarship, and are better at promoting their country's "interests." The different contributions vary in quality and hermeneutical responsibility.

6. A Further Assessment and Evaluation

1. There is no doubt that liberation theologians intend to give *the Bible* an authoritative place, in contrast to some postcolonial interpreters. Gustavo Gutiérrez, Juan Luis Segundo, and Severino Croatto see Christian theology as a dialectic between the Bible and Latin American life-contexts. Even so, they tend to begin with *questions presented by the human context*, and this places them, along with Schleiermacher, on a liberal side of the spectrum. As with Paul Tillich, we are left wondering how far the human questions actually dictate and condition what we hear from the Bible as revelation. Yet to "reduce" the Bible is not their intention. Even José Porfirio Miranda does not seek to make Christianity match Marxism, but uses Marxism to "notice" what is in the Bible. We might conclude that this is a serious danger, which sometimes but not always shapes their hermeneutics.

2. These writers seek to draw on the *resources of hermeneutics*. But if Segundo is right to claim a close parallel between de-ideologization and Bultmann's demythologizing, these writers have not chosen the best model. They profess to use Gadamer and Ricoeur, but fairly selectively. Is the *hermeneutics of suspicion* used on their own work as much as on the West or North? Does Gadamer's effective history allow too much in, when it is widely acknowledged that in spite of his insights Gadamer gives no adequate criteria of meaning for a text, other than its "application"?

3. Liberation exponents in 1968 and the early 1970s set a very good example of *solidarity with the oppressed*. But does this continue today? In opposing neoliberal "development" in favor of revolution, are they always seeking the best option for those for whom they speak? Moreover, does this become an entirely political question rather than also a theological one?

---

47. Gerald West, "1 and 2 Samuel," in *Global Bible Commentary*, p. 94.

Does it matter if the answer has to be the inclusion of politics, or is radically "leftist" politics a necessary part of Christian theology?

4. The charge of *selectivity* is frequently made, the selection of both a given class and given biblical passages. It is arguable that Exodus, Isaiah 48–55, Amos, Daniel, Matthew 5–7, and Revelation receive more than their fair share of attention. Yet might the same principle apply to some feminist hermeneutics?

5. Liberation hermeneutics is best seen as a prophetic response to its times, including the work of Vatican II. As a prophetic corrective to the imbalance and division of the poor in poor countries, it is widely perceived as having met a need. But it has now broadened into a wider social agenda and lost some of its vitality. Some describe this as dissipation.

6. The early role of *base communities* is an example that illustrates this. The Catholic Church was discovering its laity. But many Protestant churches already looked to their laity. Yet lay-led groups do not always have the expertise for a fully informed and responsible study of the Bible without including *all* gifts. This is a new kind of selectivity, and it is little wonder that Cardinal Ratzinger, now Pope Benedict, voiced concerns about the movement.

7. The spread into postcolonial interpretation arguably tends to diminish the Bible, although it is true that the Bible did not originate in Europe or America. The West and North can learn from this movement, but whether what goes under the name of "hermeneutics" is genuine or responsible hermeneutics *all* the time, rather than for some of the time, may be open to doubt. We may be prompted to consider again the hermeneutical circle, the role of biblical studies, allegorizing, and the place of suspicion and "interest" in interpretation.

7. Recommended Initial Reading

Boff, Leonardo, and Clodovis Boff, eds., *Introducing Liberation Theology* (London: Burns and Oates, 1987), pp. 11-65.

Croatto, J. Severino, *Exodus: A Hermeneutics of Freedom,* translated by Salvator Attanasio (Maryknoll, N.Y.: Orbis, 1981), pp. 1-30.

Donaldson, Laura E., ed., *Semeia* 75 (1996): *Post-colonialism and Scriptural Reading,* "An Introduction," pp. 1-15.

Kirk, J. Andrew, *Liberation Theology: An Evangelical View from the Third World* (London: Marshall, Morgan and Scott, 1979), pp. 73-92.

Thiselton, Anthony C., *New Horizons in Hermeneutics: The Theory and Practice of Transforming Biblical Reading* (London: HarperCollins; Grand Rapids: Zondervan, 1992), pp. 411-26.

CHAPTER XIV

Feminist and Womanist Hermeneutics

Feminist and womanist hermeneutics have been defined in various ways. Many stress the public visibility or leadership of women and their capacity or authority to interpret Scripture. One group sees hermeneutics largely as the retrieval of women's experience of this. Others see the Bible as a series of books all (with possibly one exception, namely, Hebrews) written by male authors, to be read largely (although not exclusively) by men. They then define feminist hermeneutics primarily as the reading of biblical texts and books through female eyes. "Womanist" hermeneutics is the name usually reserved for African or Afro-American women's movements interpreting the Bible. This network tends to see feminism as a positive but largely middle-class movement of mainly professional women. They suggest that feminists tend to neglect such resources as African or Afro-American spirituals or their distinctive problems and experience, and the distinctive African or Afro-American women's agenda.

The term "feminism" is widely associated with the blossoming of the movement in the 1960s. Nowadays "feminist hermeneutics" represents a *variety* of approaches. Many in feminist or womanist theology seek the equal rights of women, aiming at reproductive self-determination and economic justice. Extreme feminists wish "to reject the male world altogether."[1] Perhaps the one point of common agreement is that "man" is not in himself equivalent to the whole of humanity.

---

1. Ann Loades, ed., *Feminist Theology: A Reader* (London: SPCK; Louisville: Westminster John Knox, 1990), p. 1.

1. The Public Visibility and Ministry of Women from Earliest Times

If male human beings are not to be equated with the whole of humanity, it is important to see the active and sometimes distinct role adopted by women in the history of the Church and in Judaism. To highlight this role was the aim of *Women of Spirit,* edited in 1979 by Rosemary Radford Ruether and Eleanor McLaughlin.[2] Elisabeth Schüssler Fiorenza begins with an account of women's roles in the New Testament and the early Church, especially in the subapostolic era. She begins with the pre-Pauline "baptism formula" in Galatians 3:27: "As many of you as were baptized into [in allegiance to] Christ have clothed themselves with Christ." This is followed by 3:28: "There is no longer Jew or Gentile . . . slave or free . . . male and female, for all are one in Christ Jesus." She claims that wealthy women converts would have been influential in the growing house churches (Acts 12:12; 17:12). The businesswoman Lydia is singled out for mention in Acts 16:14-15 as perhaps head of her household, and Nympha appears to own the house in which the church met in Colossae (Col. 4:15). In Philemon 2 Paul greets Apphia.

Priscilla (Prisca) receives a prominent place in 1 Corinthians 16:19 and Romans 16:3-5, and may perhaps even have been the author of the Epistle to the Hebrews, as Martin Luther surmised, which would easily account for its anonymity. Paul also speaks of the household or employees of Chloe in 1 Corinthians 1:11. In 1 Corinthians 16:16 he urges that respect should be given to his "coworkers," among whom are many women. He commends Mary, Tryphosa, and Persis for their labor "in the Lord" in Romans 16:6, 12. Those who "labor" are to be respected in 1 Thessalonians 5:12. Phoebe the deacon of Cenchreae is commended in Romans 16:1.

Andronicus and Junia are explicitly called "apostles" in Romans 16:7. The argument that the best manuscripts call her "Junia" as a well-known female name has very recently been reconsidered by Eldon Jay Epp in the book *Junia* (2005). Epp is a well-known world-class specialist in textual criticism. He brings to bear textual criticism, exegesis, and reception history on this verse, and writes that the feminine reading is for him "indisputable" and "the perfectly natural reading."[3] The Greek term *diakonon* (of Phoebe) is

---

2. Rosemary Radford Ruether and Eleanor McLaughlin, eds., *Women of Spirit: Female Leadership in the Jewish and Christian Traditions* (New York: Simon and Schuster, 1979).

3. Eldon Jay Epp, *Junia: the First Woman Apostle* (Minneapolis: Fortress, 2005), p. 80.

masculine ("deacon," not "deaconess"), and she is also called *prostatis* (eminent) and a *synergos* (fellow worker).

Schüssler Fiorenza next turns to the injunction for women to remain silent in 1 Corinthians 14:33b-36. Of course, it is assumed in 1 Corinthians 11:2-16 that women will lead in prayer and in prophetic speech. But 1 Corinthians 14:33b-36 seems to forbid them to speak, but to seek religious instruction from their husbands. Elsewhere, she notes, women are also accepted as prophets, but she appears not to comment further on 1 Corinthians 14:33b-36. In my larger commentary on 1 Corinthians I have first considered, but then rejected, the view that these verses are an interpolation, in spite of Gordon Fee's advocacy of this. I have argued that these verses refer to the sifting, testing, or evaluation of prophetic speech, and that wives may have assessed their husbands' claim to be prophets in the light of their conduct in the home, which may have been wanting. Paul rejects this unusual situation of publicizing domestic events as capable of abuse, excluding family squabbles from the church.[4] In her later book *In Memory of Her,* Schüssler Fiorenza argues that Paul favors the liturgical leadership of unmarried women, or of "holy" women, but rejects the place of "ordinary" married women.[5] She rightly observes that Paul's main concern here is the protection of the Christian community, not the status of women.

With regard to what she calls the "deutero-Pauline" literature, Schüssler Fiorenza mentions the command to silence in 1 Timothy 2:9-15, because women come second in the order of creation. She asserts that this merely reflects the *patriarchal* theology of the author. She sees the beginnings of an antifeminine tradition in the Church, and hurries on to the second-century apocryphal writing the *Acts of Paul and Thecla*, which is mainly devoted to the story of this woman missionary. Thecla is converted by Paul and takes a vow of continence. She proclaims the word of God, especially at Iconium. In her chapter Schüssler Fiorenza virtually assumes the reliability of the *Acts of Paul and Thecla,* but in this apocryphal book Paul's defense of sexual abstinence is at variance with the main thrust of 1 Corinthians 7. Most scholars today rightly assume that 7:1 is a quotation from some in Corinth, against

---

4. Elisabeth Schüssler Fiorenza, "Word, Spirit and Power," in *Women of Spirit,* pp. 36-37; Anthony C. Thiselton, *The First Epistle to the Corinthians: A Commentary on the Greek Text,* New International Greek Testament Commentary (Grand Rapids: Eerdmans; Carlisle: Paternoster, 2000), pp. 1, 146-58.

5. Elisabeth Schüssler Fiorenza, *In Memory of Her: A Feminist Theological Reconstruction of Christian Origins* (New York: Crossroad; London: SCM, 1983), pp. 230-342.

which Paul argues in 7:2-8 and elsewhere in the epistle. Schüssler Fiorenza is right, however, to claim that women uttered prophetic speech, and this is even more strongly significant if David Hill, Ulrich Müller, Thomas Gillespie, and I are correct in seeing prophecy as including pastoral preaching as its main form.[6] Luke also declares that the Spirit is given to all Christians (Acts 2:17-18). In the infancy narrative Anna and Mary function as prophets. Philip has four daughters who exercise prophetic speech (Acts 21:9).

Schüssler Fiorenza also appeals to Montanism. But such were its prophetic and heretical excesses that Gwatkin declares that it set preaching back a thousand years. She is more helpful when she comments that John did not oppose "prophecy" as such, but its local form (Rev. 22:16; 2 John 4, 13). She might have said the same of 1 Timothy 2:14, but instead says it is contrary to the mainstream of the Church. We may leave aside what is said of profeminist Gnostics and antifeminine Marcionites. Despite fashion, neither is representative of the early Church.

We are on more secure ground when her chapter in *Women of Spirit* considers the Gospels. Mary Magdalene and Salome are given prominent roles as disciples. Here we find in embryonic form what is developed in Schüssler Fiorenza's later work. Mary Magdalene is mentioned in all four Gospels, and she is the first to announce the resurrection of Christ. The *Gospel of Thomas* recounts an antagonism between Peter and Mary, but not all will accept Schüssler Fiorenza's interpretation of this. She emphatically believes that a patriarchal bias in at least two of the Gospels suppresses and reduces Mary Magdalene's role as "apostle to the apostles," but we shall look at her arguments in her later work.

Rosemary Ruether considers the later patristic age in the following chapter of *Women of Spirit*. The Roman aristocracy, she writes, produced two ascetic women leaders of the church, Paula and Melania. She agrees, however, that reconstruction of their lives comes from the uncertain sources of their admirers.[7] Jerome is the primary source of information, including further comment on Marcilla. He traveled with Paula to the Holy Land and

---

6. Thiselton, *First Epistle*, pp. 956-65 and 1082-94; cf. T. W. Gillespie, *The First Theologians: A Study of Early Christian Prophecy* (Grand Rapids: Eerdmans, 1994); U. B. Müller, *Prophetie und Predigt im Neuen Testament* (Gütersloh: Mohn, 1975); and more widely and controversially Antoinette C. Wire, *The Corinthian Women Prophets: A Reconstruction through Paul's Rhetoric* (Minneapolis: Fortress, 1990).

7. Rosemary Ruether, "Mother of the Church," in *Women of Spirit*, p. 76; cf. pp. 72-98.

Bethlehem. Meanwhile Melania had traveled into Jerusalem, where she was joined by Rufinus, to build a double monastery for men and women. All this occurred in the late fourth century. Meanwhile her granddaughter, Melania Junior, followed in her grandmother's steps, first in Rome, then in Africa and the East. In 419 Jerome wrote to Augustine, mentioning greetings from their mutual friends Melania and Albina. Ruether claims that the Church never recognized the rightful place of these women.

In a chapter on medieval Christianity, Eleanor McLaughlin explores the leadership role of the abbess. This exercised a power born out of holiness. She mentions Saint Lioba (d. 779), a friend of Saint Boniface, who wrote in Latin and knew the Scriptures and the Fathers. She also mentions Mother Tetta. Christina of Markyate was a twelfth-century "holy" woman who both led and challenged the Church. She had a reputation for total obedience to Christ and was a very forceful figure in the Church. McLaughlin also mentions Catherine of Siena (1347-80), who combined contemplation and prayer with action. She was surrounded by disciples and yet embarked on a career of diplomacy, reform, and letter writing. McLaughlin, surprisingly, seems to discuss neither Hilda, abbess of Whitby (614-80), nor Hildegard (1098-1179); but perhaps these are too well known already. She speaks of the many anonymous holy women of the medieval period. She does not appear to address the question of the singleness of women leaders. Others write on related subjects, including women in Judaism. The purpose of the book is to expose the public visibility of women in leadership and ministry.

2. First- and Second-Wave Feminism and Feminist Hermeneutics

A number of writers distinguish three "waves" of feminism.[8] The first wave began in the eighteenth and nineteenth centuries, especially in America and in Britain, and was largely concerned with universal suffrage and the right to enter into legal and economic contracts. The first feminist treatise may have been by Mary Wollstonecraft, *A Vindication of the Rights of Women* (1792).

---

8. Maggie Humm, ed., *The Dictionary of Feminist Theory* (New York: Harvester Wheatsheaf, 1989), p. 251, and Rachel Muers, "Feminism, Gender and Theology," in *The Modern Theologians*, ed. David F. Ford with Rachel Muers, 3rd ed. (Oxford: Blackwell, 2005), p. 431.

She argued that women had a right to education commensurate with their position in society. Thus they could be "companions" to their husbands rather than mere "ornaments" in society. She wrote partly in response to Rousseau on the rights of man. She is acknowledged as influential for British feminism.

In America her counterpart is perhaps Elizabeth Cady Stanton (1815-1902), who championed women's right to vote, together with Susan B. Anthony.[9] She was active as an abolitionist of slavery, but after the American Civil War she concentrated on women's rights. In 1895 she published the famous *Woman's Bible.* Over the years many others joined her cause, and the so-called first wave of feminist thought is said to have ended with the Nineteenth Amendment to the United States Constitution in 1920. This extended to women the right to vote.

Second-wave feminism is widely regarded as flourishing in the 1960s and 1970s. During the Second World War many women came to experience life outside the home in a new way, with vital jobs and a new independence. Many American women were also influenced by Betty Friedan's book *The Feminine Mystique* (1963), which reflected research on the 1940s and 1950s. In 1949 Simone de Beauvoir wrote *The Second Sex* (English 1953), in which she wrote, "Man defines woman not in herself but as relative to him. . . . He is the subject. . . . She is the Other."[10] The Kennedy administration appointed a commission on the status of women, which reported in 1963. There was also much debate in America about coeducational colleges, culminating in the merger of Radcliffe College with Harvard University in 1965.

From the standpoint of feminist hermeneutics, however, apart from Elizabeth Cady Stanton's *Woman's Bible,* the first decisive step was taken by Valerie Saiving in her article "The Human Situation: A Feminine View" (1960).[11] Stanton's *Woman's Bible* alleges that in curses and blessings (Deut. 28:56, 64) women receive more curses and blame than men, but fewer blessings. Woman has no voice in the laws, the judges, or the jury. Vashti becomes

9. Cf. Elizabeth Griffith, *In Her Own Right: The Life of Elizabeth Cady Stanton* (Oxford: Oxford University Press, 1984), and Loades, *Feminist Theology,* pp. 13-23.

10. Cited by Elaine Marks and Isabelle de Courtivron, eds., *New French Feminisms: An Anthology* (Hemel Hemstead: Harvester Press, 1981); also quoted in Anthony C. Thiselton, *New Horizons in Hermeneutics: The Theory and Practice of Transforming Biblical Reading* (London: HarperCollins; Grand Rapids: Zondervan, 1992), p. 435.

11. Valerie Saiving, "The Human Situation: A Feminine View," *Journal of Religion* 40 (1960): 100-112.

a heroine in the book of Esther. Saiving argues more broadly that "man" is not to be confused with "humankind," which includes women. She firstly argues that "pride," which was identified especially by Niebuhr as the essence of "sin," is characteristic not of all sin, but of male sin. Women are more prone to distraction and even to triviality as their "sin."

Probably the next major influence on Christian feminism is Phyllis Trible's *God and the Rhetoric of Sexuality* (1978, but drawing on articles written in 1973, 1976, 1977).[12] She begins with the hermeneutical observation that a literary approach can help to bridge the divide between the church and the world. In the account of creation in Genesis 1:1–2:3 we can see a symmetrical design. Above all, "image of God" (Gen. 1:26-28) applies equally to men and women.[13] She then discusses the women who appeal to Solomon about their babies (1 Kings 3:16-28). We here discover that "womb" becomes a metaphor for compassion (Isa. 46:3, 4). The love of God is a feminine as well as a masculine quality (Jer. 31:15-22; Isa. 49:13-15), but female imagery has a decisive part (Isa. 63:15-16; cf. 27:11). Indeed, in subsequent chapters Trible makes more of female imagery to portray the love of God (Hos. 9:11-12a, 14; Deut. 32:1-43; Prov. 23:22, 25; Isa. 42:14a; 66:1-16; cf. Gen. 2:4b-19). These verses are expounded in the light of the Hebrew text.[14] Karl Barth made the point about "image" in Genesis 1:26-27 sometime earlier, in 1945-50, but is not given much credit for this exegesis.[15]

In one of her later books, *Texts of Terror* (1984), Trible retells the sad stories of Hagar, Tamar, the Levite's concubine in Judges 19:1-30, and the daughter of Jephthah. Again, she begins with hermeneutics. "Storytelling is a trinitarian act that unites writer, text and reader in a collage of understanding."[16] Hagar is a slave who is abused and rejected (Gen. 16:1-16); Tamar is a princess who is raped and discarded (2 Sam. 13:1-22); the daughter of Jephthah is a virgin who is slain and sacrificed (Judg. 11:29-40). They all accept their lot, Trible writes, like the Suffering Servant. Patriarchal hermeneutics has forgotten Tamar and the women, she argues, and glorified some of

---

12. Phyllis Trible, *God and the Rhetoric of Sexuality* (Philadelphia: Fortress, 1978).

13. Trible, *Rhetoric of Sexuality,* pp. 14-23.

14. Trible, *Rhetoric of Sexuality,* pp. 31-143.

15. Karl Barth, *Church Dogmatics,* ed. G. W. Bromiley, T. F. Torrance, and others, 14 vols. (Edinburgh: T. & T. Clark, 1957-75), III/1 (German, 1945), section 41, pp. 183-87, and III/2, section 45, pp. 222-84.

16. Phyllis Trible, *Texts of Terror: Literary-Feminist Readings of Biblical Narratives* (Philadelphia: Fortress, 1984), p. 1.

the men.[17] But Trible begins a motif that is often taken up in feminist writing. She has also edited *Feminist Approaches to the Bible* (1995) and other works.

In 1976 Letty M. Russell edited a collection of essays under the title *The Liberating Word*.[18] This was a semiofficial document of the Division of Education and Ministry of the National Council of Churches, and initially bore on the inclusive translation of various versions of the Bible. Russell modestly called it "preliminary" to more serious and developed work on feminist hermeneutics.[19] Two years earlier some short articles had appeared under the editorship of Rosemary Ruether.[20] In this volume C. Parry wrote on the theological leadership of women in the New Testament.[21] However, the real breakthrough came in 1983, with the publication of Schüssler Fiorenza's *In Memory of Her* and Ruether's *Sexism and God-Talk*.[22] These virtually established these two writers, together with Phyllis Trible, as the effective founders of the "second wave" of feminist biblical interpreters in the early 1980s. Schüssler Fiorenza had already written a chapter in Russell's *Liberating Word* in which she criticized the androcentric and patriarchal presuppositions of the biblical writers themselves. Many were "patriarchal texts" (e.g., Num. 30:2-12 concerning the vows of a wife).[23] A wife and a daughter are not the mere "property" of the husband or father, to be "used" according to his wishes.

A flood of literature on feminism and feminist hermeneutics now followed, and although many were published in the mid-1980s, some volumes were collections of essays written at an earlier date. For example, Elaine Showalter's *New Feminist Criticism*, published in 1986, incorporated essays written in 1980 by Rosalind Coward, in 1979 by Carolyn G. Heilbrun, and in 1979 and 1981 by Showalter, among others. In this collection Showalter ar-

---

17. Trible, *Texts of Terror*, p. 107.

18. Letty M. Russell, ed., *The Liberating Word: A Guide to Nonsexist Interpretation of the Bible* (Philadelphia: Westminster, 1976).

19. Russell, *The Liberating Word*, pp. 13-14.

20. Rosemary Ruether, ed., *Religion and Sexism: Images of Women in the Jewish and Christian Traditions* (New York: Simon and Schuster, 1974).

21. C. Parry, "The Theological Leadership of Women in the N.T.," in *Religion and Sexism*, pp. 117-49.

22. Schüssler Fiorenza, *In Memory of Her*; Rosemary Radford Ruether, *Sexism and God-Talk: Towards a Feminist Theology* (London: SCM, 1983).

23. Russell, *The Liberating Word*, pp. 39, 41, and 42.

gued that women bring a new and different perspective to male-authored texts, which were usually written to be read by men.[24] Feminist biblical interpretation is reading the biblical texts "through women's eyes."

3. Elisabeth Schüssler Fiorenza's *In Memory of Her:* The Argument

1. Elisabeth Schüssler Fiorenza (b. 1938) attempts a major reconstruction of Christian beginnings to around A.D. 600, concentrating especially on the New Testament era. She is an established New Testament scholar, who taught first in Germany and then at Notre Dame and Harvard. She stresses the importance of the *Sitz im Leben* of the texts. These are "the product of patriarchal culture and history."[25] She relies on "the" historical-critical method, and a hermeneutic of suspicion, and rejects both a doctrinal and a positivist approach. She stresses that texts "serve the interests of dominant classes" (p. 6). She mentions Elizabeth Cady Stanton's *Woman's Bible* and her critique of patriarchal culture within the Bible. The biblical texts are "androcentric," or written by and for a male point of view (pp. 7-14).

2. Later parts of the New Testament, including the "deutero-Pauline" texts in Ephesians, 1 Peter, and the Pastoral Epistles, and their "subordination" passages, are in Schüssler Fiorenza's view virtually beyond rescue. 1 Corinthians 11:2-16 and 14:33b-36 become interpolations. We must rid the Bible of such texts, Schüssler Fiorenza argues, as Russell, Trible, and Ruether in effect also suggest, although often with more sensitive language. We can aim to recover an authentic "remembered past" that is not androcentric. Paul proclaims female equality in Galatians 3:28, and "maleness," Schüssler Fiorenza argues, has no significance in 1 Corinthians 12:13. She suggests that the sources are divided about the role of women. Authentic Pauline letters suggest that women were apostles, prophets, missionaries, patrons, and leaders in the church and society.

3. Much of the information about origins cannot be retrieved, but Schüssler Fiorenza's hermeneutic of suspicion allows her a wide measure of *Sachkritik,* or content criticism. Patristic evidence often (but not always) sug-

---

24. Elaine Showalter, ed., *The New Feminist Criticism: Essays on Women, Literature, and Theory* (London: Virago Press, 1986), pp. 3-28, 125-48, and 225-70.

25. Schüssler Fiorenza, *In Memory of Her,* p. xv. Page numbers to this work have been placed in the text for the duration of this discussion.

gests the marginalization of women, and therefore she gathers some of her data from Montanist and Gnostic groups. This is "in order to break the hold of the androcentric text over one historical imagination" (p. 61). But she does not need to rely only on these. Phoebe of Cenchreae is a prime example. Schüssler Fiorenza turns to the social world of the New Testament, considering the work of Malherbe, Meeks, Gager, and Theissen. She follows Theissen in contrasting the itinerant missionaries of the Jesus movement with the settled "love patriarchalism" of the Pauline communities. She does not follow Theissen in every respect, but many would expect more evidence than Theissen and Schüssler Fiorenza offer for their claims. On institutionalization she turns predictably to Scroggs and especially to Weber. She argues that patriarchal "household rules" play a greater part than "biological" differences of sex or gender in determining women's roles (pp. 84-92).

4. Schüssler Fiorenza begins part 2 of her book with the alleged contrast between the pre-Pauline Jesus movement of Galilee, Jerusalem, and Antioch (Acts 11:26) and the Pauline communities. This goes back not only to Gerd Theissen, but further to Hans Lietzmann's theory about a distinction between two types of Eucharist, the fellowship meal with the risen Christ (the Jerusalem joyous type) and a Pauline remembrance of the death of Christ (the "Pauline" solemn type). Although Ernst Lohmeyer follows Lietzmann, the distinction has been decisively criticized by J. Jeremias, I. Howard Marshall, and others, and I have discussed the theory in *The Hermeneutics of Doctrine*.[26] Meanwhile Schüssler Fiorenza ascribes different environments and different goals to these two groups. She concludes, "The Gospels are paradigmatic remembrances," even if not comprehensive ones (p. 102). In many of the texts we find both a denigration of women and a simultaneous glorification of them.

The parables of Jesus, Schüssler Fiorenza believes, speak of the *basileia*, or "reign," of God, in which all come together without discrimination as co-equals. God's flock must also contain everyone (cf. Matt. 22:1-14; Luke 14:16-24). The phrase "tax collectors, sinners, and prostitutes" characterizes not a morally reprehensible group, but those of no account who are marginalized. The Jesus movement proclaims a new understanding of God on the basis of

---

26. Hans Lietzmann, *Mass and Lord's Supper: A Study of the History of the Liturgy*, ed. R. D. Richardson (Leiden: Brill, 1979); Joachim Jeremias, *The Eucharistic Words of Jesus*, trans. Norman Perrin (London: SCM, 1966), pp. 16-38; I. H. Marshall, *Last Supper and Lord's Supper* (Grand Rapids: Eerdmans, 1980), pp. 108-23; and Anthony C. Thiselton, *The Hermeneutics of Doctrine* (Grand Rapids: Eerdmans, 2007), pp. 525-29.

"the praxis of Jesus" (p. 130). The parable of the laborers in the vineyard (Matt. 20:1-16) typically articulates the equality of all, rooted in the grace of God. Drawing on the work of Norman Perrin, Schüssler Fiorenza sees the kingdom of God as a "tensive symbol," and this, she argues, draws on Wisdom Christology: "*Sophia* is justified (or vindicated) by all her children" (Luke 7:35).

It is debatable whether the feminine gender of "Sophia" is really relevant here, any more than that "child" is neuter.[27] We have seen James Barr's blistering comments on this ploy. But Schüssler Fiorenza seems to argue from this accident of language, attributing a number of sayings of Jesus to Sophia and speaking of "the reality of God-Sophia" (pp. 130-40, especially p. 135). Women's leadership, she concludes, may therefore be called "egalitarian," and involves liberation from patriarchal structures (pp. 140, and 140-52). Jesus challenges patriarchal marriage structures (Mark 10:2-9 and 12:18-27). In the eschatological future all will be like the angels. Whoever wishes to receive the kingdom of God must become as a child or slave (Mark 10:15). Jesus does not accept those who want to be "great."

5. Some of the material in Acts and the Epistles about "the Church in her (the) house" suggests the leadership, Schüssler Fiorenza argues, of women patrons or property owners. But the Acts of the Apostles is "one-sided" (p. 167). The Pauline letters give more attention to women as Paul's coworkers. These, she argues, are more like partners than assistants who occupy a subordinate status. Phoebe is called *prostatis,* sometimes translated "helper" but meaning *eminent* or *leading.* Here Schüssler Fiorenza may appeal to a growing scholarship on Paul's coworkers, including work by F. F. Bruce, E. Earle Ellis, Victor P. Furnish, D. J. Harrington, W. H. Ollrog, and Paul Trebilco.[28] The ultimate ground of coequality, however, is the gift of the Holy Spirit, who is poured upon "all flesh" (Acts 2:17-21; cf. Joel 2:28-29). This is corroborated in Paul's letters (1 Cor. 15:45; Gal. 5:25; 6:8; cf. 1 Cor. 1:24; 2 Cor. 3:17; 5:17). The community of God's people, as well as the individual Christian, constitute the holy temple of God (1 Cor. 3:16; cf. Eph. 2:22).

6. The interpretation of Galatians 3:28 receives careful attention. Paul emphasizes equality and oneness, not division. We have only to look at the

27. See the trenchant and convincing comments in James Barr, *The Semantics of Biblical Language* (Oxford: Oxford University Press, 1961), pp. 39-43.

28. For example, W. H. Ollrog, *Paulus und seine Mitarbeiter* (Neukirchen: Neukirchener, 1970), and E. Earle Ellis, *Pauline Theology: Ministry and Society* (Grand Rapids: Eerdmans, 1989).

wider context of argument to see this. 1 Corinthians 12:13 makes the same point in the context of baptism. But 1 Corinthians 11:2 and 17 and 14:33b-36 are at odds with the "pneumatic" drift of 1 Corinthians 11–14, and must be rejected as later interpretations (pp. 226-33).

7. This leads to part 3, "Tracing the Struggles." Colossians was written by a disciple of Paul, and here household codes militate against the equality of Galatians 3:28. Ephesians speaks of reconciliation and a gospel of peace (Eph. 6:15). It stresses the unity of the Spirit (Eph. 4:4-5). Schüssler Fiorenza writes, "The nonsexual monism of the divine pertains to the soul redeemed from the duality of bodily sexuality. The soul is equal and of the same essence in man and woman" (p. 277). But the Pastoral Epistles advocate a patriarchal order of being. They focus on present church order more than on the universal plan of God.

8. The climax of the book turns on the discipleship of the women and the unique apostolic role of Mary Magdalene in the Gospels. Mark presents Mary of Magdala, Mary the daughter or wife of James, Mary the mother of Jesus, and Salome as disciples. The Twelve have forsaken Jesus, whereas Acts presents the Twelve as the foremost apostolic witnesses. In John the beloved disciple is the community's apostolic authority and symbolic center, in contrast to Peter. Yet, according to John, "women — Jesus' mother, his mother's sister Mary, the wife of Cleopas, and Mary Magdalene — and one male disciple, stood by the cross of Jesus" (John 19:25-27) (p. 331). Moreover, Mary Magdalene is the last woman to appear in the Fourth Gospel. "She not only discovers the empty tomb, but is also the first to receive a resurrection appearance" (p. 332). She announces to the disciples, "I have seen the Lord," and, Schüssler Fiorenza writes, "She is the primary apostolic witness to the resurrection" (p. 332). Mary Magdalene's primacy as apostolic witness can be found in Matthew, John, and the Markan appendix; the Petrine tradition contradicts it and is found in 1 Corinthians 15:3-6.

Thus we have a dual tradition. Mary Magdalene is really "the apostle of the apostles," but a rival Petrine tradition sprung up that allegedly sought to suppress the Mary tradition. The authors of all the Epistles, Schüssler Fiorenza concludes, appeal to the authority of Paul or of Peter. But Mark and John underline the prior alternative tradition.

4. Elisabeth Schüssler Fiorenza's *In Memory of Her:* An Evaluation

Elisabeth Schüssler Fiorenza ranks perhaps with only Phyllis Trible as the most notable of explicitly feminist biblical scholars, especially since Mary Daly and Rosemary Radford Ruether work more broadly in theology than in biblical interpretation. Schüssler Fiorenza has been honored as the first woman president of the Society for Biblical Literature. Her work commands a wide consensus in many quarters, including most (though not all) feminist circles. Do her specific arguments remain above controversy or disagreement?

1. Clearly a hermeneutic of suspicion lies at the heart of Schüssler Fiorenza's work, and she draws on liberation hermeneutics for her depatriarchalizing approach. She rejects a fully conservative model of biblical interpretation that depends on something like verbal inspiration. She rejects the view that the Bible is revelation itself (p. 4). She also rejects value-neutral positivism. "Intellectual neutrality is not possible in a world of exploitation and oppression" (p. 6). Following Elizabeth Cady Stanton, she proposes depatriarchalizing in parallel to the de-ideologizing of liberation hermeneutics. But like Bultmann on demythologizing and many of the liberation theologians on de-ideologizing, she elaborates no clear *criteria* concerning which uses or occurrences of "father" or "husband" may be cultural and which uses or occurrences may be theological.

Pannenberg writes, "The words 'God' and 'Father' are not just time-bound concepts from which we can detect the true content of the message."[29] The very relation between God and Jesus is bound up with the words "Father" and "Son," however much we may use other extended imagery. It is the starting point of primitive Christian Christology, and does not ascribe gender to God. It even relates to the baptismal formula in Matthew 28:19.

2. The removal of embarrassing texts as interpretations may not be convincing without firmer evidence. Margaret Mitchell, for one, points out that various theories formulated by Walter Schmithals and others about partition and multiple sources in 1 Corinthians command no universal agreement, and her case has recently been corroborated and strengthened by David R. Hall.[30] I have argued for the contingent and contextual nature of

---

29. Wolfhart Pannenberg, *Systematic Theology,* trans. G. W. Bromiley, 3 vols. (Edinburgh: T. & T. Clark; Grand Rapids: Eerdmans, 1991-98), 1:265; cf. 1:234-327.

30. M. M. Mitchell, *Paul and the Rhetoric of Reconciliation: An Exegetical Investigation of the Language and Compilation of 1 Corinthians* (Louisville: Westminster John Knox, 1992),

1 Corinthians 14:33b-36 elsewhere, and Judith Gundry-Volf gives a convincing interpretation of Paul's aims in 1 Corinthians 11:2-16.[31]

3. Gerd Theissen's contrast between itinerant charismatic communities and "love patriarchalism" and their projection onto the New Testament is at least debatable. It may not bear the weight that Schüssler Fiorenza places upon it. In Mark 3:35 the statement "whoever does the will of God is my brother and sister and mother" does not necessarily imply a community of equals, even if Galatians 3:28 is more convincing. The very presence of leaders such as Phoebe and others in the Pauline communities suggests that "patriarchalism" overstates the case. The account of the founding of Colossians that is presented may not be entirely convincing.

4. The sheer fact that "household codes" and similar material can be found in Roman material does not imply that these are necessarily cultural rather than theological. Moreover, Sandmel's well-known "parallelomania" shows that conjunction does not necessarily imply dependency. The argument tends to be a circular one, based on dating according to a prior theory.

5. The role of Mary Magdalene as witness to the resurrection is an important one. Nevertheless, the tendency to present all the women in the Gospels as "good" defeats the point that the resurrection constituted a decisive change in the lives of those who witnessed it, to transform them to bold, forgiven sinners. This is the distinctive point about Peter, who is not necessarily a "rival" to John and Mary. But Mary does receive a distinctive role, as we have seen in the case of Junia.

6. Much of Schüssler Fiorenza's argument that women are oppressed and marginalized applies largely, but not wholly, to the Roman Catholic Church. She tends to overlook the increasing role of women's leadership in the Protestant churches. That said, she has convincingly exposed the undervaluing of women and their witness, especially in some parts of the patristic Church.

7. When we return to Schüssler Fiorenza's work on *Sophia* as a female Wisdom figure, we are constrained to consider more closely the critique of James Barr concerning confusing accidents of gender in language with the distinctive role of men and women respectively. Barr writes, "No one would suppose that the Turks, because they nowhere distinguish gender in their

---

pp. 1-99 and 198-201; D. K. Hall, *The Unity of the Corinthian Correspondence* (New York and London: T. & T. Clark/Continuum, 2003), pp. 1-86.

31. Thiselton, *First Epistle*, pp. 1146-62; J. M. Gundry-Volf, "Gender and Creation in 1 Cor. 11:2-16," in *Evangelium, Schriftauslegung, Kirche: Frt. F. Peter Stuhlmacher*, ed. J. Adna et al. (Göttingen: Vandenhoeck & Ruprecht, 1997), pp. 151-71.

language, not even in personal pronouns . . . are deficient in the concept of sexual difference; nor would we argue that the French have extended their legendary erotic interests into the linguistic realm by forcing every noun to be either masculine or feminine."[32] Accidents of linguistic form are not reliable indicators concerning concepts or thought. Even the laudable attempt of some feminists to turn "men" into "humanity" is useful only because certain sensitivities have been aroused. If the appeal is to Gnosticism, this solves different problems.

8. On the other hand, Schüssler Fiorenza's work on Paul's coworkers and the early visibility of women leaders in the church lies beyond controversy, even if she stands on the shoulders of W. H. Ollrog, F. F. Bruce, E. Earle Ellis, and others. This is beyond controversy, as is much of her work on followers of Jesus.

9. Elisabeth Schüssler Fiorenza is without doubt, together with Phyllis Trible, the most significant voice in feminist interpretation of the Bible. She is honest about the principle of marginalization and justice in liberation hermeneutics. She follows less directly Norman Gottwald in seeking to de-ideologize (or de-patriarchalize) the biblical text.[33] She is almost the last writer to hold together feminist biblical interpretation before it fragments into different themes. But some women scholars regard what Schüssler Fiorenza represents as unduly assertive, even aggressive. Janet Radcliffe Richards writes, "Feminism is not concerned with a group of people it wants to benefit, but with a type of injustice it wants to eliminate."[34] Susanne Heine is also critical of finding "feminine features," or for that matter "masculine" features too, in God.[35] We arrive, she claims, at stereotypical distortions of what each gender represents. Heine is also critical of the use of the Sophia (Wisdom) figure and Gnosticism.[36] Elizabeth Achtemeier also produced criticisms in a similar vein in 1986. I have explored these particular criticisms in *New Horizons in Hermeneutics*.

---

32. Barr, *Semantics of Biblical Language*, p. 39.

33. Norman K. Gottwald, ed., *The Tribes of Yahweh: A Sociology of the Religion of Liberated Israel* (New York: Orbis, 1979).

34. Janet Radcliffe Richards, *The Sceptical Feminist: A Philosophical Enquiry* (London: Penguin Books, 1983), pp. 17-18. Cf. Thiselton, *New Horizons in Hermeneutics*, pp. 442-50.

35. Susanne Heine, *Women and Early Christianity: Are the Feminist Scholars Right?* (London: SCM, 1987), p. 37; cf. pp. 28-52.

36. Heine, *Women and Early Christianity*, pp. 28-29; cf. Heine, *Christianity and the Goddesses: Systematic Critique of a Feminist Theology* (London: SCM, 1988).

5. The Fragmentation of the Second Wave

Schüssler Fiorenza published a number of further books on feminist interpretation after 1983. These included *Bread Not Stone* (1984); *Discipleship of Equals* (1993); *Jesus: Miriam's Child, Sophia's Prophet* (1995); *Sharing Her Word* (1998); and *Rhetoric and Ethics* (1999). This is not an exhaustive list, and the subtitles all indicate that these are studies in feminist biblical interpretation.[37] Rosemary Radford Ruether (b. 1936) and Mary Daly wrote either earlier or in the same year as *In Memory of Her*, but they addressed issues in theology more distinctively than biblical interpretation. Ruether's *Sexism and God-Talk* appeared in 1983. Like Schüssler Fiorenza, she discusses the distinctive witness of Mary Magdalene and observes female imagery concerning God.[38] Like Phyllis Trible, she discusses humanity as male and female. She then focuses on Christology, Mariology, the consciousness of evil, ministry and community, and eschatology. She is, in effect, the systematic theologian of feminism.

Ruether asks the question: "Is female to male as nature is to culture?" Women, she claims, are symbolized as "closer to nature." Female physiological processes are viewed as dangerous and polluting. Woman's social roles are allegedly regarded as inferior. She becomes "owned" by man, producing children, and dominated by the "higher" culture (p. 74). She draws on males' training in the classics to argue that in Plato and Aristotle males are above women, slaves, and barbarians. But today there is a return to nature. God or Goddess is seen as "primal matrix" or "the ground of being" (as in Paul Tillich) (p. 85). All this appears like the dated liberation theology of the 1960s, and has not much to do with hermeneutics of the biblical text. Ruether writes, "Woman through the Fall and in punishment for the Fall, lost her original equality and became inferior in mind and body" (p. 97). Eschatological feminism insists on equality in the Church. Even the life and death of Jesus of Nazareth, although "paradigmatic," is only "partial and needs to be joined by other models" (p. 115). She goes beyond a "Spirit-

---

37. Elisabeth Schüssler Fiorenza: *Bread Not Stone: The Challenge of Feminist Biblical Interpretation* (Boston: Beacon Press, 1984); *Discipleship of Equals: A Critical Feminist Ekklēsia-logy of Liberation* (New York: Crossroad, 1993); *Jesus: Miriam's Child, Sophia's Prophet; Critical Issues in Feminist Theology* (London: SCM; New York: Continuum, 1995); *Sharing Her Word: Feminist Biblical Interpretation in Contrast* (Boston: Beacon Press, 1998); and *Rhetoric and Ethics: Politics of Biblical Studies* (Minneapolis: Fortress, 1999).

38. Ruether, *Sexism and God-Talk*, pp. 8-71. Page numbers to this work have been placed in the text for the duration of this dicussion.

Christology" to one that allows *"the kenosis of patriarchy,"* namely, an androgynous Christology, or "Christ *in the form of our sister . . .* redemptive humanity" (pp. 137-38, italics in original).

In her chapter on Mariology, the Roman Catholic background of Ruether, like Schüssler Fiorenza's, shows through. "Both Mary's Immaculate Conception and her pre-figuring of the redeemed state of corporal creation reach back to the lost alternative before the Fall. Then pure nature, as it came forth from the hand of God, was totally under the power of the Spirit, and so was without evil" (p. 151). Those of more Protestant faith will simply reject these sentiments.

Ruether developed her theology and writing after 1983. She produced *Women-Church* (1985); *Gaia and God* (1992); and *Women and Redemption* (1998); as well as other works.[39] But these later works have largely taken us beyond the basic concerns of many feminists, and some see them as using *stereotypifications* of a certain type of woman or man. She moves away from "orthodox" Christianity.

6. Womanist Hermeneutics

Many Afro-American and African women writers prefer the term "womanist" over "feminist," on the ground that the latter tends to denote the interests and concerns of white, middle-class, professional or academic women of a certain type. This is in spite of Ruether's sympathy (with Schüssler Fiorenza and others) with liberation theology and the Third World. The two studies "The Community of Women and Men in the Church" (1978-83) and "Christians in Solidarity with Women" (1988-98) paved the way for a wider recognition of womanist theology, and were more ecumenical than Ruether's writings. But many date the beginnings of womanist hermeneutics from 1983, with the work of Alice Walker (b. 1944), followed shortly by Kate G. Cannon.[40]

39. Rosemary Radford Ruether, *Women-Church: Theology and the Practice of Feminist Liturgical Communities* (San Francisco: Harper and Row, 1985); Ruether, *Gaia and God: An Eco-Feminist Theology of Earth Healing* (San Francisco: HarperCollins, 1992); and Ruether, *Women and Redemption: A Theological History* (Minneapolis: Fortress, 1998).

40. Alice Walker, *In Search of Our Mother's Gardens: Womanist Prose* (New York: Harcourt Brace, 1983; London: Women's Press, 1984); cf. Kate G. Cannon, *Women and the Soul of the Black Community* (New York: Concilium, 1995; 1st ed. 1985).

By 1995 R. S. Sugirtharajah could speak of "an explosion of interest in Third-World biblical interpretation."[41] G. S. Wilmore and James Cone edited *Black Theology* in 1993, to which Benita J. Weems contributed "Women's Reflection on Biblical Hermeneutics."[42] In 2002 Stephanie Mitchem published *Introducing Womanist Theology.*[43] Kanyoro Musimbi is not an Afro-American but comes from Kenya, although she holds a doctorate in linguistics from the University of Texas. She has now written seven or eight books, including *The Power We Celebrate* (1992); *Turn to God, Rejoice in Hope* (1996); and *Claiming the Promise* (1994).[44]

Many issues affected black consciousness on the part of women. Some address "patriarchy," but questions about population, women's leadership, AIDS, and violence are prominently on the agenda. Many of the concerns overlap with those of men in the Third World. For example, Gerald West, who was born in Zimbabwe (b. 1956) but is of South African nationality, has written numerous articles and at least half a dozen books, including *Biblical Hermeneutics of Liberation* (1991), *Contextual Bible Study* (1993), and *The Bible in Africa* (2000). Vincent Wimbush has edited *African Americans and the Bible* (2001), a book of nearly 1,000 pages.[45] Kate Cannon's book sums up many of the earlier concerns: negative images of women, the promise of hope and resurrection, and womanist hermeneutics. More recently, however, this extended to violence, HIV and AIDS, and issues of population. Elsa Tamez of Costa Rica writes of the impact of liberation theology and grassroots communities. She argues that there were "anti-women customs of Hebrew culture" that are sometimes used "to prove women's marginalisation."[46]

Meanwhile, in feminist hermeneutics in the West, a plurality of themes and distinctive approaches has emerged. From the mid-1980s a flood of liter-

41. R. S. Sugirtharajah, ed., *Voices from the Margins: Interpreting the Bible in the Third World* (Maryknoll, N.Y.: Orbis; London: SPCK, 1995; 1st ed. 1991), "Introduction," p. 1.

42. G. S. Wilmore and James Cone, eds., *Black Theology: A Documentary History, 1980-1992*, 2nd ed., 2 vols. (Maryknoll, N.Y.: Orbis, 1993).

43. Stephanie Mitchem, *Introducing Womanist Theology* (Maryknoll, N.Y.: Orbis, 2002).

44. Kanyoro Musimbi, *Women, Violence and Non-Violent Change* (Geneva: World Council of Churches, 1996); Musimbi, *The Power We Celebrate* (Geneva: World Council of Churches, 1992).

45. Vincent Wimbush, ed., *African Americans and the Bible: Sacred Texts and Social Textures* (New York: Continuum, 2001).

46. Elsa Tamez, "Women's Re-reading of the Bible," in *Voices from the Margins*, pp. 49-50.

ature has emerged. Carolyn Osiek has suggested a typology of at least four or five different attitudes to the Bible.[47]

1. Osiek discusses, first, *feminist "loyalists."* These include N. A. Hardesty (1984), Patricia Gundry (1987), A. Michelsen (1986), V. R. Mollenkott (1988), Elaine Storkey (1985), and L. D. Scanzoni (1997). Scanzoni argues that Ephesians 5:22 ("Wives, be subject to your husbands as you are to the Lord") should be "revitalized" rather than rejected, for personal well-being.[48] Most of these advocate positive images of, and roles for, women but embrace all the biblical texts, albeit with attention to interpretation. Elaine Storkey, for example, traces the roots of a feminist tradition to the Reformation and its emphasis on the "companionable" aspect of marriage. She stresses the shared and complementary plurality of "made in the image of God," like Barth and perhaps Trible. She addresses "images" of women and the liberation of both men and women.

2. *"Revisionist" feminism,* as Osiek calls it, retains commitment to the Christian faith but rejects the patriarchy it finds in the Bible as culturally conditioned, contingent, and a distraction from the biblical message. This is all the clearer since writers such as Rosemary Radford Ruether, Phyllis Trible, and Ann Loades not only work in Old Testament and systematic theology, but also consciously seek to defend feminism within the Church against those who, like Mary Daly and Daphne Hampson, have come to see the Bible or Christianity as incompatible with feminism.

Ruether taught at Harvard Divinity School and later at Garrett Evangelical Theological Seminary in Evanston, Illinois. She wrote her doctoral dissertation on Gregory of Nazianzus. She criticizes the Roman Catholic Church but does not abandon it; she rejects the classical Christology of Chalcedon, but not a modified, inclusive Christology. Like Tillich, she sees

---

47. Carolyn Osiek, *Beyond Anger: On Being a Feminist in the Church* (New York: Paulist, 1986); cf. Osiek, *A Woman's Place: House Churches in Earliest Christianity* (Minneapolis: Augsburg, 2005).

48. L. D. Scanzoni, "Revitalizing Interpretations of Ephesians 5:22," *Pastoral Psychology* 45 (1997): 317-39; L. D. Scanzoni and N. A. Hardesty, *All We're Meant to Be: A Biblical Approach to Women's Liberation* (Waco, Tex.: Word, 1974; 3rd rev. ed. 1992); *Neither Slave Nor Free: Helping Women Answer the Call to Church Leadership* (London and New York: Harper Collins, 1987); A. Michelson, *Women, Authority, and the Bible* (Downers Grove, Ill.: IVP, 1986); V. R. Mollenkott, *The Divine Feminism in the Biblical Imagery of God as Female* (New York: Crossroad, 1983); and Elaine Storkey, *What's Right with Feminism?* (London: SPCK, 1985).

much theological language as symbolic. Her book *The Church against Itself* (1967) sums up her twofold attitude, unlike Mary Daly's rejection of the Church.[49] For Ruether, God is the primal motive and ground of being, to be called God/ess, and she has moved toward Gaia and ecofeminism.[50] Trible works largely with Hebrew texts, seeking to focus on positive imagery of women and inclusive discourses, but does not hesitate to reject or to "rescue" bad images and what she regards as the trappings of patriarchal culture. Loades remains a member of the Church of England and seeks justice and the avoidance of discrimination, but is an altogether more moderate and inclusive voice than Daly or even Ruether.[51] Like Letty Russell and Mary Tolbert, these writers remain within the Christian Church.

3. Osiek distinguishes the former two categories from *"liberation feminists,"* though the difference is one of degree rather than of kind. In particular, this group appeals to the claims of justice and liberation from oppression, and reflects a heavy dependence on liberation hermeneutics. The narrowness of the contrast is evidenced by the inclusion of Ruether, Schüssler Fiorenza, and Russell under this heading. We have observed Schüssler Fiorenza's use of liberation theology and her use of a hermeneutic of suspicion. Russell reports on the effect of *The Liberating Word* (1976) in the introduction to *Feminist Interpretation of the Bible* (1985).[52] She is well aware of Katherine Sakenfeld's question, "How can feminists use the Bible, if at all?" In this volume she presents the divine contribution of twelve scholars, all from the American Academy of Religion or the Society of Biblical Literature, from 1979 and 1981 onward.

Cheryl Exum takes up Exodus 1:8–2:10 in one essay as showing how women took the initiative in making possible the liberation of Israel. Pharaoh's daughter is among those who took risks. Phyllis Trible rightly argues

---

49. Rosemary Ruether, *The Church against Itself* (New York: Herder and Herder; London: Sheed and Ward, 1967); cf. Ruether, *Gregory Nazianzus: Rhetor and Philosopher* (Oxford: Oxford University Press, 1969); Ruether, *Mary the Feminine Face of the Church* (Philadelphia: Westminster, 1977); Ruether, *Sexism and God-Talk*.

50. Ruether, *Sexism and God-Talk*, pp. 47-71; Ruether, *Gaia and God*; Ruether, *At Home in the World: The Letters of Thomas Merton and Rosemary Ruether* (Maryknoll, N.Y.: Orbis, 1995).

51. Loades, *Feminist Theology*, pp. 5-10. Cf. Loades, *Searching for Lost Coins* (London: SPCK, 1987).

52. Letty M. Russell, ed., *Feminist Interpretation of the Bible* (Philadelphia: Westminster, 1985), pp. 11-18.

for a multiplicity of hermeneutical methods and related disciplines. Understanding is to be based on proper exegesis. Schüssler Fiorenza presses the need for criteria in evaluating the reader's approach to Scripture. Russell writes, "Feminist and Liberation interpreters struggle critically with the texts, using the best resources available to understand the message in the light of the biblical horizon of promise."[53] There is liberating power in the text.

4. If we may extend Osiek's typology, Mary Daly and Daphne Hampson are known as *non-Christian or post-Christian feminists.* They have come to believe that Christianity is too irredeemably patriarchal to reconcile with feminism. Mary Daly (b. 1928) once taught at Boston College, founded by the Jesuits. But her eventual rejection of the faith led to her enforced retirement. In 1968 she published *The Church and the Second Sex,* which nearly led to her leaving the college, but for public support. She refused to admit male students to some of her classes because they supposedly inhibited discussion. In 1973 Daly produced *Beyond God the Father,* loosely and critically following Tillich. *Gyn/Ecology* appeared in 1978.

Daphne Hampson (b. 1944) was educated at Harvard and Oxford, and is emeritus professor at the University of St. Andrews, Scotland. With Monica Furlong and Una Kroll she urged the ordination of women in the Church of England. But in the end she became disillusioned with the Church and rejected the patriarchalism she associated with Christianity. She regarded an objective resurrection as impossible. Her book *After Christianity* (1996) earned her the label "post-Christian feminist."[54]

5. We have already indicated that *womanist theology* has a different agenda from most feminist theology. It does, however, overlap. Susan Thistlethwaite is a feminist writer who is concerned with rape and violence. There are also many contributions from Asia.[55]

6. Many feminist writers are influenced by *French feminism.* One of the contentions of most feminist writers is that woman's role is determined not by nature or biology but by convention or culture. Roland Barthes, Jacques Derrida, and Michel Foucault have done more than any to show that often

---

53. Russell, *Feminist Interpretation,* p. 17.

54. Daphne Hampson, *After Christianity* (London: SCM, 1996); cf. Hampson, *Theology and Feminism* (Oxford: Blackwell, 1990).

55. E.g., from India, Monica Jyotsha Melanchthon, "Akkumahadeu and the Samaritan Woman: Paradigms of Resistance and Spirituality," in *Border Crossings: Cross-Cultural Hermeneutics,* ed. D. N. Premnath (Maryknoll, N.Y.: Orbis, 2007), pp. 35-54.

what look like the findings of "nature" are in fact the products of convention. Barthes, for example, showed that furniture or clothes depend on choices of social background or aspiration, rather than such "natural" phenomena as comfort to the body, or cold or heat. Foucault showed that sexuality and madness are often perceived as such contingently in the light of norms of society rather than "by nature." Baudrillard and G. Deleuze contribute further to this philosophical background.

Simone de Beauvoir, as we have seen, wrote *The Second Sex* long ago in 1949. She draws on the interface between philosophy, literature, religion, and economics to ask, "What is a woman?" She is forced by an androcentric society to become "the other." Jacques Lacan then follows Beauvoir by combining structuralism and psychoanalysis. Sexual difference plays a greater part than in American feminism, and is developed by Julia Kristeva. She came to Paris from Bulgaria, and therefore in the late 1960s made use of Russian formalism in literature. Her major work, *Revolution of Language* (1974), is only of indirect relevance, however, to biblical interpretation. French feminism, with this pedigree, is less pragmatic and more psychological than American feminism. It is also highly complex and engages with semiotics. Even recent figures, namely, Luce Irigray (b. 1930) and Michèle le Dœuff (b. 1948), have backgrounds in philosophy, literature, and psycholinguistics or semiotics, unlike most of their American and British counterparts.[56] Whereas American feminists tend to stress "equality," French feminists tend to stress "difference."

7. By contrast, Janet Radcliffe Richards stresses similarities between the sexes, especially *universal rationality*. She refuses to countenance any notion that philosophy is a "male" subject, or to stress the intuitive, personal role of women at the expense of the rational. She represents yet another type of feminism.

It is not staking too much to say that from the late 1980s or early 1990s feminism has not been "one thing" but has fragmented into a series of different approaches. It is now difficult to speak of "the" feminist approach to Scripture. In addition to our subcategories, some, perhaps like Mary Tolbert, are difficult to place and represent broadly literary feminists. Nevertheless, with this important proviso, we shall attempt a broad assessment.

---

56. Michèle Le Dœff, *The Philosophical Enquiry*, trans. C. Gordon (London: Athlone Press, 1986), and Le Dœff, *Hippardia's Choice: An Essay concerning Women and Philosophy*, trans. T. Selons (Oxford: Blackwell, 1991).

7. A Provisional Assessment of Feminist Hermeneutics

We must call this assessment "provisional" because many feminist writers deny the right of men to comment on, or to expound, their work. However, the present writer is also indebted to the varied comments of his women students over the years.

1. There is no doubt that the early writers of 1979 and the early 1980s performed a valuable work by drawing attention to *concrete examples of women's experience and leadership, and their visible profile in the Church,* in such works as *Women of Spirit.* Priscilla was a gifted and learned woman in the Pauline churches, who, we know, instructed Apollos, and she is named several times before her husband Aquila.

Probably next in importance is Junia, whom Eldon Jay Epp has decisively argued is a woman who is named as an apostle explicitly in Romans 16:7. He shows that to change the name to a masculine form, Junias, is without basis, and shows the work of later hands. Phoebe is an "eminent" leader, and John N. Collins insists that a deacon (not deaconess) is a preacher or proclaimer of the gospel or the word of God, even if a deacon is also a delegated assistant to the apostle, bishop, or overseer. Mary Magdalene is called "the apostle of the apostles" by Elisabeth Schüssler Fiorenza, because in the Johannine account she was the first to bear witness to both the cross and the resurrection to the apostles themselves. Mary, Tryphena, and Persis are "laborers in the Lord" in Romans 16:6, 12.

In the Old Testament or Hebrew Bible, positive "images of women" are shown to belong to the women who took initiatives boldly that made possible the exodus (Miriam, the daughter of Pharaoh, and the midwives), and in Judges and in the historical books Hannah, Ruth, Deborah, and Huldah. Negative images associated sometimes with Eve, the daughter of Jephthah, and Tamar are shown to be mistaken. Phyllis Trible (with Karl Barth) shows that "image of God" is the gift to humanity as a whole, and not only to men.

In her *Texts of Terror* Trible offers us an example of both promoting positive images of biblical women and correcting perceptions that may be more negative. For example, Hagar not merely represents the other-than-Sarah line, she is also despised and rejected (Gen. 16:1-16). Trible claims that this is in solidarity and continuity with the Suffering Servant of Isaiah 40–55. Tamar and the daughter of Jephthah are sacrificed and discarded (Judg. 11:29-40). The love of God is motherly as well as fatherly.

2. *The apostolic status of Junia and other women* is carefully argued by Eldon Jay Epp, who is a respected biblical scholar and textual critic. He devotes virtually the whole of a small book to defending the feminine form of the name Junia, arguing that the name is regularly applied to women in the world of Paul's day. He also traces the second-generation alteration to the masculine form Junias. He notes the absence of accents in first-century Greek, and the convincing nature of the case.

Elisabeth Schüssler Fiorenza's case for Mary Magdalene as "apostle of the apostles" is also a strong one. But she insists that a rival tradition concerning Peter and Paul as "pillar apostles" in Galatians and elsewhere is simply due to a competitive rival tradition in the early Church. There is as little evidence as F. C. Barr's alleged opposition between a "Petrine" and "Pauline" party. The reason why more is made of Peter and Paul is not only that they were males, but they were conspicuous sinners, who were transformed by the resurrection. Walter Künneth makes this point, and I have discussed it in *New Horizons in Hermeneutics*.[57] The idea of lining up John with the appendix of Mark against Luke, with possible alliance with Matthew, seems perhaps to owe more to the argument than to New Testament scholarship. Nevertheless, if we leave behind some of the more speculative theory, the basic facts about Mary Magdalene are undeniable.

3. *The use of liberation hermeneutics* has been not only acknowledged but also stated as an advantage. The shared emphasis on the importance of pre-understanding is wholly correct. It is also correct that unless a reader seeks to be open to God and to justice, readings may be distorted. Yet too often liberation theology reads into texts what it wants to find there, and its use of texts is often unduly selective. Feminist literature similarly engages often with the same agenda of texts. While writers on *liberation* theology regularly engage with Exodus, Deuteronomy, and Revelation, *feminist* writers too often engage repeatedly with Eve, Deborah, Tamar, Hannah, Hagar, Ruth, Mary the Virgin, Mary Magdalene, Junia, and Priscilla.

4. Often the *absolute rejection of "patriarchal" presuppositions* fails to carry with it any criterion of the difference between cultural baggage and theological conviction. We noted Pannenberg's careful christological discussion of why "Father" is irreplaceable. The result again is sometimes picking

---

57. Walter Künneth, *The Theology of the Resurrection* (London: SCM, 1965), pp. 89-91; cf. 92-149; Thiselton, *New Horizons in Hermeneutics,* pp. 445-50; Schüssler Fiorenza, *In Memory of Her,* pp. 315-34.

out what is agreeable. This procedure is contrary to hermeneutical theory. Gadamer speaks of being "open" to the text, and to listening to "the other" in order to be shaped and molded. Ricoeur similarly speaks of hermeneutical distance and otherness. We appropriate as "ours" what has at first seemed strange and challenging.

Dietrich Bonhoeffer writes, "Either I determine the place in which I will find God, or I allow God to determine the place where he will be found. If it is I who say where God will be, I will always find then a God who somehow corresponds to me, is agreeable to me, fits in with my nature."[58] This particularly applies to reading "God" as female, or as Sophia. Most writers rightly regard God as without gender. Can we be sure what is "cultural" and what is theological?

5. It is good and positive that some texts are read with new perspectives, often through "the eyes of women."[59] The volume edited by Wendy Robins contains a study of biblical themes on refugees and migrants, women and work, women and their bodies, justice and nonviolence, health and environment, and the universal scope of the image of God. Valerie Saiving showed that the analysis of sin and fallenness in Tillich and especially in Reinhold Niebuhr failed to take adequate account of women's point of view, in which "triviality, destructibility, diffuseness, lack of an organizing center or focus" lie closer to the heart of the matter than pride.[60] Judith Plaskow follows Saiving some twenty years later with a more detailed study.[61] Daphne Hampson criticizes Niebuhr on the ground that too often sin for women may consist of "wanting to be rid of herself."[62]

Much is right in Schüssler Fiorenza's reconstruction, although many will question her treatment of Luke-Acts, Colossians, and the Pastoral Epistles. The Church needed to attend to its structure and organization in due time, and some statements about women may depend upon local situations. Meanwhile B. Brooten (1982, 1985) attended to the leadership of women in

---

58. Dietrich Bonhoeffer, *Meditating on the Word* (Cambridge, Mass.: Cowley, 1986), pp. 44-45.

59. Showalter, *The New Feminist Criticism*, and Wendy S. Robins, ed., *Through the Eyes of a Woman: Bible Studies on the Experience of Women* (Geneva: World YWCA Publications, 1986).

60. Saiving, "The Human Situation," pp. 100-112.

61. Judith Plaskow, *Sex, Sin, and Grace: Women's Experience and the Theologies of Reinhold Niebuhr and Paul Tillich* (Lanham, Md.: University Press of America, 1980).

62. Hampson, *Theology and Feminism*, p. 123.

Judaism. Claims about Jesus' overriding of Jewish "purity laws," however, may bear reexamination, especially in the light of dating. Again, in the Hebrew Bible, narratives embody apparent violence against women (Dinah in Gen. 34:1-12; the daughter of Jephthah in Judg. 11:34-40; the episode of brutal rape in Judg. 19:23-26; and the revenge of Jehu against Jezebel in 2 Kings 9:21-26). Mieke Bal has drawn on semiotics and structuralism to offer a feminist approach to the book of Judges.[63] Phyllis A. Bird has argued that new conceptual categories must be found to restore the visibility of women in the Old Testament.[64] This becomes part of the exercise to restore "images of women" in the Hebrew Bible.

6. Carol C. Christ and several other feminists have found problems with *the maleness of Christ*.[65] She and Mary Daly are probably among the most extreme and radical feminists in believing that "God" is female, and therefore a male Christ inappropriate. This takes them outside mainline Christian thought.

7. We have seen that *womanist writings* consciously distinguish themselves from white, middle-class, professional feminists. Their concerns and their agenda are often different. There is now no longer a single "feminist" school of thought, and womanist concerns underline this. Many have broadened the agenda to include pressing problems in their region.

8. French feminism still raises some distinctive problems. Do we value feminism because women are the same as men, or because they are different from men? Biological questions have faded in much American and British feminism, which assumes that any difference between the sexes is based on conventional roles rather than on theology or physiology. But is it a matter of convention?

9. Finally the vexed and controversial question of *grammatical gender* has not yet gone away. What is its relation to female persons or deities? The figure of *Sophia, wisdom*, and the feminine gender of the Hebrew *ruach* (the comparable Greek *pneuma* is neuter) form part of the argument here. But we have noted the decisive arguments of James Barr against the relevance of this. Wolfhart Pannenberg, who rightly stresses that "Father" as applied to

63. Mieke Bal, *Murder and Difference: Gender, Genre, and Scholarship on Sisera's Death*, trans. M. Gumpert (Bloomington: Indiana University Press, 1988; reprint 1992).

64. Phyllis A. Bird, *Missing Persons and Mistaken Identities: Women and Gender in Ancient Israel* (Minneapolis: Fortress, 1997).

65. Carol C. Christ, *The Laughter of Aphrodite* (New York: Harper and Row, 1987); cf. Christ, *Rebirth of the Goddess* (New York: Routledge, 1997).

God cannot be replaced, nevertheless argues that masculine gender as applied to God is no indication of sex.

10. The tendency of a few writers to make extravagant or speculative claims for Mary the mother of Jesus will not convince many Protestants. They honor Mary for her service, sacrifice, suffering, and obedience, but fail to see her as a new Eve, or to believe in the immaculate conception or the assumption because these lack biblical evidence.

To read the Bible "through the eyes of women" adds a valuable dimension to biblical hermeneutics. But a wide array of different results comes from this. We must not forget that a minority of feminists, including Janet Radcliffe Richards, Susanne Heine, and Elizabeth Achtemeier, insist that some feminists so overstate feminism as to be their own worst enemies. Nevertheless, some moderate and well-informed feminists struggle to avoid losing some fellow feminists from allegiance to the Christian faith. There is much to learn; and much to question.

8. Recommended Initial Reading

Loades, Ann, ed., *Feminist Theology: A Reader* (London: SPCK; Louisville: Westminster John Knox, 1990), pp. 1-72.

Schüssler Fiorenza, Elisabeth, *In Memory of Her: A Feminist Theological Reconstruction of Christian Origins* (New York: Crossroad; London: SCM, 1983).

Thiselton, Anthony C., *New Horizons in Hermeneutics: The Theory and Practice of Transforming Biblical Reading* (London: HarperCollins; Grand Rapids: Zondervan, 1992), pp. 43-60, 315-34, and 430-62.

Trible, Phyllis, *Texts of Terror: Literary-Feminist Readings of Biblical Narratives* (Philadelphia: Fortress, 1984), pp. 1-64.

CHAPTER XV

Reader-Response and Reception Theory

1. Reader-Response Theory: Its Origins and Diversity

Reader-response theory places an emphasis on the active role of the reader in interpreting texts. At its simplest, it depends on the axiom that a reader, or community of readers, "completes" the meaning of a text. It rests on the assumption that even if it may speak legitimately of an author's intention, that intention is not fulfilled until a reader (or readers) appropriates the text. The text, as the "sender" of a message or other content, remains a potential until the reader actualizes it. The text remains an abstraction until it is interpreted and understood by its reader. The theory also stresses that the reader is not a passive spectator but actively contributes something to the meaning. He or she is more than a passive observer.

A parable provides a classic example of a text that a reader's response "completes." Many years ago Charles H. Dodd defined a parable proper as "leaving the mind in sufficient doubt about its precise application to tease it into active thought."[1] But many parables are extreme examples of what Umberto Eco would call "open" texts. In a "closed" text, or "engineering" text, or in a medical prescription, the freedom of the "receiver," or the engineer or pharmacist, is severely restricted, in case the intention or instructions of the author become varied or distorted. Hence "reader-response theory" may apply especially or even only to "literary" texts, or to "open" texts within the Bible. Controversy often arises because of the kind of text under discussion.

---

1. C. H. Dodd, *The Parables of the Kingdom* (London: Nisbet, 1935), p. 16.

Some claim that the first steps toward reader-response theory were taken by I. A. Richards around 1930 and Louise Rosenblatt in 1938. But a more explicit reader-response theory derives from Wolfgang Iser (1926-2007). Iser now stands at the more moderate end of a spectrum, and Norman Holland (b. 1927) and Stanley Fish (b. 1938) at the more radical end. All those exponents write primarily as literary theorists. The movement largely constitutes a conscious reaction both against Romanticism (which stressed the intention of the author to produce a meaning) and more especially against literary formalism or the New Criticism (which stressed that the text or work generated meaning in its own right). We may note, by way of anticipation, that reception theory focuses on a diachronic or historic selection of how a particular community of readers has "received," or responded to, a given text over a particular time.

The more moderate reader-response theory originates in Germany, where Iser and Hans Robert Jauss give a greater controlling element to the text than many of their American counterparts. Iser looks back to Edmund Husserl's phenomenology and to its applications to literary theory by Roman Ingarden.[2] When, for example, we look at a table, often we may observe two or three of its legs, but we should be correct to assume that it has a fourth, even though we cannot see it. We are justified in *"filling in"* what is not given, and this *"completes"* our perception of the table, or in literature, of the text. In the same way, Iser argued, we *"complete"* the text.

Even C. S. Lewis (1898-1963) partly anticipated this emphasis in 1961 in his *Experiment in Criticism*.[3] In this work Lewis considered the reader's response a better indicator of the quality of a work than an author's intention. He distinguished between an "unliterary" reader, who might be indifferent to the work, or might shrug it off with "I've read it all before," and the "literary" reader, who would fully engage with the work. A "literary" reader might even read it many times, and would perhaps identify himself or herself with its characters. Under "The Rudiments of an Aesthetic Response," Iser's parallel distinguishes between the potential of a text or work and its "concretisation" in the aesthetic response of the reader. Indeed, the "work" is not identical with the text, or the subjectivity of the reader, but with the interac-

2. Wolfgang Iser, *The Act of Reading: A Theory of Aesthetic Response* (Baltimore: Johns Hopkins University Press, 1978), pp. 112-14, 151-53, and 157-59; cf. Hans Robert Jauss, *Toward an Aesthetic of Reception,* trans. T. Bahti (Minneapolis: University of Minnesota Press, 1982), pp. xii-xvii.

3. C. S. Lewis, *Experiment in Criticism* (Cambridge: Cambridge University Press, 1961).

tion between both.[4] Iser also distinguishes between "possible actualisations of the text" by contrasting the contemporary reader with the "ideal reader."[5] Reconstruction of the real reader depends on the survival of relevant documents. This may be actual report, or a reconstruction from the conventions and social assumptions of the time. The ideal reader would share at least some of the conventions and assumptions of the author, or know of them. Thus the reader could realize the full meaning-potential of the text.[6] Iser also discusses Holland's interest in the psychological processes of the reader.

Iser supports his theory by referring also to J. L. Austin's theory of performative language, or "illusionary" utterances. These perform some action *in* the very linguistic act of *saying* them. These must also employ a shared convention. "I name this ship" must be uttered by an authorized person, such as a president, queen, or shipping magnate's wife. Again, the utterance of a text must be "completed." If I say, "I pick George," and he mumbles, "Not playing," the utterance remains unfulfilled and empty. Austin cites an archbishop saying, "I declare this library open," but the key snaps off and remains in the lock. Has the action been performed? Austin observes, the procedure must be completed. Iser discusses "filling in" a blank, within the system of the text.[7]

In her discussion of parables, Susan Wittig makes use of this idea.[8] Wittig asks how multiple meanings emerge. This may be partly due to a difference between basic goals in interpretation, but it is equally likely to arise because different readers "fill in" the text in different ways. She calls a parable proper a "duplex connotative system in which the precise significance is left unstated."[9] The reader has to fill in the blank. To "Samaritan" in Luke 10:33-36 the reader inserts "neighbor."

In the teaching and proclamation of Jesus, it is astonishing that so little attention has been given to this identity of the audience. So argued J. Arthur Baird in 1969.[10] K. L. Schmidt distinguished between enemies, the crowds, followers, and the Twelve in 1919. T. W. Manson developed "audience criti-

---

4. Iser, *The Act of Reading*, p. 21; cf. pp. 20-50.
5. Iser, *The Act of Reading*, p. 27.
6. Iser, *The Act of Reading*, pp. 28-29.
7. Iser, *The Act of Reading*, pp. 182-95.
8. Susan Wittig, "A Theory of Multiple Meanings," *Semeia* 9 (1977): 75-105.
9. Wittig, "Theory of Multiple Meanings," p. 84.
10. J. Arthur Baird, *Audience Criticism and the Historical Jesus* (Philadelphia: Westminster, 1969), pp. 5-7 and 15-31.

cism" in 1931 as a tool for deciphering hermeneutic. Baird takes this further with a careful distinction between the disciples (D), the "crowd" of disciples (DG), the opponent crowd (GO), and opponents (O). His attention to detailed passages is impressive. He then correlates the audience with Jesus' method of communication, offering twenty-seven charts of these correlations. He concludes, "We cannot really understand what the logia are saying until we understand the audience to which they are attributed."[11]

This kind of historical version of reader-response cannot be criticized. But what are we to make of readers' responses today? Readers approach a text with some kind of *expectation,* as Iser and Jauss emphasize. Susan Suleiman also addresses the place of the reader in a relatively commonsense way in the book of essays she coedited entitled *The Reader in the Text.*[12] Against the self-confidence of those concerned only with the storyteller and the story, we must consider the *interaction* between the observed and the observer. We need to move away from formalism and the New Criticism.[13] She also criticizes the era of Dilthey and Romanticism, quoting Iser. The reading subject, however, is different from the audiences identified by Baird. The reader is "transhistorical," belonging to any time, place, or situation.[14] She appeals to Norman Holland's *Poems in Persons* (1973) and *Five Readers Reading* (1975).

In *The Reader in the Text* Tzetan Todorov discusses "reading as construction." He argues that the imaginary world evoked by the author is not quite that constructed by the reader.[15] Symbolized facts are interpreted, he argues. Social conventions and values cause interpretations to vary from age to age. We need to know who the reader is who makes the constructions. In "Do Readers Make Meaning?" Robert Crosman tackles a central issue. He considers E. D. Hirsch's traditional approach, and concludes that this assumes that a text can have only one meaning.[16] The notion, he argues, that readers are *constrained* by the text is fraught with problems. We arrive at the

---

11. Baird, *Audience Criticism,* p. 134.

12. Susan R. Suleiman and Inge Crosman, eds., *The Reader in the Text: Essays on Audience and Interpretation* (Princeton: Princeton University Press, 1980).

13. Suleiman, introduction to *The Reader in the Text,* p. 5.

14. Suleiman, introduction to *The Reader in the Text,* p. 25.

15. Tzetan Todorov, "Reading as Construction," in *The Reader in the Text,* p. 73; cf. pp. 67-82.

16. Robert Crosman, "Do Readers Make Meaning?" in *The Reader in the Text,* p. 156; cf. pp. 149-64.

"author's meaning" because we *decide* that we have reached it. But is this true?

This has brought us to the more radical end of the reader-response spectrum, with Stanley Fish, Norman Holland, and David Bleich. In his book *Is There a Text in This Class?* Fish traces back his view of interpretation from 1970-80.[17] He once asked himself whether meaning is somehow embedded in the text, but after journeying, came to believe that "the reader's response is not *to* the meaning; it *is* the meaning."[18] The status of the text is put into question, he says. It is a communal decision to determine what counts as literature. He writes about the author's meaning: "I did what critics always do. I 'saw' what my interpretive principles permitted or directed me to see, and then I turned round and attributed what I had 'seen' to the text."[19] The reader "finds" what he or she puts there.

In *Doing What Comes Naturally* Fish presses his case harder. Formalism is bound to be destroyed. But it is just as illogical, he argues, to seek a halfway house. We cannot but see the world and texts from the point of view of our own interests. We cannot pause halfway down "the anti-Formalist road."[20] He attacks Wolfgang Iser, Owen Fiss, and Donald Davidson for attempting a "middle way."[21]

Norman Holland combines an interest in literary theory with psychology. He studies the stresses, fears, and needs of readers, as well as their defenses. He claims that "every reader" transforms a narrative into a wish-fulfillment fantasy, in effect, about himself or herself.[22] The ego's defenses act like a doorstop, to keep at bay invitations to interpret the text in disappointing or challenging ways. Readers differ in their response, but it is radically decisive. In *The Double Perspective* (1988) David Bleich sees the reader's response as subjective and yet so important that we must not restrict "the

17. Stanley Fish, "Introduction, or How I Stopped Worrying and Learned to Love Interpretation," in Fish, *Is There a Text in This Class? The Authority of Interpretive Communities* (Cambridge: Harvard University Press, 1980), pp. 1-17.

18. Fish, "Introduction," p. 3.

19. Fish, "Introduction," p. 12.

20. Stanley Fish, "The Anti-Formalist Road," in Fish, *Doing What Comes Naturally: Change, Rhetoric, and the Practice of Theory in Literary and Legal Studies* (Oxford: Clarendon, 1989), pp. 1-35.

21. Fish, *Doing What Comes Naturally*, p. 120; cf. pp. 68-86 and 103-40.

22. Norman Holland, *Five Readers Reading* (New Haven: Yale University Press, 1975), p. 117; cf. pp. 113-21.

reader" to an educated male graduate. We need men and women, government and people, elite and ordinary, indeed the "double perspective" of "I and you" to take the place of "the" reader.[23]

2. An Evaluation and the Application of the Theory to Biblical Studies

1. Clearly when we are dealing with "open" texts like some of the parables of Jesus, an emphasis upon the reader to "complete" the meaning is helpful. The difference, for example, between Adolf Jülicher's insistence that authentic parables are simple, obvious, and similes and Robert Funk's reply that they are indirect, await a response, and metaphors makes this point abundantly clear. If, as Jülicher thought, authentic parables function merely to "convey thoughts" in a didactic way, reader response may not be the best approach, as John Barton seems to indicate.[24] But if the parable uses indirect communication to reach outsiders by metaphor, in the parable of the prodigal son, Funk comments (alluding to Fuchs with approval), "The word of grace ... divide(s) the audience into younger sons and elder sons — into sinners and Pharisees. . . . The parables interpret him. . . . *The Pharisees are those who insist on interpreting the word of grace rather than letting themselves be interpreted by it.*"[25]

Interpreting events and actions in a narrative probably falls also under the heading of an *"open"* text. Liberation theology provides a good example of Norman Holland's notion of readers identifying themselves with those involved in the liberating event of the exodus. They see themselves as first brought to consciousness of their situation, and then experience deliverance from bondage and oppression. Severino Croatto illustrates this in his commentary on Exodus. There are quasi-symbolic and analogical parallels in typology, which depend on the readers "seeing" an event or person as typological. In *Events and Their Afterlife,* A. C. Charity shows that the Psalms have provided limitless resources for the responses of readers throughout

23. David Bleich, *The Double Perspective: Language, Literacy, and Social Relations* (New York and Oxford: Oxford University Press, 1988), pp. vii-25 and throughout.

24. John Barton, *Reading the Old Testament: Method in Biblical Study* (London: Darton, Longman and Todd, 1984), pp. 204-7.

25. Robert W. Funk, *Language, Hermeneutic, and Word of God* (New York: Harper and Row, 1966), pp. 16-17, italics in original.

the ages.[26] In Psalm 86:8, 10, when the psalmist cries, "Thou alone art God," divine transcendence and sovereignty concern all who are in bondage, or the oppressed in every age. To declare, "This is Yahweh's doing, and it is marvelous in our eyes" (Ps. 118:23), resonates with every believer who wants to voice God's praise.

2. Yet one writer suggests that when he says, "Let anyone with ears to hear, listen!" (Mark 4:9), Jesus meant *not* "Make anything that you like out of this" but "Go and work it out." Whatever Stanley Fish may say, *we know that an interpretation can be wrong, even if it is arguable that in many cases more than one interpretation may be right.* Umberto Eco has distinguished decisively between "open" and "closed" texts.[27] "Closed" texts are those where the reader's response is predetermined in advance in terms of receiving the "thoughts" or message of the author in a single way "correctly." In everyday life a pharmacist does not "interpret" a doctor's medical prescription as he or she pleases, but provides the patient with what the prescription requires. The instructions of a kit or a car manual are a "closed" text. "The water has reached three feet" is precise and unambiguous. But "The water has reached danger level" may allow a little discussion in defining "danger." What degree of risk is involved? The text is nearly closed, but also partly "open."

Many, like Charles Hodge, treat the whole Bible as consisting of "closed" texts always in propositional form. But if they are even a little "open," this invites some interpretive judgments. I have used elsewhere the example of the text in Genesis 31:49, where Laban says, "The Lord watch between you and me, when we are absent from one another."[28] This is wrongly used by many Christians to refer to committing a loved one into God's care in a person's absence. The context shows that this cannot be what the text means. Jacob and Laban have played a series of disgraceful tricks on each other. So Laban now prays the Lord to keep watch and avenge him if tricky Jacob tries it once more.

Many of the Epistles convey "the thoughts" of their author that are understood by their audience in a way that is either right or wrong. Normally for large stretches of the Epistles, reader-response theory is inapplicable, ex-

---

26. A. C. Charity, *Events and Their Afterlife: The Dialectics of Christian Typology in the Bible and Dante* (Cambridge: Cambridge University Press, 1966), especially pp. 24-34.

27. Umberto Eco, *A Theory of Semiotics* (Bloomington: Indiana University Press, 1976), pp. 56, 68-86, and 136-39, and *The Role of the Reader* (London: Hutchinson, 1981), p. 4.

28. Anthony C. Thiselton, *Can the Bible Mean Whatever We Want It to Mean?* (Chester, U.K.: Chester Academic Press, 2005), pp. 10-11.

cept in the basic sense of appropriating the text. It is insufficiently recognized, it seems, that many texts allow a reader response in a more *creative* way, *but within limits.*

This seems to be what Hugh of St. Victor, Nicholas of Lyra, and even Melanchthon were broadly suggesting when *they permitted allegorical or even anagogical and moral interpretation but insisted that the historical or literal in effect provided a "control."* We could not otherwise grade a gobbet (an extract of a text) as right, partly right, or plain wrong in a university or seminary exam paper. This does not merely mean "acceptable to the community" (often called the "guild") of biblical scholars. Even Gadamer appeals to the common sense of a community. It is possible that even Stephen Fowl, in spite of the excellence of most of his applications, does not sufficiently take account of this in the more theoretical part of his book on interpretation.[29]

Other terms in effect equivalent to "open" and "closed" texts are "literary" and "transmissive" texts. Whether a text is "literary" remains a judgment of the reader, as Nicholas Wolterstorff and John Searle argue, whereas whether a text is fiction is part of the responsibility of the author. If God or an apostle or prophet is the "sender," it is critical to decide whether the text is transmissive or literary.

One well-known example of reader-response theory comes in Robert M. Fowler's book *Loaves and Fishes.*[30] He distinguishes between the prima facie accounts of the miraculous feeding of the four thousand with seven loaves in Mark 8:1-10 and the miraculous feeding of the five thousand with five loaves in Mark 6:30-44. The pivotal verse is Mark 8:21: "Do you not yet understand?" Fowler argues that first the reader is invited to reject the literal meaning. How could the disciples be so obtuse as not to expect a second miracle if the first (the five thousand) had just occurred? Second, the author or editor knows that the disciples are slow to grasp and perceive who Jesus is. Third, the reader compares his own more adequate Christology with the foolishness of the disciples. The reader's response is that of christological confession.

There is much to admire in Fowler's theory. But in the end it is speculative and relies upon a particular redaction-critical approach. Mark is manipulating the reader, and has little interest in historical narration. It is true that

---

29. Stephen E. Fowl, ed., *The Theological Interpretation of Scripture: Classic and Contemporary Readings* (Oxford: Blackwell, 1997).

30. Robert M. Fowler, *Loaves and Fishes: The Function of the Feeding Stories in the Gospel of Mark,* Society of Biblical Literature Dissertation Series 54 (Chico, Calif.: Scholars Press, 1981), pp. 43-90 and 91-148.

we credited Mark with deploying narrative time, but this is clearly demanded by the text. There are limits to how manipulative Mark is believed to be. This is a good scenario to explore, but the evidence for it is less than Fowler claims.

American literary criticism yields reader-response theory perhaps too easily, because most of its exponents are not dealing with authoritative biblical texts. Even E. McKnight's *Bible and the Reader* mainly discusses French structuralism, Russian formalism, the narratology of Propp and Greimas, and Jauss, Hirsch, Wayne Booth, and Norman Holland more than the work of biblical specialists.[31] But Stanley Fish admits that in reader-response criticism there is no mechanism for holding interpretation in check.[32] Fish rightly stresses the interpretative community, so it is not all up to the lone individual. But there is no way of providing a critical check against the self-interests and desires of the community or what it finds "useful" to its own desires.[33] The Reformation becomes merely the preferences of one or more communities over the Roman Catholic Church. But this emphatically was not what motivated Luther, Melanchthon, Tyndale, and Calvin. Moreover, at the same time Fish doubts a serious epistemology other than a pragmatic one. Robert Corrington has shown that this distinctive pragmatism is endemic in much American hermeneutics.[34]

3. Is Allegorical Interpretation a Subcategory of Reader-Response Theory? A Suggestion

Philo and Origen, we saw, were concerned about their readers. Admittedly there were other reasons to allegorize. Some of their motives were theological. They also shared the Hellenistic notion that "body" or "history" was associated with the contingent or material realm while "soul" or "spirit" belonged to the eternal realm. For all Christian expositors, however, the incarnation challenged a sharp dualism between the two, or else the danger of Docetism threatened a firmly incarnational theology. Yet even if this con-

---

31. Edgar V. McKnight, *The Bible and the Reader: An Introduction to Literary Criticism* (Philadelphia: Fortress, 1985).

32. Fish, *Is There a Text?* p. 9.

33. Fish, *Doing What Comes Naturally*, pp. 1-33 and 68-86 (on Iser).

34. Robert S. Corrington, *The Community of Interpreters: On the Hermeneutics of Nature and the Bible in the American Philosophical Tradition* (Macon, Ga.: Mercer University Press, 1987), especially pp. 1-29.

cern had little or nothing to do with reader-response theory, the first motivation, namely, a concern that the text should be relevant to the hearers and readers, clearly does bear closely on the issue.

In interpreting the parables of Jesus, sometimes a fine line is drawn between allegorical interpretation and reader-response theory. In the Church Fathers and medieval Church, often allegory arose from imposing Church doctrine on to the text. Yet this is precisely why Andrew Louth and perhaps Henri de Lubac, among others, call for a "return to allegory."[35] We must go back to the Fathers, Louth argues, and their tradition.[36] This brings theology back into biblical interpretation. Lubac denies that Christianity is a religion of the *book* but affirms that it is a religion of the *word*.[37] Allegory is usually Christ-centered. Louth appeals to I. A. Richards, T. S. Eliot, and even Gadamer. These at times border on reader-response theory. Origen declares that the whole of Scripture and theology accord together as God's symphony. Louth likens them to polyphonic harmony. Hugh of St. Victor speaks of what Scripture means as a whole. The context is not merely the historical situation out of which a text emerges, but a life-context, which involves more than an isolated text.

Old Testament "types" presuppose a larger context. The distinction between allegory and typology is valid but should not be exaggerated. G. W. H. Lampe writes, "The saving work of Christ . . . was thus seen as the moment which gave significance to the whole course of covenant-history that had preceded it."[38] Luther would not have dissented from this, and although he came increasingly to see allegory as an unacceptable way of avoiding the plain sense of Scripture, much of his attitude depends on what Scripture passage we are expounding and for what purpose it was used. Calvin believed "Allegories ought to be carried no further than Scripture expressly sanctions: so far are they from forming a sufficient basis to found doctrines upon."[39] His chief objection in this section is to "flimsy allegories" that evade plain meaning.

35. Andrew Louth, "Return to Allegory," in Louth, *Discerning the Mystery: An Essay on the Nature of Theology* (Oxford: Clarendon, 1983), pp. 96-131.

36. Louth, *Discerning the Mystery*, p. 96.

37. Louth, *Discerning the Mystery*, p. 101.

38. G. W. H. Lampe and K. J. Woollcombe, *Essays on Typology* (London: SCM, 1957), pp. 25-26.

39. John Calvin, *Institutes of the Christian Religion*, trans. Henry Beveridge, 2 vols. (London: James Clarke, 1957), 2.5.19; p. 291.

Yet the Reformers were as aware as any that blindness and sin on the part of the self could lead to distorted interpretations of Scripture. They allowed what we might call "reader response" if it was carried out in openness to the Holy Spirit and in purity of heart. Perhaps this is akin to allegory. The plain historical sense conveys the basic foundational meaning when texts are transmissive or closed. When texts are poetic, metaphorical, or "literary," the reader's response becomes relevant. However, to claim that the effect *constitutes* the meaning of the text, as Fish does, fails to take account of what God may speak through the agency of his prophets, apostles, or Jesus, especially in didactic or prophetic literature.

4. The Recent Turn to Reception Theory and Hans Robert Jauss

Reader-response theory explores the *synchronic* response of readers at a particular time from the first audience to the present. *Reception theory* explores a *diachronic* segment of readers over a particular period, perhaps that of the Church Fathers, the Reformers, or any era of history. But it is not simply the history of interpretation. One stream of thought equates reception history with Hans-Georg Gadamer's term *Wirkungsgeschichte,* which G. Barden and J. Cumming in 1960 translated as "effective history" but Joel Weinsheimer and Donald Marshall in 1989 translated as *"history of effects."* It has also been translated, probably best of all, as "history of influences," meaning both the influence of readers on texts and the influence of text on readers, as a two-way process and method of shaping traditions.[40] Ulrich Luz declares that it includes the "history, reception, and actualising of the text in media *other* than the commentary, for example in sermons, canonical law, hymnody, art and in actions and suffering of the church." Neglect of this aspect and its relation to the interpreter's theology makes some volumes in the recent Blackwell series of "reception" disappointing.

Reception history was founded, in effect, by Hans Robert Jauss (1921-97), a former pupil of Gadamer. He was brought up in the Pietist tradition, and in the Second World War fought on the Russian front. In 1944 he began

---

40. Ulrich Luz, *Matthew 1–7: A Commentary,* trans. W. C. Linss (Minneapolis: Augsburg Fortress; Edinburgh: T. & T. Clark, 1989), p. 11; cf. pp. 95-99; Luz, *Matthew 8–20,* trans. W. C. Linss (Minneapolis: Augsburg Fortress; London: SCM, 2001); and Luz, *Matthew 21–28,* trans. J. E. Crouch (Minneapolis: Fortress; London: SCM, 2005).

his studies in Prague, and in 1948 at Heidelberg. In the early 1950s he was influenced by Heidegger and Gadamer. In 1952 he took his doctorate at Heidelberg on time and remembrance, or the relation between past and present. His *Habilitation* (postdoctoral) thesis concerned Romance philology. In 1961 he became professor in the University of Giessen, and then collaborated with Wolfgang Iser. Finally in 1966 he set up literary studies in the new University of Constance in southern Germany, where his collaborative research group of five professors, including Iser, became known as the Constance School. Jauss's 1967 inaugural lecture, "Literary History as a Challenge to Literary Theory," became the foundation document of reception theory.[41]

Jauss shared the view of Gadamer and Ricoeur that beginning with the isolated "consciousness" of Descartes, abstracted from history and social life, was fruitless. Our horizon must include the past and ideally the future, as well as our present situation. In particular, when we read a book, we bring to it "a horizon of *expectation.*" All our concerns, as Gadamer and Collingwood argued, come from *questions with motivations,* not from fixed abstract "problems." Like Gadamer, Jauss rejected a false "objectivity" and positivism, which either ignored time and history or regarded the past as "closed." In effect, he begins where Gadamer leaves off. Further work needs to be done on how "influences" affect an ongoing tradition, and its social conditions. A work of art outlasts the conditions on which it originated. Jauss accepts the principle of *"defamiliarization"* or estrangement in Russian formalism, according to which what seems familiar may by its strangeness disrupt normal perceptions. He gives more place than Gadamer to disruptive, or challenging, or even provocative elements in history. The text may live on, but readers change and bring new horizons of experience, which change the readers' perceptions from age to age. This takes us through the first twenty pages of Jauss's lecture. Now he presents seven theses.

1. The first thesis calls for a *renewal of literary history,* to see these *changes* and expose the fallacy of "objectivism." He says, "A literary event can have an effect only if those who come after it . . . respond to it."[42] This is mediated through *a horizon of expectation,* in other words, by what the reader expects in or from the work.

2. As his thesis 2 Jauss states that the reader will tend to avoid what is

41. Jauss, *Aesthetic of Reception,* pp. 3-45.
42. Jauss, *Aesthetic of Reception,* p. 22.

personally *threatening*. (This is the beginnings of "politeness theory," discussed briefly in our concluding comments.) Although Jauss does not say so explicitly, this applies especially to a liberal reading of the Bible, to liberation and to postcolonial theology, and to some feminist hermeneutics (see chapters XIII and XIV). There are psychological factors, such as we find in Holland or Bleich, in reader-response theory, and Brown and Levinson in politeness theory. The text is corrected, altered, distorted, or even reproduced.

3. The third thesis declares that the horizons of expectation will determine an influence on the audience, which it presupposes at a particular time. *A text can change our horizons.* It can satisfy, surpass, disappoint, or refute old expectations.[43] This is true, although Jauss does not mention it, of the formative power of the Bible.

4. As his fourth thesis Jauss states that reconstructing the actual horizons of expectation enables the critic or reader to pose new questions of the text and to discover how the reader *might* have *understood* the work. It brings differences between different readers fully into view. It is less subjective than Fish or Holland, for it suggests a *narrative way* of answering the questions posed by the text. It gives privilege to "the verdict of the ages," comparing cumulative verdicts with maverick readings, even though *successive* readings may differ.

5. Thesis 5 declares that this kind of exploration takes place within the *historical unfolding* of an understanding. Whatever emerges as "new" constitutes an aesthetic or artistic category, whether it relates to the surpassing, surprising, or correcting of expectations.

6. Thesis 6 underlines the synchronic and diachronic axes of linguistics. It takes account *diachronically* of changes of mind.

7. Thesis 7 declares that reception history must focus on a special history, or *special period* of history, together with the social functions of that period. In one direction this sheds light on the text; in another direction it sheds light on the readers. Jauss stresses the "*socially formative* function" of texts.[44] Among other examples, this applies preeminently to the Bible.

In his next essay Jauss discusses history, history of art, and the philosophy of history, with reference to Voltaire, Winckelmann, Herder, Droysen, Ranke, and others. He argues that the timelessly beautiful also constitutes a product of historical experience and influences. Only as the horizon of ex-

---

43. Jauss, *Aesthetic of Reception*, p. 25.
44. Jauss, *Aesthetic of Reception*, p. 45, italics in original.

pectation changes can we consider the claims of art or aesthetics.[45] Next, Jauss explores medieval literature, rejecting the value of a formalist approach. He then considers Goethe and Baudelaire, distinguishing various horizons of readings, and their poetic texts. His primary interest is in poetic literature, and he does not ask, it seems, how it applies to the Bible.

In biblical studies reception theory or reception history has recently begun to seize people's imagination, becoming a major theme at certain conferences and in certain books. Luz has applied reception theory to the Gospel of Matthew, in the Evangelisch-katholischer Kommentar zum Neuen Testament (EKK series, English, 1989-2005). In the same series Ulrich Wilckens has applied this in his commentary on Romans.[46] I have attempted various extracts under the heading "Post-history of the Text," in 1 Corinthians.[47] The Blackwell Bible Commentaries constitute a new series, which includes David Gunn on Judges, Mark Edwards on John, and Chris Rowland and Judith Kovacs on Revelation (2003-5).[48] This series is meant to be a reception history, but so far two or three of the earliest volumes do not fully measure up to Luz's definition of the subject, and the selections of historical texts seem rather arbitrary. It is as if the aim was to produce only a history of interpretation. Thomas Oden edits a series of patristic selections by InterVarsity Press.[49] This is useful, but is more a random history of interpretation. Brevard Childs produced a full, early commentary on Exodus, which regularly, but not uniformly, included a history of exegesis.[50] This movement, however, is so new that it fails to feature in the *Dictionary of Biblical Interpretation* (1999), edited by John Hoyes, and surprisingly in

45. Jauss, *Aesthetic of Reception,* p. 64.

46. Ulrich Wilckens, *Der Brief an die Römer,* 3 vols., Evangelisch-katholischer Kommentar zum Neuen Testament 6.1-3 (Neukirchen: Neukirchener, 1978-82): the volumes are on Romans 1–5 (1978); Romans 6–11 (1980); Romans 12–16 (1982); 3rd and 4th edition of vols. 2 and 3 (2003-5).

47. Anthony C. Thiselton, *The First Epistle to the Corinthians: A Commentary on the Greek Text,* New International Greek Testament Commentary (Grand Rapids: Eerdmans; Carlisle: Paternoster, 2000).

48. Judith Kovacs and Christopher Rowland, *Revelation* (Oxford: Blackwell, 2004); Mark Edwards, *John* (Oxford: Blackwell, 2004); and David M. Gunn, *Judges* (Oxford: Blackwell, 2005).

49. E.g., Thomas C. Oden, *Genesis 1–11,* ed. Andrew Louth (Downers Grove, Ill., and Leicester: InterVarsity, 2001).

50. Brevard S. Childs, *Exodus: A Commentary* (London: SCM, 1974), pp. 22-24, 40-42, 84-87, 164-68, and so on.

the *Dictionary for Theological Interpretation of the Bible*, edited by Kevin Vanhoozer.[51]

5. Reception Theory and Specific Biblical Passages

Brevard S. Childs (1923-2007) was one of the first modern commentators, if not the very first, to include a history of exegesis in a commentary (in his 1974 commentary on Exodus). Often he considered Philo and the Targums, and regularly looked at the Church Fathers, the Protestant Reformation, and modern scholarship from the eighteenth to the twentieth centuries. Admittedly this is "the history of exegesis," which is not the same as "reception criticism," although Childs seeks to show what communities of faith made of the biblical texts. Perhaps the influence of Hans Frei has colored the "Yale School," or perhaps Childs influenced Frei. At all events, both owe much to Barth. Several attempts by other writers do not give more than a history of interpretation. But they imply that the Bible serves the Church.

Exodus 2:11-25, for example, tells of Moses' slaying of an Egyptian and his flight to Midian. After discussing the Old Testament context, Childs looks at the rabbinic and Philonic tradition and then the New Testament tradition in Acts 7, which confirms Moses' authority, and sees in his "exile" a larger pattern of disobedience among God's people. In Hebrews 11:24-28 Moses refused to be called the son of Pharaoh, choosing rather to share ill treatment with the people of God. The element of choice is underlined. Rather than enjoying the "fleeting pleasures of sin, he . . . suffered for Christ." This is implicit in Exodus but explicit in the New Testament. It is a real choice made in faith.[52] The writer's boldest innovation concerns "abuse suffered for Christ," which coheres with contrast between the visible and invisible. This is more than typological; it indicates "actual participation by Moses in Christ's shame" (cf. Heb. 10:33; 13:13).[53]

In his comparisons with the Church Fathers, Childs compares Gregory of Nazianzus, *Epistles* 76; Tertullian, *Against Marcion* 4.28; and Ambrose, *On the Duties of Clergy* 1.36. In Tertullian's treatise we have to reconstruct

51. John Hayes, ed., *Dictionary of Biblical Interpretation*, 2 vols. (Nashville: Abingdon, 1999), and Kevin Vanhoozer, ed., *Dictionary for Theological Interpretation of the Bible* (London: SPCK, 2005).

52. Childs, *Exodus*, p. 36.

53. Childs, *Exodus*, p. 37.

Marcion's use of Exodus 2:13, 14, but it seems that Tertullian takes up Moses' willingness to intervene in a dispute with Christ's unwillingness to do so. But the case in the Gospels is different, Tertullian argues. Indeed, "Christ had been present in Moses . . . the Spirit of the Creator."[54] Ambrose refers to the same incident of Moses' intervention (Exod. 2:11) and sees it as an example of courage.[55] Aquinas defended Moses' action because to defend the innocent is right. Calvin argued that Moses was armed by God's command. Modern commentators speak of his sympathy for the oppressed.

Exodus 3:1–4:17 receives a very full treatment. Exodus 3:6 is cited in Matthew 22:32, Mark 12:26, and Luke 20:37. Exodus 3:6 is cited as proof of resurrection. God, the living God, is God of the living, not of the dead (Matt. 22:32). Stephen also refers to Exodus 3 in Acts 7:30. Revelation 1:8 speaks of the God who is, who was, and is to come. In Jewish exegesis Moses is the good shepherd. Most of the Church Fathers speak about Exodus 3. Irenaeus says that the "I am" has come in Christ to bring deliverance.[56] Therefore his being is declared through the Son. Ambrose speaks of "He Who Is" as being both Christ and Moses.[57] Aquinas expounds God as substance without "accidents."[58] Luther offers an allegorical interpretation, but Calvin relates it to the ontology and eternity of the Son. Only through the Mediator does God communicate.[59] In the twentieth century Barr and others see the Hebrew tense as denoting divine action rather than abstract Being, interpreting the Hebrew imperfect as an indefinite with the future meaning of "I will be."

Jauss believes that even "provocative" interpretation can be of positive value in making us think harder about the passage. In biblical studies, rather than losing heart at the variety of interpretations, it is encouraging to see *why* they arose, that is, their motivations and influences. Especially different expectations are important, and the questions asked of the text. We do not stand at an Archimedean point outside history, as Gadamer also stresses.

We take three brief examples from Ulrich Luz on Matthew. The first concerns Matthew 1:18-25.[60] Luther and Calvin address the question of whether the Hebrew ʿalmāh in Isaiah 7:14 means "young woman" or "virgin."

---

54. Tertullian, *Against Marcion* 4.28.

55. Ambrose, *On the Duties of Clergy* 1.36.180.

56. Irenaeus, *Against Heresies* 3.6.2.

57. Ambrose, *Of the Christian Faith* 1.13.83.

58. Aquinas, *Summa Theologiae,* part I, chapter 13, qu. 11.

59. Childs, *Exodus,* pp. 85-86.

60. Luz, *Matthew 1–7,* pp. 123-27.

They agree that the Hebrew means "young woman" but follow the Septuagint translation "virgin." The Christian interpretation is not referring to Hezekiah alone, but also to the Messiah. Luz himself also discusses Mary's perpetual virginity. He points out that Jerome originated this because of Mariological interests and influences. Can it be related to the intention of the text in any way? Luz argues that this passage was originally about Jesus but came to be perceived as only about Mary. It then came to function in the framework of a trinitarian doctrine of the Holy Spirit as giver of life. But in the nineteenth century Schleiermacher criticized the whole notion of a virgin birth; the passage was intended only to stress divine initiative. Many recent critical commentators associate the virgin birth with a pagan background, taking it a long way from Matthew 1:18-25.

After Vatican II, few Catholics would probably dissent from this range of views. The Biblical Commission's document *The Interpretation of the Bible in the Church* (1994) approves of all the tools used in Protestant scholarship, including "the" historical critical method, literary analysis, a sociological approach, feminist interpretation and hermeneutics.[61] But in the Anglican–Roman Catholic Agreed Statement, it is asserted that the passage is really about Jesus and the incarnation, not so much about Mary.

We take as a further example the visit of the Magi in Matthew 2:1-12.[62] Justin ascribes its origin, Luz notes, to an Arabic version of Psalm 72:10 and Isaiah 60:6, while an early tradition sees the Magi as coming from Mesopotamia or Ethiopia. In the medieval period the "three" Magi represent descendants of Ham, Shem, and Japheth. They were perceived as "kings" on the basis of Isaiah 60:3 and Psalm 72:10-11. The Reformers regarded all these views as groundless and to be rejected. The names Caspar, Melchior, and Balthasar did not emerge until the Middle Ages. In art, Caspar is a beardless young man; Melchior, a bearded old man; and Balthasar, a dark or black man. This reaches a peak of discrepancy with the text. The text itself has little influence on its reception.

In Matthew 5:1-8 (the Beatitudes) Luz sees "an immense wealth of Christian self-understanding and Christian hope."[63] Clement of Alexandria predictably sees it as seeking the purity of heart sought by the perfect Gnos-

---

61. Joseph A. Fitzmeyer, ed., *The Biblical Commission's Document "The Interpretation of the Bible in the Church": Text and Commentary* (Rome: Pontifical Biblical Institute, 1995), pp. 26-131.

62. Luz, *Matthew 1–7*, pp. 139-41.

63. Luz, *Matthew 1–7*, p. 240; cf. pp. 239-41.

tic.[64] The perfect believer has struggled victoriously against the flesh. Irenaeus takes up the promise to the pure in heart of "seeing God" and looks forward to its eschatological fulfillment in the future.[65] Gregory of Nyssa also looks forward to the end time.[66] Luther argues that the Beatitudes seek perfection in order that we may "seek God in the miserable erring and labouring" that characterizes the Christian life. Post-Reformation Pietism sees perfection as referring to the inner-worldly internal life. Athanasius is concerned for the vision of God. In all these cases we can see from their life and thought how they "influenced" the text, and were influenced by it. For Luther, grace to the poor and humble is the essence of salvation.[67] Luz himself stresses that grace alone gives the possibility of obedience, and underlines eschatological fulfillment.

Other commentaries in the Evangelisch-katholischer series give some examples of the reception theory of the Pauline Epistles. For example, we have referred to Ulrich Wilckens, *Der Brief an die Römer*. I have attempted to offer this in my commentary on the Greek text of 1 Corinthians (2000).[68] The treatment of chapter 15 on the resurrection is only one example. Less attention was given in the second century to Paul's logical and historical argument in 1 Corinthians 15:1-11 and 12-19 than to assessing the destiny of Christians or humankind, and perhaps the role of the body. In 15:35-49 we see the influence of Platonism, as if immortality were a capacity of the human soul, rather than the resurrection depending on an act of God.

Ignatius accepts that Christians will be raised in the likeness of Christ.[69] The context is partly his eagerness for martyrdom. Polycarp sees the resurrection of Christ as the guarantee for that of believers.[70] This is also based on divine promise and order. The *Didache* rightly sees the resurrection as an end-event happening at the parousia.[71] *1 Clement* takes up Paul's analogy of the seed, which is again clothed after its old body is lost.[72] We wait for the

---

64. Clement, *Stromata* 2.20; 4.6; and 5.1.

65. Irenaeus, *Against Heresies* 4.9.2.

66. Gregory of Nyssa, *On Virginity* 24; and *Against Eunomius* 3.2.

67. Martin Luther, "The Sermon on the Mount," in *Luther's Works*, ed. J. Pelikan, 56 vols. (St. Louis: Concordia, 1955-), 21:285-94.

68. Thiselton, *First Epistle*, pp. 1306-13.

69. Ignatius, *Epistle to the Trallians* 9.2.

70. Polycarp, *Epistle to the Philippians* 2.2; 5.2.

71. *Didache* 16.6.

72. *1 Clement* 24.1, 5.

dawn during sleep. Justin Martyr (d. 165) knew Platonism and Stoicism, and engaged in debate with Trypho the Jew. Justin tells him that all who live acceptably will be raised.[73] Justin argues in his *First Apology* that "God . . . can do anything we are unable to conceive," and this includes resurrection.[74] This is precisely true to the logic of Paul's argument. The Gnostic *Treatise on the Resurrection* from the Nag Hammadi library, however, clearly states, "You already have the resurrection."[75] Irenaeus explicitly attacks such a view. He defines "spiritual" persons as those who are directed by the Holy Spirit.[76] Belief in the resurrection depends on belief in God.[77] He also underlines the transformative nature of resurrection: "We shall all be changed" (1 Cor. 15:42-52).[78]

In the third century Tertullian is concerned to emphasize "bodily" resurrection, and in his Montanist period also the agency of the Spirit.[79] Origen, in effect, "demythologizes" the resurrection. He stresses how different the resurrection "body" will be, and stresses its transformation. Origen is aware of the need for caution in expounding this chapter and this concept.[80] In the fourth century Gregory of Nyssa expounds resurrection in terms of restoration, namely, the *apokatastasis* of all things. There will be a return to paradise.[81] Chrysostom correctly calls attention to continuity of identity and transformation.

Luther sees chapter 15 as integral to 1 Corinthians. So also does Karl Barth. It is "the clue to its meaning, from which place light is shed on the whole, and it (the Epistle) becomes intelligible as a unity."[82] Both identify "some have no knowledge of God" as fundamental for 1 Corinthians 15; Luther urges, "Be content. . . . Leave it to God what he will do."[83] Both relate resurrection to justification by grace through faith: human "achievement" is

73. Justin, *Dialogue with Trypho* 45.1, 2.

74. Justin, *Apology* 1.19.

75. Epistle of Rheginos, *On the Resurrection* 49.15, 16.

76. Irenaeus, *Against Heresies* 5.6.1.

77. Irenaeus, *Against Heresies* 5.3.2.

78. Irenaeus, *Against Heresies* 3.19.1.

79. Tertullian, *Against Marcion* 5.10, and *On the Resurrection of the Flesh* 34 and 48-55.

80. Origen, *De principiis* 2.7.1-4; cf. 8.1-5; and *Commentary on the Soul and Resurrection* 3.5.

81. Gregory of Nyssa, *On the Making of Man* 17.2; 22.6.

82. Karl Barth, *The Resurrection of the Dead*, trans. H. J. Stenning (London: Hodder and Stoughton, 1933), p. 11.

83. *Luther's Works*, 28:180 (in Weimarer Ausgabe, 36:647).

excluded; everything depends on the grace and sovereign power of God. Luther declares, "Let him cease to believe in himself and believe in God."[84]

We have given three sets of samples of reception theory respectively from Exodus, Matthew, and 1 Corinthians. Judith Kovacs, *1 Corinthians Interpreted by Early Christian Commentators,* remains relevant, and other treatments are emerging, such as John L. Thompson, *Reading the Bible with the Dead* (2007); David P. Parris, *Reading the Bible with Giants* (2006); and part 2 of *The Theological Interpretation of Scripture* (1997), edited by Stephen Fowl.[85] They show the contemporary interest in this subject.[86] Parris and Fowl were my former successful Ph.D. candidates. Parris begins by explaining how the variety of interpretation, far from leading to despair, can give encouragement by seeing what factors determined this.

It is also worth mentioning the work of Ormond Rush, *The Reception of Doctrine.* He appropriates Jauss and examines the complex concept of "reception."[87] He compares Grillmeier, Congar, and others on reception, and sees it as bringing together unity and plurality in the tradition. It has become one of the more positive movements in hermeneutics, showing where, how, and why diversity arises, and distinguishing mainline tradition from the merely maverick scholar. All those who write on the subject at least ask us: What *expectations* do we have of a text? How does time and history *change or mold* these?

6. Recommended Initial Reading

Fowl, Stephen E., "Making Stealing Possible" (as an example of reader-response), in Fowl, *Engaging Scripture: A Model for Theological Interpretation* (Oxford: Blackwell, 1998), pp. 161-77.

---

84. *Luther's Works,* 25:284 (in Weimarer Ausgabe, 56:291).

85. Fowl, *Theological Interpretation of Scripture,* pp. 103-389.

86. David Paul Parris, *Reading the Bible with Giants: How 2,000 Years of Biblical Interpretation Can Shed Light on Old Texts* (London and Atlanta: Paternoster, 2006); John L. Thompson, *Reading the Bible with the Dead* (Grand Rapids: Eerdmans, 2007); cf. Judith L. Kovacs, *1 Corinthians Interpreted by Early Christian Commentators* (Grand Rapids: Eerdmans, 2005).

87. Ormond Rush, *The Reception of Doctrine: An Appropriation of Hans Robert Jauss' Reception Aesthetics and Literary Hermeneutics* (Rome: Pontifical Gregorian University, 1997).

Freund, Elizabeth, *The Return of the Reader: Reader-Response Criticism* (London and New York: Methuen, 1987), pp. 90-151.

Parris, David Paul, *Reading the Bible with Giants: How 2,000 Years of Biblical Interpretation Can Shed Light on Old Texts* (London and Atlanta: Paternoster, 2006), pp. 1-23 and 191-214.

Thiselton, Anthony C., *New Horizons in Hermeneutics: The Theory and Practice of Transforming Biblical Reading* (London: HarperCollins; Grand Rapids: Zondervan, 1992), pp. 516-50.

CHAPTER XVI

Postmodernism and Hermeneutics

1. Is Postmodernity Compatible with Christian Faith? Three Possible Answers

At first sight, one might assume that all Christian people would view postmodernism in a favorable light. David Harvey defines postmodernity as a reaction against "positivist, technocratic, and rationalistic universal modernism."[1] If Harvey is correct, any dethronement of Enlightenment rationalism and positivism is to be welcomed, and those who study hermeneutics since Gadamer will welcome the de-privileging of Descartes's rationalism and David Hume's empiricism in favor of greater attention to historicality (or historical conditionedness) and the community, in contrast to "timeless" individual consciousness.

Postmodernity rejects "the standardization of knowledge" as if to suggest that all knowledge and wisdom can be measured by the natural sciences. We may agree that looking to the sciences alone yields a false notion of value-neutral "objectivity," and tends to overlook the contrast between information or knowledge and human wisdom and divine revelation. Postmodern writers share with Nietzsche and Wittgenstein the correct insight that surface-grammar can constitute an unreliable guide to meaning. Thus far, postmodernism seems to accord with Gadamer's hermeneutics, in spite of his emphasis on tradition, and with Christian faith. To our question about compatibility with Christian faith, perhaps a first possible answer is yes.

---

1. David Harvey, *The Condition of Postmodernity* (Oxford: Blackwell, 1989), p. 9.

There is more to postmodernity, however, than this. Even Harvey agrees that postmodernism fits closely in America with the rediscovery of pragmatism in philosophy, especially in the later work of Richard Rorty. In Europe the movement is initially indebted to the skepticism and antitheistic relativism of Friedrich Nietzsche, and then more specifically to the later Roland Barthes, Jacques Derrida, Jean-François Lyotard, and Michel Foucault. These writers tend to be inimical to theistic faith.

It is difficult to define postmodernity because of its complexity. Lyotard has given it a well-known definition as "incredulity toward metanarratives" (or large, universal narratives, like that which purports to support evolution or Marxism). But even he admits that this definition is "simplifying to extremes."[2] Thomas Docherty rightly observes that it represents "a mood, not a period."[3] David Lyon and Graham Ward have offered a useful distinction between *postmodernism* and *postmodernity*. The former, they suggested, represented a more philosophical or intellectual version, whereas the latter focused on sociological aspects. But most writers use either term indiscriminately.[4]

How should we characterize this mood? Harvey gives an excellent schematic comparison with modernity, which he borrows from Hassan. Modernism, he claims, is characterized by purpose and form; postmodernism by play and antiform or dysfunction. Modernism strives for coherence, hierarchy, presence, and semantics; against these, respectively, postmodernism represents chance, anarchy, absence, and rhetoric. Finally, modernism aims at metaphysics, determinacy, and transcendence; postmodernity replaces these with irony, indeterminacy, and immanence.[5] This conveys its mood well enough, although this is not an exhaustive list. If even meanings in the Bible are to remain indeterminate, and if Christian faith is based on the Bible, a second possible answer emerges to our question about compatibility, and perhaps this is no.

---

2. Jean-François Lyotard, *The Postmodern Condition: A Report on Knowledge*, trans. G. Bennington and B. Massumi (Manchester: Manchester University Press, 1984), p. 40 (French edition, 1979).

3. Thomas Docherty, "Postmodernist Theory: Lyotard, Baudrillard, and Others," in *Twentieth-Century Continental Philosophy*, ed. Richard Kearny (London and New York: Routledge, 1994), p. 479; cf. pp. 474-503.

4. David Lyon, *Postmodernity* (Buckingham: Open University Press, 1994), pp. 6-7; Graham Ward, ed., *The Blackwell Companion to Postmodern Theology* (Oxford: Blackwell, 2001), pp. xiv-xv.

5. Harvey, *The Condition of Postmodernity*, p. 43.

In my book *Interpreting God and the Postmodern Self*, I agreed that it constituted a further advantage that postmodernists also exposed the disguises of surface-grammar in language. On the other hand, we do not need postmodernity to achieve this. I showed that Thomas Hobbes, Friedrich Nietzsche, Fritz Mauthner, and Ludwig Wittgenstein strove to expose the ways in which the surface-grammar of language can serve as a disguise. The earliest of these, Thomas Hobbes (1588-1679), wrote in his book *Leviathan* that to claim "God spoke to me in a dream" is to say little more than "I dreamt that God spoke to me."[6] Friedrich Nietzsche (1844-1900) describes truth only as "a mobile army of metaphors," or "illusions we have forgotten are illusions."[7] He declares, "I fear we shall never be rid of God, so long as we still believe in grammar."[8] Fritz Mauthner (1849-1923) and Ludwig Wittgenstein (1889-1951) urge repeatedly (in the words of the latter) that philosophy "is a little against the bewitchment of our intelligence by means of language."[9]

Nietzsche, however, certainly well before his time, contributes to postmodernism. Geoff Danaher, Tony Schirato, and Jen Webb assert, "Perhaps the most important influence on Foucault's work, particularly from *The Order of Things* onward, was the German philosopher Friedrich Nietzsche."[10] Yet James K. A. Smith has recently examined postmodernism through three of its undoubted leaders, Derrida, Lyotard, and Foucault, and argued that the work of each is to the positive benefit of Christian faith.[11] He agrees that Derrida argues for "nothing but the text" but insists that this coheres with the Reformation principle of *sola Scriptura*. He acknowledges that Lyotard attacks all "metanarratives," or large, universal narratives, of which Christianity is one. But he argues that Lyotard recovers "storytelling" and narrative as the most basic biblical genre of Christian faith. Richard

6. Thomas Hobbes, *Leviathan,* ed. M. Oakeshott (Oxford: Blackwell, 1960).

7. Friedrich Nietzsche, "On Truth and Lie," in *The Portable Nietzsche,* ed. W. Kaufman (New York: Viking Press, 1968), p. 46.

8. Friedrich Nietzsche, *Complete Works,* vol. 12, *The Twilight of the Idols,* ed. O. Levy, 18 vols. (London: Allen-Unwin, 1909-13), p. 22.

9. Ludwig Wittgenstein, *Philosophical Investigations,* German and English, English text translated by G. E. M. Anscombe (Oxford: Blackwell, 1967), section 109.

10. Geoff Danaher, Tony Schirato, and Jen Webb, *Understanding Foucault* (London and New Delhi: Jage Publications, 2000), p. 9.

11. James K. A. Smith, *Who's Afraid of Postmodernism? Taking Derrida, Lyotard, and Foucault to Church* (Grand Rapids: Baker Academic, 2006).

Bauckham seems to support this view. Smith admits that Foucault sees "knowledge" and "truth" as bids to exercise power, and equates criminality merely with deviance from a conventional norm. But he sees too much kinship between the mainline Church and "the smile in the white coat" that supports the "regimes" of hospitals, schools, prisons, and armed forces as imposing their conventions on the individual.

Yet writers such as Kevin Vanhoozer see Roland Barthes and Jacques Derrida as profoundly antitheistic. "Derrida is an unbeliever in the reliability, decidability, and neutrality of the sign. He seeks to 'undo' their privileged place."[12] He is a pragmatist, who deconstructs the author, following Nietzsche's announcement of the death of God.[13] Nicholas Wolterstorff regards Derrida as entirely self-contradictory.[14]

Many universities are divided down the middle by their attitude to postmodernism. Or perhaps it would be more accurate to say that universities reflect a spectrum of views. At one end of the spectrum engineers and medics, and many in science faculties, dismiss the movement as a passing French fashion, or at worst as sheer nonsense. Yet many departments of modern languages and schools of cultural theory welcome it as full of insights, or as a useful and positive thought experiment. Sociologists, psychologists, and theologians may be divided; some are welcoming and others are cautious. Theology sometimes remains one of the few departments to remain in favor with both. For it makes claims to "universal" truth, with modernity, but sees Jesus as born of a Jewish family in first-century Israel and the Church as conditioned by history, with postmodernity.

Yet it remains a great puzzle why some are "for" postmodernism and others are "against" it. The truth is that some of its insights are of positive value to Christian faith, while other themes and aspects are not only mistaken but also seductive and disastrous. For example, James Smith can favor Lyotard because he completely overlooks and ignores his work on what he calls "the differend." We shall see in due course that "the differend" would make hermeneutics impossible. There is too readily a naïveté in some Christian scholarship that tries to force us to be "for" or "against" whatever is put

12. Kevin J. Vanhoozer, *Is There a Meaning in This Text? The Bible, the Reader, and the Morality of Literary Knowledge* (Grand Rapids: Zondervan, 1998), p. 39.

13. Jacques Derrida, *Margins of Philosophy,* trans. Alan Bass (London and New York: Harvester Wheatsheaf, 1982), pp. 207-72.

14. Nicholas Wolterstorff, *Divine Discourse: Philosophical Reflections on the Claim That God Speaks* (Cambridge: Cambridge University Press, 1995), pp. 153-70.

in front of us. But life and thought are seldom so simple. We shall see that "hermeneutics" is well served by postmodernity in certain limited respects, but becomes quite impossible in the light of others. In the end it is just as hostile to "authority" as modernity is. We might almost invest the phrase "It is right in what it affirms, and wrong in what it denies." (This aphorism is often applied to interpretations of the atonement.) Postmodernism, we may suggest as a thought experiment, may often be right in what it denies and wrong in what it affirms. A third possible answer to our question about compatibility with Christian faith is yes and no, or more strictly: in some respects, yes; in other respects, no.

We shall this time follow Smith in considering Derrida (with the later Barthes), Lyotard (with Baudrillard), and Foucault, and then turn to Rorty and American postmodernity. This is preferable to looking at postmodernity as a whole or in general for three reasons: (1) it enables us to avoid generalizations and to be accurate; (2) it is a helpful didactic method for those who approach the subject for the first time; and (3) it helps us to avoid any undue repetition from *New Horizons in Hermeneutics,* from *Interpreting God and the Postmodern Self,* and from several other essays on this subject.

2. European Postmodernism: Jacques Derrida (with the later Barthes)

Jacques Derrida (1930-2004) was born near Algiers and was expelled from school as a Jew by the Vichy French government under the Nazis. By 1949 he had begun to study the French philosophers Rousseau and Camus, as well as Nietzsche. In 1951 he studied in Paris and became friends with the Marxist Louis Althusser and with Michel Foucault. He became enthused with the phenomenology of Husserl, especially with his notion that people see everything from within a "horizon," which is relative to where they stand, but also can move and expand. He then received a grant to study at Harvard. After the war of Algerian independence from France, he was involved with the Tel Quel group of literary and philosophical theorists, and from 1960 to 1964 taught philosophy at the Sorbonne. In 1969 he published *Writing and Difference, Speech and Phenomena,* and the book that made his name, *Of Grammatology.*[15]

---

15. Jacques Derrida, *Writing and Difference,* trans. A. Bas (Chicago: University of Chi-

Since 1967 Derrida has become increasingly controversial, whether this is regarded as fame or as notoriety, and subject to much misunderstanding, for three reasons. One reason arises because he combines deconstruction with postmodernity. Christopher Norris regards deconstruction as a serious philosophy but views postmodernity with skepticism. (*Deconstruction* means undermining or erasing meanings that have been mistakenly assumed to be "natural" or fixed.) A second reason is that his later works differ from his earlier ones. A third reason why Derrida is misunderstood is that his thought remains complex. Different evaluations of "postmodern theology" add fuel to the fire.[16]

Derrida's disciple Gayatri Spirak writes in the preface to *Of Grammatology* that Nietzsche, Freud, Husserl, and Heidegger are his acknowledged precursors. Nietzsche cut away grounds of knowing; Freud asked critical questions about the human psyche, or the human subject; Husserl and especially Heidegger saw that "Being" could not be fathomed by traditional ontology, or the study of "reality." Derrida writes in *Of Grammatology* that his approach "is certainly the undoing (French, *solicitation*) of logocentrism" (or being centered on the word, or seeing a "fixed" or "given" relation between words and meanings).[17] Grammatology is a science of writing. The reason why writing cannot be centered on the word is that it does not merely stabilize, crystallize, or clothe what has been said, but always points beyond the words themselves.

This suspicion of the "logocentric" in turn occurs for two reasons. First, everything has at least a double meaning, and the first or "obvious" referent may not be the one in view. Second, the meaning is never "closed off" as if to present its application to a situation, utterance, or text yet to come. Derrida writes, "It is no longer a finished corpus of writing enclosed in a book."[18] He makes a play on the principle expounded by Ferdinand de Saussure (which

---

cago Press, 1978); Derrida, *Speech and Phenomena and Other Essays on Husserl's Theory of Signs,* trans. D. B. Allison (Evanston, Ill.: Northwestern University Press, 1973); and Derrida, *Of Grammatology,* trans. G. C. Spirak (Baltimore: Johns Hopkins University Press, 1975).

16. Terrence W. Tilley, *Postmodern Theologies: The Challenge of Religious Diversity* (Maryknoll, N.Y.: Orbis, 1995); and Graham Ward, ed., *The Postmodern God: A Theological Reader* (Oxford: Blackwell, 1997); and Kevin J. Vanhoozer, ed., *Postmodern Theology: Cambridge Companion* (Cambridge: Cambridge University Press, 2003).

17. Derrida, *Of Grammatology,* p. 74.

18. Jacques Derrida, in *Deconstruction and Criticism,* ed. H. Bloom et al. (London: Routledge and Kegan Paul, 1979), p. 84.

we saw in chapter IX) that meaning depends on *difference,* and declares that it also depends on openness-to-the-future, or on *deferment.* In French these two terms are *différence* (difference) and *différance* (deferment).[19]

The most that postponed meaning can leave is "traces" or "tracks." Moreover, a document or a "work" does not permit enough "closure" to allow the presence of the signatory. Everything is placed under "erasure." This links well with Foucault's notion that all categorizations are historically relative, and therefore constitute conventions that are imposed by those in power.[20]

It is little wonder that Vanhoozer sees all this as "undoing" Scripture, its content, and its author.[21] For him it constitutes "nihilism."[22] Yet how can James Smith see Derrida as "resonant with the Reformers' claim of *sola scriptura*" and suggest that Derrida helps us to appreciate "Abraham Kuyper, Herman Dooyeweerd, Cornelius Van Til, and Francis Schaeffer"?[23] Smith is too optimistic. But Vanhoozer is eager to engage in polemic before he has asked what we might learn from Derrida. We stressed in relation to reader-response theory (chapter XV), and even to Ricoeur (chapter XII), that what applied to *"open"* texts could not be applied to *all* texts. Some poetic portions of Scripture are "literary" and meant to be *suggestive* rather than *communicative* or *literal.* They fall under Wittgenstein's protest: Why do we so readily assume that all language is "to convey thoughts"?

It is noticeable that both writers, Smith and Vanhoozer, quote selectively, and Vanhoozer perhaps neglects Derrida's latest writings. Both speak "Christianity" and "the Bible" as if each were a monolithic system. In biblical poetry, rich in metaphor and allusion, Smith has a point in identifying its movement-toward-the-future. The more we read, the more we shall uncover fresh allusions and fresh points. After all, most Scripture is a witness to eschatological nonfulfillment or part fulfillment. The fallibility of the Church suggests that biblical interpretation is without closure. Yet Vanhoozer is right in suggesting that this is overstated, and cannot apply to all biblical material. Derrida does modify this in his later work. But why not say so from the start?

---

19. Derrida, *Speech and Phenomena,* pp. 129-60.

20. Derrida, *Writing and Difference,* pp. 31-63, on Foucault.

21. Vanhoozer, *Is There a Meaning?* pp. 37-196; but cf. Vanhoozer, *Postmodern Theology,* pp. 21-25.

22. Vanhoozer, *Is There a Meaning?* p. 73.

23. Smith, *Who's Afraid of Postmodernism?* p. 55.

Wolterstorff is equally right to say that when he declares that all Western metaphysics depends upon a mythological metaphor, Derrida is making a metaphysical statement.[24] But Derrida wrote "White Mythology" in 1974, and *Of Grammatology* and *Speech and Phenomena* in 1967. Smith and more positive interpreters cite *Limited Inc,* published in 1988, and also *The Other Heading,* published in French in 1991. "Logocentrism" for Derrida does not mean so much "word centralism" as a kind of preordained relation between word and meaning that cannot be altered. In *Positions* (1972) deconstruction is not simply overturning traditional meanings. It questions unduly privileged meanings in texts and exposes the role of what these oppose. In the long afterword to *Limited Inc* Derrida discusses J. L. Austin and responds to John Searle. Here he rejects the view that he defends total freedom of meaning.[25] He argues that *stability of meaning* exists in texts, but texts are not immutable or indestructible.

Some texts seem to resist even the notion of relative stability. The statement "Jesus was crucified under Pontius Pilate" may vary in meaning as Martin Hengel and others refine our view of crucifixion. Yet as a historic fact, does it change? Engineers may insist that in engineering, language conveys not only state of affairs but also exact procedures. Yet there are "local" factors to observe even in so-called universal sciences. David Livingstone has made a special study of this.[26] He points out that against scientists' or engineers' claims to "timeless universality," everything depends on the geographical givenness of research groups, colleagues, tools, resources, predecessors, and so on. In the light of fresh research and new colleagues, meanings and even data may change. As we noted in chapter XI, Gadamer sees *statistics* as dependent on who programmed them, and for what purpose.

When all is said and done, however, the two ends of a spectrum of genre are clear enough. J. Lotman and Umberto Eco speak of the difference between an "engineering" culture with its transmissive communication and largely "closed" texts, and a "literary" culture with multilayered communication and more "open" texts. The Bible offers both types. Gallio was proconsul in A.D. 51 or perhaps 52; this remains an immutable fact. George Caird

24. Wolterstorff, *Divine Discourse,* pp. 162-65.

25. Jacques Derrida, *Limited Inc,* ed. G. Graff, trans. J. Mehlmann and S. Weber (Evanston, Ill.: Northwestern University Press, 1988).

26. David M. Livingstone, *Science, Space, and Hermeneutics* (Heidelberg: University of Heidelberg, 2002); and Livingstone, *Putting Science in Its Place: Geographies of Scientific Knowledge* (Chicago: University of Chicago Press, 2003).

describes the symbols and poetry of the book of Revelation as resisting any attempt "to unweave the rainbow." We do not need or want mechanistic "analysis" here. The Servant Songs in Isaiah 40–53 have more than one referent, but they do represent referents. Parables create thought; commands are sometimes specific.

Yet what does seem to be lacking in Derrida is an acceptance that many texts (not all) demand an extralinguistic situation in life. Without this, our view of language becomes as impoverished as Bultmann's or Heidegger's. To be sure, not all texts are representational and descriptive, and some have multiple meaning. But in spite of his later qualifications in *Limited Inc,* there seems to be a lack of attention to the particular case, which Wittgenstein insists is not to be neglected. As Wittgenstein urges, to ask in the abstract "what is meaning?" is to start in the wrong direction.[27]

Roland Barthes also speaks of "the death of the author," while Julia Kristeva, their like-minded colleague in many other respects, demands that Derrida and Barthes attend to "the speaking subject." Some say Barthes and Derrida attack only "onto-theology." But many theologians reject *substance* theology without embracing postmodernity. Barthes admits in his later work that if "the death of the author" becomes absolutized, this becomes "counter-theological."[28] This is a long way from *Elements of Semiology* (1964), where Barthes points out that often language can function as a disguise, as in systems of furniture or of clothes. From 1966 onward, especially by 1967, Barthes began to engage in a program of postmodernism. In 1971 he distinguished "text" from "work," which presupposes the author. The text, however, is bound only to "pleasure" *(jouissance).* Thus in 1973 he wrote *The Pleasure of Text.* The text is not the result of a creative act, with order and purpose, but is simply for the sheer "pleasure" of reading it. It became a "plural" text.

From a Christian point of view, this gives control of the text to the reader, and it becomes difficult to square with Smith's appeal to the Reformers, who all too often stressed the uncomfortable and challenging aspects of Scripture. Again, it might be different if Barthes had distinguished genre and declared

---

27. Ludwig Wittgenstein, *Philosophical Investigations*, 2nd ed. (Oxford: Blackwell, 1958), sections 7, 11, 23, 29, 31, 38, 47, 92, 96, 97, 133, 166, and 304. Cf. Wittgenstein, *The Blue and Brown Books: Preliminary Studies for the "Philosophical Investigations"* (Oxford: Blackwell, 1969), p. 18.

28. Roland Barthes, "The Death of the Author," in Barthes, *The Rustle of Language,* trans. R. Howard (New York: Hill and Wang, 1986), p. 54.

that *some* texts simply serve to provide pleasure. Pleasure might lead to praise and thanksgiving. But pleasure alone suggests a directionless hedonism, or what Ricoeur calls narcissism. It does not help that Carl Raschke and Thomas Altizer find ways of calling this "theological." We need to bear in mind the three possible answers to our question about compatibility with Christian faith. These apply to Derrida and hermeneutics.

3. European Postmodernism: Jean-François Lyotard (with Jean Baudrillard)

Jean-François Lyotard (1924-98) was born at Versailles, France, went to school in Paris, and studied philosophy at the Sorbonne. He belonged to the political left wing and favored the "Socialism or Barbarianism" group. He became professor of critical theory at the University of California and visiting professor at Johns Hopkins, Yale, and Montreal. He is best known for his works *The Postmodern Condition* (French 1979) and *The Differend* (French 1983), but he also wrote other books on postmodernism, and on Kant and aesthetics.[29]

In his earlier works Lyotard addressed the problem of "incommensurability." This term is used in the philosophy of science to denote two self-consistent models or points of view that fail to allow an independent criterion for assessing one against the other. He argues that in the face of this we can learn from "paganism," which worships a plurality of gods and goddesses and rejects monotheism and "universality." He accepts that irreducible differences exist and are inevitable. In his book *Just Gaming* he defends the justice of incompatible and pluriform views, because each is based on stories, narratives, or a collection of stories.[30] If "universality" is claimed by Kant, Hegel, Marx, or Christian theists, these are all wrong. He interprets Wittgenstein as a pluralist: these are just one among a variety of "language games." People are "just gaming" when they pretend to offer universal language or truth, or that their belief system applies to everyone. Clearly this also resonates with Nietzsche in his view of truth and Christianity, and

29. Lyotard, *The Postmodern Condition,* and Lyotard, *The Differend: Phrases in Dispute,* trans. G. van den Abbeek (Manchester: Manchester University Press, 1990).

30. Jean-François Lyotard, *Just Gaming,* trans. W. Godzich (Manchester: Manchester University Press, 1985).

Rorty on Wittgenstein. We reject this pluralist understanding of Wittgenstein.[31] Meanwhile we turn to *The Postmodern Condition.*

1. Lyotard moves from "paganism" to "postmodernism," at least in name, not in content, and builds his first formulation of postmodernism in *The Postmodern Condition,* based on his previous work. It is well known that in this book he offers an admittedly simplistic definition of postmodernism as "incredulity toward metanarratives." Here "metanarrative" means a universalizing narrative such as is offered by Karl Marx, Sigmund Freud, or arguably Christian theism.[32] This is, in effect, antifoundationalism, or an attack on legitimating narratives, which apply to everyone. The first point, therefore, concerns *narratives of legitimation.*

This theme invites James Smith and perhaps Richard Bauckham to dissociate and distance biblical Christianity from the larger narratives Lyotard condemns. They stress that even the Bible contains a series of "little narratives" about specific people and events that are the primary substance of Christian life. I have discussed Bauckham's arguments in *Thiselton on Hermeneutics.*[33] While I have reservations about their optimistic assessment of Lyotard (because they are based on this one book and fail to include *The Differend*), Lyotard's main targets for attack are indeed, first, the "liberal" view of history as a steady march of *progress* toward social enlightenment; and second, the progress of "knowledge," especially in the *sciences,* toward a *unified understanding* of the world. Lyotard is utterly right that knowledge does not mean wisdom; that all governments fail to reach integrated or "joined up" thinking; that "science" is not the paradigm for all knowledge; that technology is not human understanding; and that "liberal progressism" is a mistaken myth. Much turns on "legitimation."[34] If this was the main thrust of Lyotard's thought, we could learn from him for hermeneutics.

2. Lyotard shares with Heidegger and Gadamer the view that all is not well with "*computerization.*" Even in Ph.D. theses, checking the cumulative data of Google is no substitute for original thinking. "Knowledge in the form

---

31. Cf. also Jane Heal, "Pragmatism and Choosing to Believe," in *Reading Rorty,* ed. Alan Malachowski (Oxford: Blackwell, 1990), pp. 101-36.

32. Lyotard, *The Postmodern Condition,* p. xxiv.

33. *Thiselton on Hermeneutics: Collected Works with New Essays* (Grand Rapids: Eerdmans; Aldershot: Ashgate, 2006), pp. 671-75 and 798-99; and Richard J. Bauckham, *Bible and Mission: Christian Witness in a Postmodern World* (Grand Rapids: Baker Academic; Carlisle: Paternoster, 2003), pp. 87-93.

34. This is introduced and discussed in Lyotard, *The Postmodern Condition,* chapter 2.

of an informational commodity indispensable to productive power is already
. . . the major stake in the worldwide competition for power."[35] This gives
sharper point to Foucault's work on the relation between knowledge and
power. "Knowledge" becomes a consumer commodity that can be bought
and sold to gain power. Lyotard notes the rapid change imposed on our
postindustrial, electronic society. This, again, relates well to hermeneutics.

3. This book was commissioned by the government of Montreal, and
Lyotard turns to the social implications of postmodern thought. He again
appeals to *Wittgenstein's language games*. Ordinary people often use those of
the narrative or the "little story." But this offers no legitimation. Technocrats
and scientists use the self-legitimating language game of their craft, and they
and the state appear to offer authoritative pronouncements, when these are
merely instruments of power. Lyotard writes, "Every utterance should be
thought of as a move in a game."[36] But the cognitive mapping of science or
the state disguises mere consensus as universal truth. Society is therefore becoming increasingly bureaucratic. It is also fragmented and led by "technocrats."[37] This point is ambivalent for hermeneutics. It is helpful to recall that
language is communicative action, but nothing can be authoritative for
Lyotard.

4. The fragmentation and atomization of society demand resistance to
universal legitimating claims. Lyotard tries to nurture pluriformity. In itself
this seems innocent and even liberating, but in Lyotard it also leads to his
work *The Differend*.

Lyotard regarded *The Differend: Phrases in Dispute* (1983) as his most
important work. Here again he combines "paganism" with postmodernism.
The term *differend* is a technical one, to denote a case of conflict between
two parties, which cannot be resolved. This is because one party's use of a
"language" (or of a language game) supposedly already implies the resolu-
tion of the dispute in their favor. They cannot agree on an "external" criterion. Their views are "incommensurable." The *differend* becomes, in effect, a
device to *disempower* the weaker party. One party, for example, may decide
in advance what is "reasonable" and introduce a rubric that ensures that the
"reasonable" side wins the case. Impartial judgment is impossible. A possible
example might be whether Northern Ireland is part of Britain that happens

---

35. Lyotard, *The Postmodern Condition*, p. 5; cf. chapter 1 of Lyotard.
36. Lyotard, *The Postmodern Condition*, p. 10; cf. chapter 3 of Lyotard.
37. Lyotard, *The Postmodern Condition*, chapters 4 and 5.

to be on the island of Ireland, or whether it is "Irish" and has to fight off rival British claims and the current majority population. What can stand *outside* the situation and *arbitrate?* To describe the problem is to introduce terms that presuppose a verdict.

This is another way of claiming that some language games are incommensurable. In situations of conflict, everything turns on *power:* on who is the more powerful party. Lyotard sees the answer as respecting the heterogeneity or pluriformity of all parties. The implications for *hermeneutics* are obvious. Whereas Emilio Betti claims that hermeneutics nurtures patience, tolerance, and respect for the other, Lyotard suggests premature closure because he believes that genuine negotiation is impossible. Neither the Bible nor the Church can have any "authority," because this always dictates the terms in which any conflict is resolved.

We face also the troubling question of reading and interpreting Wittgenstein in a pluralistic way. I have never read him in that way over forty years of continuous study. To be sure, a few do. Paul van Buren in his third phase of thought understands him pluralistically; William Hordern also seems to offer a pluralistic interpretation, speaking of language games as being like separate gardening actions with a hoe, a spade, a rake, and so on.[38] Richard Rorty is predictably another such interpreter. Wittgenstein does say that "the *truth* of certain empirical propositions belongs to our frame of reference."[39] But in the example of the language and action of pain, he declares, "Only of a *living human being* . . . can one say: it has sensations."[40] When language games change, he says, "there is a change in concepts, and with the concepts the meanings of words change."[41] But *all human beings* can understand shaking and uttering bleating noises as laughter. Language games differ but are not always (some may be) "incommensurable." Even Rorty prefers the metaphor of "archipelago" to self-contained "islands," although he, too, adopts an overpluralist interpretation of Wittgenstein (see section 5 below). A language game brings into prominence not its uniqueness but "the whole consisting of language and the *actions* into which it is woven."[42] The

---

38. William Hordern, *Speaking of God: The Nature and Purpose of Theological Language* (New York: Macmillan, 1964; London: Epworth, 1965), pp. 81-92.

39. Ludwig Wittgenstein, *On Certainty* (Oxford: Blackwell, 1969), section 83, italics in original.

40. Wittgenstein, *Philosophical Investigations*, section 281, 2nd ed. (1958), italics mine.

41. Wittgenstein, *On Certainty*, section 65.

42. Wittgenstein, *Philosophical Investigations*, section 7, 2nd ed. (1958), italics mine.

Investigations supply many examples of stepping out of one's frame of reference and adopting another. The same person may participate in both. The valuable element in Lyotard is his rejection of positivism and the imperialism of the sciences; but this is no reason to restrict the truth claims of Christianity to "telling one's own story." This would be reductionist.

Jean Baudrillard (1929-2007) was born in Reims, northeastern France, and studied German at the Sorbonne in Paris. He then worked in literature, sociology, and philosophy. He may more accurately be thought of as a *post-structuralist* than as a postmodernist, but is regularly associated with Lyotard, Derrida, Foucault, and G. Deleuze. He believed that measuring is based on signs, and with Saussure that it is based on difference. But as a sociologist he explored how *self-referring* language applied to society. He is often associated with Lyotard in particular because he saw society as fruitlessly searching for "total" or universal meaning. This search for coherence distracts or "seduces" humanity from genuine reality. In certain respects this search leads them away to a "virtual reality," in which consumerism becomes the new structure of power.

One positive feature of Baudrillard is his respect for the contrast between "use" and "value." This has now become assimilated, he argues, not into competitive exchange-value, as the classical Marxists argue, but into *perceived* value, or *signifying value*. Here the real world begins to disappear. Fantasy begins to take over, so that reality comes to be replaced in America by such virtual reality as Disneyland. *Simulacra* of the real world, or media constructions that are no more than virtual reality, dominate our society. The power of the media to control our perceptions offers one example. Baudrillard gave some expression to the problem of virtual reality in *The Mirror of Production* (French 1973; English 1975) and *Simulations* (French 1981; English 1983).[43] In *Forget Foucault* he agrees with Foucault about the social importance of power but stresses the related role of *simulated* knowledge.[44]

We may agree with Baudrillard about the power of simulcra and of how things are perceived in the light of the media. We may also agree with him about the seduction and power of consumerism and the power of mass advertising. Yet the whole of society is not entirely beguiled in this way, even

---

43. Jean Baudrillard, *The Mirror of Production*, trans. M. Poster (St. Louis: Telos Press, 1975), and *Simulations*, trans. P. Foss and others (New York: Semiotext(e), 1983); French edition, *Simulacres et Simulation..*

44. Jean Baudrillard, *Forget Foucault* (New York: Semiotext(e), 1987).

though the Bible (and Ricoeur) gives a place to the role of self-deception. Baudrillard is not without value for a hermeneutic of suspicion.

4. European Postmodernism: Michel Foucault; Knowledge and Power

Michel Foucault (1926-84) was born in Poitiers, the son of a surgeon. He witnessed Nazi occupation at first hand in Vichy France. He suffered acute depression and was taken to consult a psychiatrist. Medicine, hospitals, "madness," and military forces play a crucial part in his philosophy. Foucault graduated in psychology, and then in philosophy. He joined the French Communist Party in 1950 and was a close friend of the Marxist writer Louis Althusser. In 1958 he was appointed to Warsaw University, and in 1959 to Hamburg. He returned to France in 1960 and produced his *History of Madness* in 1961, published later in English in abridged form as *Madness and Civilization.* In 1965 he became visiting professor at Tunis, and published *The Order of Things* (French, *Les Mots et les choses*) in 1966. During this period he collaborated with Barthes, Lacan, and Lévi-Strauss first on structuralism and then on post-structuralism. *The Archaeology of Knowledge* appeared in 1969. From 1970 he made visits to the United States and Japan, and began *The History of Sexuality.* Gary Gutting argues that Foucault "'goes beyond' structuralism and hermeneutics."[45]

1. Foucault shows in his early work, in *Madness and Civilization* and *History of Madness,* that "madness" constitutes a variable social construct. In the ancient world, he argues, people deemed "mad" were either thought of as inspired by the gods or else hidden away as though subhuman animals. Nineteenth-century liberal reformers, however, invented the notion that madness was a "mental illness," which could be treated in asylums or so-called places of safety. This change was "abruptly reached . . . almost overnight" and constituted a "massive phenomenon."[46] It was, Foucault suggests, primarily in order to protect the bourgeois family. But what is "below the standards of reason," he argued, is judged only by the medical "regime." It imposes an arbitrary authority, with "the smile in the white coat."

45. Gary Gutting, ed., *The Cambridge Companion to Foucault* (Cambridge: Cambridge University Press, 1994), p. 2.
46. Michel Foucault, *Madness and Civilization,* trans. R. Howard (New York: Pantheon, 1965), pp. 45-46.

2. Foucault continues his critique of the authoritarian "regime" of *hospitals* in *The Birth of the Clinic* in 1963 (English 1973). In 1966 came his second celebrated major work, entitled in English *The Order of Things* (1970).[47] This deals with *language,* but within the limited tradition of German philosophy. Again, he shows how views of language have changed at different periods of history. Like Ricoeur, he also looks at correlative notions of the self. The social sciences are founded on what is relative to a particular age.

3. More significant still is *Discipline and Punish* (French 1973; English 1977).[48] The "regime" here is *the prison,* and Foucault begins with a chapter portraying torture.[49] He moves to the spectacle of the scaffold. "The Gentle Way in Punishment" includes more subtle coercion.[50] All aim to achieve the "docile body."[51] This comes upon the victim as *anonymous power,* "since it is everywhere and always alert. . . . It functions largely in silence."[52] The mood is that of *surveillance.* The whole regime produces new kinds of human subjects. They are subject to a technique of power. *There is no knowledge or truth outside networks of power relations.* Prison has become a "carceral system," which is all-encompassing in its sovereign power. It belongs to a network of "regimes" that are disciplinary. Regimes exist in "plural colonies, disciplinary battalions, prisons, hospitals, almshouses."[53] Schools are added, and some churches might be included. Police, teachers, and social workers are all accused of linking power and knowledge, and thereby producing deviants or "criminals." Clergy are not far behind.

4. Foucault's work relativizes "order" in society as nothing to do with divine decree, given for the benefit of humanity. All authority relations and values stand open to question as conventions that can be manipulated by the powerful against the weak. Sometimes Foucault might be right: there are schools and churches where an authoritarian leader may use "Thus saith the Lord" purely for his own advantage. Jesus warned against false prophets, long before Nietzsche and Foucault. We need to monitor hospitals and pris-

---

47. Michel Foucault, *The Order of Things,* trans. A. Sheridan (New York: Random House, 1970).

48. Michel Foucault, *Discipline and Punish,* trans. A. Sheridan (New York: Pantheon and Penguin, 1977); from *Surveiller et punir: naissance de la prison* (Paris: Gallimand, 1975).

49. Foucault, *Discipline and Punish,* pp. 3-31; cf. 32-69.

50. Foucault, *Discipline and Punish,* pp. 104-31.

51. Foucault, *Discipline and Punish,* pp. 135-69.

52. Foucault, *Discipline and Punish,* pp. 176-77.

53. Foucault, *Discipline and Punish,* p. 300.

ons, but they become intolerable regimes. But such a wholesale critique merely trumpets Foucault's dislike of authority in any form. Emil Brunner saw marriage and the state as divine ordinances given for the well-being of humanity. We move perilously near to Enlightenment modernity's notion "autonomy."

5. On the other hand, several writers have insisted on the usefulness of Foucault's thought for Christian theology. The best-known works are *Michel Foucault and Theology,* edited by James Bernauer and Jeremy Garrette (2004), Garrette's *Foucault and Religion: Spiritual Corporality and Political Spirituality* (1999), and many articles.[54] Elizabeth A. Castelli has written several times on Foucault and 1 Corinthians 1–4, examining his complex notions of different kinds of power, where Paul also speaks of a range of sanctions from a stick through alleged patriarchy to the power of the cross.[55] Others fasten on the danger of false prophecy and authoritarianism, rather than authority, within the Church. Yet others focus on the incarnation and "bodiliness." Foucault may speak of "docile bodies," but at least he recognizes the part played by the physical in life. Yet he offers a critique of deviant religion rather than of all religion. At its best and most subtle, it serves to alert us to highly sophisticated and often disguised networks of power. He shows us how these may become "anonymous," and how they may become connected with knowledge and surveillance. Foucault takes further what Habermas has said about "interest" or self-interest in hermeneutics, and what Ricoeur has said about unconscious desires or narcissism in hermeneutics. Foucault's work on power and knowledge can be helpful for hermeneutics. Yet difficulties also arise, not least his view that value comes from mere convention, usually of the most powerful parties.

54. James Bernauer and Jeremy Garrette, eds., *Michel Foucault and Theology: The Politics of Religious Experience* (Aldershot and Burlington, Vt.: Ashgate, 2004); and Jeremy R. Garrette, *Foucault and Religion: Spiritual Corporality and Political Spirituality* (London and New York: Routledge, 1999, 2007).

55. Elizabeth Castelli, "Interpretations of Power in 1 Corinthians," in *Michel Foucault and Theology,* pp. 19-38, and Castelli, *Imitating Paul: A Discourse of Power* (Louisville: Westminster John Knox, 1991).

5. American Postmodernism: Richard Rorty (with the Later Stanley Fish)

Richard M. Rorty (1931-2007) was born in the city of New York, married the daughter of the "social gospel" theologian Walter Rauschenbusch, and studied philosophy at the University of Chicago and at Yale. In 1961 he became professor of philosophy at Princeton University at the age of thirty, and in 1982 became professor at the University of Virginia. He was regarded as a popular figure in America, not only for his robust (some might say brash) style of writing, but also for his support for the American pragmatic tradition. His first book, *The Linguistic Turn* (1967), was a respected study of linguistic philosophy. But in his *Philosophy and the Mirror of Nature* (1979) he turned the corner to neopragmatism and postmodernism, arguing for the need to replace traditional theories of knowledge in philosophy.[56]

I have written in several books of my reservations and unease about this combination of optimistic pragmatism and postmodernism. These overlap with European postmodernism, but whereas the French thinkers generate a pessimistic mood of suspicion and critique, Rorty writes with joyous gusto in his neopragmatic version of postmodernism. Whereas the French are committed deeply to the oppressed and marginalized, Rorty postpones social concern until virtually his last book, *Philosophy and Social Hope* (2000), after he has done much of the damage (although he does express belief in liberal progressivism in *Contingency, Irony, and Solidarity*).[57] I must try to avoid repeating what I have said elsewhere.[58] In brief summary, others also draw a clear distinction between European and American postmodernity, but most contend that the left-wing suspicions of French postmodern thinkers are more seductive and inimical to Christian faith than the more optimistic American postmodernism of Richard Rorty and Stanley Fish. My view is the opposite. European postmodernity at least provides an insightful critique of inauthentic religion. But pragmatic American postmodernism tells us that all is well, whatever we believe or do, provided that it is "success-

---

56. Richard M. Rorty, *Philosophy and the Mirror of Nature* (Princeton: Princeton University Press, 1979).

57. Richard M. Rorty, *Philosophy and Social Hope* (Princeton: Princeton University Press, 1979), pp. 169-88 and 299-311.

58. Anthony C. Thiselton, *Interpreting God and the Postmodern Self: On Meaning, Manipulation, and Promise* (Edinburgh: T. & T. Clark; Grand Rapids: Eerdmans, 1995), pp. 33-34 and 111-14; *Thiselton on Hermeneutics*, pp. 519-20, 586-96, 666-70, and 796-98.

ful" for the local community. It puts success and rhetorical "winners" in the place of truth that might prove to be uncomfortable. This was precisely Paul's concern and the reason for his unease with some Corinthian Christians. It lacks any place *for self-criticism.*

In *Philosophy and the Mirror of Nature* Rorty gives an account of historical philosophers in largely narrative style. "Mirror" becomes a metaphor for a representational theory of meaning and a correspondence theory of truth, which Rorty attacks. He builds on the work of W. V. O. Quine, Wilfrid Sellars, and Donald Davidson, and favors Thomas Kuhn's early account of paradigms.[59] Again, many will welcome the equation of "science" with old-fashioned materialist positivism. He even suggests that with the demise of traditional theories of knowledge (or epistemology), hermeneutics provides "a way of coping" that fills the gap. "Rationality" is only what society or the "local" community lets us say.[60] Almost predictably he interprets the later Wittgenstein in an overpluralistic way, as Jane Heal and I have noted. Wittgenstein's friend Norman Malcolm, George Pitcher, and many others do not interpret him in this radical way.

Rorty's next major work was *Contingency, Irony, and Solidarity* (1989).[61] The first part addresses the contingency of language. Like Friedrich Nietzsche and Donald Davidson, as well as Ludwig Wittgenstein, he sees that language may use disguises. Conceptual formation is not therefore "intrinsic," but relative to our purposes. This is not distinctively "postmodern." But then Rorty urges the contingency of the self, appealing again to Nietzsche, Wittgenstein, and Heidegger. (Whether the appeal to Wittgenstein is justified remains open to question.) The contingency of the community follows. Here he becomes political and rejects (or tries to reject) the charge of moral relativism. He discusses the ethics of cruelty, and believes that we progress to a more liberal society. With this one cannot help comparing Foucault's attitude to bureaucracy; to the *regimes* of prisons, hospitals, or the armed forces; and to torture; and Lyotard's attitude to the "myth" of liberal progressivism and Darwinianism.

In part 2 Rorty considers *irony.* Proust, Nietzsche, Heidegger, and especially Derrida are models of the "ironic man."[62] Derrida does not attempt

---

59. Rorty does refer to the second edition of Kuhn's book, on pp. 322-35 and 343-47, but does not appear to take Kuhn's caution very seriously.

60. Rorty, *Mirror of Nature*, pp. 342-47 and 366-69.

61. Richard M. Rorty, *Contingency, Irony, and Solidarity* (Cambridge: Cambridge University Press, 1989).

62. Rorty, *Contingency, Irony, and Solidarity*, pp. 122-37; cf. pp. 96-121.

metaphysics or traditional epistemology. Stanley Fish endorses Rorty's views, which he discusses explicitly. He prefers to turn "rhetoric" to "irony," but the two terms are close. He states with astonishingly bold and robust generalization: "There are . . . two ways of thinking about various things. . . . It is the difference between serious man and rhetorical man."[63] The first half of the quotation comes from Rorty. Fish and Rorty almost outdo each other in brash generalization and optimism about what most regard as open to question.

In part 3 Rorty discusses social solidarity with reference also to cruelty. George Orwell was an old-fashioned liberal, he claims, who all the same denies the liberal hope of progressivism. In his last section he reduces ethical evaluations to "we" statements made on behalf of a particular community. For there is no "natural" self. "It is part of the Christian idea to treat everyone . . . as a fellow sinner. . . . Secular ethical universalism has taken over this attitude from Christianity."[64]

Rorty develops these themes in *Objectivity, Relativism, and Truth* (1990) and *Essays on Heidegger and Others* (1991). These were designated volumes 1 and 2 in *Philosophical Papers,* with the third volume, *Truth and Progress,* appearing in 1998 and a fourth and final volume, *Philosophy as Cultural Politics,* in 2007. (All are published by Cambridge University Press.) In the first essay of *Truth and Progress,* Rorty makes considerable use of the American pragmatists William James and John Dewey. He agrees with James that "The true is the name of whatever proves itself to be good in the way of belief."[65] There is no task of "getting reality right."[66] The essays come from 1995. In the final essay Rorty expresses his esteem for Davidson, Wittgenstein, and Derrida.

It would repeat my critique to say something about pragmatic philosophy in America. But in very brief summary, I refer here to Robert Corrington's excellent account of American hermeneutics.[67] The key is al-

---

63. Stanley Fish, *Doing What Comes Naturally: Change, Rhetoric, and the Practice of Theory in Literary and Legal Studies* (Oxford: Clarendon, 1989), pp. 501-2; cf. pp. 471-502.

64. Rorty, *Contingency, Irony, and Solidarity,* p. 191.

65. Richard Rorty, *Truth and Progress: Philosophical Papers,* vol. 3 (Cambridge: Cambridge University Press, 1998), p. 21.

66. Rorty, *Truth and Progress,* p. 25.

67. Robert S. Corrington, *The Community of Interpreters: On the Hermeneutics of Nature and the Bible in the American Philosophical Tradition* (Macon, Ga.: Mercer University Press, 1987), pp. 1-46.

ways to look for "progress," and even "success" and "winners," and to talk about "the community." Benjamin Franklin (1706-90) looked for "the benefits of humanity," while Ralph Waldo Emerson (1803-82) called his party "the Party of the Future." The double criterion was always the benefit and the consensus of the community. Royce was the American Hegel, who expounded "the community" and "progress." Rorty sweeps everything away as "rubbish," which does not accord with pragmatic criteria. This is reminiscent of the 1930s, when A. J. Ayer dismissed as "non-sense" all that did not meet his empirical criterion of verifiability. His dismissive attitude seduced thousands in Britain, just as Rorty and Fish do in America. It is no accident that Ayer was Britain's most stylish and brash philosopher at the time. Those who struggle with large questions without taking shortcuts are less popular. We look back on logical positivism as naive empiricism. We suggest that the other is naive pragmatism.

Terrence Tilley examines with some skepticism such terms as "postmodern," "postchristian," "postcolonial," "postindustrial," "postanalytic," "post-structural," and so on.[68] Similar titles and terms are *Beyond Objectivism* and *After Freud.* He calls this a "post-age" stamp! The present is always thought to yield to a greater and better future. Yet one problem is that all these theories are historically relative. What will come after the postmodern or poststructuralist? Rorty is sufficiently concerned about being regarded as an elitist relativist to call his philosophy "local" or *ethnocentric* rather than relativist. But he actually agrees that his thought amounts to relativism, although he dislikes the term. But he cannot have it both ways.

Rorty's "criterion" of truth encourages competition, consumerism, and technology. In this sense it returns to the Enlightenment. It will have become apparent that in spite of his claims for "hermeneutics," Rorty's work is of relatively little value for hermeneutics in the sense in which the term is usually used. By contrast the European thinkers do hold out certain insights and warnings, which may cause some necessary heart searching in our hermeneutical endeavor. More specifically Rorty, Fish, and Lyotard (because of *The Differend*) go too far to remain useful for hermeneutics. Derrida, Barthes, Baudrillard, and Foucault can provide insights for hermeneutical reflection, but we view some aspects of their thought with extreme caution. We cannot generalize about postmodernism.

---

68. Terrence Tilley, "The 'Post-Age' Stamp," in *Postmodern Theologies,* pp. vi-vii.

6. Recommended Initial Reading

Critchley, Simon, and Timothy Mooney, "Deconstruction and Derrida," in *Twentieth-Century Continental Philosophy*, edited by Richard Kearney (London and New York: Routledge, 1994), pp. 441-71.

Haber, Honi Fern, *Beyond Postmodern Politics: Lyotard, Rorty, Foucault* (New York and London: Routledge, 1994), pp. 9-42 and 73-134.

Lyon, David, *Postmodernity* (Buckingham: Open University Press, 1994), pp. 1-19.

Rorty, Richard, *Truth and Progress: Philosophical Papers*, vol. 3 (Cambridge: Cambridge University Press, 1998), pp. 1-42.

Thiselton, Anthony C., "The Bible and Postmodernity" and "Retrospective Appraisal," in *Thiselton on Hermeneutics: Collected Works with New Essays* (Grand Rapids: Eerdmans; Aldershot: Ashgate, 2006), pp. 643-81.

CHAPTER XVII

Some Concluding Comments

1. Divine Agency and the Authority of Scripture

I am aware that in this book I have not fully addressed the problem of how divine agency in the inspiration of the Bible relates to human reading and interpretation. The nearest we came to this issue was in chapters V, VI, and VII, from the New Testament to the eighteenth century, and in chapter X, which included the theology of Karl Barth. Barth considers that the Holy Spirit will mediate the Word of God, although human faith and human expectations play a part. The earlier Church Fathers state their view of inspiration by the Holy Spirit, but this often remains a separate issue from their practical comments on reading or hearing and interpretation.

Recently Mark Bowald, as we noted, criticized Enlightenment theories of knowledge, Kant's philosophy, and the rise of biblical criticism, for obscuring or avoiding this question in studies of hermeneutics.[1] Jens Zimmermann makes a similar point about divine agency in Scripture. He urges that we ought to recover the pre-Enlightenment emphasis on contemplation of God as a primary condition for right interpretation.[2] But their plea for faith to be a presupposition of interpretation first ignores much work on *pre-understanding,* and second, ignores the multiform nature of biblical criticism, which encourages not (singular) *a* method, but (plural) method*s*. One must

1. Mark Alan Bowald, *Rendering the Word in Theological Hermeneutics* (Aldershot and Burlington, Vt.: Ashgate, 2007), pp. 16-25 and 163-83.
2. Jens Zimmermann, *Recovering Theological Hermeneutics: An Incarnational-Trinitarian Theory of Interpretation* (Grand Rapids: Baker Academic, 2004), throughout, but especially pp. 160-80.

do justice to the fact that Semler, Strauss, and F. C. Baur stand at one end of a spectrum, while Westcott, Lightfoot, and Hort, and more recently such writers as C. F. D. Moule, B. S. Childs, and F. F. Bruce, stand at the other.

In any case, we risk committing a category mistake. To put it crudely, how God chooses to inspire Scripture is God's concern, not so much ours, once we agree that this is the work of the Holy Spirit. This is not to say that human inquiry is irrelevant or unimportant; it is to say that it offers no more predictable or easy answers than any questions about the nature of the Holy Spirit. Even Karl Barth says about the gifts of the Spirit that we must focus on *whence* rather than *how*. "What we are really concerned with is not (spiritual) phenomena in themselves, but with their whence? and whither? to what do they point? to what do they testify?"[3]

This is even further complicated by the self-effacing operation of the Holy Spirit. God is at work, but this activity is seen only from its effects (John 3). It is no accident that the *how* has escaped writers' attention from earliest times. Bowald's diagrams and models do not help us very much. Wolterstorff has provided *one* possible model of divine agency.[4] But this is a different subject from hermeneutics, and it is a pity that Bowald is so critical of attempts to avoid fusing them together, with its related perils. Our attitude toward "spiritual gifts" is that the Spirit gives them "as he wills" (1 Cor. 12:11). The same can be said of the *how* of inspiring so many different biblical genres in different ways.

J. T. Burtchaell writes, "What confounds scholars in so many areas [is] the manner in which individual human events are jointly caused by both God and man. . . . The root problem is the incarnation."[5] We must avoid the equivalent of both Docetism and Arianism.

2. Advances in Linguistics and Pragmatics: Politeness Theory

Some probable future developments in hermeneutics may be mentioned. But perhaps these are too new to include in full detail as part of a textbook,

3. Karl Barth, *The Resurrection of the Dead*, trans. H. J. Stenning (London: Hodder and Stoughton, 1933), p. 80.

4. Nicholas Wolterstorff, *Divine Discourse: Philosophical Reflections on the Claim That God Speaks* (Cambridge: Cambridge University Press, 1995), especially pp. 1-8 and 95-129.

5. James T. Burtchaell, *Catholic Theories of Inspiration since 1810: A Review and Critique* (Cambridge: Cambridge University Press, 1969), p. 279.

not least because our prediction remains speculative. Even though the later Derrida qualifies his earlier remarks about an autonomous text, and although Barthes is not alone in speaking of the "death of the author," nevertheless this approach will be no more than a passing fashion. Wittgenstein makes it clear that a language game regularly consists "of language and the actions into which it is woven." He declares, "To imagine a language means to imagine a form of life." "Speaking . . . is part of an activity, or a form of life." "Commanding, questioning, recounting, chatting are as much a part of our natural history as walking, eating, drinking, playing."[6] The problem is that we are tempted to generalize and abstract, asking questions like "What is language?" or "What is meaning?" in the abstract.

To recognize that language often involves actions and settings brings us to the brink of what J. L. Austin calls *"performative" or "illocutionary" language.* Wittgenstein saw that the utterance "We mourn our brother" in the setting of a funeral service is not a statement describing an activity, but a performative utterance or illocutionary expression, which presupposes the fact of someone's death.[7] Austin explicitly showed also that performatives rest on the use of shared and accepted conventions. The adjective "true or false" does not apply to the performative itself, but to the situation it presupposes. In such examples as "I name this ship" or "I open this fete" or "I baptize this infant," the person who utters the performative or illocutionary utterance must be duly authorized to do so. A given procedure must also be fully executed. What happens if the archbishop declares, "I open this library," and the key snaps in the lock? Or what happens if I say, "I pick George," and he mumbles, "Not playing"?[8]

D. D. Evans develops this idea very well with reference to God's act of creation.[9] There is a hint of the parallel between conventions in everyday life and covenant in the context of divine word, action, or decree. John Searle modifies Austin's classifications and refines them, pointing out that performative verbs do not always correspond with performative actions. My former doctoral candidate Richard S. Briggs has further applied performa-

---

6. Ludwig Wittgenstein, *Philosophical Investigations,* German and English, English text translated by G. E. M. Anscombe (Oxford: Blackwell, 1967), sections 7, 19, 23, and 25.

7. Wittgenstein, *Philosophical Investigations,* part II, ix, p. 189.

8. John L. Austin, *How to Do Things with Words* (Oxford: Clarendon, 1965), pp. 11-38.

9. Donald D. Evans, *The Logic of Self-Involvement: A Philosophical Study of Everyday Language with Special Reference to the Christian Use of Language about God as Creator* (London: SCM, 1963), especially pp. 11-79.

tive language to confessions of faith, absolution, and teaching.[10] There is no doubt that this is fruitful territory for further exploration in hermeneutics, provided that we remember, unlike some German scholars, that performatives presuppose facts or imply statements, as well as conventions or perhaps covenant.

This leads to a further cognate subdiscipline in linguistics and pragmatics known in the discipline as *"politeness theory."* This emphasizes the situational background of language but observes especially that language and its contexts often pose either a threat or a face-saving device to the speaker. It calls on detailed work in biblical "introduction." In linguistic theory it rests heavily upon the work of Penelope Brown and Stephen Levinson.[11] It suggests that when we use language, our concern is largely to defend the "face" that we project, or have projected, and therefore we use face-saving language against possible "threats" provided by the conversation. It depends on earlier work on *conversional implicature* and on *speech acts* or *performatives.*[12] "Politeness" involves saving face for another. Positive face is the desire to be liked or appreciated. Some strategies aim to minimize threats, or constitute technically a "Face-Threatening Act" (known as FTA in the books).

William Olhausen, another of my successful Ph.D. candidates, has recently advanced these researches with reference to 1 Corinthians.[13] It is an irony that some in biblical studies focus on "the sociology of the New Testament" while others focus on Derrida, post-structuralism, or "rhetoric," when the text is often abstracted from its setting. Politeness theory offers a way forward. But often developments in other fields are greeted with great enthusiasm ten or twenty years after they have reached their peak in other disciplines and begun to wane. It is possible, however, that this approach will quickly enter hermeneutics.

10. John R. Searle, *Expression and Meaning: Studies in the Theory of Speech Acts* (Cambridge: Cambridge University Press, 1979), pp. 1-57, and Richard S. Briggs, *Words in Action: Speech Act Theory and Biblical Interpretation; Toward a Hermeneutic of Self-Involvement* (Edinburgh and New York: T. & T. Clark, 2001), especially part 2, pp. 147-292.

11. Penelope Brown and Stephen C. Levinson, *Politeness: Some Universals in Language Usage* (Cambridge: Cambridge University Press, 2003).

12. Stephen C. Levinson, *Pragmatics* (Cambridge: Cambridge University Press, 1983), pp. 97-166 and 226-83.

13. At the time of writing his only work to my knowledge in print is William Olhausen, "A 'Polite' Response to Anthony Thiselton," in *After Pentecost: Language and Biblical Interpretation,* ed. Craig Bartholomew and others, Scripture and Hermeneutics Series, vol. 2 (Grand Rapids: Zondervan; Carlisle: Paternoster, 2001), pp. 121-30.

3. Brevard Childs and the Canonical Approach

Another area I might have included in this textbook is "the canonical approach" of Brevard S. Childs (1923-2007). Childs commented in a recent interview that he disliked the term "canon criticism" as a description of his approach, because he had not produced a new critical method or methodology. He also stressed that neither we nor the Church "makes" a book canonical, but can "acknowledge" its canonical status.[14] F. F. Bruce has made the same correct point. Childs does attend, however, to communities of readers, and for much of life has also attended to "the reception" of texts by Judaism and the Church, as he did preeminently in his commentary on Exodus, which we have discussed.

Childs has always opposed the illusion of value-free neutral scholarship, and it is disappointing, to say the least, that Heikki Räisänen queried whether his scholarship was "sound," purely because they disagreed on this matter. In his *Introduction to the Old Testament as Scripture* (1979), Childs set himself the task of seeing what difference it made to interpret a biblical book in the light of its place in the canon.[15] Hosea's language on the triumph of love goes beyond his immediate situation. I studied this book with a group of clergy, and we agreed that the result was variable but very positive in some cases.

In 1984 Childs did the same with New Testament books. For example, we cannot ignore Luke's use of Hannah's song of praise when we come to the Magnificat of Mary (Luke 1:46-55; cf. 1 Sam. 2:1-10).

Childs pursued the theme further in *Old Testament Theology in a Canonical Context* (1985) and *Biblical Theology of the Old and New Testaments* (1992). He seeks to redefine biblical theology. Sometimes it is alleged that Childs has not been sufficiently attentive to biblical criticism. That, at least, has not been his intention. I have not provided a full section on Childs, first, because a textbook cannot include everything, and second, because it was only two years ago that I wrote on Childs.[16]

14. Brevard S. Childs, *Biblical Theology in Crisis* (Philadelphia: Westminster, 1970), p. 105.

15. Brevard S. Childs, *Introduction to the Old Testament as Scripture* (London: SCM; Philadelphia: Fortress, 1979).

16. Anthony C. Thiselton, "Canon, Community and Theological Construction," in *Canon and Biblical Interpretation*, ed. Craig G. Bartholomew and others, Scripture and Hermeneutics Series, vol. 7 (Grand Rapids: Zondervan; Carlisle: Paternoster, 2006), pp. 1-30.

4. Fuller Meaning, Typology, and Allegorical Interpretation

The question of "fuller meaning," or *sensus plenior*, of Scripture raises again the perennial question of the legitimacy of allegorical interpretation. We raised this question in chapters V, VI, and XV, especially in VI, "From the Third to the Thirteenth Centuries." During this discussion we noted Robert Markus's observation that Gregory could be less cautious than Augustine about allegory, because in the era of the Church Gregory was permitted a narrower worldview. Today things have turned full circle, and we are compelled, like Augustine, to hold a wider worldview and theory of signs.

Yet it is a pity that writers like Andrew Louth and perhaps Henri de Lubac commend allegory as an entirely positive, almost all-or-nothing view. The best biblical interpreters of the Church, including Augustine and Luther, have permitted allegory, but with careful reserve and caution. The answer seems to depend not on whether we disapprove of allegory or fully commend it, but on the purpose for which we are using Scripture, and whether we are interpreting an "open" or "closed" text. There is much precedent for allowing a contemplative use of allegory, but for not allowing its use to settle doctrinal conflicts. This explains much of the Reformer's suspicion of allegorical interpretation. Further, Calvin poses a dilemma for some of us when he insists that the Bible yields one single clear meaning *(unus et simplex)*. We might assume that he speaks primarily of doctrinal passages or of descriptive reports. But no one could imagine that poetic passages or the verses about the Suffering Servant have only one clear and simple meaning.

5. Catholic Biblical Scholarship and Two Great Turning Points

Relatively few of those discussed in this book stand in the Roman Catholic tradition, except that Catholics and Protestants would both claim as "theirs" the writers before the Reformation. To speak of Origen, of Augustine, of Nicholas of Lyra, or of Thomas Aquinas is to include our common Christian forebears. From the Reformation up to Vatican II, it happens that the most creative writers in hermeneutics have been Protestant scholars. But we have mentioned the inclusivity of the recent Pontifical Biblical Commission's *The Interpretation of the Bible in the Church* (Rome, 1994) and its introduction by

Joseph A. Fitzmyer.[17] This is a remarkably ecumenical document, prefaced by the then Joseph Cardinal Ratzinger, now Pope Benedict.

This document welcomes all the tools and methods of biblical scholarship, and is warm and positive about hermeneutics. From a Protestant viewpoint many of the joint statements are most encouraging, although the documents of Vatican II still insist on the immaculate conception and assumption of Mary, often claiming that these doctrines have a symbolic rather than "literal" meaning. The decisive step forward in much Catholic theology is to regard Mariological statements as statements about Christ and the incarnation. With few obvious exceptions, the Bible is treated similarly to that which Protestantism accords to it.

There is an equal omission at the other end of the spectrum. I have not included many other figures, for example, from Dean Freiday's *The Bible: Its Criticism, Interpretations, and Use in Sixteenth and Seventeenth Century England* (except Tyndale), which includes Richard Baxter and others. But again, a textbook must be selective about its content.

Schleiermacher and Gadamer do represent two crucial turning points in the subject. Together especially with Paul Ricoeur, they deserve, and have received, special attention. It is notable that, together with Karl Barth, Gadamer has so much about *"listening"* to the text. It is my hope that readers may come to the Bible not only in a "listening" way, but also with appropriate *expectations,* as Jauss emphasizes. Listening and expectancy would do much to give to the Bible the place it deserves in public and private reading. The "authority" of the Bible will thereby become a practical matter of experience as well as a doctrine.

17. Joseph A. Fitzmyer, *The Biblical Commission's Document "The Interpretation of the Bible in the Church": Text and Commentary* (Rome: Pontifical Biblical Institute, 1995).

Select Bibliography

Those books or articles that some think of as textbooks are marked with an asterisk (*). Books referred to here as significant for their contribution to hermeneutics are marked (+).

Aageson, J. W., *Written Also for Our Sake: Paul and the Art of Biblical Interpretation* (Louisville: Westminster John Knox, 1993).

*Achtemeier, Paul J., *An Introduction to the New Hermeneutic* (Philadelphia: Westminster, 1969).

+Alter, Robert, *The Art of Biblical Narrative* (New York: Basic Books, 1981).

+Apel, Karl-Otto, *Understanding and Explanation: A Transcendental-Pragmatic Perspective* (Cambridge: MIT Press, 1984).

Aquinas, Thomas, *Commentary on John,* translated by J. A. Weisheipl and F. R. Larcher, Aquinas Scripture Commentaries 3 and 4 (Albany, N.Y.: Magi Books, 1966, 1998).

———, *Commentary on the Epistle of Paul to the Ephesians,* translated by F. R. Larcher, Aquinas Scripture Commentaries 2 (Albany, N.Y.: Magi Books, 1966).

———, *Summa Theologiae,* Latin and English, Blackfriars edition, 60 vols. (London: Eyre and Spottiswood; New York: McGraw-Hill, 1963 onward).

Assmann, Hugo, *A Practical Theology of Liberation,* translated by Paul Burns, introduction by Gustavo Gutiérrez (London: Search Press, 1975).

*Atkinson, James, *Martin Luther and the Birth of Protestantism* (London: Penguin Books, 1968).

Attridge, H. W., *Commentary on the Epistle to the Hebrews* (Philadelphia: Fortress, 1989).

+Austin, John L., *How to Do Things with Words* (Oxford: Clarendon, 1992, 1965).

+Baird, J. Arthur, *Audience Criticism and the Historical Jesus* (Philadelphia: Westminster, 1969).

*Baird, William, *History of New Testament Research,* 3 vols., vol. 2, *Jonathan Edwards to Rudolf Bultmann* (Minneapolis: Fortress, 2003).

Bal, Mieke, *Murder and Difference: Gender, Genre, and Scholarship on Sisera's Death,* translated by M. Gumpert (Bloomington: Indiana University Press, 1988; reprint 1992).

Balthasar, Hans Urs von, *Theo-Drama: Theological Dramatic Theory,* translated by G. Harrison, 5 vols. (San Francisco: Ignatius, 1988-98).

Barr, James, *The Bible in the Modern World* (London: SCM, 1973).

+————, *The Semantics of Biblical Language* (Oxford: Oxford University Press, 1961).

+Barth, Karl, *Church Dogmatics,* edited by G. W. Bromiley, T. F. Torrance, and others, 14 vols. (Edinburgh: T. & T. Clark, 1957-75).

+————, *The Epistle to the Romans,* translated by E. C. Hoskyns (Oxford and London: Oxford University Press, 1933).

————, *The Resurrection of the Dead,* translated by H. J. Stenning (London: Hodder and Stoughton, 1933).

————, "Rudolf Bultmann — an Attempt to Understand Him," in *Kerygma and Myth: A Theological Debate,* edited by Hans Werner Bartsch, 2 vols. (London: SCM, 1953), 2:83-132.

*————, "The Strange New World within the Bible," in Barth, *The Word of God and the Word of Man* (London: Hodder and Stoughton, 1928), pp. 28-50.

————, *The Theology of Schleiermacher: Lectures at Göttingen, 1923-24,* translated by G. W. Bromiley (Grand Rapids: Eerdmans, 1982).

*————, *The Word of God and the Word of Man,* translated by D. Horton (London: Hodder and Stoughton, 1928).

Barthes, Roland, "The Death of the Author" (1968), in *Image-Music-Text,* translated by Stephen Heath (London: Fontana, 1977).

————, *Elements of Semiology* (London: Jonathan Cape, 1967).

*————, *Mythologies* (London: Jonathan Cape, 1972).

————, *The Rustle of Language,* translated by R. Howard (New York: Hill and Wang, 1986).

+————, "A Structural Analysis of a Narrative from Acts X-XI," in *Structural-*

ism and Biblical Hermeneutics: A Collection of Essays, edited and translated by Alfred M. Johnson (Pittsburgh: Pickwick, 1979), pp. 109-39.

Barton, John, *Reading the Old Testament: Method in Biblical Study* (London: Darton, Longman and Todd, 1984).

*Bauckham, Richard J., *Bible and Mission: Christian Witness in a Postmodern World* (Grand Rapids: Baker Academic; Carlisle: Paternoster, 2003).

Baudrillard, Jean, *Forget Foucault* (New York: Semiotext(e), 1987).

——, *The Mirror of Production,* translated by M. Poster (St. Louis: Telos Press, 1975).

+——, *Simulations,* translated by P. Foss and others (New York: Semiotext(e), 1983); French edition, *Simulacres et Simulation.*

+Bauman, Zygmunt, *Hermeneutics and Social Science: Approaches to Understanding* (London: Hutchinson, 1978).

Bernard, L. W., *Justin Martyr: His Life and Thought* (Cambridge: Cambridge University Press, 1967).

Bernauer, James, and Jeremy Garrette, eds., *Michel Foucault and Theology: The Politics of Religious Experience* (Aldershot and Burlington, Vt.: Ashgate, 2004).

*Berryman, Phillip, *Liberation Theology* (London: Tauris, 1987).

*——, *The Religious Roots of Rebellion: Christians in the Central American Revolutions* (London: SCM, 1984).

+Betti, Emilio, *Allgemeine Auslegungslehre als Methodik der Geisteswissenschaften,* German translation and edition of the Italian (Tübingen: Mohr, 1967).

Bible and Culture Collective, *The Postmodern Bible* (New Haven: Yale University Press, 1997).

Bird, Phyllis A., *Missing Persons and Mistaken Identities: Women and Gender in Ancient Israel* (Minneapolis: Fortress, 1997).

*Blackman, E. C., *Biblical Interpretation* (London: Independent Press, 1957).

Blank, Josef, in *Rudolf Bultmann in Catholic Thought,* edited by Thomas F. O'Meara and Donald M. Weisser (New York: Herder and Herder, 1968), pp. 78-109.

Bleich, David, *The Double Perspective: Language, Literacy, and Social Relations* (New York and Oxford: Oxford University Press, 1988).

Bleicher, Josef, *Contemporary Hermeneutics: Hermeneutics as Method, Philosophy, and Critique* (London and Boston: Routledge and Kegan Paul, 1980).

*Blomberg, Craig L., *Interpreting the Parables* (Leicester: Apollos, 1990).

Boesak, Allan, *Black and Reformed: Apartheid, Liberation, and the Calvinist Tradition* (Maryknoll, N.Y.: Orbis, 1984).

Boff, Leonardo, *Jesus Christ Liberator: A Critical Christology of Our Time*, translated by Patrick Hughes (Maryknoll, N.Y: Orbis, 1978; London: SPCK, 1980).

*Boff, Leonardo, and Clodovis Boff, eds., *Introducing Liberation Theology* (London: Burns and Oates, 1987).

Bonhoeffer, Dietrich, *Meditating on the Word* (Cambridge, Mass.: Cowley, 1986).

Bonner, Gerald, "Augustine as Biblical Scholar," in *The Cambridge History of the Bible,* edited by P. R. Ackroyd and C. F. Evans (Cambridge: Cambridge University Press, 1970), 1:541-63.

Boucher, Madeline, *The Mysterious Parable: A Literary Study* (Washington, D.C.: American Catholic Biblical Association, 1977).

Bovon, François, introduction to *Exegesis: Problems of Method and Exegesis in Reading (Genesis 22 and Luke 15),* edited by François Bovon and Grégoire Rauiller, translated by D. G. Miller (Pittsburgh: Pickwick, 1978).

————, *Luke the Theologian,* 2nd ed. (Waco, Tex.: Baylor University Press, 2006).

Bowald, Mark Alan, *Rendering the Word in Theological Hermeneutics* (Aldershot and Burlington, Vt.: Ashgate, 2007).

+Briggs, Richard S., *Words in Action: Speech Act Theory and Biblical Interpretation; Toward a Hermeneutic of Self-Involvement* (Edinburgh and New York: T. & T. Clark, 2001).

+Brown, Penelope, and Stephen C. Levinson, *Politeness: Some Universals in Language Usage* (Cambridge: Cambridge University Press, 2003).

+Bultmann, Rudolf, *Faith and Understanding,* vol. 1 (London: SCM, 1969).

————, *History of the Synoptic Tradition,* translated by John Marsh (Oxford: Blackwell, 1963).

————, "Is Exegesis without Presuppositions Possible?" in *Existence and Faith: Shorter Writings of Rudolf Bultmann,* edited by S. M. Ogden (London: Collins, 1964), pp. 342-52.

*————, *Jesus Christ and Mythology and Other Essays,* edited and translated by Schubert Ogden (Philadelphia: Fortress: 1984).

+————, "New Testament and Mythology," in *Kerygma and Myth: A Theological Debate,* edited by Hans Werner Bartsch, 2 vols. (London: SCM, 1953), 1:1-44; retranslated in Bultmann, *New Testament Mythology and Other Ba-*

sic Writings, selected, edited, and translated by Schubert M. Ogden (Philadelphia: Fortress, 1984), pp. 35-36.

+―――, "The Problem of Hermeneutics," *Zeitschrift für Theologie und Kirche* 47 (1950): 47-69; reprinted in Bultmann, *Essays Philosophical and Theological* (London: SCM, 1955), pp. 234-61.

Burrows, Mark S., and Paul Rorem, eds., *Biblical Hermeneutics in Historical Perspective: Studies in Honour of Karlfried Froehlich on His Sixtieth Birthday* (Grand Rapids: Eerdmans, 1991).

Burtchaell, James T., *Catholic Theories of Inspiration since 1810: A Review and Critique* (Cambridge: Cambridge University Press, 1969).

Caird, George B., *The Language and Imagery of the Bible* (London: Duckworth, 1980).

Cairns, David, *A Gospel without Myth? Bultmann's Challenge to the Preacher* (London: SCM, 1960).

Calvin, John, *The Epistles of Paul to the Galatians, Ephesians, Philippians, and Colossians*, translated by T. H. L. Parker (Edinburgh: Oliver and Boyd, 1965).

+―――, *Institutes of the Christian Religion*, translated by Henry Beveridge, 2 vols. (London: James Clarke, 1957).

+―――, preface to *The Epistles of Paul to the Romans and the Thessalonians*, translated by R. Mackenzie, edited by T. F. Torrance (Edinburgh: Oliver and Boyd, 1964).

―――, *The Second Epistle of Paul to the Corinthians; the Epistles of Paul to Timothy, Titus, and Philemon*, translated by T. A. Smart (Edinburgh: St. Andrews Press, 1964).

Cannon, Kate G., *Women and the Soul of the Black Community* (New York: Concilium, 1995; 1st ed. 1985).

Carson, Donald A., *Biblical Interpretation in the Church: Text and Context* (Exeter: Paternoster, 1984).

Castelli, Elizabeth, *Imitating Paul: A Discourse of Power* (Louisville: Westminster John Knox, 1991).

―――, "Interpretations of Power in 1 Corinthians," in *Michel Foucault and Theology: The Politics of Religious Experience*, edited by James Bernauer and Jeremy Garrette (Aldershot and Burlington, Vt.: Ashgate, 2004), pp. 19-38.

Chadwick, Henry, *The Enigma of Philo* (London: Athlone, 1969).

Charity, A. C., *Events and Their Afterlife: The Dialectics of Christian Typology in the Bible and Dante* (Cambridge: Cambridge University Press, 1966).

Childs, Brevard S., *Biblical Theology in Crisis* (Philadelphia: Westminster, 1970).

+————, *Exodus: A Commentary* (London: SCM, 1974).

+————, *Introduction to the Old Testament as Scripture* (London: SCM; Philadelphia: Fortress, 1979).

Chilton, Bruce D., *A Galilean Rabbi and His Bible: Jesus' Use of the Interpreted Scripture of His Time* (London: SPCK, 1984).

*————, "Targum," in *Dictionary of Biblical Interpretation,* edited by John H. Hayes, 2 vols. (Nashville: Abingdon, 1999), 2:531-34.

Christ, Carol C., *The Laughter of Aphrodite* (New York: Harper and Row, 1987).

————, *Rebirth of the Goddess* (New York: Routledge, 1997).

+Christianson, Eric, *Ecclesiastes through the Centuries,* Blackwell Bible Commentaries (Oxford: Blackwell, 2007).

+Corrington, Robert S., *The Community of Interpreters: On the Hermeneutics of Nature and the Bible in the American Philosophical Tradition* (Macon, Ga.: Mercer University Press, 1987).

*Court, John M., ed., *Biblical Interpretation: The Meanings of Scripture — Past and Present* (London and New York: T. & T. Clark and Continuum, 2003).

Cranfield, Charles E. B., *The Gospel according to St. Mark: A Commentary,* Cambridge Greek Testament (Cambridge: Cambridge University Press, 1959).

+Croatto, J. Severino, *Exodus: A Hermeneutics of Freedom,* translated by Salvator Attanasio (Maryknoll, N.Y.: Orbis, 1981).

Crossan, John Dominic, *Cliffs of Fall: Paradox and Polyvalence in the Parables of Jesus* (New York: Seabury Press, 1980).

+————, *In Parables: The Challenge of the Historical Jesus* (New York: Harper and Row, 1973).

————, *Raid on the Articulate: Comic Eschatology in Jesus and Borges* (New York: Harper and Row, 1976).

Danaher, Geoff, Tony Schirato, and Jen Webb, *Understanding Foucault* (London and New Delhi: Jage Publications, 2000).

Daube, David, "Rabbinic Methods of Interpretation and Hellenistic Rhetoric," *Hebrew Union College Annual* 22 (1949): 234-64.

Derrida, Jacques, in *Deconstruction and Criticism,* edited by H. Bloom et al. (London: Routledge and Kegan Paul, 1979).

————, *Limited Inc,* edited by G. Graff, translated by J. Mehlmann and S. Weber (Evanston, Ill.: Northwestern University Press, 1988).

+———, *Margins of Philosophy,* translated by Alan Bass (London and New York: Harvester Wheatsheaf, 1982).

———, *Of Grammatology,* translated by G. C. Spirak (Baltimore: Johns Hopkins University Press, 1975).

+———, *Speech and Phenomena and Other Essays on Husserl's Theory of Signs,* translated by D. B. Allison (Evanston, Ill.: Northwestern University Press, 1973).

———, *Writing and Difference,* translated by A. Bas (Chicago: University of Chicago Press, 1978).

+Dilthey, Wilhelm, *Gesammelte Schriften,* vol. 7 (Leipzig and Berlin: Teubner, 1927), pp. 213-14; translated in *Selected Writings,* edited by H. P. Rickman (Cambridge: Cambridge University Press, 1976), pp. 226-27.

+———, *Gesammelte Werke,* vol. 5, *Die geistige Welt: Einleitung in das Philosophie des Lebens* (1924).

———, "The Rise of Hermeneutics," translated by Frederick Jameson, *New Literary History* 3 (1972): 229-441.

*Dobshütz, Ernst von, "Interpretation," in *Encyclopedia of Religion and Ethics,* vol. 7, edited by James Hastings (Edinburgh: T. & T. Clark, 1926), pp. 391-95.

*Docherty, Thomas, "Postmodernist Theory: Lyotard, Baudrillard, and Others," in *Twentieth-Century Continental Philosophy,* edited by Richard Kearny (London and New York: Routledge, 1994).

Dodd, Charles H., *According to the Scriptures* (London: Collins/Fontana, 1965).

*———, *The Parables of the Kingdom* (London: Nisbet, 1935).

Doeve, J. V., *Jewish Hermeneutic in the Synoptic Gospels and Acts* (Assen: Van Gorcum, 1954).

Donaldson, Laura E., ed., *Semeia 75: Postcolonialism and Scriptural Reading* (n.p.: Society of Biblical Literature, 1996).

*Dussel, Enrique, ed., *The Church in Latin America, 1492-1992* (London: Burns and Oates; New York: Orbis, 1992).

Ebeling, Gerhard, *An Introduction to a Theological Theory of Language* (London: Collins, 1973).

———, "Time and Word," in *The Future of Our Religious Past: Essays in Honour of Rudolf Bultmann,* edited by James M. Robinson (London: SCM, 1971); translated from *Zeit und Geschichte* (1964).

———, *Word and Faith,* translated by J. W. Leitch (Philadelphia: Fortress; London: SCM, 1963).

————, *The Word of God and Tradition,* translated by S. H. Hooke (London: Collins, 1968).

Eco, Umberto, *The Role of the Reader* (London: Hutchinson, 1981).

+————, *A Theory of Semiotics* (Bloomington: Indiana University Press, 1976).

Entrevernes Group, *Signs and Parables: Semiotics and Gospel Texts,* with a study by Jacques Geninasca, postface by A. J. Greimas, translated by Gary Phillips, Pittsburgh Theological Monograph 23 (Pittsburgh: Pickwick, 1978).

Epp, Eldon Jay, *Junia: The First Woman Apostle* (Minneapolis: Fortress, 2005).

Erb, Peter C., *Pietists: Selected Writings* (London: SPCK; New York: Paulist, 1983).

Eriksson, Anders, *Tradition as Rhetorical Proof: Pauline Argumentation in 1 Corinthians* (Stockholm: Almqvist & Wiksell, 1998).

*Evans, Craig A., "Targum," in *Dictionary of Biblical Criticism and Interpretation,* edited by Stanley E. Porter (London and New York: Routledge, 2007), pp. 347-49.

+Evans, Donald D., *The Logic of Self-Involvement: A Philosophical Study of Everyday Language with Special Reference to the Christian Use of Language about God as Creator* (London: SCM, 1963).

Evans, Gillian R., *The Language and Logic of the Bible: The Road to the Reformation* (Cambridge: Cambridge University Press, 1965).

+Fish, Stanley, *Doing What Comes Naturally: Change, Rhetoric, and the Practice of Theory in Literary and Legal Studies* (Oxford: Clarendon, 1989), pp. 1-35.

+————, *Is There a Text in This Class? The Authority of Interpretive Communities* (Cambridge: Harvard University Press, 1980).

Fitzmyer, Joseph A., ed., *The Biblical Commission's Document "The Interpretation of the Bible in the Church": Text and Commentary* (Rome: Pontifical Biblical Institute, 1995).

Flannery, Austin P., O.P., ed., *Documents of Vatican II* (Grand Rapids: Eerdmans, 1975).

Foerster, Werner, *Gnosis: A Selection of Gnostic Texts,* translated by R. McL. Wilson, 2 vols. (Oxford: Clarendon, 1972).

Forbes, G. W., *The God of Old: The Role of Lukan Parables in the Purpose of Luke's Gospel,* Journal for the Study of the New Testament, Supplement Series, no. 198 (Sheffield: Sheffield Academic Press, 2001).

*Ford, David F. (with Rachel Muers), *The Modern Theologians,* 3rd ed. (Oxford: Blackwell, 2005).

Ford, J. M., "Towards the Reinstatement of Allegory," *St. Vladimir's Theological Quarterly* 34 (1990): 161-95.

Foucault, Michel, *Discipline and Punish,* translated by A. Sheridan (New York: Pantheon and Penguin, 1977).

————, *Madness and Civilization,* translated by R. Howard (New York: Pantheon, 1965).

————, *The Order of Things,* translated by A. Sheridan (New York: Random House, 1970).

*Fowl, Stephen E., ed., *The Theological Interpretation of Scripture: Classic and Contemporary Readings* (Oxford: Blackwell, 1997).

Fowler, Robert M., *Loaves and Fishes: The Function of the Feeding Stories in the Gospel of Mark,* Society of Biblical Literature Dissertation Series 54 (Chico, Calif.: Scholars Press, 1981).

France, R. T., *Jesus and the Old Testament* (London: Tyndale Press, 1971).

*Frei, Hans, "David Friedrich Strauss," in *Nineteenth Century Religious Thought in the West,* edited by Ninian Smart et al. (Cambridge: Cambridge University Press, 1985), 1:215-60.

Friere, Paulo, *Pedagogy of the Oppressed* (New York: Herder and Herder, 1970).

Froehlich, K., *Biblical Interpretation in the Early Church,* translated by W. G. Rusch (Philadelphia: Fortress, 1984).

Frye, Northrop, *The Great Code: The Bible and Literature* (New York and London: Harcourt Brace Jovanovich, 1982).

+Fuchs, Ernst, "The Hermeneutical Problem," in *The Future of Our Religious Past: Essays in Honour of Rudolf Bultmann,* edited by J. M. Robinson, translated by C. E. Carlston and R. P. Scharlemann (London: SCM, 1971), pp. 267-78.

————, *Hermeneutik,* 4th ed. (Tübingen: Mohr, 1970).

+————, "The New Testament and the Hermeneutical Problem," in *New Frontiers in Theology,* vol. 2, *The New Hermeneutic,* edited by James M. Robinson and John B. Cobb, Jr. (New York and London: Harper and Row, 1964).

————, *Studies of the Historical Jesus,* translated by A. Scobie (London: SCM, 1964).

*Funk, Robert W., *Language, Hermeneutic, and Word of God* (New York: Harper and Row, 1966).

Gadamer, Hans-Georg, *Hermeneutics, Religion, and Ethics,* translated by Joel Weinsheimer (New Haven: Yale University Press, 1999).

+———, *Philosophical Hermeneutics,* translated by David Linge (Berkeley: University of California Press, 1976).

+———, "Reflections on My Philosophical Journey," in *The Philosophy of Hans-Georg Gadamer,* edited by Lewis Edwin Hahn (Chicago and La Salle, Ill.: Open Court, 1997).

+———, *Truth and Method,* 2nd English ed. (London: Sheed and Ward, 1989).

Garrette, Jeremy R., *Foucault and Religion: Spiritual Corporality and Political Spirituality* (London and New York: Routledge, 1999, 2007).

Geffré, Claude, *The Risk of Interpretation: On Being Faithful to the Christian Tradition in a Non-Christian Age* (New York: Paulist, 1987).

Goba, Bonganjalo, *An Agenda for Black Theology: Hermeneutics for Social Change* (Johannesburg: Skotaville, 1988).

Gollwitzer, Helmut, *The Existence of God as Confessed by Faith,* translated by James W. Leitch (London: SCM, 1965).

*Goppelt, Leonhard, *Typos: The Typological Interpretation of the Old Testament in the New,* translated by D. H. Hadvig (Grand Rapids: Eerdmans, 2006).

*Gottwald, Norman K., ed., *The Bible and Liberation: Political and Social Hermeneutics* (Maryknoll, N.Y.: Orbis, 1983).

*Grant, Robert M., *A Short History of the Interpretation of the Bible,* 3rd ed. (London: Black, 1965; rev. ed., Philadelphia: Fortress, 1984).

Green, Joel, *The Gospel of Luke* (Grand Rapids: Eerdmans, 1997).

Greenslade, S. L., ed., *The Cambridge History of the Bible,* vol. 3, *The West from the Reformation to the Present Day* (Cambridge: Cambridge University Press, 1963).

Greimas, A. J., *Sémantique Structurale: recherche de méthode* (Paris: Larousse, 1966; reprint, Paris: Presses Universitaires, 1986).

Grelot, P., *What Are the Targums? Selected Texts* (Collegeville, Minn.: Liturgical Press, 1992).

Grobel, Kendrick, *The Gospel of Truth: A Valentinian Meditation on the Gospel* (London: Black, 1960).

*Grondin, Jean, *Hans-Georg Gadamer: A Biography,* translated by Joel C. Weinsheimer (New Haven and London: Yale University Press, 2003).

Gundry, Patricia, *Neither Slave Nor Free: Helping Women Answer the Call to Church Leadership* (London and New York: Harper Collins, 1987).

Gundry, Robert H., *The Use of the Old Testament in St. Matthew's Gospel with Special Reference to the Messianic Hope* (Leiden: Brill, 1967).

Gunn, David M., *Judges*, Blackwell Commentaries (Oxford: Blackwell, 2005).

+*Gutiérrez, Gustavo, O.P., *A Theology of Liberation: History, Politics, and Salvation*, translated by Sister Caridad Inda and John Eagleson (London: SCM, 1974).

Gutting, Gary, ed., *The Cambridge Companion to Foucault* (Cambridge: Cambridge University Press, 1994).

+Habermas, Jürgen, *Knowledge and Human Interest*, 2nd ed. (London: Heinemann, 1978).

+———, *The Theory of Communicative Action*, translated by Thomas McCarthy, 2 vols. (Cambridge: Polity Press, 1984-87).

Hagner, Donald H., *The Gospel of Matthew*, 2 vols. (Dallas: Word, 1993).

Hampson, Daphne, *After Christianity* (London: SCM, 1996).

———, *Theology and Feminism* (Oxford: Blackwell, 1990).

+Hanson, Anthony Tyrrell, *The Living Utterances of God: The New Testament Exegesis of the Old* (London: Darton, Longman and Todd, 1983).

+*Hanson, R. P. C., *Allegory and Event: A Study of the Sources and Significance of Origen's Interpretation of Scripture* (London: SCM, 1959), pp. 11-64.

Haroutunian, Joseph, and Louise Pettibone Smith, eds., *Calvin's Commentaries*, Library of Christian Classics, vol. 23 (London: SCM; Philadelphia: Westminster, 1958).

Harvey, David, *The Condition of Postmodernity* (Oxford: Blackwell, 1989).

Hayes, John, ed., *Dictionary of Biblical Interpretation*, 2 vols. (Nashville: Abingdon, 1999).

Heal, Jane, "Pragmatism and Choosing to Believe," in *Reading Rorty*, edited by Alan Malachowski (Oxford: Blackwell, 1990), pp. 101-36.

Heidegger, Martin, *Being and Time*, translated by John Macquarrie and Edward Robinson (Oxford: Blackwell, 1962).

———, *Introduction to Metaphysics* (New Haven: Yale University Press, 1959).

Heine, Susanne, *Christianity and the Goddesses: Systematic Critique of a Feminist Theology* (London: SCM, 1988).

———, *Women and Early Christianity: Are the Feminist Scholars Right?* (London: SCM, 1987).

Henderson, Ian, *Myth in the New Testament* (London: SCM, 1952).

Hepburn, R. W., "Demythologizing and the Problem of Validity," in *New Essays in Philosophical Theology*, edited by A. Flew and A. MacIntyre (London: SCM, 1955), pp. 227-42.

*Hodges, H. A., "Selected Passages from Dilthey," in *Wilhelm Dilthey: An Introduction* (London: Oxford University Press, 1944).

Holgate, David, and Rachel Starr, *Biblical Hermeneutics* (London: SCM, 2006).

Holland, Norman, *Five Readers Reading* (New Haven: Yale University Press, 1975).

Holland, Tom, *Contours of Pauline Theology: A Radical New Survey of the Influences on Paul's Biblical Writings* (Fearn, Scotland: Christian Focus, 2004).

*Humm, Maggie, ed., *The Dictionary of Feminist Theory* (New York: Harvester Wheatsheaf, 1989).

*Hunter, A. M., *Interpreting the Parables* (London: SCM, 1964).

*———, *The Parables Then and Now* (London: SCM, 1971).

+Iser, Wolfgang, *The Act of Reading: A Theory of Aesthetic Response* (Baltimore: Johns Hopkins University Press, 1978, 1980).

+———, *The Implied Reader: Patterns of Communication in Prose Fiction from Bunyan to Beckett* (Baltimore: Johns Hopkins University Press, 1974).

*Jasper, David, *A Short Introduction to Hermeneutics* (Louisville and London: Westmister John Knox, 2004).

+Jauss, Hans Robert, *Toward an Aesthetic of Reception,* translated by T. Bahti (Minneapolis: University of Minnesota Press, 1982).

*Jeanrond, Werner G., *Theological Hermeneutics: Development and Significance* (London: Macmillan, 1991).

*Jensen, Alexander, *Theological Hermeneutics,* SCM Core Text (London: SCM, 2007).

*Jeremias, Joachim, *The Parables of Jesus,* translated by S. A. Hooke, rev. ed. (London: SCM, 1963).

Jewett, Robert, *Letter to Pilgrims: A Commentary on the Epistle to the Hebrews* (New York: Pilgrim Press, 1981).

Johnson, Alfred M., ed., *Structuralism and Biblical Hermeneutics: A Collection of Essays* (Pittsburgh: Pickwick, 1979).

Johnson, Roger A., *The Origins of Demythologizing: Philosophy and Historiography in the Theology of Rudolf Bultmann* (Leiden: Brill, 1974).

Jonas, Hans, *The Gnostic Religion: The Message of the Alien God and the Beginnings of Christianity,* 2nd ed. (Boston: Beacon Press, 1963).

Jones, Geraint Vaughan, *The Art and Truth of the Parables* (London: SPCK, 1964).

Kant, Immanuel, *Critique of Judgement,* translated by Werner Pluhar (Indianapolis: Hackett, 1987).

Käsemann, Ernst, *The Wandering People of God: An Investigation into the Epis-

tle to the Hebrews, translated by R. Harrisville and A. Sandberg (Minneapolis: Augsburg, 1984).

Kearney, Richard, *On Paul Ricoeur: The Owl of Minerva* (Aldershot and Burlington, Vt.: Ashgate, 2004).

Kierkegaard, Søren, *Concluding Unscientific Postscript to the Philosophical Fragments* (Princeton: Princeton University Press, 1941).

Kim, Seyoon K., *The "Son of Man" as the Son of God* (Tübingen: Mohr, 1983).

King, J. Christopher, *Origen on the Song of Songs as the Spirit of Scripture: The Bridegroom's Perfect Marriage Song* (Oxford: Oxford University Press, 2006).

*Kirk, J. Andrew, *Liberation Theology: An Evangelical View from the Third World* (London: Marshall, Morgan and Scott, 1979).

Kissinger, Warren S., *The Parables of Jesus: A History of Interpretation and Bibliography* (Metuchen, N.J., and London: Scarecrow, 1979).

Kittel, Gerhard, and Gerhard Friedrich, eds., *Theological Dictionary of the New Testament,* translated by G. W. Bromiley, 10 vols. (Grand Rapids: Eerdmans, 1964-76).

Klein, William W., Craig L. Blomberg, and Robert L. Hubbard, Jr., *Introduction to Biblical Interpretation* (Dallas: Word, 1993).

*Klemm, David E., *Hermeneutical Inquiry,* 2 vols. (Atlanta: Scholars Press, 1986).

————, *The Hermeneutical Theory of Paul Ricoeur: A Constructive Analysis* (London and Toronto: Associated University Press, 1983).

Kovacs, Judith L., *1 Corinthians Interpreted by Early Christian Commentators* (Grand Rapids: Eerdmans, 2005).

Kovacs, Judith, and Christopher Rowland, *Revelation,* Blackwell Bible Commentaries (Oxford: Blackwell, 2004).

Künneth, Walter, *The Theology of the Resurrection* (London: SCM, 1965).

Kusimbi, Kanyoro, *Women, Violence, and Non-Violent Change* (Geneva: World Council of Churches, 1996).

+Laeuchli, Samuel, *The Language of Faith: An Introduction to the Semantic Dilemma of the Early Church,* introduction by C. K. Barrett (London: Epworth, 1965).

Lambrecht, Ian, *Once More Astonished: The Parables of Jesus* (New York: Crossroad, 1981).

Lampe, G. W. H., and K. J. Woollcombe, *Essays on Typology* (London: SCM, 1957).

Lane, William L., *The Epistle to the Hebrews*, 2 vols., Word Biblical Commentaries, vol. 47 (Dallas: Word, 1991).

Leach, Edmund, "Structuralism and Anthropology," in *Structuralism: An Introduction*, edited by David Robey (Oxford: Oxford University Press, 1973), pp. 37-56.

Levinson, Stephen C., *Pragmatics* (Cambridge: Cambridge University Press, 1983).

Lewis, C. S., *Experiment in Criticism* (Cambridge: Cambridge University Press, 1961).

Linnemann, Eta, *Parables of Jesus: Introduction and Exposition*, translated by John Sturdy from 3rd edition (London: SPCK, 1966).

Livingstone, David N., *Putting Science in Its Place: Geographies of Scientific Knowledge* (Chicago: University of Chicago Press, 2003).

———, *Science, Space, and Hermeneutics* (Heidelberg: University of Heidelberg, 2002).

*Loades, Ann, ed., *Feminist Theology: A Reader* (London: SPCK; Louisville: Westminster John Knox, 1990).

Lonergan, Bernard J. F., *Method in Theology* (London: Darton, Longman and Todd, 1972).

Longenecker, Richard, *Biblical Exegesis in the Apostolic Period* (Grand Rapids: Eerdmans, 1975).

Louth, Andrew, "Return to Allegory," in Louth, *Discerning the Mystery: An Essay on the Nature of Theology* (Oxford: Clarendon, 1983).

Lubac, Henri de, *Medieval Exegesis*, vol. 2, *The Four Senses of Scripture*, translated by E. M. Maeierowski (Grand Rapids: Eerdmans; Edinburgh: T. & T. Clark, 2000).

Lundin, Roger, ed., *Disciplining Hermeneutics: Interpretation in Christian Perspective* (Grand Rapids: Eerdmans; Leicester: Apollos, 1997).

Luther, Martin, *Commentary on the Epistle to the Hebrews*, in *Luther's Early Theological Works*, edited by James Atkinson, Library of Christian Classics, vol. 16 (London: SCM; Philadelphia: Westminster, 1962).

+———, *The Heidelberg Disputation*, in *Luther's Early Theological Works*, edited by James Atkinson, Library of Christian Classics, vol. 16 (London: SCM; Philadelphia: Westminster, 1962).

+———, *Luther's Works*, edited by J. Pelikan, 56 vols. (St. Louis: Concordia, 1955-).

+Luz, Ulrich, *Matthew 1–7: A Commentary*, translated by W. C. Linss (Minneapolis: Augsburg Fortress; Edinburgh: T. & T. Clark, 1989).

+————, *Matthew 8–20,* translated by W. C. Linss (Minneapolis: Augsburg Fortress; London: SCM, 2001).

+————, *Matthew 21–28,* translated by J. E. Crouch (Minneapolis: Fortress; London: SCM, 2005).

*Lyon, David, *Postmodernity* (Buckingham: Open University Press, 1994).

Lyotard, Jean-François, *The Differend: Phrases in Dispute,* translated by G. van den Abbeek (Manchester: Manchester University Press, 1990).

————, *Just Gaming,* translated by W. Godzich (Manchester: Manchester University Press, 1985).

————, *The Postmodern Condition: A Report on Knowledge,* translated by G. Bennington and B. Massumi (Manchester: Manchester University Press, 1984; French edition, 1979).

*McKim, Donald K., ed., *Dictionary of Major Biblical Interpreters* (Downers Grove, Ill., and Nottingham: IVP, 2007).

McKnight, Edgar V., *The Bible and the Reader: An Introduction to Literary Criticism* (Philadelphia: Fortress, 1985).

Macquarrie, John, *An Existentialist Theology: A Comparison of Heidegger and Bultmann* (London: SCM, 1955).

————, *The Scope of Demythologizing: Bultmann and His Critics* (London: SCM, 1962).

Marks, Elaine, and Isabelle de Courtivron, eds., *New French Feminisms: An Anthology* (Hemel Hemstead: Harvester Press, 1981).

Markus, Robert, *Signs and Meanings: World and Text in Ancient Christianity* (Liverpool: Liverpool University Press, 1996).

Marlé, René, "Bultmann and the Old Testament," in *Rudolf Bultmann in Catholic Thought,* edited by Thomas F. O'Meara and Donald M. Weisser (New York: Herder and Herder, 1968), pp. 110-24.

Michelson, A., *Women, Authority, and the Bible* (Downers Grove, Ill.: IVP, 1986).

Miegge, Giovanni, *Gospel and Myth in the Thought of Rudolf Bultmann,* translated by Stephen Neill (London: Lutterworth, 1960).

Miranda, José Porfirio, *Being and Messiah: The Message of St. John,* translated by John Eagleson (Maryknoll, N.Y.: Orbis; London: SCM, 1977).

+*————, *Marx and the Bible: A Critique of the Philosophy of Oppression* (Maryknoll, N.Y.: Orbis, 1974; London: SCM, 1977).

Moberly, R. W. L., *The Bible, Theology, and Faith: A Study of Abraham and Jesus* (Cambridge: Cambridge University Press, 2000).

Mollenkott, V. R., *The Divine Feminism in the Biblical Imagery of God as Female* (New York: Crossroad, 1983).

Moo, Douglas J., *The Old Testament in the Gospel Passion Narratives* (Sheffield: Almond, 1983).

*Morgan, Robert (with John Barton), *Biblical Interpretation* (Oxford: Oxford University Press, 1988).

Mosala, Itumeleng J., *Biblical Hermeneutics and Black Theology in South Africa* (Grand Rapids: Eerdmans, 1989).

*Mueller-Vollmer, Kurt, ed., *The Hermeneutics Reader* (Oxford: Blackwell, 1985).

Neill, Stephen, and Tom Wright, *The Interpretation of the New Testament, 1861-1986*, 2nd ed. (Oxford: Oxford University Press, 1988).

+Nida, Eugene A., "The Implication of Contemporary Linguistics in Biblical Scholarship," *Journal of Biblical Literature* 91 (1972): 23-90.

Oduyoye, Mercy Amba, *Introducing African Women's Theology* (Sheffield and New York: Continuum, 2004).

Oduyoye, Mercy Amba, and Elizabeth Amoah, eds., *People of Faith and the Challenge of HIV/AIDS* (Ibadan: Sefer, 2005).

*Oeming, Manfred, *Contemporary Biblical Hermeneutics: An Introduction*, translated by J. Vette (Aldershot and Burlington, Vt.: Ashgate, 2006).

Ogden, Schubert, *Christ without Myth: A Study Based on the Theology of Rudolf Bultmann* (New York: Harper and Row, 1961).

Olhausen, William, "A 'Polite' Response to Anthony Thiselton," in *After Pentecost: Language and Biblical Interpretation*, edited by Craig Bartholomew and others, Scripture and Hermeneutics Series, vol. 2 (Grand Rapids: Zondervan; Carlisle: Paternoster, 2001), pp. 121-30.

Oliver, J. M., ed., *Diodore: Commentary on the Psalms*, in *Corpus Christianorum, Series Graeca*, 6 vols. (Turnhout: Brepols, 2006).

*Osborne, Grant R., *The Hermeneutical Spiral: A Comprehensive Introduction to Biblical Interpretation* (Downers Grove, Ill.: InterVarsity, 1991).

Osiek, Carolyn, *Beyond Anger: On Being a Feminist in the Church* (New York: Paulist, 1986).

————, *A Woman's Place: House Churches in Earliest Christianity* (Minneapolis: Augsburg, 2005).

Pagels, Elaine, *The Gnostic Paul: Gnostic Exegesis of the Pauline Letters* (Philadelphia: Fortress, 1975).

————, *The Johannine Gospel in Gnostic Exegesis* (Nashville and New York: Abingdon, 1973).

*Palmer, Richard E., *Hermeneutics: Interpretation Theory in Schleiermacher, Dilthey, Heidegger, and Gadamer,* Studies in Phenomenology and Existential Philosophy (Evanston, Ill.: Northwestern University Press, 1969).

+Pannenberg, Wolfhart, "Myth in Biblical and Christian Tradition," in Pannenberg, *Basic Questions in Theology,* translated by R. A. Wilson (London: SCM, 1970-73), 3:1-79.

+————, *Systematic Theology,* translated by G. W. Bromiley, 3 vols. (Edinburgh: T. & T. Clark; Grand Rapids: Eerdmans, 1991, 1994, 1998).

Parker, T. H. L., *Calvin's Old Testament Commentaries* (Edinburgh: T. & T. Clark, 1986).

Parratt, John, *An Introduction to Third World Theologies* (Cambridge: Cambridge University Press, 2004).

*Parris, David Paul, *Reading the Bible with Giants: How 2,000 Years of Biblical Interpretation Can Shed Light on Old Texts* (London and Atlanta: Paternoster, 2006).

Parsons, Mikeal, "Allegorizing Allegory: Narrative Analysis and Parable Interpretation," *Perspectives in Religious Studies* 15 (1988): 147-64.

Patte, Daniel, *Early Jewish Hermeneutic in Palestine,* Society of Biblical Literature Dissertation Series 22 (Missoula: Scholars Press, 1975).

*————, *What Is Structural Exegesis?* (Philadelphia: Fortress, 1976).

————, ed., *Global Bible Commentary* (Nashville: Abingdon, 2004).

————, *Semiology and Parables: Exploration of the Possibilities Offered by Structuralism for Exegesis* (Pittsburgh: Pickwick, 1976).

Plaskow, Judith, *Sex, Sin, and Grace: Women's Experience and the Theologies of Reinhold Niebuhr and Paul Tillich* (Lanham, Md.: University Press of America, 1980).

Poland, Lynn M., *Literary Criticism and Biblical Hermeneutics: A Critique of Formative Approaches* (Chico, Calif.: Scholars Press, 1985).

*Porter, Stanley E., ed., *Dictionary of Biblical Criticism and Interpretation* (London and New York: Routledge, 2007).

Reventlow, Henning Graf, *The Authority of the Bible and the Rise of the Modern World,* translated by John Bowden (London: SCM, 1984).

Richards, Janet Radcliffe, *The Sceptical Feminist: A Philosophical Enquiry* (London: Penguin Books, 1983).

+Ricoeur, Paul, *The Conflict of Interpretations: Essays in Hermeneutics,* translated by D. Ihde (Evanston, Ill.: Northwestern University Press, 1974).

+*————, *Essays on Biblical Interpretation,* edited by Lewis S. Mudge (Philadelphia: Fortress, 1980; London: SPCK, 1981).

————, *Fallible Man,* revised and translated by Charles A. Kelbley (New York: Fordham University Press, 1985).

————, *Figuring the Sacred: Religion, Narrative, and Imagination,* translated by David Pellauer and Mark I. Wallace (Philadelphia: Augsburg Fortress, 1995).

————, *Freedom and Nature: The Voluntary and Involuntary* (Evanston, Ill.: Northwestern University Press, 1966).

+————, *Freud and Philosophy: An Essay on Interpretation,* translated by Denis Savage (New Haven: Yale University Press, 1970).

————, *Hermeneutics and the Human Sciences: Essays on Language Action and Interpretation,* edited and translated by John B. Thompson (Cambridge: Cambridge University Press, 1981).

————, "Intellectual Biography," in *The Philosophy of Paul Ricoeur,* edited by Lewis E. Hahn (Chicago: Open Court, 1995).

+————, *Interpretation Theory: Discourse and the Surplus of Meaning* (Fort Worth: Texas Christian University Press, 1976).

————, *The Just,* translated by David Pellauer (Chicago and London: University of Chicago Press, 2000).

+————, *Oneself as Another,* translated by Kathleen Blamey (Chicago and London: University of Chicago Press, 1992).

————, *Reflections on the Just,* translated by David Pellauer (Chicago and London: University of Chicago Press, 2007).

————, *The Rule of Metaphor: Multi-Disciplinary Studies of the Creation of Meaning in Language,* translated by Robert Czerny with Kathleen McLaughlin (London: Routledge and Kegan Paul, 1977).

————, *The Symbolism of Evil* (Boston: Beacon Press, 1969; 1st English ed. 1967).

+————, *Time and Narrative,* translated by Kathleen Blamey and David Pellauer, 3 vols. (Chicago and London: University of Chicago Press, 1984, 1985, 1988).

Ricoeur, Paul, and André LaCocque, *Thinking Biblically: Exegetical and Hermeneutical Studies,* translated by David Pellauer (Chicago and London: University of Chicago Press, 1998).

Robins, Wendy S., ed., *Through the Eyes of a Woman: Bible Studies on the Experience of Women* (Geneva: World YWCA Publications, 1986).

Robinson, James M., "Hermeneutics since Barth," in *New Frontiers in Theology,* vol. 2, *The New Hermeneutic,* edited by James M. Robinson and John B. Cobb, Jr. (New York and London: Harper and Row, 1964), pp. 1-77.

Rogerson, John, *Old Testament Criticism in the Nineteenth Century: England and Germany* (London: SPCK, 1984).

Rorty, Richard M., *Philosophy and Social Hope* (Princeton: Princeton University Press, 1979).

————, *Philosophy and the Mirror of Nature* (Princeton: Princeton University Press, 1979).

+————, *Truth and Progress: Philosophical Papers*, vol. 3 (Cambridge: Cambridge University Press, 1998).

Ruether, Rosemary Radford, *Gaia and God: An Eco-Feminist Theology of Earth Healing* (San Francisco: HarperCollins, 1992).

————, *Women-Church: Theology and the Practice of Feminist Liturgical Communities* (San Francisco: Harper and Row, 1985).

————, ed., *Religion and Sexism: Images of Women in the Jewish and Christian Traditions* (New York: Simon and Schuster, 1974).

+Ruether, Rosemary Radford, and Eleanor McLaughlin, eds., *Women of Spirit: Female Leadership in the Jewish and Christian Traditions* (New York: Simon and Schuster, 1979).

+Rush, Ormond, *The Reception of Doctrine: An Appropriation of Hans Robert Jauss' Reception Aesthetics and Literary Hermeneutics* (Rome: Pontifical Gregorian University, 1997).

+Russell, Letty M., ed., *Feminist Interpretation of the Bible* (Philadelphia: Westminster, 1985).

————, *The Liberating Word: A Guide to Nonsexist Interpretation of the Bible* (Philadelphia: Westminster, 1976).

Saiving, Valerie, "The Human Situation: A Feminine View," *Journal of Religion* 40 (1960): 100-112.

Saussure, Ferdinand de, *Course in General Linguistics,* edited by C. Bally and A. Sechehaye, translated by R. Harris (London: Duckworth, 1983).

Scalise, Charles J., *Hermeneutics as Theological Prolegomena: A Canonical Approach* (Macon, Ga.: Mercer University Press, 1994).

Scanzoni, L. D., "Revitalizing Interpretations of Ephesians 5:22," *Pastoral Psychology* 45 (1997): 317-39.

Scanzoni, L. D., and N. A. Hardesty, *All We're Meant to Be: A Biblical Approach to Women's Liberation* (Waco, Tex.: Word, 1974; 3rd rev. ed. 1992).

+Schleiermacher, Friedrich, *Christmas Eve: A Dialogue on the Incarnation,* translated by T. N. Tice (Richmond, Va.: John Knox, 1967).

+*————, *Hermeneutics: The Handwritten Manuscripts,* edited by Heinz

Kimmerle, translated by James Duke and Jack Forstman (Missoula: Scholars Press, 1977).

————, *On Religion: Speeches to Its Cultured Despisers,* translated by John Oman (reprint, New York: Harper and Row, 1959).

*Schmithals, Walter, *An Introduction to the Theology of Rudolf Bultmann,* translated by John Bowden (London: SCM, 1968), pp. 38-39.

*Schubeck, Thomas L., S.J., "Liberation Theology," in *The Encyclopedia of Christianity,* edited by Erwin Fahlbusch, Jan Milič Lochman, et al., translated by G. W. Bromiley, 5 vols. (Grand Rapids: Eerdmans, 1999-2008), 3:258-65.

Schüssler Fiorenza, Elisabeth, *Bread Not Stone: The Challenge of Feminist Biblical Interpretation* (Boston: Beacon Press, 1984).

————, *Discipleship of Equals: A Critical Feminist Ekklēsia-logy of Liberation* (New York: Crossroad, 1993).

+————, *In Memory of Her: A Feminist Theological Reconstruction of Christian Origins* (New York: Crossroad; London: SCM, 1983).

————, *Jesus: Miriam's Child, Sophia's Prophet; Critical Issues in Feminist Theology* (London: SCM; New York: Continuum, 1995).

————, *Sharing Her Word: Feminist Biblical Interpretation in Contrast* (Boston: Beacon Press, 1998).

Scott, Bernard B., *Hear Then the Parable: A Commentary on the Parables of Jesus* (Minneapolis: Fortress, 1989).

Searle, John R., *Expression and Meaning: Studies in the Theory of Speech Acts* (Cambridge: Cambridge University Press, 1979).

+Segundo, Juan Luis, *Liberation of Theology,* translated by John Drury (Dublin: Gill and MacMillan, 1977).

Selwyn, Edward G., *The First Epistle of St. Peter: The Greek Text with Introduction, Notes, and Essays,* 2nd ed. (London: Macmillan, 1947).

Shotwell, Willis A., *The Biblical Exegesis of Justin Martyr* (London: SPCK, 1965).

Showalter, Elaine, ed., *The New Feminist Criticism: Essays on Women, Literature, and Theory* (London: Virago Press, 1986).

Silverman, Hugh, *Gadamer and Hermeneutics: Science, Culture, Literature* (New York: Routledge, 2001).

*Smalley, Beryl, *The Study of the Bible in the Middle Ages* (Oxford: Blackwell, 1952, 1964).

Smart, James, *The Interpretation of Scripture* (London: SCM, 1961).

Smith, James K. A., *Who's Afraid of Postmodernism? Taking Derrida, Lyotard, and Foucault to Church* (Grand Rapids: Baker Academic, 2006).

Souter, A., *A Study of Ambrosiaster*, Texts and Studies 7 (Cambridge: Cambridge University Press, 1905).

Stanley, Christopher D., *Paul and the Language of Scripture: Citation Technique in the Pauline Epistles and Contemporary Literature*, Society for New Testament Studies Monograph Series, no. 69 (Cambridge: Cambridge University Press, 1992).

*Stein, Robert H., *An Introduction to the Parables of Jesus* (Philadelphia: Westminster, 1981).

*Stiver, Dan R., *Theology after Ricoeur: New Directions in Hermeneutical Theology* (Louisville and London: Westminster John Knox, 2001).

Storkey, Elaine, *What's Right with Feminism?* (London: SPCK, 1985).

Strauss, David F., *The Life of Jesus Critically Examined,* translated and edited by P. C. Hodgson (Philadelphia: Fortress; London: SCM, 1973).

Stuhlmacher, Peter, *Historical Criticism and Theological Interpretation of Scripture,* translated by R. A. Harrisville (Philadelphia: Fortress, 1977).

*Sturrock, John, ed., *Structuralism and Since: From Lévi-Strauss to Derrida* (Oxford: Oxford University Press, 1979).

Sugirtharajah, R. S., *The Bible and the Empire: Postcolonial Explorations* (Cambridge: Cambridge University Press, 2005).

————, *The Bible and the Third World* (Cambridge: Cambridge University Press, 2001).

————, ed., *Asian Faces of Jesus* (Maryknoll, N.Y.: Orbis; London: SCM, 1993).

————, *Voices from the Margins: Interpreting the Bible in the Third World* (Maryknoll, N.Y.: Orbis; London: SPCK, 1989, 2006).

+Suleiman, Susan R., and Inge Crosman, eds., *The Reader in the Text: Essays on Audience and Interpretation* (Princeton: Princeton University Press, 1980).

*Tate, Randolph W., *Biblical Interpretation: An Integrated Approach* (Peabody, Mass.: Hendrickson, 1991).

Theissen, Gerd, *Psychological Aspects of Pauline Theology,* translated by J. P. Galwin (Philadelphia: Fortress; Edinburgh: T. & T. Clark, 1987).

Thielicke, Helmut, "The Restatement of the New Testament Mythology," in *Kerygma and Myth: A Theological Debate,* edited by Hans Werner Bartsch, 2 vols. (London: SCM, 1953), 1:138-74.

Thiselton, Anthony C., "Authority and Hermeneutics: Some Proposals for a More Creative Agenda," in *A Pathway with the Holy Scripture,* edited by

Philip E. Satterthwaite and David F. Wright (Grand Rapids: Eerdmans, 1994), pp. 107-41.

————, "Canon, Community and Theological Construction," in *Canon and Biblical Interpretation,* edited by Craig G. Bartholomew and others, Scripture and Hermeneutics Series, vol. 7 (Grand Rapids: Zondervan; Carlisle: Paternoster, 2006), pp. 1-30.

*————, *Can the Bible Mean Whatever We Want It to Mean?* (Chester, U.K.: Chester Academic Press, 2005).

————, *The First Epistle to the Corinthians: A Commentary on the Greek Text,* New International Greek Testament Commentary (Grand Rapids: Eerdmans; Carlisle: Paternoster, 2000).

+————. *The Hermeneutics of Doctrine* (Grand Rapids: Eerdmans, 2007).

*————, "The New Hermeneutic," in *New Testament Interpretation,* edited by I. H. Marshall (Exeter: Paternoster, 1972), pp. 308-31.

————, *New Horizons in Hermeneutics: The Theory and Practice of Transforming Biblical Reading* (London: HarperCollins; Grand Rapids: Zondervan, 1992).

*————, "Reader-Response Hermeneutics, Action Models, and the Parables of Jesus," in Roger Lundin, Anthony C. Thiselton, and Clarence Walhout, *The Responsibility of Hermeneutics* (Grand Rapids: Eerdmans; Exeter: Paternoster, 1985), pp. 79-115.

+————, *Thiselton on Hermeneutics: Collected Works with New Essays* (Grand Rapids: Eerdmans; Aldershot: Ashgate, 2006).

+————, *The Two Horizons: New Testament Hermeneutics and Philosophical Description with Special Reference to Heidegger, Bultmann, Gadamer, and Wittgenstein* (Grand Rapids: Eerdmans; Exeter: Paternoster, 1980).

Thiselton, Anthony C. (with R. Lundin and C. Walhout), *The Promise of Hermeneutics* (Grand Rapids: Eerdmans; Carlisle: Paternoster, 1999).

Thompson, John B., *Critical Hermeneutics: A Study in the Thought of Paul Ricoeur and Jürgen Habermas* (Cambridge: Cambridge University Press, 1981, 1983).

Thompson, John L., *Reading the Bible with the Dead* (Grand Rapids: Eerdmans, 2007).

Tilley, Terrence W., *Postmodern Theologies: The Challenge of Religious Diversity* (Maryknoll, N.Y.: Orbis, 1995).

Tolbert, Mary Ann, *Perspectives on the Parables* (Philadelphia: Fortress, 1979).

Torjesen, Karen Jo, *Hermeneutical Procedure and Theological Method in Origen's Exegesis* (Berlin: Walter de Gruyter, 1986).

Torrance, Alan J., *Persons in Communion: An Essay on Trinitarian Description and Human Participation with Special Reference to Volume One of Karl Barth's "Church Dogmatics"* (Edinburgh: T. & T. Clark, 1996).

Torrance, Thomas F., *Divine Meaning: Studies in Patristic Hermeneutics* (Edinburgh: T. & T. Clark, 1995).

*———, *Karl Barth: An Introduction to His Early Theology, 1910-1931* (London: SCM, 1962).

Tracy, David, *The Analogical Imagination: Christian Theology and the Culture of Pluralism* (London: SCM, 1981).

+Trible, Phyllis, *God and the Rhetoric of Sexuality* (Philadelphia: Fortress, 1978).

+———, *Texts of Terror: Literary-Feminist Readings of Biblical Narratives* (Philadelphia: Fortress, 1984).

Trigg, Joseph W., *Origen: The Bible and Philosophy in the Third-Century Church* (London: SCM; Louisville: John Knox, 1983, 1985).

+Tyndale, William, *A Pathway into the Holy Scripture*, in Tyndale, *Doctrinal Treatises and Introductions to Holy Scripture* (Cambridge: Cambridge University Press, Parker Society, 1848).

Ullmann, Stephen, *Principles of Semantics*, 2nd ed. (Oxford: Blackwell, 1963).

———, *Semantics* (Oxford: Blackwell, 1962).

Vanhoozer, Kevin J., *Biblical Narrative in the Philosophy of Paul Ricoeur: A Study in Hermeneutics* (Cambridge: Cambridge University Press, 1990).

+———, *Is There a Meaning in This Text? The Bible, the Reader, and the Morality of Literary Knowledge* (Grand Rapids: Zondervan, 1998).

*———, ed., *Dictionary for Theological Interpretation of the Bible* (London: SPCK, 2005).

*———, *Postmodern Theology: Cambridge Companion* (Cambridge: Cambridge University Press, 2003).

Via, Dan Otto, "The Parable of the Unjust Judge: A Metaphor of the Unrealised Self," in *Semiology and the Parables: An Exploration of the Possibilities Offered in Structuralism for Exegesis,* edited by Daniel Patte (Pittsburgh: Pickwick, 1976), pp. 1-32.

+———, *The Parables: Their Literary and Existential Dimension* (Philadelphia: Fortress, 1967).

Walker, Alice, *In Search of Our Mother's Gardens: Womanist Prose* (New York: Harcourt Brace, 1983; London: Women's Press, 1984).

Wall, John, *Moral Creativity: Paul Ricoeur and the Poetics of Possibility* (Oxford: Oxford University Press, 2005).

Wallace, Mark, *The Second Naïveté: Barth, Ricoeur, and the New Yale Theology* (Macon, Ga.: Mercer University Press, 1990).

*Ward, Graham, ed., *The Blackwell Companion to Postmodern Theology* (Oxford: Blackwell, 2001), pp. xiv-xv.

*———, *The Postmodern God: A Theological Reader* (Oxford: Blackwell, 1997).

+Warnke, Georgia, *Gadamer: Hermeneutics, Tradition, and Reason* (Cambridge: Polity Press, 1987).

Warnock, J. G., "Every Event Has a Cause," in *Logic and Language*, edited by A. G. W. Flew, 2nd ser. (Oxford: Blackwell, 1966), 1:95-111.

+Watson, Francis, *Text and Truth: Redefining Biblical Theology* (Edinburgh: T. & T. Clark, 1997).

+———, *Text, Church, and World: Biblical Interpretation in Theological Perspective* (Edinburgh: T. & T. Clark, 1994).

Weber, Otto, *Karl Barth's "Church Dogmatics": An Introductory Report*, translated by A. C. Cochrane (London: Lutterworth, 1953).

+Weinsheimer, Joel C., *Gadamer's Hermeneutics: A Reading of "Truth and Method"* (New Haven: Yale University Press, 1985).

Wellek, René, and Austin Warren, *Theory of Literature* (London: Jonathan Cape, 1949; 3rd ed., Pegasus, 1973).

Wenham, David, *The Parables of Jesus: Pictures of a Revolution* (London: Hodder and Stoughton, 1989).

Wilder, Amos N., *Early Christian Rhetoric* (Cambridge: Harvard University Press; London: SCM, 1964); the second edition of *Jesus and the Language of the Gospel* (Philadelphia: Fortress, reprinted 1976, 1982).

———, "The Word as Address and the Word as Meaning," in *New Frontiers in Theology*, vol. 2, *The New Hermeneutic*, edited by James M. Robinson and John B. Cobb, Jr. (New York and London: Harper and Row, 1964).

Wilmore, G. S., and James Cone, eds., *Black Theology: A Documentary History, 1980-1992*, 2nd ed., 2 vols. (Maryknoll, N.Y.: Orbis, 1993).

Wimbush, Vincent, ed., *African Americans and the Bible: Sacred Texts and Social Textures* (New York: Continuum, 2001).

Wimsatt, W. K., and Monroe C. Beardsley, "The Intentional Fallacy," *Sewanee Review* 4 (1946): 468-88; revised and republished in Wimsatt and Beardsley, *The Verbal Icon: Studies in the Meaning of Poetry* (Lexington: University Press of Kentucky, 1954), 3-18.

Wittgenstein, Ludwig, *The Blue and Brown Books: Preliminary Studies for the "Philosophical Investigations"* (Oxford: Blackwell, 1969).

———, *On Certainty*, German and English (Oxford: Blackwell, 1969).

+————, *Philosophical Investigations,* German and English, English text translated by G. E. M. Anscombe (Oxford: Blackwell, 1967).

Wittig, Susan, "A Theory of Multiple Meanings," *Semeia* 9 (1977): 75-105.

+Wolterstorff, Nicholas, *Divine Discourse: Philosophical Reflections on the Claim That God Speaks* (Cambridge: Cambridge University Press, 1995).

Wood, James D., *The Interpretation of the Bible* (London: Duckworth, 1958).

+Work, Telford, *Living and Active: Scripture in the Economy of Salvation* (Grand Rapids: Eerdmans, 2002).

Wycliffe, John, *On the Truth of the Holy Scripture* (Kalamazoo, Mich.: Mediaeval Institute, and Western Michigan University, 2001).

————, *The Pastoral Office,* translated by F. L. Battles, Library of Christian Classics, vol. 14 (London: SCM; Philadelphia: Westminster, 1963).

*Yarchin, William, *History of Biblical Interpretation: A Reader* (Peabody, Mass.: Hendrickson, 2004).

Zaharopoulos, Dimitri Z., *Theodore of Mopsuestia on the Bible: A Study of His Old Testament Exegesis* (New York: Paulist, 1989).

Zimmermann, Jens, *Recovering Theological Hermeneutics: An Incarnational-Trinitarian Theory of Interpretation* (Grand Rapids: Baker Academic, 2004).

Index of Names

Bold *pages denote those important for the subject.*

Aageson, J. W., 77-78
Abelard, 118
Achtemeier, Elizabeth, 293, 305
Achtemeier, Paul, 195
Akiba, Rabbi, 63
Albert the Great, 120
Alcuin of York, 118
Alliende, Salander, 259
Alter, Robert, 28
Althusser, Louis, 331, 341
Altizer, Thomas, 336
Alves, Rubem, 263, 268
Ambrose of Milan, **102-3**
Ambrosiaster, **102-3**
Andrew of St. Victor, 21, 119
Anscombe, Elizabeth, 27
Anscombe, G. E. M., 243
Anselm of Canterbury, 190
Anthony, Susan B., 284
Apel, Karl-Otto, 9, 248
Apollos, 80
Aquila, 87, 89
Aquinas, Thomas, **120-22**, 188, 354
Aristides, 68
Aristotle, 207, 220, 224, 231, 233, 238, 239, 261
Arius, 110

Ast, Friedrich, **14**, **153**
Astruc, Jean, 139
Athanasius, **108-10**
Augustine of Hippo, 10, 51-52, 93, 95, **114-17**, 354
Austin, John L., 176, 180, 191, 193, 235, 251, 308, 334, 351
Ayer, A. J., 347

Bach, J. S., 140
Bacon, Francis, 162
Baird, J. Arthur, 308-9
Baird, William, 146-47
Bakhtin, Mikhail, 221
Bal, Mieke, 304
Barden, G., 316
Barr, James, 26, **203-4**, 205, 289, **292-93**, 304
Barrett, C. K., 68
Barth, Karl, 148, 154, 183, **185-90**, 191, 204, 205, 355
Barthes, Roland, 25, **197-99**, **202**, 235, 299, 328, 330, **335-36**, 341
Barton, John, 28
Bartsch, Hans-Werner, 182
Bauckham, Richard, 330, 337
Baudrillard, Jean, 300, **340-41**, 347

381

Index of Subjects

Bold type denotes either the importance of the entry or an explanation of the meaning of a term.

Index of Scripture and Other Ancient Sources